SERVICE ECONOMIES

SERVICE ECONOMIES

*Militarism, Sex Work, and
Migrant Labor in South Korea*

JIN-KYUNG LEE

UNIVERSITY OF MINNESOTA PRESS

MINNEAPOLIS • LONDON

Portions of chapter 1 were previously published as "Surrogate Military, Subimperialism, and Masculinity: South Korea in the Vietnam War, 1965–1973," in *positions: east asia cultures critique* 17, no. 3 (Winter 2009): 655–82. Portions of chapter 4 were previously published in Korean as "Hawijegukjuŭi sidaeŭi chaehan ijunodongjawa hangukinŭi isan: Pak Pŏm-sinŭi *Namaste*" [Immigrant/Migrant Labor and Korean Diaspora in the Age of Subimperialism: Pak Pŏm-sin's *Namaste*], in *Munhak Tongne* [Literature World] 48 (Fall 2006): 458–69; and as "Minjok, hawijegukjuŭi, ch'ogukgajŏk nodong: hangukŭi ijunodongjadŭlgwa migukŭi hanguk iminjadŭl" [Ethnicity, (Sub)Empire, and Transnational Labor: Asian Migrant Workers in South Korea and South Korean Immigrants in the United States], in *Hwanghae Munhwa* [Hwanghae Culture] 50 (Spring 2006): 284–95.

Published by the University of Minnesota Press
111 Third Avenue South, Suite 290
Minneapolis, MN 55401-2520
http://www.upress.umn.edu

Library of Congress Cataloging-in-Publication Data

Lee, Jin-kyung.
Service economies : militarism, sex work, and migrant labor in South Korea / Jin-kyung Lee.
p. cm.
Includes bibliographical references and index.
ISBN 978-0-8166-5125-2 (hc : alk. paper)—ISBN 978-0-8166-5126-9 (pb : alk. paper)
1. Service industries—Korea (South). 2. Sex-oriented businesses—Korea (South).
3. Militarism—Korea (South). 4. Korea (South)—Economic policy. 5. Korea (South)—
Foreign relations—United States. 6. United States—Foreign relations—Korea (South). I. Title.
HD9987.K62L43 2010
363.4´4095195—dc22
2010001663

Printed in the United States of America on acid-free paper

The University of Minnesota is an equal-opportunity educator and employer.

Contents

Acknowledgments

I have benefited from the generous spirit of many who guided me along the way to the completion of this book. Although this project began as a separate and different project from my dissertation, it is still very much a product of my training in both East Asian studies and comparative literature, and my deepest gratitude goes to my teachers at UCLA. John Duncan has been a scholar and a teacher to be emulated from the first day I arrived in the early 1990s at UCLA until today, having continually challenged and reshaped my ideas about Korea and Korean studies. With the help of my Japan history teachers, Leslie Pincus and the late Miriam Silverberg, I was prodded to think about Korean history and literature in ways that would not have been possible otherwise. Chungmoo Choi and Shu-mei Shih provided lasting intellectual stimulus for my work. Along with much that I have learned about Buddhism and Korean Buddhism in his classes, Robert Buswell has offered indispensable support as a mentor over the years. My teachers from comparative literature, Ross Shideler, Kathleen Komar, Katherine King, and Samuel Weber, lent both intellectual inspiration and professional guidance during graduate school years and beyond.

At the University of California, San Diego, I have been very fortunate to be surrounded by the most encouraging coworkers and the most exciting group of scholars. Takashi Fujitani, Rosemary Marangoly George, Stephanie Jed, Lisa Lowe, Don Wayne, Lisa Yoneyama, and Yingjin Zhang have been unstinting in their hard work on my behalf to guide both my intellectual work and professional life. Others on the UCSD campus have been cordial, caring, and dependable colleagues to whom I have turned at various points for their help. They include John Blanco, Lisa

Bloom, Robert Cancel, Jim Cheng, Jaime Concha, Page Dubois, Fatima El-Tayeb, Yen Espiritu, Heather Fowler, Stephan Haggard, Larissa Heinrich, Nancy Ho-Wu, Tara Javidi, Sara Johnson, Milos Kokotovic, Todd Kontje, Susan Larson, Jeyseon Lee, Margaret Loose, the late Masao Miyoshi, Max Parra, Roddey Reid, Lucinda Rubio-Barrack, Rosaura Sánchez, Shelley Streeby, Stefan Tanaka, Daniel Widener, Wai-lim Yip, Jong-Sung You, and Oumelbanine Zhiri.

The growing community of Korean studies in North America and others in Asian studies lent intellectual and moral support along the way. I would like to thank Nancy Abelmann, Hyaeweol Choi, Kyeong-Hee Choi, Ja Hyun Kim Haboush, Kelly Jeong, Chong Bum Kim, Namhee Lee, John Lie, Seungsook Moon, Pori Park, Janet Poole, Naoki Sakai, Andre Schmid, Toshiko Scott, Gi-Wook Shin, Yuki Terazawa, Rumi Yasutake, and Alison Yeung. Over the past years, many colleagues, friends, and teachers working in South Korea and Europe extended themselves to provide crucial corrections, generous criticisms, invaluable dialogues, and hospitality. I am greatly indebted to the kindness of Baek Mun Im, Hwang Jongyon, Kim Chul, Kim Jae-yong, Kim Jongmyung, Kim Uchang, Kwon Youngmin, Lee Kyung Hoon, Lee Sang-kyung, Lim Jie-hyun, Paik Won-Dam, Shin Hyung Ki, John Frankl, Michael Kim, and Vladimir Tikhonov. This project has also benefited much from my interaction with enthusiastic and accomplished undergraduate and graduate students in the Department of Literature at UCSD over the years.

I would like to thank the Korea Foundation and UCSD for offering fellowships and grants that enabled me to take time off from teaching during my years at the university. My sincere gratitude goes to Richard Morrison, my editor at the University of Minnesota Press, for his interest in this project in its inchoate stages, for his exacting and generous professional guidance, and for his extraordinary patience through the entire process.

Last but not least, completing this book would not have been possible without the love and support of my family: my father, Myung-Jae Lee; my mother, Hwa-Suh Park; my partner, Ted Hughes; and all of our nieces and nephews on both sides of our extended families.

Introduction

Proletarianizing Sexuality and Race

GLOBAL AND LOCAL MOBILIZATION: MILITARY, INDUSTRIAL, AND SEXUAL PROLETARIANIZATION

In the post-1945 period, as the United States emerged as a superpower it created and implemented expansive programs of economic development in the Third World, often accompanied by military force. With the end of World War II, the United States immediately engaged in two consecutive hot wars against communism: first, on the Korean peninsula, and then in Vietnam and the larger Southeast Asian region as it simultaneously confronted in a cold war its most important Asian enemy, communist China. The U.S. wars in Asia, the "production of destruction,"[1] a lucrative business in and of itself, also laid the indispensable groundwork for the United States' future international productivity, that is, its economic domination in the region. As a direct and indirect result of U.S. militarism, various locations in Asia, including South Korea and Vietnam in the short and long run, came to function as places of low-wage labor for U.S. capital since the 1970s. Confirming once more that war and market were intrinsic extensions of each other in U.S. global expansionism, a series of Asian states continue to operate as a mass of offshore military-industrial complexes for the United States.

Rather than further affirm the "success" of South Korean development as a "miracle,"[2] this book seeks to demystify the exceptionality of the South Korean case, first, by situating South Korean industrialization from the 1960s to the present in the context of the interplay between the United States' military engagement in the Korean peninsula and in Southeast Asia, and its economic supremacy in these regions. In viewing the post-1945 historical trajectory of South Korea as an integral part of the United States' global expansion in Asia, I locate major South Korean historical events and processes—South Korean participation in the Vietnam War, the U.S. military presence in South Korea, the South Korean diaspora to the United States, rapid industrialization, South Korea's rise as a subimperialist power, and the recent Asian labor migration to South Korea—in the always already transnational space between the United States, Asia, and South Korea. Secondly, this book attempts to de-exceptionalize South Korean development by highlighting four marginalized working-class labors, which occupy a central position in connecting U.S. imperialism in Asia to South Korea's successive and overlapping positions, from a U.S. neocolony to a subempire.

The four different labors of the period between the mid-1960s and the present—all of which have occupied, paradoxically, highly visible and yet invisible places in South Korea—serve as the topics of each chapter: South Korean military labor in the Vietnam War; female sex labor and sexualized service labor for domestic clientele; South Korean military prostitution for the U.S. troops from the industrializing era; and immigrant and migrant labor, from Asia and other areas, in contemporary South Korea. The book's focus on these labors draws further attention to two dimensions that have been overlooked in the studies of South Korean development: sexuality and race. The chapters explore what I call the "proletarianization" of sexuality and race, that is, the ways in which sexuality and race, in necessary articulation with each other, Korean ethnonationality, and transnational racial hierarchy, become aspects of productive and socially reproductive labors that are constructed for specifically gendered, classed, ethnicized or racialized, and nationalized collectives in the transnational context.

The existing historiography of South Korean modernization, both in South Korea and in the United States, has centered largely on industrial labor, that is, manufacturing labor (female labor for light industry and male labor for heavy industry), as constituting the very core of the economic development. While they have been objects of scholarly investigation as discrete and distinct topics in more recent years,[3] none of the three labor experiences of the industrializing era that I deal with in this book (military labor in Vietnam, domestic sex work, and military prostitution) has been understood as having a structural relation to the more mainstream industrial labors and as transnational proletarianization of sexuality and race. Although the subject of migrant labor has started to draw some scholarly attention, again it is not being sufficiently grasped as having a structural continuity with the transnational racialization of the South

Korean labors of an earlier era that I discuss in the first three chapters. Thus, I argue in this book that these marginal transnational proletarian labors, which are premised on commodifying the transformation of sexuality and race into labor power, constitute an essential dimension of South Korean modernization. I further maintain that these particular labors help us locate the specificity of South Korean industrialization in its linkage to the United States, while also illustrating the more universal patterns of post-1945 Third World development.

In writing about the long process of European modernization and industrialization since the eighteenth century, Paul Virilio puts forth two important theses that are relevant to our understanding of the South Korean development that took place a couple of centuries later. First, Virilio's notion of "dromology," or mobilization, specifically refers to the movement of laboring bodies, subjugating them to the governing forces as human resources or objects. He calls this modern deployment of people a "dictatorship of movement."[4] Second, calling attention to the structural continuity between the "production of destruction" and the production of wealth, that is, the indissoluble linkages between modern European militarism and capitalism, Virilio points to the consequent processes that he calls "industrial proletarianization" and "military proletarianization," which are again entwined with each other: "available, enrolled in a single, great army serving by turns in war, in trade and in land-development activities"; "the 'nation on the march' of the mass army's military proletariat sent out on the 'highway territory' and an industrial proletariat, a 'worker's army' . . . that remains enclosed in the vast camp of the national territory."[5] Virilio further discerns another related mobilization—that of female sex work: "the cloistered body of the woman put in a harem or brothel, her sex sold or rented, even put under lock and key, as a source of profit for her temporary owner."[6] Following Virilio's concepts of military and industrial proletarianization, we will call this process sexual proletarianization. We can extend Virilio's transnational discussion of modern European contexts to the global colonial and neocolonial contexts, thus further complicating these three forms of proletarianization through their intersection with race. In the increasingly globalized context of the last few decades, we have seen this continuing trend of an internationally divided and racially hierarchized process of triple proletarianization accelerate. Just as Southeast Asian economies depend on tourism, and tourism-related sex and sexualized service labors, the United States deploys its ethnic minorities, racialized immigrants, and working-class whites to the world over as its "voluntary" high-tech military force.

While Virilio lays out three types of proletarianization in relation to one another, Kathleen Barry's work focuses on female sexual proletarianization, elaborating the historical connections between prostitution and global colonial and neocolonial militarized modernization. Understanding prostitution as a necessarily transnational phenomenon that exploits gender, class, race, and national hierarchy, Barry distinguishes three successive stages in its development in modern globalized history. After tracing the ideological premise of modern prostitution to feudal patriarchy and its trafficking of women, Barry posits that the first stage of modern prostitution, the "militarization of sex," comes with militarized colonial or neocolonial occupation of a country or region. Under such circumstances, women either resorted to prostitution as the only means of survival or were subjected to a more systematized mobilization for military prostitution. The Japanese colonial state's conscription of "Comfort Women" during the Asia–Pacific Wars, drawn from the population of the Korean peninsula and the other areas of Asia it occupied, is one historical example. During the 1950s, in the aftermath of the Korean War, female orphans, widows, and other impoverished women catered to occupying American soldiers. In the subsequent decades of industrialization, the 1960s and '70s, a sector of female rural migrants came to fill the demand for military prostitution for U.S. troops who continued to be stationed in South Korea. In the case of South Korea, the stage of militarized prostitution largely overlapped with the next phase, what Barry describes as the "industrialization of sex," that has accompanied the economic development of the Third World. Barry characterizes this stage of prostitution as based less on forced trafficking or physical coercion and more upon economic motivations and conditions, under which women's already devalued labor power makes them more vulnerable and exposed to the prostitution industry. Barry describes the "industrialization of sex" as the "production of a product, sex . . . for the purpose of market exchange," that is, as a "massive commodity production." She situates the industrialization of sex as a historical consequence of the earlier or simultaneous stages in the transnational militarized capitalization process, specifically foreign military occupation, the development of tourist industries, and export-oriented economic development in export processing zones (EPZs).[7] Keeping in mind Barry's historicization of modern prostitution in the global context, chapters 2 and 3 explore, respectively, representations of "domestic" prostitution (or industrial prostitution for domestic clientele) and military prostitution for the U.S. military.

MOBILIZING THE "PRODUCTIVE POTENTIAL": NECROPOLITICAL LABOR

"Proletarianization" usually means a transformation of the traditional peasantry, or those engaged in feudal subsistence agricultural labor, into the modern industrial workforce as wageworkers.[8] This book attempts to revise the concept of proletarianization in four ways. Following Virilio, it first expands the notion of proletariat beyond the normative industrial sector to include soldiering, prostitution, and military prostitution as invisible types of proletarianization. Second, subsequent chapters examine and highlight the ways in which the intersecting relations between transnational racialization and gendering and sexualities form constitutive dimensions of these marginal proletarian labors. Third, in recognizing proletarianization as mass mobilization, this book explores proletarian labors as part of a process of scattering, that is, local and global, or intranational and transnational, "diasporas," and argues that the proletariat occupies a space shared among vagrants, refugees, and economic migrants, that is, local and global "diasporics." Lastly, in considering these particular four labors—soldiering, sex work, military sex work, and migrant work—this book describes proletarian labor in general as necropolitical labor, a concept whose derivations I explain below.

Michel Foucault has drawn our attention to a critical shift that took place in modern Europe from the governance of the population via the threat of death to governance via productive control and management over life, a shift he termed "bio-power." Simultaneously, Foucault has also pointed to certain extreme and yet continuous examples of bio-power, that is, the fostering of life (of some) to the point of extermination of the life of others, largely based on the state and other kinds of organized racism, such as Nazi Germany's extermination of Jews and the American enslavement of Africans. This particular aspect of bio-power, necropolitics, has been further explored, most prominently by Agamben and Mbembe, among others.[9]

Linking this notion of necropolitics to certain kinds of labor, especially those I deal with in this book, I would like to reconceptualize both the notions of bio-power and labor through their connection to death or possibilities of death and call it necropolitical labor. Thus, necropolitical labor means the extraction of labor from those "condemned" to death, whereby the "fostering" of life, already premised on their death or the disposability of their lives, is limited to serving the labor demands of the state or empire. While those in the Nazi concentration camps were put to death eventually, they were also simultaneously put to work both to sustain their own lives in the camps and to contribute to the larger economy and war effort. Although, technically, African slaves in the Americas cannot be considered as "condemned to death" in the way that those in the concentration camps were, given the conditions of slavery that were premised on the disposability of their lives and their bodies as human commodities, slaves can be said ultimately to have been condemned to death, while at the same time being allowed, and even encouraged, to reproduce the next generation of slaves.[10] I would like to emphasize the ways in which both of these necropolitical contexts must be conceptualized as consisting of a fundamental linkage between the extraction of labor and the conditions of condemnation to a "living death" perpetrated by the state and capital. The notion of necropolitical labor highlights an intermediate stage where the extraction of labor is related to and premised on the possibility of death, rather than the ultimate event of death itself. Put another way, we can also think of necropolitical labor as the most disposable labor, that is, the ultimate labor commodity or worker, something or someone to be thrown out, replaced, and/or (both literally and figuratively) killed after or as the labor is performed. If we extend this notion of necropolitical labor to both ends of the spectrum, we find, at one end, the Nazi uses of dead bodies or body parts for medical and other purposes, or the contemporary organ trade as a type of necropolitical "labor"—a posthumous labor.

We can conceptualize soldiering or military labor as one kind of necropolitical labor, a job that can be carried out only by necessarily risking one's life. I explore military labor as occupying an inherently paradoxical and contradictory position with its simultaneous roles as the agent of the state's necropolitical power and as the state's very potential victims. On the one hand, military labor carries out the will of the state in conquering and subjugating the enemy, but it also carries the risk of being exterminated by the enemy. In the state's ability to mobilize a sector of the population as military workers who are potentially expendable, I argue that the state already constructs them as subject to its own necropolitical authority. Other manufacturing labors that are most dangerous and often result in injury, disability, and death can also be conceptualized as types of necropolitical labor at the other end of the spectrum. These dangerous jobs in the industrial sector are most often performed by migrant workers in South Korea—as discussed in chapter 4—and in other industrialized countries. Prostitution, one type for the domestic market (which I discuss in chapter 2) and another for U.S. military clienteles (which I address in chapter 3), I argue, can be conceptualized as another kind of necropolitical labor. Sex work and the sex worker, that is, the commodified body and acts of a prostitute, is one of the most disposable (labor) commodities. Prostitution involves, at one level, a figurative erasure or symbolic murder of the prostitute's subjectivity, in preparation for, and as a consequence of, the psychological, physical, and sexual violence and injury incurred by the commercialization of sex. The frequency of murder among sex workers, which indeed appears to be a universal and cross-cultural phenomenon, can be viewed as a material extension of this figurative violence. Under multiply coercive conditions—economic, physical, and psychological— "selling sex" exists in an inherent continuum with "sexual violence," which always carries the risk of death. Like the other necropolitical labors I mention above, the possibility of death, the ultimate disposability, is an integral element of prostitution as an occupation. In the more extreme case of Comfort Women (the Japanese empire's military sexual slaves during World War II), though essentially continuous with the more mundane contexts of all prostitution, this disposability was eminently brought out in the attitudes of the Japanese military toward the sexual slaves who became "useless" due to disease or insanity: if they could not be restored to a "usable" condition, they were to be discarded.[11]

We can define "proletarian" labor as broadly necropolitical labor, that is, as an expendable and disposable labor or life; as a graduated combination or intersection of fostering, maintenance, or reproduction of life; and as an extermination of life or condemnation to death. Another way to define necropolitical labor is to think of broadly proletarian labor—work itself— as necessarily incurring injury and harm to the body and mind; in other words, work as trauma, violence, and mutilation that indeed lies in continuum with death.[12] Work can be thought of as not simply performing an action or activity, or as a series of gestures or behaviors, but as a process of bearing the forces that are exerted on the laborer. Simultaneously, then, work comprises institutionalized forces, such as mechanized physical forces in the case of manufacturing or social and psychological disciplinary forces in all jobs, that injure, harm, and traumatize the body and psyche. Trauma and violence on the job, especially those that I deal with in this book, function as part of a disciplinary mechanism, a productive force: the process of getting used to the continuing violence, and yet not getting quite used to it, is the very experience of such traumatic work. While working at such jobs means bearing or reacting to such external forces, this does not mean that the worker becomes simply a passive object, but rather an agent, both active and passive, who is transformed by, and transforms, such injuring and violent forces. Injuries and permanent damage to the body and psyche, as a form of slow death or erosion of living beings, constitute a continuum in the expendability of laborers as human subjects. In those jobs that incur physical and psychological mutilation, disability, and trauma, work is necessarily a trade-off between labor that destroys the laborer and the rewards for work; in return for the injuries received, wages provide food and shelter, enabling the laborer to continue to live. The working subject is fragmented and divided against him- or herself, torn between harming him- or herself and surviving.

The notion of necropolitical labor demonstrates to us the ways in which the economy of bio-power, fostering the life of some, operates by destroying and harming the lives of others. It also shows bio-power to be a manipulation and management of death in the form of necropolitical labor, extracting labor and deferring death in the meantime. I would argue that necropolitics is not just one extreme kind of bio-power, but rather necropolitics *as* necropolitical labor is always already a constitutive dimension of bio-power. From the point of view of workers who must perform necropolitical labor, such labor is always a form, or a means, of surviving.

Proletarianizing Sexuality

Foregrounding gender and sexuality as a major site of subject formation,[13] this book challenges the ways in which ethnonationality (*minjok*) and ungendered conceptions of class—that is, the ethnonationalized working-class male as the sovereign subject of the dissident politics of the 1970s and '80s—have been privileged. In my attempt to reconceptualize gendered sexualities in their particularized form as sex work or sexualized labors—military labor in Vietnam, domestic prostitution, and military prostitution for U.S. troops—I explore in this section the particular appropriation of working-class sexuality as a form of labor that is not fully figured into Foucault's writings on bourgeois sexuality and bio-power. Then, combining Foucault's notion of microphysical disciplinary power with the more classical Marxian concepts of labor, I discuss these gendered sex and sexualized labors as service labor. While I argue that service labor as a whole can be viewed as a prototype of all labors, in terms of the production of disciplined bodies and behaviors, my discussion will also point to military, sex, and military sex work as a particular type of service labor—what I call a surrogate or prosthetic labor.

Foucault: Bourgeois and Proletarian Sexualities

Sexuality occupies a central place in Foucault's conception of modern bio-power as concerning itself more with "explicit calculations" and "knowl-edge-power" over life than with "dominion over or threat of death."[14] Sex, as a "means of access to both the life of the body and the life of the species,"[15] is vitally connected to such areas as reproduction, public health, hygiene, and longevity. To a large extent, Foucault's discussion in *The History of Sexuality* highlights the formation of bourgeois sexuality and its deployment vis-à-vis traditional ruling elites, paying little attention to the issues of labor in general or working-class sexuality or proletarian labor in particular.[16] Foucault's characterization of the modern reconstruction of sexuality as occurring in four different social and sexual sites or bod-ies—"hysterization of women's body, pedagogization of children's sex, socialization of procreative behavior, and psychiatrization of perverse pleasures"[17]—does not seem to address the specificities of the transition into modernity of the working class's experiences, that is, the ways in which the very creation of the modern working class was connected to mobiliza-tion of their sexualities and sexualized bodies as labors and commodities.

One of the few places where he does contemplate the relation between labor and sexuality—pertaining to both the bourgeoisie and the working class, we assume—is his description of the "first phase" of industrialization in nineteenth-century Europe, where he argues that the politico-economic need to mobilize the labor force resulted in an "elision of sex," or "its re-striction solely to the reproductive function." He further argues that the formation of the labor force took place through "avoid[ing] any useless expenditure, wasted energy."[18] I would argue here that the Foucauldian notion of elision of sex as expenditure or restriction of sex to reproduction must be conceptualized in specific relation to respective classes, by posit-ing that the bourgeoisie's sexual expenditure was carried out in the form of proletarian sexual labor, that is, prostitution. Jeffrey Weeks and Judith

Walkowitz, among others, have demonstrated that the European cities of the Victorian age were thoroughly saturated with the ongoing commercialization of sex. The ideological iconography—and its manifestation in reality—of the Victorian lady as sexually pure and virtuous was physically and economically joined to the vast "underbelly of prostitution."[19] I would argue also that for the working class of South Korea during the initial stages of industrialization—as well as for the colonized proletariat under Japanese rule during the Asia–Pacific Wars—sex was not "elided" or "restricted to reproduction," but rather the "violent and physical constraints"[20] on the body were produced as gendered sex and sexualized labors, as military work, nonmilitary (or industrial) sex labor, and military sex work.

For Foucault, sex in modern Europe became a thing "to be managed, inserted into systems of utility, regulated for the greater good of all."[21] Since he implicitly conceives of the utility of sex as limited to such areas as health, longevity, and reproduction, the value of sex is ultimately economic, restricted to reproduction and the maintenance of the labor force and productivity. I would like to consider another kind of utility for sex and sexuality, in its commercialized and commodified form, as "play" or "recreation." This particular function of sex and sexuality as a "recreational" activity necessarily involves hierarchized power relations between groups determined by varied and shifting articulations of classes, genders, and races—for example, relations between bourgeois male and proletarian female, or those between proletarian male and proletarian female—in which the "playful" utility of sex and sexuality for one group necessarily becomes a form or dimension of labor as sex and sexualized labor for another. I would argue that commercialized and commodified sex and sexuality function as a particular form of social reproduction, in which the utility of the "playfulness" of sex and sexuality lies in the maintenance of bourgeois and proletarian industrial and military (male) workforces. "Playfulness" of commodified sex and sexuality displaces, reenacts, and reinforces the necessary violence that constitutes the hierarchized power relations between consumers and providers of commodified sex and sexuality. If "sex was a means of access both to the life of the body and the life of the species,"[22] then the truth of sex varied for the state, bourgeoisie, and working class. For national and global militarism and economic development, the bodies of the proletariat were differently invested, deployed, and consumed from those of the bourgeoisie. Furthermore, prostitution in globalized contexts became a major site where interracial, interclass, and intergender power relations played out. These chapters on military, sex, and military sex work situate sexualized working-class labors and the sexual dimensions of nonsexual labors as the very sites of an "especially dense transfer point for relations of power,"[23] in which multiple forces converge and intersect, such as neocolonial global capitalism, the developmental state, authoritarian nationalism and subimperialism, patriarchy, and masculinism.

Microphysical Discipline, Docility-Utility, and Sex Work or Sexualized Labors

Although Virilio's theorization of mobilization remains, for the most part, at the macro level of a "dictatorship of movement," he also refers to proletarianization as a "dictatorship of motor function."[24] He conceptualizes both military and industrial proletarianization as a process that engages the human subject at the level of bodily movements—"kinetics"—and produces workers as "mobile machines."[25] His notion of the production of proletarian labor at the micro level as "gestural" readily lends itself to comparison with Foucauldian concepts of discipline, and "docility-utility" in particular. For Foucault, as well as for Virilio, the soldier becomes the prototype of the modern worker, and the military serves as the model for modern discipline.[26] Foucault writes, "By the late eighteenth century, the soldier has become something that can be made, the machine required can be constructed . . . making it pliable . . . turning silently into the automatism of habit."[27] The system of disciplinary mechanisms produces differentiated, specified types of activities and behaviors as various "docility-utilities," regulating and modulating each movement for efficiency.[28] Foucault's notion of docility-utility, as exemplified by a military worker, or Virilio's notion of the laboring body as a set of dictated gestures, helps us deconstruct the distinction between productive (manufacturing) and reproductive (service) labors and rethink all labors as types of service labor.

Service Labor as a Prototype: Production of Behaviors

In this book, I address four different kinds of labor: military labor, (industrial) sex work, military sex work, and migrant industrial labor. The first three are types of service labor, while the last is normally classified as a productive labor. While Marxist theories tend to privilege commodity manufacturing over service labor, any kind of hard and fast distinction between productive and reproductive labor is difficult to maintain. As all labors produce either services or commodities that service, all labors are, at a fundamental level, "service labors." Service labor produces the human body, human body parts, and human behavior as commodities, but the manufacturing labor that produces commodities cannot be performed without, first, a process of discipline and domination that transforms a human subject into a worker. What constitutes the ideological and material basis and impetus of capitalism is, ultimately, the disciplinary system that converts human labor power into a labor commodity. Furthermore, if we consider commodities themselves as different extensions of the human mind or body, as prosthetics, so to speak—that is, if we can think beyond the dichotomy between the human subject and the inanimate object— then the manufacturing labor that produces commodities that "perform services" overlaps with service labor. In this sense, service labor exemplifies the capitalist construction of the human body and mind as disciplinable labor power and an exchangeable labor commodity.

I do not mean to suggest, of course, that service labor in general, and the three particular labors I discuss in this book, do not have characteristics that distinguish them from productive labors. A worker in a manufacturing industry exerts him- or herself, producing a commodity that represents the externalization of his or her time, effort, and skill into an alien object; in contrast, a service worker exerts him- or herself in order to produce him- or herself as a commodity.[29] In this sense, service labor as a particular kind of labor illustrates to us the most severe contradiction: the fact that the producer (the subject of labor) and the produced (the object of labor) are one and the same being. The "externalization" of labor that gets embodied in the very body, behavior, and activities of the worker as an alien object represents the most profound kind of alienation. Service labor has been characterized as a labor that is immediately consumed in the act of its exchange, or "exhausted in its performance," thus "abetting the forgetting of labor."[30] (Our discussion focuses on low-skilled, menial service labor and excludes professional service labor, which carries a completely different social and economic value and status.) In contrast to commodity production, in which human labor is preserved and transformed into the object produced, service labor, in its very re-productive capacity, must erase itself on behalf of the other who consumes the labor. The very evaporation of service in its performance sustains the consumer. If human labor is externalized in the product through the manufacturing process, labor externalized in the form of service is soon internalized by the consumer.

The magical disappearance of the labor in the process of absorption or transfer of service into the consumer also results in loss or damage to the service laborer's subjectivity, that is, in being forgotten.

I would further argue that the paradoxical nature of service lies in its contradiction between the materiality of service labor—the exertion of human labor—and the immateriality or the abstractness of its result. In contrast to manufacturing, where mechanization has become an essential dimension, replaceablity through machines is much more limited in service labor, although service labor can be enhanced or partially replaced by machines. To a large extent, human labor is an absolute necessity in service labor, as it requires human contact, a body's engagement with another body, and therefore necessarily involves an affective dimension. Due to these particularities, I maintain that low-skilled service labors are necessarily a type of surrogate labor. Service laborers become extended surrogate bodies, or body parts, to those who utilize the service. Service labors are labors that are replaceable only by human surrogates. Both military and sex workers are such service laborers, functioning as absolutely indispensable and eminently disposable human surrogates. Both military and sex labor require bodily performances and activities that are usually linked to socially constructed gendered behaviors. While the affective dimension is an inalienable element in these labors—obviously one cannot kill enemies, or have sex with a stranger, without having one's emotions involved at some level—the service simultaneously requires that the physical aspect of the labor be severed and compartmentalized from its inevitable affective engagement. The end goal of military labor as destruction of the enemy also necessarily includes the possibility, and perhaps inevitability, of being destroyed by the enemy. Military work that requires putting at risk one's life is the ultimate service labor, since it literally erases one in the act of performing the labor. Death in military service labor is the ultimate reproductive and surrogate labor, as it enables someone else to live. A military worker works and dies as a surrogate. This is why the economic and social aspect of military "service," that is, the particularities of it *as* a labor, must be occluded and obfuscated: military service (labor) is nationalized, sacralized, and memorialized, thus, forgotten.

Disciplined Body as a Surrogate

Dipesh Chakrabarty interprets Marx's notion of abstract labor as being grounded upon the Enlightenment conception of the human subject as bearer of juridical freedom and abstract and universal equality. Chakrabarty further argues that such a notion of abstract labor is embedded in the contradictory situation of modern labor, which is "juridically free and yet socially unfree." According to him, the idea of abstract labor makes it possible to "extract from peoples and histories that were all different a homogeneous and common unit for measuring human activity."[31] Put another way, it is the notion of abstract equality that creates a marketplace of labor commodities and, in turn, undergirds the possibility of surrogate and prosthetic labor. When we consider the premodern contexts, both Western and Asian, where one's "economic" activities were necessarily integrated into one's "social" status, it is only in the modern marketplace of labor power, where one's labor is abstractly and fantastically separated out from other aspects of one's identity (such as class, race, and nationality), that we can have a group of people (proletarian, nonwhite, non-Korean, peripheral) performing labor as surrogates for another group (bourgeois, white, Korean, core or semiperipheral). Therefore, the differences between labor commodities that Chakrabarty speaks of do not disappear but articulate themselves as racial, class, or national surrogacies in the global labor market in various forms. In other words, surrogate labor operates by the paradox of simultaneous sameness or equivalence and difference or hierarchy of race, class, and gender. If abstract equality renders the substitutability of labor possible, the unfree and unequal conditions of race or nationality, class and gender are articulated as the proletarianization of sexuality and race. The substitutability of surrogate labors—performed by racialized or gendered populations for the relatively universalized subjects—and unsubstitutability are simultaneously acknowledged and erased by the cheaper wages contracted for them. The im/measurable and in/calculable difference between races, genders, or classes are measured and calculated as monetary differences.

TRANSNATIONAL PROLETARIANIZATION OF RACE

I will explore here, first, what I call the proletarianization of race, that is, the economic and social appropriation of racialization for production of labor, often organized and regulated through state racism or by the racial state.[32] Reading Foucault's scattered notions of the relations among race, sexuality, and the state, Ann Stoler concludes that the state's bio-political powers are a "crucial feature of racism."[33] Second, I will further elaborate the notion of the proletarianization of sexuality discussed in the previous section by examining the necessary intersection of sexuality with ethnicity and race, what Joane Nagel calls "ethnosexualities," that is, the ways in which "ethnosexualities"—as "sites where ethnicity is sexualized and sexuality is racialized, ethnicized, and nationalized"—become the object of transnational proletarianization.[34] This book examines three working-class labors—South Korean military labor in Vietnam, South Korean military prostitution for the U.S. troops, and Asian and other migrant labor in contemporary South Korea—as instances of the transnational proletarianization of race.

The presupposed isomorphism between homogeneous ethnicity, based on a biologistic notion of common ancestry, and such elements as long-standing territorial boundaries and shared language and culture, has helped to lay the foundation for Korean nationalism since the onset of modernity. However, when we look into the historical processes that constructed Korean ethnicity, as a modern political and cultural category Korean ethnicity has always been, from its very inception, a product of transnational and transethnic interactions. As such, Korean ethnicity is an ideological construct that has undergone a series of changes, as the very transnational contexts of what constitutes "Korea" have fluctuated through the rapid changes of the colonial and postcolonial eras. Rising out of the context of Japan's colonization of Chosŏn in the early twentieth century, Korean anticolonial ethnonationalism mirrored various dimensions of Japan's imperial nationalism in form, while supplying "uniqueness" in content. Korean ethnicity's essential linkage to the nation-state was forged as Chosŏn— a premodern monarchy whose ideological bases were not ethnic—was transformed into a proto-ethnic nation in the very moment of its demise. Korean nationalism at this particular transnational moment was built on the resistive assertion of ethnic purity that performatively helped create unity and solidarity around a single ethnicity. Put another way, Korean ethnic nationalism was a reaction to the Japanese empire's production of Koreans as an ethnicized or racialized collective. While the colonial proletariat, as a further racialized sector, had made up the bottom strata of the imperial workforce for the Japanese colonial state and capital since the beginning of the annexation, with Japan's entry into the full-scale Asia–Pacific Wars in the early 1930s the status of Korean ethnicity—and Korean ethnic nationalism—underwent certain modifications in relation to the colonial state's assimilationist policies, employed for the purpose of total mobilization. The assimilationist policies that were to engineer a multiethnic, multicultural empire under wartime imperatives further helped produce the ethnosexualities of Korean male and female working-class populations as a military-industrial proletariat (as imperial soldiers and industrial workers) and as military-industrial sex workers (as Comfort Women). The colonial mobilization during the assimilationist period generated ambivalent and contradictory effects in that, while it was premised on certain further intensifications of the racialization of the colonized— rather than a lessening of it—at the same time, the state's effort to multiethnicize and multiculturalize the empire loosened the essentialized linkage between ethnicity and the nation or empire. In other words, as the Japanese empire became multiethnic, with Korean ethnics incorporated as members (albeit second class), I would argue that this was the first historical precedent that pried Korean ethnicity away from the Korean nation-state, to be imagined now and to be built later, after independence. If this possibility of separating Korean ethnicity from the Korean nation-state was performed for the racialized and colonized by the Japanese empire, we will see how this decoupling of Korean ethnicity from the nation-state takes place again in the new century, as South Korea begins to emerge as a subempire that needs to incorporate a multiethnic workforce into its population.

Although postcolonial nation-building in South Korea was an intensely ethnonationalized, or ethnonationalizing, process, it was, again, a product of transnational history. Most important, the very existence of South Korea as a political entity owed itself to the United States' determination not to lose Asia to the powerful dominance of indigenous communists in various postcolonial locations in the immediate post–World War II era. Although South Korean ethnic nationalism was thus born of a confluence of transnational forces, such as the new U.S. imperialist impulse, the global cold war conflict, and the South's ideological confrontation with the communist North, postcolonial South Korean ethnic nationalism precluded the considerations of such transnational historicity. The postcolonial context, in which liberation from Japan brought Korean ethnicity and the nation-state form "back" together for the first time, seemed to compel South Koreans to accept this coincidence of ethnicity and the nation-state as a "natural" condition more readily and more firmly. The ubiquitous imperative, called the "Modernization of Our Nation" (choguk kŭndaehwa), under successive South Korean regimes between the early 1960s and 1980s, which thoroughly saturated the South Korean populace, neglected to take note of the fact that the very process of nationalist economic development was necessarily that of transnationalizing the South Korean economy, through South Korea's integration into global capitalism. This historical equivalence between economic development on the one hand and post-colonial nation-building on the other has tended to suppress the simultaneously constitutive transnational dimension of modernization in South Korea. The presumed nonviability of industrialization, via the 1950s strategy called Import Substitution and its 1960s replacement of export-oriented industrialization, marked the South Korean economy's integration into global capitalism, with the international division of labor built into it. For the antigovernment left-leaning and radical leftist dissidents of the industrializing era, South Korea's subordinated relations with the United States occasioned critical historiography and cultural productions that are intensely anti-American and fervently ethnonationalist, rather than prompting considerations of the transnationality of South Korea and the more radical implications in terms of ethnicity, race, nation-state, and global militarism and capitalism. In other words, the deconstructive potential of recognizing the transnationality of South Korea's neocolonized relations with the United States was recuperated back into, or reconstructed as, South Korean leftist ethnic nationalism.

Although capitalism became even further transnationalized starting in the late 1960s, many agree that the nation-states have not relinquished their control over a range of spheres, such as citizenship, law, security, and the economy.[35] One of the most vital roles that the South Korean state has played since the era of industrialization is its role in the production and management of the labor force. The South Korean governments in the 1960s, '70s, and '80s worked hard at maintaining a cheap, docile, and abundant workforce through their use of laws and state violence so as to attract foreign investors and retain jobs in the EPZ plants. The state also played varying roles in the more marginal national and transnational working-class labors that I discuss in this book: first, it functioned as a transnational labor broker in exporting military labor to the Vietnam War; second, it participated in promoting and managing military prostitution in camp towns; and finally, in conjunction with institutions in the private sector, it helps to import, manage, and control the migrant and immigrant worker population in contemporary South Korea. If the South Korean state of the earlier era contributed in significant ways to the creation of a transnational labor force, its reliance on ethnonationalism was essential in precisely obfuscating the transnational dimension of this mobilization. The contemporary South Korean government now deploys multiculturalist and multiethnic subimperialist nationalism in domesticating South Korea's new transnational labor, that is, migrant and immigrant workers.

During the U.S. wars against Asian communism in the post-1945 era in Korea, Vietnam, and Southeast Asia, American anticommunism as a state ideology operated in conjunction with its anti-Asian state racism. U.S. state racism was a significant contributing factor in escalating the scale of the American destruction of Asian peoples and territories in the post-1945 era. However, American state racism was perpetrated not only against its Asian enemies, but also against its own Asian allies—South Korean and other Southeast Asian surrogate forces—and against its own racialized minorities who made up the majority of the draftees. Similarly, the atrocities committed by the South Korean military against Vietnamese civilians must also be traced back to the more systematic racism made possible by the South Korean state and its military authorities. The South Korean military's relationship with military prostitution in Vietnam also resembles the close linkage between the U.S. military's appropriation of South Korean women's ethnosexualities and American state racism. In both cases, the South Korean military in Vietnam and the U.S. military in South Korea, I examine the cultural productions that delineate the ways in which state racisms articulate themselves as bio-political measures that regulate the movement, the body, and the health of soldiers and sex workers.

As South Korea's position moved from periphery to semiperiphery, the South Korean export of labor power was substituted with two forms of non-ethnic Korean labor: foreign offshore labor in various locations and migrant labor in South Korea from more peripheral economies. South Korea itself now replaced the bottom strata of its working class with a racialized surrogate labor force. South Korean camp towns for the U.S. military, where South Korean working-class women and men once lived and worked as internally diasporized Koreans and deterritorialized workers for the United States, have been replaced with migrant sex and sexualized service workers, again deterritorialized and diasporized from their own native locations, such as Russia and the Philippines. The last chapter of this book concentrates on the proletarianization of the racialized migrant population, largely male industrial labor, while also touching on female migrants' sexualized labors. It highlights various aspects of the South Korean state's governance over the migrant population, that is, its role as a "racial state" to borrow Omi and Winant's term.[36] The South Korean state plays contradictory functions in regard to racialized minorities; on the one hand, the state helps to normalize, acculturate, and assimilate immigrants and migrants into the "domestic" workforce through the use of various official channels, such as setting up Korean language training, legalizing the education of children of undocumented workers, and promoting, in general, liberal multiculturalism. On the other hand, the state is a main agent, in collusion with South Korean businesses, in structuring foreign labor migration through the legislation of racist, discriminatory laws that regulate and restrict all aspects of the lives of the racialized workforce.

If the South Korean working class once experienced transnational racialization vis-à-vis its external core counterparts, contemporary South Korea is undergoing a process of internal racial formation.[37] While Korean ethnicity was never a stable entity in the earlier modern periods, as we have seen above, it is now being reformulated and reconceptualized in much more radical ways, in the context of the intensifying globalization of the South Korean economy and the consequent multiethnicization of its population. Only very recently has Korean identity, Koreanness, or the Korean nation and nationality begun to be delinked from its exclusive attachment to ethnicity. We are witnessing the very incipient stage of a process of gradual de-ethnicization of Koreanness, as Korean identity is being broadened to include plural cultures and multiple ethnicities. While a reconceptualization of Koreanness as multiple, heterogeneous, and hybrid, to borrow Lisa Lowe's formulation,[38] is on the one hand a political and intellectual necessity now and a goal to strive for in the future, on the other hand we also know too well, from the U.S. context, the ways in which such radically inclusionary conceptions of a national identity can be domesticated, coopted, and recuperated by hegemonic multiculturalism to serve imperial interests. As I mention above, a similar strategy of assimilationist multiculturalism was adopted by the Japanese empire through its most violent expansionist period at the end of World War II. The dissolution of South Korea as a mono-ethnic nation-state, attended by an inclusive expansion of Koreanness, is not only a symptom of South Korea's changed status as a subempire, but also a strategy for its maintenance and further extension. In this latest context, where Korean ethnicity comes to occupy a quasi-universal or subuniversalist position in regard to the racialized minority migrant worker populations, the "original" Korean ethnicity

or "Korean" Koreanness, as opposed to other varieties of Koreanness—
that is, multiethnic, multicultural, and minoritized Koreanness—comes to
represent a dominant Koreanness, that is, one equipped with full citizenship and full ethnic cultural authenticity. On the other hand, dominant
Koreanness also comes to be defined in relation to or as a result of anti-
Korean sentiment or anti-Koreanism, as a collective resistive movement
rises among the minorities. This dominant Koreanness has already begun
to function in the similar way that whiteness does in the United States.

These new trends that are beginning to reconceptualize Koreanness, I
would argue, are connected to two concepts that connect South Korea to
broader global contexts. First, the hierarchized notion of Korean identity
is connected to an emergent pan-Asianism. If the South Korean move
toward pan-Asianism parallels other Asian nation-states' ongoing con-
solidation of themselves as a regional economic power bloc, it is also
related to South Korean capital's racial diversification of its workforce,
both domestic and overseas, which consists largely of pan-Asian populations. This pan-Asianist tendency, whether it is associated with the government or with more progressive NGOs, seems to be reminiscent of its
previous manifestation, wartime Japanese imperialist pan-Asianism, that
was necessarily predicated on a civilizational hierarchy and suborien-
talizing racialization of other Asians. Rather than promise much difference,
the contemporary South Korean version appears to be another historical
repetition.

Another aspect of this expansive and diverse Koreanness is growing pan-
Koreanism. If pan-Asianism recuperates the essentialism of Korean identity by means of hierarchization, pan-Koreanism represents a subimperial
desire to re-essentialize Korean ethnicity. Pan-Koreanism, as an ideology
becoming gradually pronounced in the mass media, and as a more explicit
policy and concerted practice in the South Korean government and corporations, is, in part, related to the newfound usefulness of overseas diasporic ethnic Korean populations as human resources in multiple locations
in the age of globalization. This newly emergent deterritorialized Korean
identity is also related to the continuing emigration and fast-growing
cosmopolitanism of middle-class and elite South Koreans to various locations, including North America and Australia. While the very value of
overseas Koreans lies in their cultural diversity and hybridity, it is their re-
essentialized Korean ethnicity that qualifies them as global agents of the
subempire. Although the cultural boundary is expanded in this inclusive

definition of diasporic "Koreans" as Korean, pan-Koreanism redraws the subimperial—no longer national—boundary around the core, that is, the "essential" Koreanness. As historical circumstances metamorphose in rapid and complex manners, essentialist notions of Korean ethnicity seem to adapt themselves in a similarly flexible and strategic fashion. In its role either as an agent of racializing and assimilating migrant workers, or as that of renationalizing and re-essentializing overseas Korean diasporics, South Korea as a nation-state must now operate transnationally, across national borders, while simultaneously reinforcing the boundaries of ethnicity. In other words, the concept of "Koreanness" that can include overseas Korean diasporics is exclusively ethnically defined, excluding their cultural diversity, while another concept of "Koreanness," beginning to emerge, that can include (racialized) immigrants and migrants is culturally defined. The South Korean state and capital are finding both definitions of "Koreanness," either multiracial and transethnic Koreanness or pan-Korean, diasporic and translocal Koreanness, instrumental in appropriating the transnational labors of both groups.

DEVELOPMENTALISM AND MILITARISM IN SOUTH KOREA UNDER PARK CHUNG HEE

Developmental Authoritarianism and Militarism

South Korea's development began in earnest only after a young general named Park Chung Hee mounted a military coup in 1961 and eventually succeeded in getting himself elected president of the Republic of Korea in 1963. Only when we situate Park Chung Hee's fervor for development during the two decades of his rule, from 1961 until his assassination in 1979, in the larger context of the United States' invention, promotion, and purveying of "development" as an ideology and policy in the Third World,[39] are we then able to grasp the urgency of development felt by the Park regime, not as an exception but rather as an instance that squarely fits with the global trend of the time. As the American ideology of development was inventing the Third World, South Korea under Park Chung Hee's leadership reinvented itself as a "developing country" (*kaebal tosangguk*) at this time.

The period of Park Chung Hee's rule between 1961 and 1979, commonly known as the era of industrialization (*sanŏphwa sidae*), resulted in unprecedented social and economic changes in South Korean history.

Critical South Korean scholarship has characterized Park's leadership as "developmentalist authoritarianism" (kaebal tokjae), while others in South Korea and the United States have also described the period under Park as "militarized modernization."[40] Both concepts refer to Park's rule as a dictatorship that exploited the global and national injunction for economic development for the purpose of justifying his authoritarian governance.[41] The path of developmentalist authoritarianism on which Park placed South Korea was maintained by his successor, Chun Doo Hwan, a military dictator who seized power in a bloody coup d'état in 1980 and ruled the country until 1987. After South Korea began to make its gradual transition to liberal democracy in the late 1980s, and throughout the 1990s, the very recent past of military dictatorship and militarized development continued to be a significant legacy that needed to be documented, researched, analyzed, and overcome. Therefore, I begin my contextualization of the transnational labors of South Korea by inquiring into the two interrelated historical dimensions of the era of industrialization: developmentalism and militarism.

Developmentalism as an Ideology

Park Chung Hee's personal connections to Japanese colonialism—his brief career as a young soldier in the Japanese army in Manchuria and his frank admiration for the Meiji Reform—have often been cited by Korean scholars as one of the explanations for his military dictatorship and his fascistic pursuit of development. While there is validity in recognizing such connections, it would serve us better to understand the historical relations between the Japanese colonial modernization and Park Chung Hee's postcolonial version in broader terms. In contrast to many other extraction colonies of the late nineteenth and early twentieth centuries under European rule, the Korean peninsula was a colony that was developed and industrialized especially through the 1930s and '40s. Colonial Korea occupied an exceptional place in modern colonial history when it was allowed to join the expanding Japanese empire as a junior partner.[42] One of the most important factors in historicizing South Korean development is the extent to which the colonial elites were assimilated into the imperial power structure, and, further, the ways in which their partial integration became a historical opportunity for their interpellation into the ideologies of modernization. Unlike the majority of colonies under Western rule, in which biologistic conceptions of racial hierarchy minimized the possibility of development,[43] Japan's incorporation of Korean elites into its political and economic power structure in effect initiated the upper stratum of the colonized into recognizing the eminent possibility of modernization on their own.

Not only for the Park regime and its Western-educated elite teams of bureaucrats and technocratic experts, but also for the majority of the South Korean population, the ideology of development and modernization was soon to become an internalized imperative. Park Chung Hee availed himself of the already existing ethnonationalism, born of anticolonial resistance prior to liberation from Japanese rule and further heightened during Syngman Rhee's rule after liberation, and joined it to developmentalism. Park's formula of ethnonationalizing developmentalism was very effective in mobilizing the population, as it was proffered as a decisive strategy of overcoming the nation's historical collective oppression, that is, that of decolonization. The Park regime's revival of neo-Confucian ideals, such as filial piety *(hyo)*, loyalty to the state *(ch'ung)*, and spirit of mutual aid *(sangbu sangjo)*, further lent support to mobilizing ethnonationalism for modernization. The traditional concept of the state as a familial entity was particularly useful in helping to build solidarity within the ethnonational collective that would transcend class divisions, while other values, such as patience, ability to endure suffering, and willingness to sacrifice, were also called upon for the purpose of creating a docile modern workforce.[44] The regime's ability to forge an absolute linkage between the welfare of the ethnonational collective on the one hand, and economic development on the other, was essential in advancing economic development as a national ideology.

Slogans such as "Let's Live Better!" *(Chalsara bose!)* and "If We Try, We Can Do It" *(Hamyŏn toenda)* were widely disseminated by the Park regime and deeply internalized in the minds of South Koreans. The first catchphrase, "Let's Live Better!" with its presumption of poverty, produced the rationale for development, while the policies for development were, in fact, destroying subsistence living in the countryside and further impoverishing the urban working class, as we will see below. The other phrase, "If We Try, We Can Do It," operated by promoting self-empowerment and self-responsibilization of the population. It effectively put to use the strategy of voluntarization that had already become an important marker of modern subjectivity in the colonial period.[45] Together with the Confucian values, such slogans created desires and disciplined the emotions of South Koreans as developmental subjects. Developmental ideology operated in an ambivalent way; it successfully subjugated the populace in the state mobilization of the workforce, while energizing and motivating (that is, subjectifying) them to be modern ethnonational subjects as never before. In propagandizing the ideology of development, the government used an extensive network of various interconnected channels, such as state-controlled mass media, educational institutions, neighborhood associations, and economic organizations. Under Park, the ideology of developmentalism became a "cultural system" in which such multiple actors came to take part.[46] As a cultural system that went beyond mere state policies and penetrated into the material practices and consciousness of people's daily lives, the Park regime was relatively successful in generating a sense of unity as an ethnonational collective, integrating different segments of society and surmounting class lines. Reaching the status of unquestionable social certainty soon to be realized,[47] the ethos of development, "modernization of our country" (choguk kŭndaehwa), became a historical mission for all South Koreans to take upon themselves, in order to achieve a "renaissance of the Korean people" (minjok chunghŭng), another catchphrase of the Park era.

Development as a Policy

Through the period of South Korea's industrialization, between the mid-1960s and the mid-1980s, the sole advantage South Korea, a country with few natural resources, had over its competitors was its abundant cheap labor.[48] It would not be an exaggeration to say that industrialization for South Korea equaled the economic imperative to create and manage a modern workforce, that is, to utilize effectively the only resource it had. Starting in the early 1960s, the South Korean government began pursuing the key policy of keeping the prices of agricultural products low—a policy designed to systematically pauperize the rural area and make staples affordable for the urban working class. The class of small farmers was affected most severely, and the younger members of this class, both male and female, came to supply the majority of the industrial labor. The constant oversupply of cheap labor for the industrial sector was the result of continuing migration from the countryside to the urban centers throughout the 1970s.[49] Through consecutive stages—the "take-off" period in the latter half of the 1960s, the concentration on "light industry" from the early to mid-1970s, and the period of transitioning into "heavy industry" in the late '70s and the first half of the '80s—one of the most important roles for the South Korean state was to sustain this vital supply of cheap labor for domestic businesses and for foreign companies and investors.[50] The intimate relationship between the South Korean state—under Park Chung Hee, as well as under the subsequent military dictators, Chun Doo Hwan and Roh Tae Woo—and family-owned big businesses, known as *chaebŏl* (*zaibatsu* in Japanese), is a subject that has been much researched and well-documented.[51] The state saw its role as protecting and fostering conglomerates through organizing and distributing foreign capital, offering legal and taxation benefits, helping to accumulate domestic capital and channeling it to them, and systematically preventing the organization of labor and suppressing labor activism.[52] While labor laws in the South Korean constitution, modeled after that of the United States, were liberal, not only were they never enforced, but the military dictatorships instituted other executive laws and regulations that seriously curtailed the rights of workers.[53] Until the end of authoritarian rule, South Korean workers did not have the basic three labor rights to strike, organize, and engage in collective bargaining.[54] The rate of unionization of workers was very low throughout the 1970s, as the state and corporations mobilized public and private forces—the police, KCIA, and thugs—to prevent, interrupt, and punish efforts to organize labor.[55] The authoritarian style of South Korean corporate management and the militarized discipline of workers in the factories kept the workers in line. The label of "communism" was an ever ready and powerful apparatus for the South Korean state in suppressing labor activism. As accumulation of capital resulted from the exploitation of labor, the state and capital formed a "powerful alliance against labor."[56]

While the South Korean state's policy on domestic industrial labor, though draconian and militarized, still falls more or less within the range of the role played by other developmental nation-states, the South Korean state's function in regard to the nation's military labor in Vietnam (see chapter 1) and contemporary migrant labor (see chapter 4) goes further. In the case of the former, the South Korean state operated more or less as a labor broker, mobilizing, maintaining, and negotiating with another government, the United States. In the case of the latter, it also played a major role as an agent, this time in importing labor from contributing countries. The state also played a significant role in mobilizing and legislating working-class women's sexuality, that is, in industrializing sex. The Park Chung Hee government set up a series of laws, regulations, and legal mechanisms throughout the 1960s and '70s that were indirectly designed to facilitate the enlistment of working-class women into the profitable sex tourism industry.[57] This is another common thread this book will trace through the following four chapters: the government-led proletarianization of military labor, sex work for domestic and foreign clienteles, military and business, and migrant work, through intersecting state masculinism, state sexism, state classism, and state racism.

Below, I attempt to explore the various ways in which sex work interconnects with other mainstream labors in the broader context of the state-led industrialization in South Korea. As I mention above, the late 1960s and '70s saw the exodus of young men and women from peasant households to urban centers and industrial complexes. Of this migrant population, young women in their late teens and early twenties outnumbered their male counterparts. While the majority of these young women found work in factories and in middle-class homes as domestics, a larger percentage of the young men moved to Seoul seeking higher education. Other young women found jobs in the service industry as bus conductors and restaurant servers, as well as in sex and sexualized service industries, including full-time prostitution. In the South Korean context, where nuclear and extended families functioned as economic units, if the burden of carrying out agricultural labor fell on the shoulders of older women after young people departed for the city, young women's labor in factories, middle-class homes, restaurants, bars, and houses of prostitution and their meager wages also contributed to the household economy. As social mobility was perceived to be a collective matter for the family as a unit, rather than an individual achievement, daughters' labor more often than not served the goal of financing the higher education of sons, whose success, in turn, would push the entire family into a higher economic stratum. The idea of a filial daughter's sexual sacrifice for the sake of her male siblings or her parents was a familiar and sacralized Confucian custom, sarcastically dubbed by some the "Sim Ch'ŏng phenomenon."[58] Young women's sex and sexualized service labors were thus mobilized initially at the level of family and the domestic sphere through the intersecting ideologies of familism and patriarchy. The state's call for modernization would be translated into a massive mobilization of young women into sex and sexualized service industries by such traditional ideologies. Their contribution to the family income, which helped to sustain the general survival of the family as an economic unit, was, of course, necessarily an integral part of the South Korean national economy. As the wages from sex and the sexualized service jobs of young unmarried women were slated for their male siblings' education, they made a specific economic contribution to the production of South Korea's next generation of a higher-skilled, educated (male) labor force. What made capital accumulation possible, which later led to South Korea's "graduation" into heavy industries (understood in gendered terms as "masculine"), was women's labor in all areas.[59] As in many other industrializing contexts, South Korea was no exception: modernization was made possible through women's unpaid and low-paid labor.[60] My intention here is to bring attention to the ways in which invisible labors are necessarily intertwined with mainstream labors as an integral part of the national and transnational economy. Indeed they have been barely considered "labors": soldiers in Vietnam were national heroes, but not workers; prostitution was ubiquitous, and yet sex work, counting only as sexual degradation, remained clandestine; migrant workers are a growing presence, but their "illegal" status renders them into nonworkers, workers without rights. If the wealth of cheap human labor was one of the most significant driving forces behind the "miracle" of South Korean industrialization and the postindustrial South Korean state and capital must continue to wager its future success on finding cheaper labor now outside its national boundary (including North Korea), then the "cheapness" of labor is determined by multiple ideological factors that concern race, gender, and a nation-state's development level in the international context. South Korean soldiers in Vietnam cost the United States a mere fraction of what its own troops cost. The U.S. military, stationed in South Korea, expressed its incredulity at how "cheap" South Korean women sex workers were in the 1960s and '70s. Now South Korean men go on sex tours in search of "cheap" women in Southeast Asia. Domestically and internationally, cheap labor has been an ideological creation of the policies of the developing states and the neocolonial First World that transformed the peasantry in subsistence living into the urban poor, generating desperate economic conditions that, in turn, produced a psychological willingness to work for cheap wages. Cheap industrial labor is also produced by the support of other kinds of labors provided cheaply or without pay, that is, by women's labors; cheap labor is made possible by even cheaper labor in the stratification of labor.

Militarism, Anti-communism, and Militarization for Development

Although the connection between militarism and modernization must be traced back to the Japanese colonial occupation, "militarized modernity" came into its own with Park Chung Hee as the first official military ruler and became a postcolonial "sovereign" practice.[61] I situate South Korean development—and its transnational labors, the topic of this book—in its intimate relations with the militarization of South Korean society, South Korean submilitarism in Vietnam, and the U.S. cold war militarism that involved greater Southeast Asia. South Korea's decision to dispatch troops to the Vietnam War in 1965 was a linchpin in locking South Korea into a position as one of the junior partners in the U.S.-led global capitalist network. In helping to support U.S. hegemony in the greater Asian region, South Korea's submilitarism in Vietnam—subordinated to U.S. militarism—jumpstarted South Korean industrialization in its beginning stages.[62] As the historical role of South Korea's participation in the Vietnam War is inextricably linked to the subsequent rise of South Korea in the 1990s as a subimperial power, South Korea's overall development, which took place during the cold war, must also be located in relation to its geopolitical strategic indispensability to the United States' anticommunist militarism in Asia. The close relationship between militarism and economic development in the South Korean domestic context is well illustrated by the twin slogans that Park Chung Hee put forth as soon as he seized power: "Autonomous Economy" and "Autonomous Defense."[63] Park's idea of "Autonomous Defense" pointed to the historical shift that South Korea underwent, from engaging in a hot war against the communist North to a cold war confrontation with the same.

Although the most frequently studied aspect in the historical examination of Park's military dictatorship is the militarization of the political sphere,[64] recently, more scholars have begun to pay more attention to the generalized nature of militarism, that is, the militarization of South Korean society that penetrated deeply into the everyday life of the villages and cities, accomplished through dissemination of militarist nationalist ideologies in schools, factories, and companies, through various programs and policies at all levels and venues of South Korean society.[65] Just to name a few examples, not only did South Korean companies adopt military and militarized tactics to discipline their workers, but the South Korean state's collaboration with big business also consisted of militarized control of labor resistance.[66] The Park government's founding of a civilian reserve force, Hyangt'o yebigun (Homeland Security Reserve), and its introduction of compulsory military education as part of the high school and university curriculum, did much to further transform South Korea into a thoroughly militarized and totally mobilized "country on the verge of development" *(kaebal tosangguk)*.[67] The general militarization of South Korean society was again aided a great deal by the public's memory of the Korean War and the ongoing cold war confrontation with the North.

Park Chung Hee proposed economic development and modernization as a strategy of contending with communism and continued to exploit it throughout the course of his successive presidencies. Park pronounced, "The foremost task for us, besieged by chronic impoverishment, is to eliminate poverty, and that is the only way to defeat and overcome communism."[68] If the threat of communism was a compelling argument for development in the broader global context,[69] South Koreans, who had already experienced a war with the communist North, did not need much persuasion that modernization could be an effective weapon against communism. Anticommunist development, or developmentalist anticommunism, was reformulated as freedom from communism; development was freedom.[70] The problem of opposing ideologies between North and South Korea— what had once taken the form of a military conflict on the peninsula—was being offered an economic solution. The success of South Korean development, a victory in the economic front of the war against communism, was to serve as an ideological role model for the rest of the Third World.[71] The extent of support that Park's military rule was able to garner for itself from the population—or the relative absence of opposition to the regime— can be attributed to a complex of historical factors and Park's effective manipulation of them: the Korean War and Park's use of the memory of the Korean War; the post–Korean War elimination of the left, and Park's thorough anticommunization of South Korean society; and the potential threat of another war with the North, which Park proposed to win by economic development.

South Korea as an Ideological Model Minority

For the entire Park era and beyond—even amid the most vehement protests against military dictatorships—modernization, economic development, and industrialization had no rivals as the inevitable and eventual social realities to be achieved as the future of the Korean people. Arturo Escobar refers to the dominance and authority that the discourse of developmentalism gained in the Third World countries as a "colonization of reality."[72] South Korean development soon became an example, serving as a model minority in the broader context of the United States' neocolonial "under-development and impoverishment" of countries in Latin America and Africa.[73] The most recent evidence of South Korean victory over the communist North is South Korea's transformation of the North Korean city Kaesŏng into an "Export Processing Zone"—a contemporary version of the 1970s and '80s South Korean EPZs under the hegemony of the core economies—where North Korean workers share with other migrant and offshore laborers a contribution to South Korean and global capital as cheap labor.

South Korea's authoritarian development can be usefully compared to the Japanese colonial state's total mobilization efforts in the late colonial period during the Asia–Pacific Wars. Under a new legal provision in the late 1930s, the colonial state mobilized Korean men and women as part of Chŏngsindae, whose literal meaning in translation is "Volunteering Body Corps," for labors of all kinds, including factory and mining work, military support labor, military labor, and sex work. Female sex workers for male military and industrial workers were called Comfort Women.[74] Without necessarily equating the Japanese colonial state's imperialist militarism and industrialization with the postcolonial South Korean state's modernization, the parallel we note between these two historical processes—along with significant differences—is remarkable, especially when we consider mobilization of the four different labors—military labor, (domestic industrial) sex work, military prostitution for the United States, and migrant labor—that this book examines. If the assimilated Korean elites of the colonial period already acted as "self-"colonizing agents in this process, we could further argue that South Korean military dictatorships and their partners are postcolonial extensions of such autocolonizing agents of the earlier era in the changed, neocolonial context of the period after World War II. We might, in fact, be able to define neocoloniality precisely as a type of colonization that takes place through the dominated group's internalization of colonizing discourses and governmentality as their own, without necessarily underestimating the significance of authoritarian development as a self-empowering, autonomizing process that resulted in South Korea's rise as a subimperial power.

Conclusion: Mobilization, Mobility, and Transnational Labors

When the South Korean economy was relatively more dependent on the political and economic hegemony of the core countries, South Korean working-class labor was not only serving the national power bloc, the South Korean state, and its close partner, South Korean capital, but also the transnational counterpart of the core nations. During this period, South Korea exported various kinds of cheap labor, including soldiers to Vietnam, nurses and miners to West Germany, construction workers to the Middle East, and emigrants to North and South America. South Korean female and male labor in EPZs, and military prostitution and other service labors performed in camp towns, were also types of labor "export." Since the 1990s the South Korean economy, the eleventh largest in the world, has required both offshore and migrant labor in order to maintain its growth and profitability. In considering this historical shift in the last part of the introduction below, first I inquire into the nature of the recent changes in South Korean labor—the postcolonial and neocolonial origins of all "South Korean" labor and the radical impact on the "South Korean" "national" community as a result of migrant and immigrant labor—in relation to the broader global context. Second, I explore another conceptual framework of this book, mobilization and mobility, that organizes the four respective chapters individually and as an interconnected historical narrative, intersecting with the central framework—the transnational proletarianization of sexuality and race.

Global labor migration and immigration from periphery to core nations, both of which have accelerated in the past three decades or so, have been understood as phenomena that trace their roots to the history of colonialism, as a postcolonial return of the ex-colonized "back" to the metropole. South Korea represents an interesting variation as a postcolonial location that has moved, only very recently, from a neocolony whose own migrants' and emigrants' "return" was destined for the United States, to a subempire to which other ex-colonized peoples of Asia migrate, short of reaching metropoles. This particular postcolonial movement to South Korea must be, once again, traced back to South Korea's neocolonial relations to the United States in the post-1945 era, as South Korea's emergence as a subempire itself is due to its paradoxically profitable domination by the United States. To the extent that South Korea now functions as a subordinate partner to the U.S. empire, Southeast and South Asians' "return" to South Korea is a detoured "return" to the United States on "Korean" soil. South Korean immigration to the United States in the period between the 1950s (after the Korean War) and the 1980s had strong ties to U.S. intervention in the Korean War, the subsequent U.S. military presence, and the U.S.–

South Korean relations of domination and cooperation, but the recent influx of Vietnamese workers and "immigrant brides" (*kyŏlhon ijuja*) into South Korea is a latter day manifestation of the earlier historical triangulation among Vietnam, South Korea, and the United States. Occupying the position of subempire entails performing a series of surrogate labors for the empire. South Korea "develops" peripheral nations, including North Korea, by "technology transfer," by disciplining the labor force in the offshore locations as subcontracting firms for the United States and other core economies, and by creating a consumer population with "made in Korea" products. In its role as a surrogate (sub)empire, South Korea also absorbs part of the formerly colonized populations who would have traveled further to the metropole.

The first three chapters of this book attempt to reconceptualize the mobilization of military work, (industrial) sex work, and military sex work—what had been narrativized within an intensely ethnonationalized context in the earlier era—as transnational. The postcolonial and neocolonial mobilization of these labors was a matter either of the movement of workers within the domestic boundary (as in industrial and military sex work) or of a symbolic bringing back of transnational laborers into the fold of the ethnic nation, if they had to cross a physical boundary (as in the case of South Korean military work in Vietnam) or the forgetting and excluding of others who chose to leave South Korea permanently (as in the cases of emigrants to North and South America or migrant workers who settled in places like Germany). In other words, these national and transnational mobilizations of labor were constantly being recuperated back into the ethnic nation. However, in contemporary South Korea and beyond, the very nature of transnational mobilization—the speed, volume, directionality, intensity, and complexity of people's movement—has changed. The most significant change for South Korea is the fact that it has become a receiving country of migrant workers. This new kind of transnational mobilization that South Korea is now experiencing has already transformed South Korea into an immigrant subimperial nation-state. On the one hand, South Korea as a new immigrant nation-state operates according to the conventional and still powerful conceptions of the nation-state and its sovereign rights to regulate its border. South Korea's status as a nation-state is simultaneously challenged by its changing position as what Arjun Appadurai calls a "transnation,"[75] whose characteristics are less formal and legal and more social, economic, and cultural. Appadurai defines transnation as "no longer a closed space for the melting pot to work its magic but yet another diasporic switching point."[76] South Korea as a transnation functions as a site that is open in its intimate network with other locations. Appadurai's concept of transnation views ethnic enclaves of migrants and immigrants not simply as isolated sites of racialized exploitation, but rather as transnational spaces with active linkages stretching out and connected to multiple global locations.

I began this introduction with Virilio's notion of dromology, the historical process of modern mobilization and proletarianization in Europe, finding its broad applicability to South Korean proletarianization as a transnational mobilization of male and female peasants in military and sex labors through the period of industrialization from the mid-1960s to the 1980s. Tracing the historical transition of the South Korean mobilization of transnational labors brought us to migrant and immigrant labor in contemporary South Korea. I would like to end the introduction by comparing the concept of dromology with the notion of mobility suggested in Appadurai's discussion of globalization. While Virilio's theorization of dromology offers much explanatory power by relating the simultaneously destructive and productive processes of state militarisms and capitalist accumulation to the governing forces that converted and deployed peasantry into a modern workforce, I find problematic the aspect of his thought that tends to regard the modern proletariat as sheer objects of mobilizing and disciplinary powers. This book inquires further into a couple of aspects that constitute this process of modern proletarianization. First, I argue that the modern production of the proletarian workforce is also a process of construction of a voluntaristic subject, a subject that has been formed through the Western liberal ideologies of free will, abstract equality, and self-reflexivity. This process of production of voluntaristic subjectivity is further intertwined in the South Korean context with psychological indoctrination and interpellation via such multiple ideologies as nationalism, anticommunism, developmentalism, and masculinism. The proletarian subject, like the bourgeois subject, is produced through the process of internalizing the governing ideologies as one's own. Second, the following chapters also explore the ways in which such voluntarized interpellation is simultaneously an imbrication with the resistive dimensions of this subjectivity. South Korean cultural productions represent these racialized and gendered or sexualized proletarian labors as constituted not only by the governing forces that deploy, discipline, and exploit them, but also by their resistive dimensions that contemplate and counter domination. The focus of this book, in exploring the literary and popular cultural productions of South Korea from the mid-1960s to the 1990s, is precisely to highlight a fundamentally conflictual, multilayered proletarian subjectivity, one that is formed through the thoroughly entwined processes of governmentalities, voluntarization, and resistance.

In Arjun Appadurai's work, the concept of mobility appears to rise out of, and apply to, the specific context of the contemporary mobilization of transnational labor in the age of intensified globalization. As the further polarized global economy resulted in a more severely unequal international division of labor, new technologies have come to enable complexity and frequency of movement of people, ideas, and cultures at a level that was unprecedented in the earlier phase of modernity. In this way, Appadurai's specific concept of mobility is most relevant to the last chapter of this book, which deals with contemporary migrant and immigrant labor in South Korea, but I would like to consider the more general significance of the notion of mobility in the context of the earlier era of South Korean industrialization, highlighting the agency and active resistance of the proletarian subject in contrast to Virilio's notion of mobilization as producing a proletariat that is mechanical, passive, and subjugated. When we consider both Virilio's and Appadurai's respective conceptions of mobilization and mobility together, the former tends to underscore the governing forces without giving due consideration to the agency of those who are mobilized, while the latter seems reluctant to investigate the new and varied strictures and structures placed on the globalized proletariat. In other words, my discussion of the cultural productions will pay close attention to mobilization in considering mobility and will take mobility into account when considering mobilization, both in the earlier era of industrialization in South Korea, as well as in postindustrial contemporary South Korea. A South Korean writer, Cho Sŏn-jak, whose work I will discuss in both chapters 1 and 2, calls the heroine of his novel, one who enters a brothel as a full-time prostitute after her valiant struggle during her sojourn in Seoul, a *nanmin*, a refugee: "Soon it became nighttime and Ŭn-ja was committed to one of the vacant rooms downstairs. That's right. There is no other word to describe it than to say, 'committed.' We usually call those who have lost their possessions and homes due to war, fire or flood, refugees. Refugees are supposed to be 'committed.' . . . As long as we are trying to understand Miss Yang Ŭn-ja as a refugee, we might as well make it clear what the disaster for her was. Wasn't it the blast of wind, the so-called modernization?"[77] However, by the time Cho Sŏn-jak makes this pronouncement of his heroine as a "refugee" at the end of the novel, he has already devoted about four hundred pages to constructing her as an agent of free will, though severely constrained—indeed, an agent of the modernization of herself and life. In other words, he combines a representation of his heroine as both an economic refugee and economic migrant, if we endow the term "migrant" with more voluntarism than the sense of determination associated with the word "refugee." Similar to sex workers for the domestic clientele (treated in chapter 2), South Korean volunteer soldiers for the Vietnam War, military sex workers for the U.S. troops, and migrant workers in contemporary South Korea (respectively the topics of chapters 1, 3, and 4) can also be understood as representing a varying ratio of intersecting forces of determination and resistive agency, that is, simultaneously as objects of governing and mobilizing powers and as subjects of mobility.

The first chapter, "Surrogate Military, Subempire, and Masculinity: South Korea in the Vietnam War," explores the critical redefinitions of masculinity by analyzing literary representations of South Korean military labor in Vietnam as a gendered and sexualized service labor that was masculinizing or emasculating and racializing or racialized in the context of stratified ethno-masculinities. It further examines the militarized masculine bodies' sexualized relations with racialized military sex workers. I conclude the chapter by considering the (dis)connections between remembrance of the war and searching for possible reconciliation and reparation on the one hand, and the current South Korean economic and cultural "interests" in Vietnam on the other. Chapter 2, "Domestic Prostitution: From Necropolitics to Prosthetic Labor," examines varying masculinist perspectives on the economic, social, and symbolic value of prostitution: neo-Confucian subsumption, sublimation, and elision of female sex work for patriarchal family, class, and nation; prostitution as a social work for the national (male) collective; and commoditization of feminine sexuality as a cultural emblem for the urbanization process. The chapter contrasts these views to politicized representations that understand domestic sex work's fluid boundary with other working-class women's and men's labors, its connection or disconnection to military sex work for U.S. troops, and its place in the national and transnational industrialization process. The third chapter, "Military Prostitution: Gynocentrism, Racial Hybridity, and Diaspora," focuses on the recent revisionist literary representations of camp towns for U.S. troops in South Korea. They de-allegorize the camp town lives, from three different perspectives—those of the working-class camp town patriarchy, feminist writers and activists, and biracial children of camp towns— by foregrounding the gynocentric and lesbian and homosocial dimensions of women's lives and the racial hybridity and cultural transnationality of children. Finally, the chapter assesses the changes brought about by the influx of Filipina and Russian migrant sex workers into South Korean camp towns. The last chapter, "Migrant and Immigrant Labor: Redefining Korean Identity," examines the ways in which the recent multiethnicization of South Korea with the growing population of migrants and immigrants is redefining "Koreanness" and "Korean" identity. It treats diverse issues, such as discrimination against racial minorities, interracial marriages, biracial children, naturalization and citizenship, multicultural education, anti-Koreanism, and the re-internationalization of South Korean labor activism in relation to its new status as a multiethnic and multicultural subempire. Lastly, the chapter offers a critical reflection on the South Korean middle class's "education emigration," the rising cosmopolitanism of elites, and a newly emergent pan-Koreanism accompanied by the re-nationalization and re-essentialization of Korean identity.

1 Surrogate Military, Subempire, and Masculinity

South Korea in the Vietnam War

It is a little-known fact in the U.S. remembrance of the Vietnam War that between 1965 and 1973 the Park Chung Hee regime of South Korea dispatched a total of over three hundred thousand troops and over one hundred thousand civilian workers to Vietnam.[1] Of the nations that responded to President Lyndon Johnson's call for an international coalition and commitment of combat troops—Australia, New Zealand, Thailand, the Philippines, and South Korea—South Korea emerged, by far, as the largest contributor, helping the United States deflect the charges of a racist war.[2] In the current U.S. war in Iraq, South Korea has supplied, once again, the second largest number of ground troops after the United States, despite a furious controversy that forced the South Korean public to be reminded of the legacy of their involvement in the Vietnam War. Until 2000, when a South Korean newspaper began to report on civilian massacres by South Korean soldiers during the war, the Vietnam War had largely receded in the South Korean collective memory.[3] After the Vietnamese government's policy of Doi Moi (Reform) was put in place in 1986, South Korea's economic entry into Vietnam also became an opportunity for South Koreans to remember the war that they had forgotten, as South Korean businesses relocated their factories to Vietnam, and Vietnamese migrant workers were brought to South Korea.

In reconsidering South Korean military involvement in the Vietnam War, this chapter focuses on the multivalent relationship between military labor and masculine sexuality in the overlapping contexts of class stratification, nationalist economic development under the military dictatorship of Park Chung Hee, the rising transnational anticommunism of the era, and the U.S.-led neocolonizing capitalization of the greater Asian region.

In this chapter, my discussion of South Korean participation in the Vietnam War is premised on three different ways of conceptualizing military labor. First, in linking South Korean military labor in Vietnam to the contemporary process of economic development and industrialization, I propose to analyze South Korean military labor in Vietnam as a type of sexual proletarianization. Deriving from and modifying Paul Virilio's notion of a "military proletarianization" that accompanied industrial proletarianization in the modern European context, I define sexual proletarianization as a process of mobilizing respectively gendered sexualities into various working-class service labors, such as military labor, military and industrial sex work, and other sexualized service work.[4] Military labor is a particular kind of sexual proletarian labor, where certain aspects of masculine sexuality are (re)constructed, (re)appropriated, and deployed as a range of tasks. I will discuss South Korean literary representation of the militarization of masculinity and their implications for alternative conceptions of masculinity.

I also explore military labor as occupying an inherently paradoxical and contradictory position—that is, its simultaneous roles as the agent of the state's necropolitical power and as its very potential victim.[5] On the one hand, military labor carries out the will of the state in conquering and subjugating the enemy, that is, those "deemed worthy of being exterminated,"[6] while soldiers—especially or exclusively those who fill the lower ranks—carry the risk of themselves being exterminated by their enemy. In the state's ability to mobilize a sector of population as military workers who are potentially expendable, I argue that the state already constructs them as subject to its own necropolitical authority.

This chapter then conceptualizes military labor as a particular instance of surrogate labor by examining literary and cinematic representations of death in combat and war in terms of personal, communal, and national surrogacy or substitutability. While the modern nation-state's power of exercising universal military conscription (as well as the colonial state's power for labor conscription for even wider purposes such as plantation work, industrial labor, and prostitution in the late nineteenth and early twentieth century) formed an "exception" in the capitalist labor market, where an individual is compelled to dispose of his or her labor power "freely," the recent shift from a universal draft to a volunteer army in the post–Vietnam War United States, and South Korea's use of volunteers during its involvement in the Vietnam War, illustrate to us these governments' efforts to modify the system toward a more effective model, where the only coercive force is an economic one. In this new market model, a universal draft can be dispensed with in order to substitute the entire (male) population, viewed as equally potential agents or victims of its necropolitics, with a racialized and underclass surrogate population, both domestic and overseas. If abstract equality renders the substitutability of labor possible, the unequal conditions of class, race, gender, and nationality are articulated as a proletarianization of sexuality and race. The substitutability and unsubstitutability of surrogate labors are simultaneously acknowledged and erased by the cheaper wages contracted for the gendered, classed, and racialized population, who take the place of relatively universalized subjects. The measurable and calculable, and immeasurable and incalculable differences between races, genders, and classes are measured and calculated as monetary differences. South Korean military labor in the Vietnam War functioned as intranational class surrogate labor for South Korea and as transnational racialized surrogate labor for the United States, while the South Korean state simultaneously reconstituted such military proletarian labor as a supra-class, ethnonationalist, and masculinist service.

This chapter is organized around two related axes: first, the South Korean developmental state's role in the mobilization of working-class male sexuality as military labor in Vietnam;[7] second, literary representations of military labor that deconstruct such state appropriations. The chapter first examines the ways in which a certain material disjunctiveness in the surrogacy of military labor is elided and military labor is elevated into military service or duty by a complex of (supra)ideological causes such as ethnonationalism, heterosexist masculinism, racism, and transnational anticommunism. By delinking the economic dimension of military labor from the causes it was supposed to serve, and obfuscating the national commodification of working-class masculinity, the state's representations of the South Korean military venture in Vietnam exceptionalized military labor during the war, and then obliterated it after the war. The second part of the chapter explores South Korean critical literary representations of military labor that de-exceptionalize military labor by situating it back in the broader continuum of sexual proletarianization—that is, in the context of the production of other developmentalist sexual-labor-commodities that were less visible, such as female prostitution and other masculine (a)sexualized service labors. The third section examines literary and popular culture representations of the relations between South Korean servicemen in

Vietnam and Vietnamese women as subimperialist versions of the "camp town fiction" genre. The fourth and fifth sections of the chapter deal with the issue of race and masculinity in the multiracial context of the Vietnam War. In considering the collusive linkages between U.S. militarisms and its economic aggressions worldwide after 1945, articulated as an idea that an armed war is only a pretext for an economic war—a war of "commodity imperialism"—in Hwang Sŏk-yŏng's novel *The Shadow of Arms,* the chapter maintains that South Korean submilitarism in Vietnam was a significant contributing factor in securing its position as a subimperial force within the U.S.-dominated global capitalism in the years following the end of the Vietnam War.[8] I close the chapter with a brief examination of recent South Korean cultural productions that (dis)remember the Vietnam War.

MILITARIZING DEVELOPMENT AND RE-MASCULINIZING THE NATION

Ideologies of the Vietnam Deployment: Anti-communization and Developmentalization under Park Chung Hee

Recent years have witnessed a surge of scholarly investigation into the Park Chung Hee regime (1961–79), focusing on the crucial links between its militarism and industrialization, most often conceptualized as "authoritarian developmentalism" or "militarized modernization."[9] The Park regime's twin banner of "construction" *(kŏnsŏl)* and "national defense" *(kukbang)*— widely popularized in the slogan "Let us build our nation as we fight" *(Ssaumyŏnsŏ kŏnsŏlhaja)*—encapsulates the ways in which the dual axes of militarism and development began to organize South Korean society beginning in the mid-1960s.[10] South Korea's military participation in the Vietnam War was to serve as a model for working toward achieving the twin goals of "peaceful reunification" and a "prosperous tomorrow."[11]

The Park regime put forth the cause of anticommunism, in support of South Vietnam and the United States, as the most urgent reason for the deployment. Highlighting the similarities between a divided Vietnam and a divided Korean peninsula,[12] Park sold South Korea's participation as a way of preventing another communist invasion from the North; not helping South Vietnam to win its war could result in the communization of South Korea, or "Chŏkhwa t'ongil" (red reunification), as the anticommunist frontline in "Free Vietnam" was said to be directly connected to the line dividing North and South Koreas.[13] A military marching song for the

Brave Tigers Division stated that the presence of South Korean soldiers in Vietnam made possible the "sweet sleep of (their) parents and siblings" in Korea; the distinction between the Korean peninsula and Vietnam could be erased insofar as anticommunists were fighting the communist "Red Horde."[14] Furthermore, participation in the Vietnam War was considered a valuable "actual war experience" that allowed the South Korean military to develop its "courage and confidence" in preparation for another potential war in its own country. The memory of the Korean War, which had ended in a stalemate only about a decade before, effectively aided in transforming Park Chung Hee's exploitation of anticommunism for his political power into a quasi-religious cause, articulated in the two most common slogans for the South Korean military in Vietnam: "crusaders of peace" and "crusaders of freedom."[15] Through the Vietnam War military venture, Park was able to stabilize and solidify his still new and insecure military dictatorship by gaining U.S. support and rallying the country, justifying and displacing militarized politics in the domestic arena to militarism on foreign soil. For subsequent eras, through the end of Park's near twenty-year rule and into the seven years of the next military dictator, Chun Doo Hwan, the Vietnam War passed on the legacy of the thorough anticommunization of South Korea, where a permanent anticommunist revolution was to be waged.

Another sacralized cause, that of economic development, played an equally important role in the Park regime's decision to deploy its military. By now, it is readily accepted that Park's deployment to Vietnam jumpstarted the South Korean economy and funded its industrialization in the crucial initial stages. South Korea was promised and received, in return for committing combat troops, vast financial compensation and profit in the form of soldiers' salaries, grants, loans, and contracts for supplying and building for U.S. forces in Vietnam. For a period of nine years, South Korea earned, on average, 200 million dollars per year from the Vietnam War.[16] The revenue from combat military labor made up about 40 percent of the total amount earned from South Korean export during this period.[17] For some of South Korea's largest conglomerates, the lucrative contracts that they secured from U.S. military-related construction and business became the foundation of their subsequent growth and success.[18] If South Korea operated as an offshore military-industrial complex for the United States during the Vietnam War years and beyond, South Korea's military-industrial relations with Vietnam functioned in a similar way, compelling us to trace

South Korea's current economic subimperialism in Southeast Asia back to South Korea's submilitarism in the Vietnam War.

State Ceremonies and the Spectacularization of Ethnonational Masculinity

From the very first "farewell ceremony" in 1965 in Yŏŭido Square to the last "welcome ceremony" in 1973 in Tongdaemun Stadium, public ceremonies for sending soldiers off to Vietnam and welcoming them back—events staged by state and local governments and reminiscent of the ones performed during the Asia–Pacific Wars under Japanese colonial rule—came to have a far-reaching impact on militarizing the lives of the South Korean people. Broadcast on radio and television, they were national events with tens of thousands of mobilized students and citizens, speeches by government dignitaries, and entertainers offering floral wreaths to the soldiers marching through the streets of downtown Seoul. At these ceremonies, as well as through incessant publicity broadcasts, Park Chung Hee made explicit connections between South Korea's military deployment to Vietnam and ethnonational masculinity.[19] Calling the troops the "descendants of Hwarang," an elite male youth corps of a premodern dynasty, Park exhorted them to "demonstrate the bravery of Korean manhood to the world."[20] He declared the deployment to be a historic landmark that signified Korea's emergence as a "sovereign, mature adult nation"; it was now in a position to help other nations, rather than being the recipient of the help of others, as it had been in the past.[21] The idea that the Vietnam War was the very first occasion where Korea, in its long, five-thousand-year history, sent its troops overseas is emphatically reiterated in the state publicity discourses as a historical achievement that should "deeply stir all Koreans."[22]

An enormously popular song from the early 1970s, titled "Sergeant Kim Who Returned from Vietnam," echoes the idea of masculine maturation that Park's government propaganda exploited for the war.[23] The pop song depicts the transformation of a "youthful troublemaker Kim," through his military experience in the Vietnam War, into a "reliable" and "dignified" Sergeant Kim with a medal. Kim's masculine development is clearly marked by the shift in his appellation, from *ch'onggak,* used to refer to the status of an unmarried young man as a minor, to "Sergeant Kim," now a marriageable bachelor, ready to step into the role of a patriarch, as the song is revealed to be from a young village woman's perspective by its end: "Dashing Sergeant Kim who's come back / I fell in love with. Reliable Sergeant Kim who's come back / I fell in love with." Sergeant Kim's adulthood mirrors and projects South Korea's (ethno)national advancement—imagined as masculine and developmentalist—brought about by its Vietnam experience. The slogan for the welcoming ceremony that marked the withdrawal of South Korean troops in 1973, "They've Returned Victorious,"[24] offers us a glimpse into the value of the Vietnam War for the Park regime, that is, the victory of South Korean masculinity, that renders irrelevant the historical fact of South Korea fighting on the side of the United States, whose defeat was imminent.

These public ceremonies appear to have been very effective in suppressing the initial reluctance and opposition to the military involvement. The images from these ceremonies, featuring mass games, military marching songs, motorcades and ticker-tape parades, and a mobilized public at attention, were spectacles widely circulated via newspapers, newsreels, and television. The ceremonies and their images were overwhelmingly affirmative, imposing, and uncontestable,[25] compelling the South Korean public to identify with the departing or returning soldiers, who were in turn closely associated with the authority of the leader, Park, and then ultimately with the state and the ethnonation. The military spectacles, and their aesthetic of collective masculinity to be interiorized by the population, could then be reproduced as militant posturing in daily life, which was regimented by various rituals in schools, factories, and offices.[26] The spectacularized military masculine image, with its close links to the state, race, anticommunism, and developmentalism, operated as a major apparatus of "visual domination" for the South Korean state until the late 1980s.[27]

Park's tactic of associating the prestige and status of the nation with the enhancement of collective masculinity was enormously effective in the context of a South Korean patriarchy that had suffered political, economic, and military subordination to the United States since 1945, when the Korean peninsula was liberated from Japanese colonialism and the southern half was inserted into the United States' sphere of influence. For the Park regime, and for the majority of the South Korean public, who either supported the war eagerly or acquiesced quietly, South Korean participation in the Vietnam War became a chance to remasculinize the patriarchal national community. The Vietnam War became an occasion where ideologies such as ethnonationalism, masculinism, militarism, anticommunism, and developmentalism, inherited from the colonial period, were successfully reintegrated and reconfigured in the new contexts of a postcolonial nationalism and the global cold war. The effective melding and mutual legitimation of these ideologies became the complex organizing structure for South Korean society under Park Chung Hee and the military dictators who followed him in the 1980s.[28]

Transnational and National Military Proletarianization and Class and Racial Surrogacy

While we recognize the specific conditions for the rise of authoritarian development in South Korea, we must also note the inextricable linkages between militarism and industrialization, which form a continuity between the "early" (advanced or imperialist) and "late" (Germany, Japan, and then South Korea, among others) developing countries—the ways in which the "production of destruction" was associated with the "production of wealth," and the ways in which mass mobilization of labor resulted in a simultaneous "military proletarianization" and "industrial proletarianization" in the modern era.[29] Just as Japan's mobilization for the industrial-military sectors in the 1930s and '40s was transnational, involving Korean and other colonial subjects, the mobilization of South Korean labor during the Vietnam War and beyond in the age of neocolonialism must be situated within this expanding globality of militarized development in general, and within the changed hierarchy of the United States–Japan–South Korea in particular. South Korea's involvement in the Vietnam War, through its military proletarianization, served the goal of nation building on one level, and that of supplying a transnational labor force for the U.S. empire on another level. For South Korea, Vietnam became a "highway territory" where its military proletariat labored to bring in "foreign" capital—along with other labor commodities, sent abroad as nurses, miners, engineers, construction workers, and emigrants to various locations around the globe under Park Chung Hee and his successor, Chun Doo Hwan, as governmental labor export ventures—while the South Korean state simultaneously mobilized a "workers' army," or "industrial warriors," consisting of female factory workers first in the 1960s and '70s, and then of male industrial workers in the '70s and '80s, in the "vast camp of the national territory."[30] Despite the very high percentage of female labor in industrial sectors in the '60s and all the way up to the mid-'70s, the state and social discourses centered on both the military labor of the '60s and early '70s, and male industrial labor in the subsequent period (late '70s and '80s), making the masculine body the fulcrum of militarized modernization. Starting in the mid-1960s, South Korean militarization and industrialization transformed the largely agrarian population into varieties of a transnational and national proletariat. Some physically crossed national borders, while others crossed borders of different kinds—economic, cultural, and social—in camp towns, EPZ factories, and the tourist and prostitution quarters of Seoul. Either way, a large portion of the South Korean working class came to occupy a place in the fourth world of "transnational" and "migrant" workers.[31]

This "trans/nationality" and "migrancy" or "mobilizability" of the South Korean military proletariat in Vietnam must be understood in terms of class and racial surrogate labor, both within the domestic and global contexts. While South Korea required, and still does, mandatory military service of all able-bodied young men, the South Korean military personnel dispatched to Vietnam consisted of volunteers from this larger pool of conscripts. The majority of those who volunteered for Vietnam service came from a rural peasant background, drawn to the economic advantages of service in Vietnam, which was financed by the Unites States. Given the impoverished conditions of the South Korean working-class men who were already conscripts during the '60s and early '70s, the prospect of "eating American food, wearing American underwear, getting paid in dollars" and making additional income by dealing in U.S. commodities on the black market was a sufficiently attractive incentive.[32] Militarized masculinity became an instrument of socioeconomic mobility for those working-class young men who viewed Vietnam as an economic opportunity. The combination of harsh constraints and a slim pick of options already skewed the direction of their decisions. The government promotion of masculinist nationalist militarism further appealed to working-class young men, whose vulnerable masculinity could always use more reinforcement. Under such circumstances, the South Korean government never had trouble filling the quota for Vietnam duty. South Korean soldiers in Vietnam were working-class domestic surrogates for their urban middle-class counterparts—they were military labor commodities, exported by the South Korean state, which performed the role of a contractual labor broker.

Contemporary military strategy defines a "surrogate army" as a military "arm" that is part of joint operations but is not part of coalition forces. While in traditional coalition forces a foreign army would assist and augment the U.S. ground force, a surrogate army, advocated as a superior strategy, becomes the primary ground force, standing in for the U.S. military, filling in the gaps created by U.S. strategic choices and necessities.[33]

While South Korean and other Asian militaries certainly did not wholly replace the U.S. ground troops in the Vietnam War, the strategic choices for dangerous and difficult combats and missions positioned South Korean servicemen and other Asians, such as Hmongs, Filipinos, Laotians, and Cambodians, as surrogates. For the United States, there were many advantages to employing the South Korean military. South Korean soldiers were a cheap replacement, earning a dollar a day, one-twentieth of their American counterparts' wages.[34] Members of the younger generation of South Koreans, who grew up in the aftermath of the Korean War, were indoctrinated as staunch anticommunists, willing soldiers to fight for the cause. Hungry and poor, they were eager to prove their masculinity. The use of this particular surrogate army turned out to be hugely successful; they were a most effective unit for the United States, and a brutal enemy for the North Vietnamese. The United States also deployed domestic surrogates. The inequitable draft system allowed deferments for white middle- and upper-class draftees, leaving predominantly African Americans, Latino Americans, immigrants, and the white working class to fill the ranks of Vietnam service. Similarly, minority soldiers were assigned to combat duties in disproportionate numbers.[35] Both the "domestic" racialized and working-class force and the "international" force formed a continuum as a state-produced, state-controlled transnational migrant labor. The South Korean "volunteer army" in the Vietnam War, and the U.S. "volunteer army" in the current Iraq War, share an important characteristic: the only coercive force in the constitution of free labor is economic.[36] As military labor is nationalized, sacralized, and memorialized and forgotten as military service, the nation's or empire's role in commodifying this particular sexual-proletarian labor, that is, its production of national and imperial "mercenaries" as "volunteer armies," must also be occluded.

South Korean Submilitarism and Subimperialism in Vietnam

While we acknowledge, on the one hand, that the South Korean military functioned as a neocolonized surrogate force—"national mercenaries,"[37] in other words—for the U.S. imperialist war in Vietnam, on the other hand, our understanding of the Park regime's mimetic ambitions for political, economic, and military aggrandizement, and our recognition of Vietnam as a victim of South Korean invasion must reposition the South Korean military in Vietnam in a radically opposing way, that is, as submilitarist and subimperialist. To the South Korean public the Park regime portrayed the

South Korean military in Vietnam as "exalting the national prestige over-seas," or "enhancing our national pride." The rhetoric of government dis-course, summed up in key phrases and concepts such as the "vanguard of the nation," "creation of a new history," and "prosperity and glory," evi-dently point to the relations posited between South Korean participation in Vietnam and South Korean development and its ambitions in the global arena.[38] The idea that Korea was "helping" another country, and the sense of "recovery" of ethnonational masculinity, closely bordered the senti-ment of South Korea's supremacy and dominance over Vietnam and the Vietnamese. The pride in (sub)militarism in Vietnam was often frankly acknowledged as (sub)imperialist satisfaction, a particular kind of mascu-line national pride of a subempire, vengefully mimetic and reiterative.

For the purpose of managing relations with the "native population" and for the South Korean public's consumption, South Korean media reported on the various services that the military performed for the Vietnamese people, offering humanitarian aid—medical services and food distribution; building roads, parks, and schools; teaching Korean and Taekwondo; and even arranging entertainment for village seniors. Many of these elements— the pictures of these "humanitarian" activities; the imposing Western-style building surrounded by barbed wire occupied by the headquarters for the South Korean Military in Vietnam; Korean entertainers' performances for the troops, resembling the USO concerts; and the Vietnamese camp towns and prostitution districts, reserved exclusively for South Korean soldiers— cannot help but remind us of the presence of the United States military in South Korea. The South Korean Military in Vietnam (Chuwŏl hangukkun), said to "have planted peace and freedom everywhere they went," was a mimetic and miniaturized version of the U.S. Military in South Korea (Chuhan migun), emblematic of its status as a subempire within an em-pire. A contemporary South Korean documentary on the war, seemingly having preserved the Park era ideologies intact, does offer one updated interpretation of South Korea's military involvement in Vietnam when it pronounces it as the first instance of "internationalization" or "globaliza-tion" (kukjehwa) that "took us beyond the Korean peninsula and put us on a path to the world."[39] In the South Korean state's formulation of overseas labor as a nationalist economic activity, male bodies were conceived as territorializing agents abroad, whether in Vietnam, Saudi Arabia, or Brazil, for the isomorphism posited between masculine bodies and territories of the nation. The transformation of their status from labor commodities for neocolonial capital into agents of subimperialism for South Korea always hovered on the horizon for South Korea and its leaders, even in those early days, only to be much more explicitly formulated in the latter days of the 1990s when subempire was no longer just a dream for South Korea.

The South Korean military in the Vietnam War was a highly contradictory instance of extreme visibility (elevated as international anticommunist crusaders and patriotic masculinist icons) and extreme invisibility (functioning as surrogates and prostheses—bodies and body parts that substituted for the absent ones—and as surrogate labor whose consequences, such as deaths and injuries, were elided). They occupied and traveled through these visible and invisible spaces and routes (state ceremonies, parades, and newsreels on the one hand, and the villages, jungles, and the Ho Chi Minh trail of Vietnam on the other). When we think of the multiple Asian nations—South Korea, Vietnam, the Philippines, Thailand, and Japan—that provided military and support labor (construction, production and supply of commodities, recreation, and military prostitution) for the Vietnam War as a continuous, integrated, but hierarchized territory, it was the laboring bodies—surrogate and prosthetic—that bridged the separated territories to constitute Asia as a colossal military-industrial complex for the United States—an "empire of bases."[40]

SOLDIERING AS GENDERED AND SEXUALIZED LABOR

From Folk Hero to Male Prostitute:
Sexual Proletarianization in "The Dream of a Hero"
Hwang Sŏk-yŏng's story "The Dream of a Hero" (1974) at first glance appears to be an odd tale that deals with the unusual topic of a young peasant from the countryside who becomes a male prostitute in the city. However, the implications of the story become more discernible when we juxtapose it with Hwang's other works from the same period, which address the larger themes of the rural population's exodus into urban centers and the hardships they find there, the incipient labor movement, and military labor in Vietnam. I argue below that "The Dream of a Hero" instantiates the process of sexual proletarianization, that is, the transformation of traditional peasant masculinity into sex and sexualized labors.

The story narrates the tale of a young man, Il-bong, who migrates from the countryside to Seoul to realize his dream of becoming a professional wrestler. We are told that he comes from a lineage of folk heroes, *changsa*, Herculean creatures who would save the community by exerting super-natural physical power and performing miracles in times of crisis. Unable to find a job worthy of his lineage and his magnificently masculine body, the young man must bus tables in restaurants or scrub other people's bodies at public baths. He is also disappointed to learn that wrestling, once his dream, is merely a choreographed game, a fraudulent entertainment. One day a fortune-teller divines that he will "sell his body and become a celebrity that everyone adores."[41] Soon, while at work at the public bath, he is "discovered" by a small-time pornography director. His impressive physique affords him a career in the porn industry for a brief period of time, until he runs away with his female costar. When his lover, unwilling to endure poverty without their fairly lucrative jobs in the porn business, leaves him, he finds well-paying work as a freelance male prostitute, catering to middle- and upper-class housewives. Finding himself "castrated" in his job as a prostitute, he resolves to leave the city to return to his native village.

Hwang's nostalgic reconstruction of premodern martial heroes, Il-bong's ancestors, emerges in relation to the modern changes that Il-bong is facing. Il-bong embodies the virile ancestry of mythical times, when the peasant male body and its folk masculine sexuality were fully woven into the community and served its sacral causes. However, Il-bong has now been torn out of such social fabric and turned loose into an industrializing economy. In his various service jobs in the city, he finds his anachronistic masculinity, which had joined labor, sexuality, and communal meaning to one another, now reduced to sheer corporealization, that is, the mechanis-tic value of the body's asexual and emasculating labor capacity. On the other hand, he also finds that the very sexuality of his magnificent body can now be put to work. In both cases, Il-bong's sexuality has been sepa-rated out as various uses and values that can be produced, circulated, and consumed in the labor market. The value of his alienated masculinity exists only as the sexual commodity that he is, or as his asexualized labors. As Il-bong is reconstituted as a sexualized laboring subject, the aura of folk masculine sexuality, conjured by the modern leftist nationalist literary imagination, can only be recovered in its degraded form, in the glamour of his celebrity as a porn star. Foucault's assertion that the truth of an individ-ual is accessed through his or her sex in modernity can be altered in the case of the working class, for whom sexuality is appropriated, disciplined, and transformed by or into their labor.[42] In comparison to the bourgeoisie, whose sexuality is regulated through multiple social institutions, such as family, school, and medicine, and yet is confined to the "private" sphere, the truth of working-class subjectivity lies in this indissociability of their sexuality and their labor, both of which are appropriated in the "public" economy.

Il-bong finds that all of his jobs—as a bathhouse worker, a porn star, or a prostitute—have a peculiar effect on his body. He feels his body becoming like a "piece of wood," or "moving like a machine."[43] His work as a porn star and a prostitute leaves him further feeling that his "flesh" is becoming inanimate and is being drained of its life force: "I found out that I was castrated. . . . [I was] no more than a mere several pounds of flesh."[44] And yet we also realize, from Il-bong's description of his female porn star partner on the set, that resistance is already immanent in the process that produced the deadened flesh: "Ae-ja was magnificent. . . . Her expression was always the same. It said, 'Look, people! I am alive. I am moving proudly like this to live.'"[45] Their lovemaking becomes another way of reclaiming their sexuality and subjectivity from the commodifying forces and restoring it to the "private" sphere, now resignified for the sexual proletariat as a resistive space "outside" the public or market sphere: "we believed that we could take back our flesh that we had lost through their gaze."[46] He attempts to breathe life back into his inert body: "Come back to life, my flesh. Then you will hurl all your enemies down and you will take the bull by the horns." Just as he imagines the pleasures of the country life, he experiences the "miracle of [his] penis rising with vigor like the front paw of a tiger."[47]

"The Dream of a Hero" portrays the making of the modern working class as that of transition from the (imagined) communal, sacral integration of labor and sexuality, to sexual proletarianization in which sexuality, reconceptualized as being inherently linked to the very ontological vitality of the subject, must be reconstituted as (a)sexualized laboring subjects. Just as Hwang regards this process of sexual proletarianization as producing disenchanted bodies and lifeless zombies for the dispossession of their sexuality, for Hwang sexuality also becomes the authentic and magical locus of a proletarian subjectivity that is fundamentally a sexual-vitalistic subject.

Getting the Job Done: The Masculinization of Killing and Torturing

If male sex labor is a less common or less visible type of sexual proletarianization, military labor, in contrast, is the most universal form of masculine sexual proletarianization. Militarization of male subjects and bodies deploys the variously constructed dimensions of masculine gender and sexuality as skills and tasks. Below I discuss Hwang Sŏk-yŏng and An Chŏng-hyo's literary works, which illustrate to us the complex ways in which the context of the Vietnam War intensified the conglomeration of multiple ideological factors, such as nationalism, racism, (heterosexist) masculinism, militarism, and anticommunism, to produce working-class masculinity as a militarized gendered and sexualized labor.

An Chŏng-hyo's *White Badge* (1983) in part lets us access the kind of popular masculinism that prevailed in the South Korean military in Vietnam.[48] The first-person narrator of *White Badge* came to Vietnam believing that war was a "sanctuary of masculine strength, while the merciless conflict to the death was an ascension of ordinary man towards divinity."[49] The young recruits' first combat experience is likened to a first sexual encounter, and a victory in a battle to a sexual climax: "Like young boys gone to a whorehouse for the first time, the soldiers resumed their jabber, asking one another, what did you feel, what did you think during the shelling?"; "For the winners, war was a breathless joy and excitement, an ejaculation of male ecstasy.... They were jubilant ... the individual companies competing with one another in killing. The commanding officers repeatedly inquired of subordinate officers how many more they had killed."[50] This relation posited between masculine sexuality and military activity exceeds a simple metaphor. In both sexual and military acts, to different degrees, aggression, violence, and power to subjugate the other are defined as constituting the central values of masculinity,[51] while weakness or submissiveness is associated with the feminine gender, or with effeminacy or homosexuality. Military prowess is sexualized or conflated with sexual prowess; military labor as a sexualized labor eroticizes killing and other related tasks. Killing is experienced as "profoundly sexual and exhilarating";[52] killing is similar to sexual acts to the extent that pleasure is derived from symbolic or material vanquishing and elimination of the other. In the military's appropriation of masculine sexuality, Robin Morgan argues, "maleness itself becomes the weapon of destruction."[53]

Literary representations of the Vietnam War, even the most critical ones, convey to us the prevailing sense among South Korean soldiers that "Vietcongs" are to be disparaged as a racially inferior, effeminate enemy in comparison to a robust South Korean masculinity. Interrogation and torture further bring out the relations of sexuality, power, and violence

already inherent in combat. In a sexualized torture, the interrogator or torturer (re)affirms his identity constituted through a complex of intersecting
ideologies, such as racism, nationalism, and (heterosexist) masculinism,
by transforming the POW into a racialized and feminized or castrated
enemy-other. While tortures and sexualized tortures are carried out in
order to maintain the state of disidentification with the enemy, this other-
ing process, at least for some, has a strange way of simultaneously further
escalating the identity or interchangeability of the subject positions of the
captor or torturer and the captive or tortured, as illustrated by a scene from
Hwang Sŏk-yŏng's story "One Who Returned."

In Hwang's story, a Vietnam veteran back in Korea recalls a torture ses-
sion carried out by his squadron on a POW named Than. Than, a former
middle-school teacher turned guerrilla, put up the fiercest resistance. South
Korean soldiers, infuriated, start taunting him, and the taunting eventually
leads to sexual assault and torture. When one of the South Korean soldiers
tries to put a burning cigarette on Than's penis, Than bites the soldier's
hand. As a punishment, the soldiers all beat Than severely, and the tor-
turers soon discover, to their surprise, that Than is dead.[54] Just as killing
another human being in ground combat is necessarily an intimate act, in
which elemental identification and disidentification with another human
being take place,[55] Hwang Sŏk-yŏng's Vietnam veteran recalls this vertigi-
nous slippage between his and his victim's positions: "Whenever I met
his cold and tense stare, I would suddenly feel lonely. I couldn't stand the
fact that he hated me. When I thought of the value of his life, the values he
holds dear and his efforts at preserving his own dignity, I felt in my bones
my own resistance to him."[56]

In White Badge, when the protagonist's squadron seizes a female guerrilla who happens to be a young beautiful woman, the task of dealing with
a POW coincides with the South Korean soldiers' heterosexual conquest of
Vietnamese women. Once the guerrilla is captured, the fact of her militant
resistance is obliterated, and she is transformed into a military sex worker
serving her enemy. Their job of searching the prisoner turns into a "strip-
tease" show amid the lewd laughter of the soldiers. As she stands "totally
exposed," one of the soldiers suggests that they search her private parts:
"Who knows? She might be hiding a bazooka in that tunnel." The narrator
defends this idea by explaining the rumor that female Vietcongs carry a
lethal poison in their genitals.[57] This episode in White Badge portrays the
severe sexual assault that the female Vietnamese POW suffers at the hands

of South Korean soldiers as the more-or-less harmless, juvenile, good-natured sexual fun and excitement to which young soldiers are entitled. South Korean soldiers are described as treating her as a beauty queen, "Miss Vietcong," showering her with gifts and admiring her beauty and softness. The novel blithely negates the sexual violence Korean male captors commit upon the Vietnamese female captive: "What they wanted from her was not slimy grunting sex, but warmth and comfort and peace."[58] This particular scene from a fiction must be read against the numerous cases of actual rapes and other sexual war crimes committed by South Korean servicemen, which have been documented and attested to by Vietnamese victims and witnesses.[59] Commercial sexual relationships with, or sexual violence upon, Vietnamese women (both enemies and allies) is considered by South Korean soldiers as a type of service work—sexual, emotional, and social; in short, Vietnamese women function as "comfort women" for them. Sexual violence committed against the enemy women can further be used as a reward for victory or as a strategy to weaken the enemy psychologically, by devaluing and damaging "enemy property," that is, their women.[60] In other words, acts of sexual violence in military and militarized contexts are encouraged to function as a continuation of military labor.

If the South Korean state was able to remasculinize itself through this military venture, working-class men who fought in the war and survived suffered horrible, emasculating effects of injuries, disabilities, and psychological trauma.[61] Hwang Sŏk-yŏng's and An Chŏng-hyo's stories unravel the myth of militarized masculinity as embodying power, authority, and domination: "The fight was without honor or dignity, without even masculinity—the base acts of a cowardly war. We simply murdered our own species in the most despicable, contemptible, dastardly way. Here even death was insulted."[62] For both Hwang's and An's characters, the job of killing another human being is a cowardly act that becomes the source of their infinite shame.[63] In disrupting the connection between the male body and the nation or (sub)empire, these critical works begin, in incipient ways, to reclaim masculinity from its association with violence, to demilitarize masculinity.[64] If "military valor" indicates the successful interpellation of men into military labor commodities who will perform sanctioned violence, then a soldier's "effectiveness," we can argue, is the very extent to which they *fail to resist* the dominant ideologies of the state and society. The examples I have discussed in this section attest mostly to the overall success of the system, but the next section highlights the various ways in which the failure of dominant ideologies occurs through soldiers' identification with their female sexual proletarian counterparts, that is, prostitutes.

(Male) Military Labor and/or as (Female) Prostitution in "Birds of Molgaewŏl" and "Yŏng-ja's Heyday"

Let us now explore the representations of close affinity between male military work and female prostitution in Hwang Sŏk-yŏng's "Birds of Molgaewŏl" (1976) and Cho Sŏn-jak's "Yŏng-ja's Heyday" (1973), two works that stand out for their attention to working-class camaraderie over gender hierarchy between (former) soldiers and female military and non-military prostitutes. "Birds of Molgaewŏl" is set in a domestic camp town (in contrast to camp towns for U.S. troops), named Molgaewŏl, which exclusively serves South Korean soldiers bound for Vietnam. The story captures the peculiar mood of such a camp town, where soldiers sojourn anxiously before their departure for Vietnam and prostitutes who have drifted into the town from all corners of the nation "with nowhere else to go" are nightly "harassed by soldiers headed for battlegrounds."[65] The story by no means negates the tension between soldiers and prostitutes as the above quote illustrates, but nonetheless, it consistently endeavors to acknowledge and value the connection the two groups attempt to establish between themselves. Beyond offering an explanation of this kinship as based on their shared social and economic background, it further portrays their acute sense of affinity as being generated by the harsh, militarized environment. They are enveloped together in the extraordinary atmosphere of abandonment, desolation, and desperation in a remote town in the wilderness. Soldiers' unspoken fear of the possible imminence and anonymity of their death—"the worry that I might die without anyone knowing it crossed my mind"[66]—mixes with the more routinized sense of terror that the town prostitutes experience in their lives of extreme material and emotional hardship. Both groups, living as if condemned, communicate and interact with each other in this palpably heavy atmosphere. On a rainy night out on the camp town, the narrator finds a dead-drunk prostitute "thrust into a sewage ditch." It is precisely a woman in such a state, a "corpse-like" woman, who "aroused his desire,"[67] and yet at the same time, it is the soldier's sense of identification with the prostitute that also prevents him from having sex with her. With exasperation, he thinks to himself how he could possibly "eat someone" who now came to feel like "family."[68]

Like "Birds of Molgaewŏl," Cho Sŏn-jak's "Yŏng-ja's Heyday" also underscores the sense of solidarity that a Vietnam veteran feels toward his girlfriend, a (nonmilitary) prostitute, Yŏng-ja, and her colleagues, who live and work in one of the cheapest prostitution districts of Seoul, while being much more exacting in its conceptualization of the relations of power, violence, and sexuality that structure both soldiering and prostitution. The first-person narrator is a young man who earned the "medal of honor for having torched seven Vietcongs to death."[69] However, upon his return to the outskirts of Seoul, the only job that he managed to obtain was that of a "body scrubber" at a public bath, like Il-bong from "The Dream of a Hero." When our unnamed protagonist visits a prostitution district, he happens to run into Yŏng-ja, an old acquaintance from his days as an apprentice welder, who had been at the time a domestic at his boss's house. To his shock, Yŏng-ja is now not only a prostitute, but she has also lost her arm in an accident when she was working as a bus conductor. The Vietnam vet and Yŏng-ja form a relationship, as he helps her with her business, in particular by making a gift of a homemade artificial arm to her. Just when Yŏng-ja's business takes a turn for the better, with the prosthetic arm that conceals her disability, the prostitution quarters are subjected to a governmental crackdown. Yŏng-ja escapes the police chase, but when she returns to the district to collect the wages she was owed, she becomes the victim of a fire that engulfs the block of brothels.

From beginning to end, the short story is structured by a thorough interweaving of the veteran's recollection of the Vietnam War with Yŏng-ja's experience in the prostitution quarters of Seoul, and by a constant comparison between the male narrator's experience as a soldier in Vietnam and Yŏng-ja's life as a prostitute in Seoul. Upon buying her, the narrator describes his feelings as "the same kind of cruel pleasure that I used to feel when I killed a person." In his mind, the naked body of a prostitute bought and the lifeless corpse of an enemy killed become conflated: "I looked down upon Yŏng-ja's torso with complex ambivalence, as I would upon a dead body that I had just killed."[70] He is further reminded of an incident in Vietnam:

One time when we pacified a village, there were only women left in it. A sergeant pulled my ear and whispered into it, "A fantastic opportunity." The village girls readily opened their legs to the demands of my comrades. That time too, I had bought an ugly girl, frozen with terror, with a box of emergency rations, which was not even necessary. She had a thin neck. She resisted, shaking her neck that looked like a dried up reed. What a happy man would I have been, had I been rude and ignorant enough not to understand her sad resistance! Yeah. I dreadfully feared the terrible pain that would assail the girl's genitals. I took care of the member that was violently erect outside of the girl. Foolishly thinking of the pain that would attack Yŏng-ja's private parts, I deeply occupied Yŏng-ja.[71]

On the one hand, his conflation of buying a prostitute with killing an enemy once again reaffirms the sexualized nature of military labor, where the subject/victor assumes the position of a male, while the enemy/defeated is assigned that of a female, just as it bears out the nature of sex work as a structure of violent power relations that approximates that of a battle premised on a (racialized, classed) gender hierarchy. On the other hand, I would like to attend to the fragile and tenuous but not insignificant sense of identification that the male narrator feels toward his female Vietnamese enemy and rape victim, as well as toward a Korean prostitute. His transethnic and transgendered identification is enabled by a certain degree of failure of the interlocking and mutually reinforcing ideologies that constitute his subjectivity and legitimize his actions as a soldier in Vietnam or a consumer of sex work back in Korea. He succeeds, to a modest degree, in disidentifying with "himself," thus disrupting the structure that defines his hierarchized differences from the respective women.

In addition to the more general source of the camaraderie between soldiers and prostitutes, such as the similarities in class position and militarization we saw portrayed in "Birds of Molgaewŏl," we can trace this affinity to a couple of other, more particular commonalities shared by military work and sex work. A Korean soldier's reflection upon a Vietnamese prostitute's body in another story by Hwang Sŏk-yŏng—"a brown chunk of flesh flapping about pathetically . . . sad like my body"[72]—points to what appears to be an unmediated commodification that transforms the body and its respectively gendered sexualities into monetary values, both in military labor and sex work. Both sexual-proletarian labors produce their bodies themselves as commodities, despite other skills and services that may be part of their labors.[73] There is a sheer bodiliness that is translated into economic value in both labors. As (military) prostitution renders "several pounds of meat" into currency, the U.S. government offers monetary compensation to South Korean soldiers for their lives or dead bodies. The soldiers in An Chŏng-hyo's *White Badge* speak of the "dollars" that their families would collect for their deaths, the money that would make them "filial sons."[74] Pak Yŏng-han's characters in *Distant Ssongba River* (1978) must resign themselves to the "measly $500" that their deaths or lives are worth to their employer, the U.S. government, complaining about the much larger amount that their U.S. counterparts are worth. A soldier says, with sympathy and resentment toward the South Korean government who was their negotiator: "Well, that was the best our government could do for us anyway."[75] Military labor, like prostitution, seems to be constituted through an inherently contradictory logic whereby laboring bodies—compensated for the value of the sheer surrogacy of those bodies, bodies that stand in for those of others—are simultaneously absolutely indispensable, and yet eminently disposable.

Another commonality is a sense of figurative deformity that seems to be brought on by these labors to a person's body, sexuality, and subjectivity. The male narrator in "Yŏng-ja's Heyday" expresses his resentment toward the women he classifies as "those women who are not prostitutes," describing them as *"pŏndŭt pŏndŭthan,"* an odd, therefore meaningful, choice of adjective. As *pŏndŭt pŏndŭthan* connotes a state that is "straight," "square," or "intact," the narrator suggests that women prostitutes—and by extension their femininity and sexuality, which is determined by their occupation, sex work—are by contrast queer, distorted, misshapen, deformed, or damaged. It is through his identification with prostitutes that the male narrator suggests the damaged nature of his own sexuality and subjectivity, conjuring up clandestinely the historical fact of the South Korean soldiers, approximately sixteen thousand, who were injured and disabled in the Vietnam War.[76] This impaired-ness of working-class militarized masculinity, not only literal and physical but symbolic and psychological, I would argue, is displaced onto its female counterpart, that is, Yŏng-ja's disability, her one-armedness, which is—in addition to being a mark left by a physically demanding job due to her material privation—a symbol of her own sexual proletarianization, her damaged sexuality and subjectivity. The mutilation working-class masculine bodies incurred in the Vietnam War seems to have been muted, remaining below the surface of public consciousness, for the duration of the war in South Korea. By comparing Yŏng-ja to the "one-armed" heroes of Hong Kong martial arts films, which were immensely popular in 1960s and '70s South Korea precisely among young working-class men like our protagonist, Cho Sŏn-jak's "Yŏng-ja's Heyday" establishes

Yŏng-ja as a (female) symbolic surrogate for the damaged working-class male sexuality and subjectivity of the Vietnam era. In fact, her escape from the prostitution quarters under police attack is successful due to her male drag.

Yŏng-ja's temporary triumph, or her "heyday," when her business was thriving thanks to the artificial arm that the narrator made for her, also substitutes then for the spectacular display of the supernatural powers of disabled protagonists—often one-armed and sometimes one-legged or one-eyed—of these Hong Kong (and South Korean) martial arts films.[77] Yŏng-ja's prosthesis, which at first points to the subalternity of her sexuality and subjectivity, I would argue, is transformed in the course of the story into a magical fetish, a surrogate that is the very source of re-creative, regenerative life. By affirming the sexually proletarianized body as an assemblage of body parts—arms, legs, eyes, fingertips, backs, and sexual organs—that operate as surrogate laboring bodies and body parts, Yŏng-ja's triumphant prostheticization reverses, though temporarily, the hierarchy between the original or intact body and the surrogate or damaged bodies, body parts, and sexualities. Yŏng-ja's prosthetic arm—and the invisible prosthetic arms and legs of superheroes, and heroines occasionally, that perform miracles in martial arts films—fulfills the promise of a "righteous arm," the literal meaning of the most common term for a prosthetic arm in Korean, ŭisu. Yŏng-ja's "righteous arm" (or Yŏng-ja as a righteous prosthesis) functions as the very impossible political ground—the surrogate that takes the place of the original—that must be established and yet destroyed.

"Yŏng-ja's Heyday" concludes with the male narrator's further intensified sense of disempowerment that he shares with the prostitutes when he imagines the prostitution district under the police crackdown metamorphosing into the battlegrounds of the Vietnam War: "The rumor had it that the authorities planned on completely wiping out prostitution in this area, just like our squadron used to mount mop-up operations against the leftover Vietcongs. They were calling it a 'bulldozer operation.'" Soon the state deploys additional military forces, cornering the prostitutes like "rats in a vat." Yŏng-ja's blackened body, burned to death in a fire in the state's "war" against prostitutes, reminds him of the images of "Vietcongs torched by a flame thrower."[78] It is through double identification, transgender and transethnic or transnational, with (South Korean) prostitutes who are in turn associated with his former (Vietnamese) enemies that the veteran of the Vietnam War is able to accurately situate himself in the position of the South Korean state's official enemy, Vietnamese communist insurgents. He recognizes himself to be the target of the state's power, its violence and militarism, like the "Vietcongs" that he himself killed at the call of the state.[79]

If the short story "Yŏng-ja's Heyday" concludes with the South Korean veteran's disidentification with the state, one of the most popular Hollywood representations of the Vietnam War, the Rambo trilogy, quickly contains the subversiveness of the veteran's similar recognition of his position as a soldier in relation to his government and nation. Rambo's relationship with the state is generally marked by his sense of extreme betrayal and abandonment, and the absence of reciprocity he feels for the service he rendered his country for the "love" of his country. In the second film of the trilogy, *Rambo: First Blood, Part II* (1985), Rambo, on a secret mission to rescue American POWs still held in Vietnam, explains to a female native guide his understanding of his government's perspective on soldiers and veterans like himself in one particular word: "expendable." Its verb form, to "expend," articulates two opposing and yet related meanings. To "expend" conveys one meaning, "to employ for a given purpose," while at the same time it also means "to use up material or strength."[80] The dialogized ambivalence of the word "expend" seems to echo Rambo's knowledge of military workers' dual function for the state: first, that of the agent of necropolitical power to be "employed" for the given goal of eliminating the enemy population; and second, that of the (potential) victims of necropolitical power of the state's own military agenda, to be "used up" in such a process. Rambo does understand that his role as a military worker is to be used and then discarded, and yet the film, in a predictable and predetermined fashion, contains this dangerous perception via the character of a paternal colonel who asks Rambo and the audience to make a distinction between the government, figured as a villainous bureaucrat, and the country, which remains only an absolutely abstract entity with a hollow ring. In place of his earlier bitter and deadly recognition, Rambo, on behalf of veterans, can only plead meekly, "We would like [our country] to love us as much as we love it."[81] An Chŏng-hyo defines an enlisted man, a *somop'um*, which may be translated as "expendable supplies," as "a human being who was deprived of his right to know about his fate and his life, that is what a soldier in a war is. An enlisted man, that was truly like an expendable commodity."[82] In early modern Europe, as well as in South Korea under Park Chung Hee, convicts were mobilized as soldiers; as they were not worthy of living, they were perfectly worthy of laboring to kill or laboring to risk being killed.[83] Military labor is a paradoxical instance where a worker, as part of the modern process of the "industrialization of death," is required to destroy another human life, and in doing so a soldier constitutes another kind of the modern living dead.[84]

SOUTH KOREAN GIS AND VIETNAMESE WOMEN: WAR ROMANCE, SEXUAL BILDUNGSROMAN, AND SUBIMPERIALIST CAMP TOWN FICTION

Regardless of the varying degrees of their critical stance on many issues, the representations of the Vietnam War by all three writers, Hwang Sŏk-yŏng, An Chŏng-hyo, and Pak Yŏng-han, share an implicit assumption that male soldiers' commercialized sexual and/or noncommercial "romantic" relationships with local women are a constituent part of their sanctioned tasks.[85] Nonetheless, despite this general assumption, the treatment of this issue in two novels, An Chŏng-hyo's *White Badge* and Pak Yŏng-han's *Distant Ssongba River*, reveals significant differences. In *White Badge*, the contradiction between the novel's critical awareness of South Korea's position as an invasion force—a subordinate national military serving U.S. imperialism and its own subimperial and national-mercenary desires—and the novel's inability to recognize South Korean men's sexual and romantic relationships with Vietnamese women as colonizing sexual exploitation, remains a glaring blind spot throughout the novel. *Distant Ssongba River's* not only uncritical, but rather celebratory, accounts of sexual and romantic relations between South Korean soldiers and Vietnamese women amount to what we might call a subimperialist camp town fiction, a counter example of a South Korean literary subgenre, camp town fiction *(kijich'on munhak)*, explored in chapter 3 of this book. Camp town fictions represented South Korean military sex workers' bodies as a figurative site of the United States' neocolonial domination, seeking to protest, discursively, U.S.–South Korean relations via masculinist nationalist allegories. While camp town fiction as a subgenre features prominently the nexus between state power—both U.S. and South Korean—and military prostitution as an object of critique, these literary representations of Vietnamese prostitution for the South Korean military, for the most part, elide such linkages, with the significant exception of acknowledging the presence of a South Korean military-run medical facility in Vietnam, a space of ethnosexual decontamination and purification, set up to treat South Korean soldiers' sexually transmitted diseases (STDs) prior to their return home.

Indeed, *White Badge* itself contains a small-scale South Korean camp town story within the larger narrative about South Korean participation in the Vietnam War. South Korean military sex workers were allowed to enter Vietnam "to entertain" U.S. troops, forming South Korean camp towns for American GIs in Vietnam. The first-person narrator, Sergeant Han, tells us that they were publicized as "Korean entertainers actively working on international stages," while he knows better: it is no more than "international prostitution." The protagonist's reaction to seeing South Korean military prostitutes with American GIs is one of violent outrage at the women themselves, accompanied by a sense of attack on his ethnonational masculinity: "Perhaps it was because I believed the land of war was a sanctuary for the male human species, but I always felt ashamed and humiliated, like a boy caught masturbating, whenever I saw that Korean women I met in Vietnam were of the kind that brought disgrace and infamy to my nationality and my personal self-esteem." Sergeant Han also takes note of Vietnamese camp towns for South Korean soldiers: "The sign 'R&R Center' in red paint on the broad plank . . . a piece of deserted sandy beach segregated by barbed wire entanglements to keep off the Vietnamese, as if it was a pocket of Korean territory."[86] The R&R Center for the South Korean military in Vietnam is structurally identical to that of American camp towns in Korea, a quasi-extraterritorial space for the occupying military.[87] However, the novel refuses to recognize the transposability between South Korean GIs in Vietnam and American GIs in South Korea. Pak Yŏng-han's *Distant Ssongba River* does register the protest of a Vietnamese man who decries South Korean soldiers' relationships with Vietnamese women, but only as a caricature; the Vietnamese man's "racial castration"[88] merely amounts to a laughably pathetic gesture to South Korean soldiers. The novel turns a blind eye to the parallel between South Korean GIs or "Ttaihans" (as local Vietnamese yell, "Ttaihan go home!") and American GIs (as local South Koreans have done many times, "Yankee go home!").[89]

White Badge's treatment of Vietnamese prostitution for the South Korean military can be characterized as a war romance, revolving around the relationship of the first-person narrator, Sergeant Han, with a Vietnamese woman, Hai. Hai is a young widow who takes in occasional customers at her shack in her desperate efforts to survive. Her young son, who is less than ten years old, works the streets of the area around the Korean base, often begging or sometimes peddling what he can. He brings Sergeant Han to his mother. While in the end he does admit to himself that he was "unwilling to love her" and that he was only seeking her company for "consolation," the novel is unable to recognize the opposing and yet mirroring logic of (South Korean) anti-neocolonial masculinist nationalism (vis-à-vis the United States) and (South Korean) masculinist subimperialism (vis-à-vis Vietnam). If South Korean camp town fictions protest American imperialism via their critique of its emasculating effect on Korean masculinity, then its remasculinization occurs via the Korean military's mimetically (sub)imperialist military-sexual-economic conquests of Vietnamese women. A bestseller at the time of its first publication in 1978, Pak Yŏng-han's *Distant Ssongba River* is absolutely unabashed as a popular war romance novel, in which all South Korean male fantasies are explored and realized. Overwhelmingly occupied with romantic, sexual relations between South Korean military personnel and Vietnamese women, and necessarily eliding the commercial aspects of such relations, the novel includes a dimension of what we could call sexual bildungsroman. For the protagonist, Sergeant Hwang, military service in Vietnam was an opportunity to escape the mundane and unsatisfactory life of a young college student, disillusioned with both the corrupt military dictatorship and the youthful opposition of students. Considering both of these conditions that he faces to be "shameful to the fire of youth," his volunteering was a challenge to a life that would be more worthwhile because of its confrontation with death. The novel essentially amounts to a chronicle of Sergeant Hwang's "transformation" into an "adult" through the course of the war, from a young man frightened before a woman, to a man who now thinks that "woman is only one of the subjects that I want to study in life."[90] The psychosexual maturation he undergoes in the course of the novel is necessarily the consequence of his experience with a seemingly endless succession of Vietnamese women, who are, in turn, exotic, beautiful, and Westernized, and yet primitive and inferior. This psychosexual education of a South Korean male is carried out through a suborientalized space of Vietnam, just as that of American men would be in the neocolonized Orient. *Distant Ssongba River,* as a sexual bildungsroman, narrativizes the national masculine sexual development that President Park Chung Hee's declaration—that South Korea has become a "mature adult nation" with its military deployment to Vietnam—once projected in speech.

STRATIFIED MASCULINITY AND CLASS SURROGACY: BLOOD MONEY, ONE BLOOD/ONE NATION, BLOOD ALLY

Like the South Korean state's experience of the disjunction between its juridically sovereign decision to send troops to Vietnam and the international political and economic constraints that compelled it to make that choice, South Korean volunteers for the Vietnam War faced the similarly contradictory conditions of being "juridically free and yet socially and economically unfree."[91] Given their limited options, many working-class recruits perceived Vietnam service as an opportunity, offering various financial advantages and perks:

> Vietnam isn't as dangerous as the DMZ in Korea. . . . The life for enlisted men is easier in Vietnam, I think. And you must remember how hungry you used to be at the Korean frontline camps. But you'll never go hungry in Vietnam and you'll have fancy Western meals, beef and all, every day. You certainly tasted the American C-rations they sell in black markets. . . . You will get much more pay because you'll be paid by both the US and ROK governments, and you can see a foreign country. How else could you even dream of touring a foreign country in your miserable lifetime as a poor country boy? Do I have to list any more reasons why you have to love this war?[92]

However, the promise of "striking it rich" (hanmok chapda) in Vietnam,[93] as in a sarcastic comment made by a passerby watching a group of returning Vietnam veterans on the streets of Pusan, did not really materialize for most soldiers dispatched to Vietnam. Hwang Sŏk-yŏng's short story "A Neighbor" (1972) portrays the most probable trajectory after discharge for a Vietnam veteran from a rural proletarian background. Having spent five months back in his home village, he migrates to Seoul. Vietnam service seems to have put him squarely back where he had started, with no money, no skill, and no hope of social or economic mobility—no different from other rural migrants. He finds life in Seoul to be extremely harsh, and he drifts from place to place, unable to find a steady job. One day, a fellow day laborer teaches him how to make easy money: one can sell one's blood. To his own amazement, he finds this particular commodification of his body to be "addictive."[94] Not only does he regularly return to the hospital to sell his blood, but he also agrees to do a blood transfusion for a wealthy man who desires a healthy young man's blood for its supposed restorative and rejuvenating effects. If Hwang's text from the mid-1970s literalizes the metaphor of the "blood money" that the South Korean working class earned for their ruling elites—figured as the vampire-like old man in the story—in the Vietnam War, it was long after the war that it could be articulated much more directly in An Chŏng-hyo's *White Badge*: "The blood money we had to earn at the price of our lives fueled the modernization and development of the country. And owing to our contribution, the Republic of Korea, or at least a higher echelon of it, made a gigantic stride into the world market. Lives for sale. National mercenaries."[95]

The habit of earning his living from selling his blood only pushes the protagonist of "Neighbor" further into a life of poverty, depression, and violence. One day he steals a bicycle and uses it to buy a prostitute. When he feels that he has been cheated out of the money that was exchanged for the bicycle by the brothel owner, he becomes enraged and stabs a neighborhood night security man to death. He defends his murder in this way to the police interrogator:

That's how the kitchen knife thrust itself into someone. But actually I didn't have any ill feelings toward him . . . because he was the same type of man as me anyway. When I have endured everything in the battlefields, in Seoul, in the construction sites and at the blood bank, I don't understand why I couldn't restrain myself with him. What? It's a sign of affection? . . . I walked around with a knife without knowing where the end of the knife should be directed at. *It's true that he was killed by me but maybe I didn't kill him. It doesn't feel like I stabbed him. Just like my gun that was wielded in the distant land doesn't feel like it was me who wielded it.*[96] (emphasis added)

This Vietnam veteran, whose experiences connect the geographical locations—rural Korea, Vietnam, and Seoul—and the kinds of labors he performed—agricultural, military, and industrial—to one another, says, "No one knows what I went through. I've seen everything. At this age, I've killed several tens of people already. Of course that was in the war."[97] Hwang Sŏk-yŏng's character points to the social forces underlying the seemingly voluntary acts of combat or murder: in both instances, he was no more than a proxy holding a knife in Seoul or a gun in Vietnam. Both An Chŏng-hyo's *White Badge* and Hwang Sŏk-yŏng's stories on the Vietnam War remember the war as mass killing—a sanctioned, organized mass murder. Their stories are counternarratives to South Korean official

history of its participation in the Vietnam War, encapsulated as state propaganda in such slogans as "dauntless warriors of democracy" or "vanguards
of peace" or "expeditionary forces of the Korean crusade to Vietnam for
preserving peace and freedom in Indochina." The materiality of the blood
shed by South Korean soldiers for national profit ("or at least a higher
echelon of it") dissolves the abstract homogeneity of the Korean ethnos,
the idea succinctly captured in a password in combat in *White Badge:* "One
blood—One nation."[98] Like the case of the blood transfusion, the young
veteran's murder of a night watchman, again replicating and displacing
the blood shed in the Vietnam War, illustrates differentiated and stratified
"blood" according to class. The young veteran's recognition that we shed
only each other's blood—he killed merely a fellow working-class man, a
night watchman in a slum—can also be extended: South Korea succeeded
in becoming a "blood ally" *(hyŏlmaeng)* of the United States, by shedding
merely each other's blood, its own and Vietnamese blood, at the behest of
the United States.

AMBIVALENT ETHNIC IDENTIFICATIONS AND RACIAL SURROGACY

Multiple Racial Identifications: South Koreans in the Middle

Hwang Sŏk-yŏng's understanding of the U.S. wars in Asia as wars of conquest coincides with the most critical U.S. interpretations of its imperialist history. The Vietnam Wars, to borrow Marilyn Young's expression,
were extensions of the genocidal wars against the indigenous tribes that
expanded the U.S. territory westward; thus, Asia became a territorial extension of the "wild" American West, and Asians became "Indians abroad."[99]
However, the ambiguous and contradictory position of South Korea as a
subimperialist force in the Vietnam War is articulated as South Korean soldiers' ambivalent racial identifications or ethnic transgressions in Hwang
Sŏk-yŏng's works. Hwang's "Birds of Molgaewŏl" portrays the Vietnam-
bound South Korean soldiers who are stationed in Molgaewŏl, a rural
camp town in South Korea, as identifying with both white conquerors and
"Indians." This remote military camp town is fantastically transformed
into a scene from the historical American West, as the first-person narrator
"feels as if he were a desperado who shows up in a Western town in search
of gold," and his buddy is identified by his nickname as *ch'ujang,* a word
most often associated with *indiŏn ch'ujang* (Indian chief), "for his long

nose."[100] When South Korean soldiers arrive in Vietnam, their close work-ing relations with Americans and their proximity to the American lifestyle seem to give rise to their racial mimicry or "racial transvestism."[101] Hwang's stories illustrate several instances of South Korean soldiers' desire for racial upward mobility, through their identification with white Americans.[102] On the other hand, South Korean soldiers are also compelled to identify themselves with the Vietnamese, beyond the ideological distinctions— North and South, or communist and anticommunist—while fighting on the side of Americans. Another story by Hwang, "Pagoda" (1970), thema-tizes their racial affinity toward the Vietnamese through the South Kore-ans' refusal to blow up a pagoda in defiance of a U.S. order to do so: a white American officer utters in disgust, "I can't understand these yellows."[103] These examples illustrate the conflicting pressures on South Korean sol-diers in Vietnam that align them with different racial, national, and his-torical groups, ranging from white Americans and Native Americans, to Vietnamese and other Asians.

Camp Towns/Boom Towns in Vietnam

In Hwang Sŏk-yŏng's stories, camp towns, both for the Vietnam-bound South Korean soldiers and for the U.S. military bases in South Korea, meta-morphose into American Western boom towns, haunted by the ghosts of "Indians" and by the mythical promises of gold and fortune.[104] For the South Korean government and its corporate partners, the prospect of striking it rich in the camp towns/boom towns of Vietnam was rela-tively solid. However, they held out much more tenuous economic prom-ise for South Korean working-class soldiers and other civilian workers, such as construction workers, petty traders, and sex workers in Vietnam. In another story by Hwang Sŏk-yŏng, "Eye of a Camel" (1972), set in Pusan, the largest port city in Korea, where the returning South Korean and American soldiers from Vietnam arrive, the camp town area of this city, where both South Korean and American soldiers mix, is transformed into a "chinatown," an ethnic ghetto, an internal colony within U.S. terri-tory, in the words of a song moaned by a blonde Korean prostitute: "the Chinese street in the foreign land of America . . . America . . . merica, mer-ica . . ."[105] As the protagonist, a Vietnam veteran, listens to her murmuring, in front of his eyes the streets of Pusan turn into a fantastic landscape of the American West: "Gigantic sand columns began to shoot up one by one and then they collapsed all at once in front of my eyes. Then, bleak, empty cities where only dry dust was whirling around floated up. Land like parched lips dying of thirst unfolded in front of me infinitely."[106] Both the song of a female prostitute who sells her labor to the American military in a South Korean camp town, and the vision of a South Korean military worker who fought in Vietnam place their bodies and labors—though deterritorialized—"within" the American empire, within its landscape. Their bodies and labors, which serve the empire, connect Vietnam and South Korea, physically and figuratively, to the territory of the United States proper. Hwang's work grasps these South Koreans as neocolonized *and* subimperial subjects; they are laboring subjects of the U.S. empire and South Korean subempire, as territorialized or deterritorialized and indigenized or "diasporized" in South Korea or Vietnam—their own or a foreign country. However, when these subjects are able to recognize their relation to the empire, the sand columns begin to crumble in an instant, leaving only the ashen traces of ruined cities. The mirage that a South Korean Vietnam veteran conjures up performs the prophetic ending of an empire and also turns the subimperial territory into a wasteland.

Vietnam as a Sexual Prosthetic

Hwang Sŏk-yŏng's short story "Eye of a Camel" contains the first-person narrator's flashback to an unforgettable, disturbing experience he had during his service in Vietnam. The title refers to something like a sexual prosthetic that was being made and sold by Vietnamese street vendors to foreign soldiers. The object is supposed to be a camel's eye with camel hair around it, but Korean soldiers conjecture that what is passing for a camel's eye is probably something like a piece of sliced dog's tail. Such a "camel's eye," authentic or not, put on a male penis, is supposed to enhance male sexual performance: "It drives women crazy."[107] When the narrator was on a furlough in Vietnam, he encountered a group of Vietnamese boys who were selling pornographic pictures, condoms, and camels' eyes. They used the Korean word for "camel's eye," *nakt'a nukkal*, with a clear pronunciation, as they made lewd gestures, snickering among themselves. Foucault's notion of "pedagogization" of children's sexuality in the modern European bourgeois context diverges sharply from the kind of sexual knowledge and learning that enables these children's barest living in the war economy. What disturbed him more than the fact that they forced camels' eyes on him was the children's taunting chant of "Ttaihan" (South Koreans), the only other word he could understand.

Shortly after, at a bus stop, he and an African American soldier come across a group of young girls who sell souvenirs. One of them snatches the African American soldier's magazine, and when he goes after her, all of the girls start pointing fingers at both of them and making gestures. They point at different parts of their bodies, arms, noses, and ears and pretend to eat them. Then, they seem to be asking, "How many do you eat, two, five, or ten?" They also say, "You are like Papa. . . . Baby chop chop." As the children's taunting of the soldiers becomes more intense, the angry African American soldier slaps one of the girls on the face, and finally a local police officer is brought in as crowds gather around them. The scene ends with an altercation between the Vietnamese police officer and the African American soldier.[108]

In the story, South Korean Vietnam veterans, now back in Pusan, consider these camels' eyes to be "precious" spoils of the war. If the sexual prosthetic seems to symbolize a masculinizing force for the largely working-class South Korean soldiers and for the South Korean subimperial state then the taunting by the militarized and sexualized children, who must survive by selling "camel's eye" to the occupying forces, subverts the masculine and masculinizing power invested in it. Their gestures, which imitate eating body parts, seem to suggest a link between sexuality, which the children sell to soldiers to make a living, and military power, which the soldiers embody. And such sexualized military power, or militarized sexuality, their gestures argue, is cannibalistic. The South Korean soldier-narrator understands that "Ttaihan" became the Vietnamese children's curse—an utterance of resistance at South Korean soldiers. He leaves Vietnam with the memory of the "shame" that the children made him feel. When his friend shoves the camel's eye in his mouth as they wait for a prostitute back in Pusan, he vomits it out into a toilet: "Someone was staring at me as I was gagging repeatedly. That was the camel's eye sitting on top of the deep hole of the toilet. The camel's eye that became a rotten, mangled blind eye of the dead and its bottomless darkness seem to be quietly gazing at me."[109]

South Korean military engagement in the Vietnam War restored its ethnosexual potency; Vietnam functioned as a sexual prosthetic that would counteract a masculinity diminished under the pressures of neocoloniality and industrialization. However, in this last scene of the story, the spectacle of the sexual prosthetic that became a dead man's eye interrogates such an ideological conglomeration, that is, subimperializing militarized ethnonational masculinity, which was once spectacularized by the state.

War for Commodities: Hwang Sŏk-yŏng's The Shadow of Arms

A picture of an American soldier in the current Iraq war handing out chocolate bars to a group of children surrounding him could be from many other previous U.S. wars since 1945, including the Korean War and the Vietnam War. Hwang Sŏk-yŏng's two-volume novel *The Shadow of Arms* was completed in 1989, over a decade after the end of the Vietnam War, a few years after Vietnam's launch of its "Reform" policy, and at the beginning of the end of the cold war.[110] This later work on the Vietnam War by Hwang offers us an interpretation of the ubiquitous image I mention above. The novel focuses almost exclusively on the "economic" dimensions of the war, specifically on the black market operations by all groups—Vietnamese, Americans, Koreans, and others—and the U.S. military's interest in, and control over, them. The novel's main character is a South Korean officer, working in a joint team with the U.S. military, set up to investigate the black marketing of goods that flow out of the commissaries (a.k.a. the PX or postal exchange). The novel's argument, in sum, locates an intimate nexus between U.S. militarism and its economic expansionism— what Anne McClintock calls "commodity imperialism"—as the very crux of the Vietnam War.[111]

The Shadow of Arms not only confirms the obvious fact that the goal of any U.S. military incursion is ultimately economic, but it further contends that the Vietnam War and other U.S. wars were primarily a pretext to begin the economic war. The military invasion becomes an opportunity to forcibly suspend the normal economic activities of the country: its own production system and distribution network. During wartime, the Vietnamese, both in the North and South, had to rely on black marketing, not only in terms of consumption of U.S. goods for everyday necessities (actual U.S. goods could only be bought and consumed by middle- and upper-class Vietnamese), but more importantly, the entire wartime Vietnamese economy centered around the profits generated through black market operations.[112] While the U.S. military pretended to be cracking down on such operations, crackdowns were used to exert more control over black markets. In fact, they mounted their own "black markets," in addition to other kinds of more "legitimate" economic operations, such as "economic aid," "humanitarian aid," or "reconstruction."[113] Military occupation became an economic occupation. The novel also notes Japan's role, in contrast to South Korea's, in the Vietnam War. If South Korea sold their young men—their raw labor power—in the form of combat troops, the novel notes (with chagrin) that Japan sold their manufactured goods.[114] The protagonist is surprised at the fact that a large percentage of commodities circulating in Vietnam are Japanese. Following the model of Japan thirty years earlier in Vietnam, South Korea is now the subject of commodity (sub)imperialism, a manufacturer and purveyor of goods circulated in Vietnam, Southeast Asia, and South Asia—and in the current Iraq War, as a junior partner, once again, to the United States.

However, the most important aspect of this economic war in Hwang's representation is its "cultural" dimension, "commodity imperialism." Hwang calls the PX, serving the U.S. military personnel stationed overseas, a "Disneyland in a large tin warehouse," where "a tired soldier would buy the dream of possession, created by the mass industrial society, with their military currency stained with blood."[115] The novel explores the ways in which the PX functions as a connecting point between U.S. capitalism and the local economy. At first glance, the mundane commodities, such as soap, candies, perfumes, and canned foods, in which PXs deal seem trivial and even form an incongruous contrast with the U.S. "military capabilities that could turn three hundred acres of land in only four minutes into a wasteland where no plants or animals could live."[116] But Hwang's novel wants to underscore the PX's most important function, as a disciplinary institution, one that introduces the taste, feel, smell, color, and sound of the empire to the "natives." To describe the trafficking of materials from PXs into the local economy, Hwang uses the term "offensives in materials/resources" (*mulyang kongse*). The PXs become bases for launching a "commodity war":

What is a PX? . . . [I]t is a general goods store . . . that turns the natives into ridiculous clowns, one that makes them go crazy and drunk and shell out all their money. . . . A PX teaches civilization to the dirty Asian slopeheads, who would have lived happily with each other, with their bananas and just a handful of rice. It teaches them how to wash their faces with milky white soaps, and the taste of Coca Cola that refreshes their heart. It pours perfumes and rainbow-colored candies, lacy lingeries, high-quality wristwatches, and gemstone rings over the barracks that have been bombed to pulp. Now

Asians will have cheese on their table, instead of their own smelly foods, and the condoms that slipped out from between girls' legs will dance on the tender fingers of children playing.[117]

The commodity war on the native body and its senses works by offering pleasure and comfort. The native body and its senses succumb to the powerful seduction of things that are softer, sweeter, cooler, more colorful, and more fragrant, although the successful conquest of the natives' taste does not take place simply due to the material superiority of the commodities themselves; rather, the magical fetishism of commodities is further enhanced by their association with the empire and its military might. In a story by O Chŏng-hŭi, a South Korean girl in a camp town whispers to her friend, "They are made in America, you know."[118]

The commodity war is a new kind of opium war in which "conquest" takes places through the construction of the body's desires: "If you have once been entranced by the taste, smell, and feel of those things, you cannot forget it even after your death. Products will reproduce the loyalty of the natives to the producers of the products. Those who have touched the American fortune will have 'U.S. Military' branded on their brain. The children who grow up eating the candies and chocolate handed to them and humming their songs will trust their compassion and optimism. . . . [T]he PX is the most powerful weapon that America possesses."[119] Not unlike a Hollywood movie, a chocolate bar can narrate the story of fantastic America. Commodities, "lying on the threshold of culture and commerce,"[120] discipline the enemy's taste; to learn to consume is to be colonized. Hwang continues, "The prodigious buying power in the market, the booming urban economy, and the enthusiasm and raptures in the alleys, they all are directly proportionate to the heat of the war."[121] Even as the Vietnamese were winning the war on the military front, Americans were winning the war of commodities by creating consumers first, to be later transformed into workers. Hwang's novel concludes that the fundamental premise that undergirds these scattered global locations is the transnational imaginary and material community of consumers erected through the circuits of American commodities.

What seems like an unusual U.S. military strategy during the Vietnam War, the establishment of the so-called Phoenix Villages, is completely consistent with this interpenetration of economic expansion and militarism. According to the novel, they were officially called in Vietnamese

"New Life Villages" (*sinsaenghwalch'on*). Unofficially they were called "Settlement Villages" (*chŏngch'akch'on*) or "Strategic Villages" (*chŏllyakch'on*) by the Korean military and South Vietnamese government who jointly administered the program with the U.S. military, while the Vietnamese people called them *mikkuŏdo* or "American Villages." They were planted in strategic locations, so that their residents would be able to perform multiple functions—as farmers to grow food, as potential soldiers to fight the guerrilla forces, and as cultural-ideological model villagers. The American Villages that promoted and enforced the American ways of life were a future brought to the present, a future that they were fighting for. American Villages, at the other end of Manifest Destiny across the Pacific, transformed the Vietnamese peasantry into surrogate homesteaders, or auto-proxy-colonizers. Not unlike the world exhibitions, which conveyed the "promise of social progress for the masses without revolution," the material and virtual world of American commodities as a "unified system of cultural representations" at the PXs and in American Villages,[122] was already waging another kind of revolution during the Vietnam War. A Vietnamese character, a black marketeer, comments in *The Shadow of Arms*, "Isn't war the cruelest form of business [*changsa*]?"[123] For the intimate nexus between military and economic conquest, the novel offers us the metaphor of U.S. dollars as "blood-red fungus flowers,"[124] exploding multiply and globally.

REMEMBERING THE VIETNAM WAR IN CONTEMPORARY SOUTH KOREA

This last section of the chapter discusses some of the recent South Korean cultural productions that deal with the memory of the Vietnam War. They come in a wide variety of media and genres, ranging from politicized literary works to popular literature, memoirs, horror film, and television dramas.[125] If a small number of these productions are critical of South Korea's past and present relations with Vietnam, the more mainstream popular culture products are oblivious to such issues and problems in their erasure of history and exoticization of Vietnam. Pang Hyŏn-sŏk, a labor activist and writer of the 1980s who recently turned his attention to relations between South Korea and Vietnam, writes, "What I was able to confirm in areas where the South Korean military occupied was that after twenty-six years, the people living there did not forget anything and everything remained recorded. Just because we want to forget, that certainly does not mean that everything will be forgotten."[126] For Pang, then, Koreans' own remembering of the war must become a "listening" to the Vietnamese remembrance.

"Contemporary" South Korea-Vietnam Labor Relations: The Problem of Anachronism

Pang Hyŏn-sŏk's novella *The Time of Eating Lobster* (2003) depicts Vietnamese and South Koreans, who fought one another in the battlefields, once again confronting one another thirty years later in South Korean factories located in Vietnam.[127] Vietnamese men who were once teenage guerrilla fighters are now middle-aged factory workers, policemen, and local party officials. South Korean men who were once young recruits in the war are now managers and supervisors of South Korean factories that employ Vietnamese workers. These roles that both Vietnamese and South Korean characters play in the novel embody the historical trajectory of the fateful transition from South Korea's surrogate militarism—its destruction of the Vietnamese population—to Vietnam's victory, which then turned into its submission in offering surrogate bodies to South Korean transnational capital. Pang's story locates the logic of the intimacy between militarism and global industrialism in their changed roles; the battle between invading soldiers and insurgent guerrillas is now transformed into struggles on the shop floors of South Korean multinational factories in Vietnam. Pang's *The Time of Eating Lobster* complexly weaves memories of South Korea's past submilitarism in Vietnam and those of South Korea's "domestic" labor struggle of the 1980s with its problematization of current South Korea–Vietnam labor relations. The protagonist, Kŏn-sŏk, works for a South Korean shipbuilding company whose factory is located in Vietnam. In dealing with labor disputes with Vietnamese workers, South Korean management resorts back to its 1970s practices: "Isn't it the case that the way these people live and think is similar to the way we were twenty years ago? Why don't we just use the same method we used to use twenty years ago?"[128] The management routinely searches the Vietnamese workers for parts and tools that they suspect the workers steal. After the workers' bitter protest against this practice, the company eventually installs a metal detector. However, one particular worker continues to set off the metal detector every day, even after they completely strip him. When X-rayed, his body reveals thirty-two pieces of shrapnel, remains from his years as a guerrilla fighter. The alarm set off by the "Iron Man"—so named by his coworkers—brings together two temporalities, the past and the present, in which the South Korean history as an invading force is lodged as metal in the body of a Vietnamese guerrilla-turned-factory-worker.

The protagonist's family history adds another layer to the complex relations between South Korea and Vietnam. Kŏn-sŏk's father, a Vietnam War veteran, brought back a son that he had with a Vietnamese woman. Kŏn-sŏk and his older half-brother, Kŏn-ch'an, grew up together. As a half-Vietnamese, half-Korean boy, Kŏn-ch'an suffered a great deal of discrimination. However, under the care of his Korean stepmother, who grudgingly but responsibly raises him, Kŏn-ch'an grows up to be a skilled worker at a major industrial company in the early 1980s. Kŏn-ch'an, as a model filial son and a responsible older brother, supports the protagonist, Kŏn-sŏk, through his college education. When Kŏn-ch'an joins the labor movement, he declares to his family that he has found, for the first time in his life, a community where he feels like he belongs, that is, the community of fellow workers and labor organizers. Despite his mother's pleas to quit his labor activism, he continues his participation until he is found dead one day after a long day's demonstration. Kŏn-sŏk carries around a great deal of guilt for his older brother's death, for not interfering, as well as for his sad and unhappy memories of his brother's difficult life as a biracial child growing up in Korea. Through "revealing" that one of the many martyred labor activists was a biracial person, born out of the context of South Korea's involvement in Vietnam, the novella retroactively rewrites the highly ethno-nationalized labor activism of the earlier era as transethnic; it links the transethnic labor activism of the past to its contemporary transnational counterpart, set in Vietnam this time.

Symbolic Surrogate Labor: The Sexual Economy of Remembering the War

The Time of Eating Lobster uses the metaphor of a lobster's supposed ability to cut off the damaged parts of its body and then live on as a contrast to the impossibility of South Korea to find redemption for itself, and to offer reparation for the atrocities it committed against the Vietnamese population during the war. However, the novella's simultaneous inclusion of a Vietnamese female character whose love for Kŏn-sŏk presents the possibility of reconciliation seems to undermine the novella's other argument— that South Korea must learn to live with pain, that is, with the profound historical awareness and responsibility for the past. Kŏn-sŏk's Vietnamese lover, Lien, serves literally as an intervening space between the memories of the war and the current labor problems, between critical, hostile

Vietnamese people and Kŏn-sŏk, a "good" Korean man. She teaches him about the war and her people, offering him historical, intellectual, and political lessons and sexual comfort.[129] The protagonist's tortured reflection on the impossibility of amputating the past is contradicted and transcended by Lien, who will chop up lobster and cook it as a soup for her Korean lover.

The appropriation of the Vietnamese female body in a South Korean film *R Point* (2004) forms an interesting contrast with Pang Hyŏn-sŏk's literary works. Set in 1972 during the Vietnam War, the film is about a squadron of South Korean soldiers who are sent on a special mission to find another squadron that seems to have "vanished." As a horror film that makes use of every formula, *R Point* turns the Vietnam War into material for the particular pleasures the audience is incited to derive from the genre, thus undermining its general antiwar message and its critique of South Korean participation. At its center, *R Point* places a rather clichéd formula— a beautiful, vengeful female ghost in a traditional Vietnamese costume, a white aodai—in order to figure the Vietnamese victimhood wrought by South Korean militarism. In turn, it is this Vietnamese female ghost who drives the squadron mad, leading all of them to mutual destruction; the mission to find the missing soldiers turns into a suicide mission. The film ends with the suggestion of the female ghost's eternal return, that the vengeful ghost will continually suck South Koreans into the nether world. Although the film's particular depiction, which feminizes, sexualizes, aestheticizes, and suborientalizes Vietnam, further contributes toward depoliticizing the memories of the Vietnam War, the unrelenting and unconciliatory female ghost does diverge from the gestures toward reconciliation figured through the female body of Lien in *The Time of Eating Lobster*.[130]

CONCLUSION

This chapter has explored South Korea's submilitarism in Vietnam, under the tutelage of U.S. imperialist expansionism in Southeast Asia. Domestically, South Korean military involvement contributed to the militarization of the entire workforce, as soldiers became a prominent cultural signifier of the era for three successive decades, from the 1960s to the 1980s. Internationally, in a matter of two decades South Korean participation in the Vietnam War firmly placed South Korea on track for its eventual rise as a subimperial nation, not only through the financial profit it gained from the war, but also through its forging of intimate political and economic relations with the United States. Since the normalization of relations between South Korea and Vietnam in recent years, there has not been any official discussion of apologies or reparations on the part of the South Korean government for the war crimes committed by its military, and its contribution to the genocidal war that destroyed nearly 10 percent of the Vietnamese population. During South Korean president Roh Mu Hyun's visit to Vietnam in 2004, he only obliquely alluded to South Korea's military involvement in the Vietnam War in his mention of the "debt in our people's heart" to Vietnam. The controversy caused by a retired colonel's testimony in 2000 about a civilian massacre that he and his men committed, however, opened a public debate that resulted in media investigations, scholarly research, and activist movements, apart from the more or less complete official silence on the matter of the South Korean military's civilian massacres in the Vietnam War.

Other veterans, who corroborated these narratives of civilian massacres, have pointed to the South Korean state and its military authority in Vietnam as responsible for not educating soldiers against racism and actively sanctioning racist policies and strategies in combat. For South Korean veterans, the concept of state racism was something they themselves experienced as its very agent.[131] Koreans' demand for redress of the historical injustices committed during Japan's colonization of Korea must be accompanied by South Koreans' need to seek Vietnamese forgiveness. Since the topic of South Korean war crimes has been broached, progressive activist and cultural organizations have made efforts to conceive and work toward reconciliation between the two countries and peoples, and to educate South Koreans about the part of their history that they have suppressed and forgotten. Critical cultural productions have dealt with such issues as Korean and Vietnamese victims of Agent Orange, and the generation of children of South Korean soldiers left behind in Vietnam.[132]

In contrast, the South Korean mass culture industry has generated a variety of products that, once again, erase history and celebrate South Korea's current subimperialist status over Vietnam. As newspapers inform readers of the South Korean domination of the Vietnamese market—whether it be cell phones, or construction businesses, or television dramas—popular culture translates economic domination, once again, into a figurative gendered hierarchy between South Korean men and Vietnamese women. In the material sphere, Vietnamese men and women work in South Korean factories relocated to Vietnam, as they have also entered South Korea as migrant workers. Vietnamese women cater to South Korean sex tourists, and others come to Korea as immigrant wives of South Korean farmers.[133]

Just as relations between South Korea and Vietnam seem to be repeating their historical precedents in many spheres, South Korea's Roh Mu Hyun regime once again dispatched its troops to Iraq in another ongoing U.S. war. The sentiment that in order to join the ranks of superpowers, South Korea must fight terrorism alongside the United States seems to be generally accepted by mainstream South Korean society. South Korea's role in contributing to the further entrenchment of what Neferti Tadiar calls the "free world fantasy"[134] has been significant: South Korea is often touted as a model Third World nation that has now become one of the world's largest economies. Just as much of post-1945 American history took, and is taking, place abroad—in Korea, Vietnam, and Iraq, just to name a few locales—South Korean history also took place in the Vietnam War, and is taking place in (relation to) contemporary Vietnam.

2 Domestic Prostitution

From Necropolitics to Prosthetic Labor

This chapter explores literary and popular culture representations of "domestic prostitution" from 1970s South Korea. By situating "domestic prostitution"—in contradistinction to prostitution for the U.S. military, the topic of the next chapter—in the context of the massive mobilization of young female labor under the military dictatorship of Park Chung Hee, this chapter considers the "transnationality" of nontransnational work, or the ways in which "domestic" prostitution existed in inextricable relation to the more obviously transnational labors involved in the process of globalizing industrialization. By contextualizing prostitution in relation to other female working-class labors, the chapter also seeks to illuminate the permeable boundary among sex work, sexualized work, and nonsex or nonsexualized work.

The massive commercialization of working-class female sexuality of the 1970s was a historical phenomenon that South Korea shared with other industrializing nations, what Kathleen Barry calls the "industrialization of sex."[1] Barry distinguishes this period of the global sexual proletarianization of Third World women as being propelled by economic conditions and motivations, both at the level of workers and at that of the Third World societies, from the preceding age, when the process of sexual proletarianization was much more closely tied to territorial colonialism and military occupation. In the case of South Korea, one sector of prostitution, that is, military prostitution for U.S. troops, was still at least partially tied to U.S. neocolonial interests in South Korea and its military manifestation, although this "privatized" prostitution was still a marked shift from the Japanese imperial system of Comfort Women during World War II.

Given Barry's understanding of prostitution as a global and globalizing industry, this chapter seeks to recognize "domestic" prostitution in the context of South Korea during the 1970s as a "national" segment of a transnational phenomenon, that is, an intranational and intraethnic exploitation that actually takes place as part of the greater chain of compounded international and interracial, gendered and sexualized, and classed exploitation. Another dimension that historically distinguishes this era of the "industrialization of sex" is its scale, the geographically unbounded production of female sexuality as a commodity, its ubiquity, both nationally and globally, and the temporal rapidity of the proliferation of the sex industry. This chapter offers a glimpse into the magnitude of the domestic sex industry that is structurally linked to the greater transnational prostitution market.

As state-led industrialization kicked into high gear, starting in the early 1970s, South Korea saw even further accelerated migration of the rural proletariat into urban areas. Many of the writers of the 1970s, the majority of whom were critical of Park Chung Hee's authoritarian regime and sympathetic to the newly formed urban proletariat, began to write about their plight and the urban slums. It would not be an exaggeration to say that these works indeed constitute the bulk of the South Korean literary canon of the 1970s. They are part of what came to be known as the Minjok Munhak Movement, or National Literature Movement, an intensely ethnonationalized version of Marxist literature in the postcolonial and neocolonial context of South Korea. However, the topic of (domestic) prostitution remained largely outside of their purview. Hwang Sŏk-yŏng and Cho Sŏn-jak, whose works on prostitution I discuss in this chapter, are exceptions to the broader literary omission of prostitution as a social phenomenon and proletarian labor problem. If it is rare to find sustained representation of domestic prostitution in the leftist literature, simultaneously it was a topic monopolized by the mass-market literature, popular film, and tabloid journalism of the 1970s.[2] This chapter examines a few of the most celebrated examples of such popular cultural representation of commercialized feminine sexuality.

This chapter is divided into three sections. The first section offers a tentative definition of prostitution as a kind of necropolitical labor, while simultaneously contextualizing its emergence and proliferation in the specific period of South Korean industrialization in the 1960s and '70s, which was simultaneously nationalist and transnationalizing. The second section deals with the masculinist appropriations of female sexuality in both canonical and popular literary works, in which women's sex work and sexual service are not only materially utilized by the (masculine) family, (masculine) proletarian class, and (masculine) ethnic nation-state, but the symbolic value of a woman's sex or sexualized labor as a filial daughter, a national Comfort Woman, and an icon of modernization and its social ills serves a crucial function in further shoring up the masculinist ideologies of family and nation. This section is followed by my reading of more critical representations of prostitution, including those by male authors from the 1970s.[3] In these more materialist works, prostitution is situated back into street life and into the very bottom strata of the working-class environment; within such a context, these works are interested in probing prostitution as a particular type of work, that is, gendered, classed, and sexualized work, as work of survival, prosthetic resistance, and clandestinity. This chapter attempts to recover and restore the continuity between two categories of prostitution, "domestic" and "military," that have been differentiated in the South Korean context, while noting the discontinuity. This chapter also traces the links between domestic prostitution and military labor (addressed in chapter 1) and military sex work (to be considered in chapter 3), as well as parallels between strategies for the proletarianization of sexuality in prostitution and those for the proletarianization of race in the migrant workforce (the subject of chapter 4).

"DOMESTIC" PROSTITUTION IN THE NATIONAL AND TRANSNATIONAL CONTEXTS

Prostitution and Death

If we first exclude the extremely small percentage of prostitutes and their advocates who argue that prostitution is a freely chosen profession, one that is an expression of their will, desire, and self-fulfillment, and if we further eliminate from our consideration the minority of elite sex workers who exercise a comparatively higher degree of control and autonomy over their lives and interaction with their clients, we can define prostitution as an institution in which a person, most often a woman, belonging to an underclass and often a racialized population, both in national and transnational contexts, is compelled to "allow clients to secure temporarily certain powers of sexual command" over themselves in exchange for "money and/or other material benefits." For the majority of sex workers globally, prostitution is an occupational "choice" that is largely forced on them as a matter of bare subsistence and survival, over other even more dire situations such as poverty, physically dangerous and/or low-paying jobs, violence, or death. While recognizing fully Julia O'Connell Davidson's critical intervention that the essential dimensions of prostitution—mutual consent and voluntary exchange between sex workers and their clients—separate prostitution from rape and other sexual violence,[4] we also want to acknowledge prostitution as an institutionalization of sexual violence via commercialization, for the ways in which the "consent" is forcibly manufactured out of unequal social and economic relations among sex workers, their employers, and their clients. In other words, considering this inherent coerciveness and structural violence built into prostitution, I would like to conceptualize prostitution as another kind of necropolitical labor. I have defined necropolitical labor as extraction of labor from those "condemned" to death, whereby the "fostering" of life, already premised on an individual's death or disposability of her or his life, is limited to serving the labor needs of the state or empire and capital. The notion of necropolitical labor highlights the intermediate stage where extraction of labor is related to, and premised on, the possibility of death, rather than the ultimate event of death itself. Incurring psychological, physical, and sexual violence and injury, prostitution involves, at one level, a figurative erasure of the sex worker's subjectivity. The very frequency of the murder of sex workers, indeed appearing to be a universal, cross-cultural phenomenon, can be viewed as a material extension of this figurative violence. Like the other necropolitical labors I discuss or mention in the previous chapters, such as slavery, concentration camp labor, and military service, the possibility of (physical) death is an integral part of prostitution as an occupation.

A brief discussion of a recent U.S. film, *Monster* (2003), will help illustrate my conception of sex work as a necropolitical labor. Based upon the true story of a female "serial killer," *Monster* reconstructs and interprets the killings of the protagonist, a street hooker-turned-serial killer, Aileen "Lee" Wuornos.[5] It is not difficult to agree with the film's point of view that sex workers, especially those who work the streets, are commonly exposed to extreme violence and danger, including the possibility of being murdered on their job. The first prostitute user Lee kills is shown anally raping her multiple times using various instruments, subjecting her to other kinds of severe torture after tying her down, including bashing her head and face and pouring water and alcohol on her bleeding body parts. This particular character, a rapist and user, repeatedly asks as he rapes and tortures Lee, "Do you want to fucking die? Do you want to die?" Clearly his desire to "have sex" with her is his desire to murder her. While we cannot claim that wanting to kill one's sex partner is necessarily limited to those who buy sex, buying sex is too often linked to killing the sex worker. In this scene, Lee reacts to this vicious assault upon her by shooting him multiple times, killing him.

What Julia O'Connell Davidson calls the "social death" of prostitutes can also be interpreted as a necrophilic dimension of commercialized sex[6]: prostitute users' necrophilia is satisfied by sex workers' necropolitical labor. Another way to define necropolitical labor is to think of broadly proletarian labor, that is, work itself, as necessarily incurring injury and harm to the body and mind—work as trauma, violence, and mutilation that indeed lies in continuum with death. In one of the film's key scenes, a self-explanation, Lee's voice-over narrates the following: "The thing that no one ever realized about me was that I could learn, I could train myself into anything. People always look down their noses at hookers. Never give you a chance, because they think it's an easy way out. No one can imagine the willpower it takes to do what we do, walking the streets, night after night, taking the hits, still getting back up. But I did. They all missed out. They had no idea what I could discipline myself to do."[7] If necropolitical labor means a state of being exposed to constant and continuing physical and psychological injuries, leading to or contributing to death, as is often the case in prostitution, the protagonist of *Monster*, Lee, defines her "reaction" itself to such a state as a kind of labor in a much more broadly meaningful sense. Prostitution as a necropolitical labor includes not just a series of actions or activities, but also "reactions" that are not passive but resistive, and "discipline" that is not just an acquisition of skills or behaviors, but also a much more profound existential and fundamental—both mental and physical—forbearance and fortitude.

From Sexualized Work to Sex Work

The film *Monster* portrays sex work at its most dangerous and violent, thus illustrating the deadly potential that it embodies as a necropolitical labor. I now return to situating prostitution within the specific context of South Korea in the late 1960s and 1970s, where we began to see a wildly polymorphous array of sexualized services emerging. In placing full-time prostitution, first, in relation to nonsex or nonsexualized labors, such as factory work and domestic service, and then in relation to part-time prostitution and sexualized service work, this section explores the porous and ambiguous boundaries between the broader female working-class labors. Contemporary South Korea has seen by now a fairly extensive accumulation of historiography on state labor policies and labor movements of the industrializing era. More recently, women factory workers and their achievements have also begun to receive attention from feminist scholars. However, many of these extremely valuable studies tend to focus on female manufacturing labor as a distinct and separate category of labor, without exploring the structural linkage it has to other kinds of feminine proletarian labors: domestic service work, sex work for both domestic and foreign clientele, and other kinds of sexualized and nonsexual service labor.[8] The works of writers such as Hwang Sŏk-yŏng, Cho Sŏn-jak, and others from the 1970s, which this chapter discusses, narrate the stories of women who worked simultaneously in these various sectors or serially moved between them.[9]

Shannon Bell tells us that the specificity of the modern prostitute lies in the overall historical shift in which women's sexuality and women's labor became commodified, when they came to be subjected "en masse [to] the wage relation."[10] In other words, sex work and other female nonsex labors necessarily came into existence simultaneously and in relation to one another. Sexual proletarianization of working-class women in the 1970s took place along with simultaneous historical changes affecting the middle-class women of South Korea. On the economic level, it was the availability of the cheap labor of young female migrants to the city—as domestic servants and as various service workers, restaurant servers, bus conductors, and sales assistants—that made possible the process of housewifization in the newly industrializing economy. The typical roles of postcolonial, modern, normative, feminine sexuality, such as "college girls" and middle-class housewives, whose activities included supporting the careers of their husbands, managing the children's education, and participating in the informal economy through real estate investment, necessarily co-emerged along with the entry of rural working-class women into the urbanizing and developing economy, due to the simultaneous pauperization of the countryside.[11] Under the new economic policies of the Park Chung Hee regime, which further impoverished the rural areas, making subsistence living impossible, young girls and women who had previously contributed to family farming and domestic work were now compelled to

leave for the urban centers. There, they would be able to make more contributions to family finances, by supporting themselves and sending the
rest of their income home to help with their male siblings' education.[12]
The traditional undervaluing of daughters placed the burden of helping
to educate the male heirs of the family on the shoulders of these young
women, as male members' acquisition of higher education was expected
to elevate the social and economic status of the family as a whole.[13]

Prostitutes contributed clandestinely to the family economy, yet were disavowed by their families. The "voluntary" prostitution of female sexuality in
times of family crisis has been an archetypal mode of female conduct in the
Confucian tradition. Some literary works portray the ways in which politicization of sex workers begins by detaching themselves from their (patriarchal) family, and further disassociating themselves from their (masculinist)
ethnonation.[14] As discriminatory social practices and inequity in pay, education, and job availability—all sanctioned by the state—helped to produce
the prostitution labor market, scholars have argued that prostitution must
be understood as an aspect of the broader systematic gender injustice.[15]

In the mid-1970s, South Korean society began to see the accumulated
effects of the serious industrialization efforts that had started in the mid-
1960s. While the absolute standard of living had gone up for the general
population, the uneven distribution of capital accumulation and the sense
of relative deprivation began to register with the working class. One of the
ways in which the increasing polarization of classes began to be felt was
the rise of the service industry for the middle class in general. In particular,
the thriving entertainment and sex and sexualized service industry, targeted
at middle-class, white-collar male workers, was a symptom of this larger
economic and social trend, what Kathleen Barry calls the "industrialization
of sex," that is, the development of well-organized and interrelated businesses
that supported and profited from prostitution.[16] In addition to the sheer
enormity of the growth of the sex and sexualized service industry, it was also
the polymorphousness of the industry's proliferation that seemed to astound
even contemporary tabloid magazines, whose soaring popularity at the time
relied on reporting on all manner of the commodification of feminine sexuality.[17] The overall emergence in the 1970s of a consumer culture and a mass
culture industry in the form of films, TV, and tabloid magazines was also
another significant factor that contributed to the mass migration of young,
rural women, whose "seduction" into modernization was made possible by
turning them into consumers of popular culture and consumer products.

Successive generations of young women from rural areas who would arrive in Seoul through the late 1960s and the '70s in search of economic opportunities became a social category. They were called *mujakjŏng sanggyŏng sonyŏ*, literally translated as "a girl who came to the capital without any plans." Many girls showed up at their friends' boarding houses or workplaces, or at the doorsteps of their relatives who had migrated to Seoul earlier. They would find jobs as domestics, factory workers, or other low-skilled service workers, such as bus conductors, golf caddies, sales assistants, and so forth. Others who simply arrived at the Seoul Railroad Station without anyone to turn to would find themselves at one of the many employment agencies that advertised in the newspapers. The surplus young female labor that could not be absorbed into the usual occupations would be produced as a new "social-sexual" category of working-class women, that is, as prostitutes on the margins of rapidly industrializing South Korean society,[18] as large sections of Seoul and other urban centers were transformed into prostitution districts in the late 1960s.

While domestic labor as live-in housekeepers was regarded, by working-class families themselves and the society at large, as providing more supervision and moral-sexual protection in a family-like atmosphere for young women, most of the young women themselves preferred the social independence and financial autonomy that factory work promised them, especially when the demand for female factory work increased rapidly in the early 1970s. If domestic work was experienced as isolated, imprisoning, and anachronistic, young female rural migrants felt that wage labor in factories or at shops would afford them an opportunity to extricate themselves from the patriarchal and domestic constraints imposed on them. Factory work and other kinds of service labor lured them with the anticipation of individual and social freedom that domestic labor could not bring them. Contrary to the purported protection it should have offered young women, domestic labor could, in fact, turn out to be a sexually predatory situation. Cho Sŏn-jak's short story "Yŏng-ja's Heyday," discussed in chapter 1, traces the reason for her "fall" and her turn to prostitution to her first job as a domestic in a middle-class home, where she was subjected to nightly sexual assaults by male members of the family. Another story, Kang Sŏk-kyŏng's "Days and Dreams," also points to brutal sexual—and economic—exploitation of a young maid by her male employer as the cause of her entry into sex work.[19] The sexual abuse of young female domestics is difficult to document, especially in the context of South

Korean society in the 1970s, when the notion of sexual harassment or sexual violence did not exist for even middle-class women, let alone for working-class women. We can only surmise the prevalence of such occurrences, and the gravity of such offenses, from anecdotal evidence, such as young women's desperate pleas seeking advice in the newspaper columns.[20]

For the period from the 1960s through the 1980s, we need to pay attention to the interchangeability between sex work and factory work by young women, that is, the subterranean and yet evident connections between the economic exploitation of factory workers, which appropriated patriarchal constructions of femininity and feminine sexuality, and the sexual exploitation of economically disadvantaged working-class women in the prostitution industry. For some female factory workers, casual and occasional sex work was a means of earning additional income to supplement their meager salaries. In Hwang Sŏk-yŏng's short story "A Dream of Good Fortune," for example, we meet factory girls who "moonlight" at the local inns, with their male superiors as their customers.[21] The women who engaged in this type of "casual sex work" clearly had more control over who they accepted as customers, or how often they had sex for money, or even how much they would ask for, than women who were full-time sex workers in Seoul's many prostitution districts. Given the hierarchies of power, the lines among romantic affairs, sexual harassment, and prostitution became rather blurred in some cases. In other cases, this type of casual sex work could, of course, lead to full-time sex work. Some of them kept their factory jobs as a cover for their "primary" occupations as bar hostesses or call girls.[22] The fact that they maintained their factory jobs during the day, while also working in sex or sexualized industries at night, functioned often more as a kind of "psychological comfort" for them.[23] For factory workers who did not succumb to part-time or full-time prostitution, their psychological consolation was to "feel pride in living a clean life."[24] If some women were entrapped, immediately and directly, into full-time prostitution upon their arrival in Seoul and other cities, others were first led into sexualized service labors, such as working as servers in restaurants, tea rooms, and bars. These jobs were often an entry into casual or part-time prostitution, known in Korean as *kyŏmŏp maech'un.* Tearoom attendants *(leji)*[25] or bar hostesses were by no means considered full-time sex workers, but their sexualized services, such as sitting and chatting with male customers, were necessarily part of their job. As in other national contexts, the boundary between prostitution and certain kinds of service jobs, such as female workers in barbershops and massage parlors, was extremely ambiguous. Therefore, in such a context, prostitution itself, an even more lucrative business, was always encouraged by their employers.[26]

Most literary representations of prostitution overwhelmingly attribute the main reason for women to enter prostitution to poverty, but this still does not quite answer the question of why, under similar circumstances, some women chose to enter prostitution while others did not. For some, childhood abandonment, broken homes, or sexual molestation further facilitated their entry into prostitution. As we will see later more in detail, female migrants' descent into prostitution was not a matter of simple victimization, but a complex process of their negotiation with multiple varying circumstances—that is, it arose as a result of carefully and painfully made choices in the midst of extremely limited opportunities. For the majority of South Korean working-class young women, who internalized the Confucian norms of female sexual purity, opting for sex work or even sexualized service labor was a difficult decision with countless moral obstacles. On the other hand, the "advantages" of such work also presented a seductive alternate route at every turn in their harsh lives as domestics, factory workers, and other low-skill service laborers. Some of these "advantages," severely offset by moral degradation and social stigma, were escaping long hours of physically excruciating labor at factories, avoiding the humiliation of domestic service, and perhaps most important, earning a higher income. Some young women concluded that prostitution would be the fastest way to afford their economic independence; they desperately dreamed of saving up money and leaving prostitution for a normal life "outside." Eventually, they calculated, a temporary sexual degradation in the present could afford them financial autonomy, leading to social respectability in the future. As South Korea was making the transition to a modern capitalist society, where money and material possessions were a measure of one's status, their calculation in some ways was not so unreasonable. Nonetheless, the harsh reality of the business made such dreams virtually impossible to achieve.

"Domestic" Sex Work and Other Transnational Working-Class Female Labors

In addition to the flow of working-class female labor from factories to sexualized service and prostitution industries, we find another kind of interchangeability and "migration" between domestic prostitution and other kinds of transnational working-class female labors: female manufacturing labor in EPZs, military sex work for the U.S. troops, and "kisaeng sex tourism," catering mostly to Japanese businessmen.[27] As in other developing national economies, and as in other sectors of the South Korean economy, the state played a major role in planning and legislating the utilization of working-class female sexuality as a human resource.[28] Contradicting its promulgation of "Laws on the Prevention of Prostitution" in 1961,[29] the Park Chung Hee government set up a series of laws, regulations, and legal mechanisms throughout the 1960s and '70s that promoted the sex tourism industry and were indirectly designed to facilitate the mobilization of working-class women into the sex industry. This state-led, "export-oriented" sexual proletarianization articulated itself in multiple forms, but one of the more significant and interesting roles it took upon itself was that of "educating" sex workers who served the foreign clientele, namely foreign tourists and U.S. military personnel, under the euphemistic title of "cultural lectures." This government-sponsored "education" consisted of, first, inculcating them about their "patriotic" duty to contribute to the national economy, and second, compelling their adaptation and assimilation into the foreign cultures they came in contact with on their jobs.[30]

While the occupations held by female migrants might have been distinct, they were, in fact, social spaces, structurally linked to one another, where the femininity or feminine sexuality of young women of peasant background could be variously proletarianized by the nexus between the South Korean state, transnational capital, and U.S. neocoloniality. In fact, EPZs and U.S. military bases shared much in common; in the former, a foreign company relocated its factory, while in the latter, a foreign military occupied a segregated, circumscribed part of another country's otherwise sovereign territory.[31] The presence of EPZs or military bases in South Korea was a result of complex negotiations and calculations of cost and profitability for both the host country and the occupying countries, whether their end goal was national security and economic development or neocolonial military and economic expansionism.

The anticommunist developmental state of South Korea has benefited from such a military and economic arrangement with the United States, as it also has become the agent of structuring the exploitation of South Korean female working-class labor. It is possible to argue, along with Julia O'Connell Davidson, who writes about sex tourism industry in the contexts of many developing nations, that in the nationalizing and transnationalizing context of South Korean industrialization, female prostitution, whether serving a domestic or foreign clientele, military or industrial, contributed to maintaining an artificial low-wage economy. This economy served the interests of multinational corporations on the one hand, while functioning as a kind of "alternative welfare system" that reduced the state expenditure on the other, as women's sex work provided subsistence living for themselves and the rural and urban households they supported.[32]

The postwar Japanese economic hegemony over South Korea, under the aegis of U.S. leadership, has occupied a less prominent spot in the South Korean masculinist imagination, in their gendered and sexualized conceptions of national identity and empires, although Japanese sex tourism in South Korea did draw some attention and protest from the student movement and South Korean feminists.[33] In comparing military prostitution for U.S. troops and sex tourism for Japanese businessmen, we are reminded of the intimate connection between militarism and tourism as "cause and effect," astutely pointed out by Cynthia Enloe.[34] The military "tour" in South Korea, for example, as in other countries such as Thailand or the Philippines, has necessarily included "R & R," that is, sex tourism.[35] Just as South Korean women's military prostitution serving the Americans in the post–Korean War era served the transnational market interests of the United States and South Korea, the end of Japanese colonialism and its militarized sexualization of Korean working-class women as Comfort Women did not exactly discontinue in the postwar era. They continued to serve the former colonial power in their civilian guise, in the "market-time" sex tour,[36] and this time they did so with their own sovereign government's sanction.

In the previous chapter, we explored the similar connections between the South Korean use of military prostitution during the Vietnam War and contemporary South Korean men's market-time sex tourism in Vietnam and other Southeast Asian countries. If overseas sex tourism and overseas military service are marketed on the basis of a set of ideological assumptions about masculinity, adventure, and pleasure, the colonial Japanese, neocolonial United States, and postcolonial South Korean governments have been willing partners, sharing similar ideas about the appropriation of working-class women's sexuality.[37]

In trying to think through the significance of the relationship between sex work and an ethnonational masculine identity, one of the important points of departure is the decisive separation of these two different kinds of prostitution in South Korean literature. What I am calling literary representations of "domestic" prostitution can be named as such only in opposition to what has come to form a literary subgenre, "camp town literature," which exclusively deals with military prostitution for U.S. servicemen, the topic of the next chapter. The premise of camp town literature is an allegorization of the female prostitute body as the symbolic site of the United States' infringement upon South Korean political, economic, and military sovereignty. In protesting this, camp town literature's ideological goal is to restore the damaged and diminished Korean national identity, conceived as masculine. In contrast, South Korean literature or cultural criticism has not investigated "domestic" prostitution, sex work that services Korean men, as a matter of ethnonational identity or ethnonational (masculine or feminine) sexuality. This chapter, in conjunction with the following chapter, inquires into the ideological motivations for why representations of domestic sex work and military prostitution must be separated in the masculinist imaginary of the ethnonation.

ETHNONATIONAL MASCULINITY AND COMMERCIALIZED SEX IN POPULAR CULTURE

This section offers a reading of three different types of masculinist representation of female "sex work" in major literary and popular texts of the 1970s: sex work as a filial sacrifice, as ethnonational social work, and as an allegory for commoditizing urbanization.

Prostitute as a Filial Daughter: Sexual Voluntarism and Leftist Nationalism in "A Dwarf Launches a Little Ball"

The practice of sacrificing a daughter's sexuality in the form of marriage or prostitution during family crises, for the benefit of family or of a male heir, had been a longstanding Confucian tradition. *A Dwarf Launches a Little Ball* (1978), arguably the most celebrated literary work of the leftist nationalist canon of the 1970s, blithely continues this custom, in spite of, or along with, its fierce call for a class revolution. A short story titled "A Dwarf Launches a Little Ball" is the central chapter of a linked novel (*yŏnjak sosŏl*) by the same title.[38] The short story consists of three sections, each of which is narrated by one of the three teenage children, two older boys and a daughter, of the "Dwarf," the patriarch of a working-class family. It tells the story of their eviction from their "unauthorized shack" in a neighborhood that was designated as part of the "redevelopment area" of the expanding city of Seoul. The City Redevelopment Project was a program initiated by the Park Chung Hee regime and continued during the succeeding eras under Chun Doo Hwan and others.³⁹ The project aimed at ridding the city of what were commonly known as *p'anjach'on* (literally a "village of wooden panels"), slum areas that mushroomed in various parts of the city. *P'anjajip,* or wooden shacks, were mostly built and occupied by squatters—rural migrants to the city—and the redevelopment projects intended to replace such working-class neighborhoods with middle- and upper-middle-class housing, that is, high-rise apartments, wherever they could, in order to accommodate the fast-growing urban middle-class population.

The first two sections, narrated by the Dwarf's two sons, tell us the story of their father's and neighbors' struggle with local government authorities and real estate developers, and of the violent process of eviction from and demolition of their house. The last section of the story reveals what happened to the teenage daughter, who, the reader was told in the earlier sections, was kidnapped by "aliens." The girl, Yŏng-hŭi, the first-person narrator of the conclusion of the short story, is about fifteen years of age. We are told that she went with a young man who works for a development company as a broker; he buys the rights to the new apartments to be built from those who are being evicted from their shacks and sells them to the prospective middle-class buyers for a significant profit. Since slum residents cannot afford to buy these new apartments, the only thing they can do is sell their rights. Yŏng-hŭi allows herself to be picked up by the young man, with the intention of somehow retrieving her family's "apartment rights," which they had sold to the man earlier. Confined to his apartment, she serves temporarily as his sexual slave until she is able to steal the documents from his safe and return to her family.

First we note the striking contrast between the South Korean literary establishment's celebration of Cho Se-hŭi's "A Dwarf Launches a Little Ball" as one of the most progressive literary achievements, and the traditional role assigned to its heroine by the text—that of the sexually self-sacrificing female. The sexual martyrdom of Yŏng-hŭi is offered not only to the male-led family, but, by extension, also to the masculine-identified working class as a whole and ultimately to the masculinist ethnonation *(minjok),* as redefined by leftist nationalism. In other words, while inheriting the traditional nexus between the family and the state,⁴⁰ the daughter's filiality in Cho's work, manifested as her sexual voluntarism, is also altered to fit the modern leftist nationalist ideology, which redefines the (masculine) working class as the ethnonation's sovereign subjects (*chuch'e*). In Cho Se-hŭi's "A Dwarf Launches a Little Ball," the sexual exploitation of working-class women is transposed to become a triumphant exploit, an act of sacrifice and martyrdom, voluntarily conceived and heroically executed by the teenage girl. It is through her filial motive and through an aestheticized and sacralized representation of her actions as a prostitute that the short story effectively empties out the sexual content—her sexual degradation as a labor performed for family, class, and ethnonation—of Yŏng-hŭi's relationship with the broker, a representative of the dominant class as a grandson of a conglomerate. The leftist nationalist masculinist recuperation of exploited working-class female sexual labor as an act of proletarian nationalist revolution, in fact, obfuscates and assists in the conservative state's and capital's collusion.

As a contrast, the short story does offer another instance of a young teenage girl, Myŏng-hŭi, who becomes a sexual victim rather than a martyr. Myŏng-hŭi, who moved from one kind of service job to another—some of them sexualized services—becomes pregnant as a result of sexual assault, often the eventual and inevitable end for many in similar circumstances. If Yŏng-hŭi's valiant self-sacrifice for her family seems to, fantastically, redeem her from physical sexual defilement, Myŏng-hŭi's suicide also endows her with agency to purify herself as her female ancestors had done when they found themselves subjected to sexual victimization. Cho Se-hŭi's leftist nationalist text recreates the archetypal heroines of the past, who willingly and lovingly sacrifice their sexuality for the greater cause of the clan, the state, and their men; now their descendants surrender theirs for the family, the class, the ethnonation, and their men. In this context, prostitution is not only condoned but encouraged as a uniquely feminine contribution to the righteous cause. Yŏng-hŭi's feminine sexuality in its purity, accomplished precisely through its sacrificial degradation, is an articulation of leftist nationalist masculine will, shared by their right-wing counterparts. The very essence of (masculinist) leftist nationalism lies precisely in its will and ability to claim, mobilize, and sanction working-class feminine sexuality for sacrificial prostitution and ultimately to sanctify it as a dissident national act.

Sex as Social Work in Winter Woman

If Cho Se-hŭi's "A Dwarf Launches a Little Ball" "modernizes" the Confucian notion of female sexuality as a family property by its representation of the voluntarized commandeering of the body of a working-class woman for the (proletarian) class and the (leftist) ethnonation, Cho Hae-il's popular novel *Winter Woman* (1975) accomplishes a different kind of moderniza-tion: it attempts to liberate women's sexuality from familism's proprietary relationship with it, and to reinsert feminine sexual labor directly into the ethnonation. The ethnonation in *Winter Woman* is in vague opposition to the right-wing military state portrayed in the novel and yet it is still largely conservative, thus strangely overlapping with the state. *Winter Woman*, along with Ch'oe In-ho's *Hometown of Stars*, which I discuss next, was one of the most popular serialized newspaper novels of the 1970s. Its popular-ity was explosive, and the novel is said to have rescued practically single-handedly the *Chosŏn Daily*, where it was serialized, from the losing battle with its rival at the time, the *Tonga Daily*. A film version, released in 1977, was also a huge box office hit. Though some of Cho Hae-il's works are included in the South Korean literary canon, the classification of *Winter Woman* as popular fiction is undisputed. Unlike his camp town story, "America," on military prostitution, where, as I discuss in the next chapter, his ideological stance falls more or less in line with the leftist nationalist camp, *Winter Woman* is essentially a bourgeois nationalist text in its con-ceptualization of the relations between the elite class, especially intellectu-als, and the masses, despite some sympathetic gestures toward the student movement and the dissident faction who opposed Park Chung Hee's mil-itary dictatorship.

The novel begins with the protagonist of the novel, I-hwa, still in high school.[41] With her father as a pastor and school chaplain of a girls' high school in Seoul, she grew up in a Christian household, morally impeccable and economically comfortable. She happens to be a striking beauty, whose spiritual purity is said to shine through, apparent to anyone who comes in contact with her. One day she receives an anonymous letter from a young admirer. Soon they meet and get to know each other, but she with-holds herself sexually and emotionally, as befits a young woman with good breeding. His unexpected death makes her feel guilty about her concep-tions about herself and her values concerning sexual chastity.

She is soon an object of pursuit by another young man, Sŏk-ki, when she enters college. Their relationship progresses to a point where the in-creasing pressure he puts on her for a sexual relationship results in what is essentially his date rape of her. This "rape" becomes a turning point in her spiritual and sexual life, an experience of suffering that awakens and enlightens her to the "sadness of the world." In fact, the young man acts as if he raped her in order to teach her a philosophical and religious life lesson. His dying words to her—this second young man also dies, while serving in the military—are that she must recognize the reality "how poor and sad our country is, and how poor and sad our people are": "I-hwa, you must love your countrymen, as many as you can. Become their lover."[42] Her sexual experience, combined with her experience of two men's deaths, seems to release her from the conventional social norms into sexual free-dom. From this point on, she has a series of "sexual-spiritual" relation-ships with men, but she is not romantically and emotionally attached as an individual woman to another individual man. She insists that she will never marry anyone, vehemently rejecting what she calls "family centrism" *(kajok igijuŭi)*. Her sexual relations with men are narrated in terms of reli-gious iconography—Christian in particular; each sexual act is repeatedly described as her offering water to a thirsty man.

After graduating from college, she works as a reporter for a woman's magazine. While doing an investigative article on the lives of factory women, she meets a man, Kwang-jun, who runs a night school for children in a poor neighborhood. His work as a teacher and caretaker is closer to that of a volunteer social worker or a charity worker, as distinct from the work of the contemporary student movement activists. Although the student movement did perform such social work, their message and ultimate aim were acutely political. The novel concludes with her joining Kwang-jun to help with the children and the poor.

Winter Woman can be read at one level as a female sexual bildungsroman, a story of the rite of passage of a teenage girl into adult femininity, predom-inantly centering on her sexual awakening and her subsequent sexual, "romantic" relations with men. As I mentioned earlier, these "romantic" relationships are not quite romantic, since romance by definition is a rela-tionship between individuals. I-hwa's relationships with each man acquire, progressively, a more collective, social meaning. Although in fact I-hwa has sexual relations with only four men in the course of the novel, she vows that she will provide sexual service to "as many [Korean] men as possible." The lessons two men's deaths impart to her are symbolically represented as a spiritual rebirth for her,[43] just as Sŏk-ki's rape of her was also a decisive moment in her rebirth as a sexually emancipated woman who must serve all Korean men.[44] The very last man she gives herself to in the novel is pre-cisely a man who himself serves the wretched of the ethnonation. As the novel progresses, her awareness of the nation's social problems grows. Simultaneously, her recognition of the need for her sexual service follows from her social awareness; her sexual service to each man, which serves the entire Korean male public through the medium of a serialized newspaper novel, is narrated in increasingly more maternal and saintly terms. Thus the novel's portrait of I-hwa's sexual-moral-religious education, offered to male readers, serves as an instrument of socialization for female readers, to transform each woman to give herself sexually, openly, and liberally, to South Korean men, without asking for anything in return.

While I-hwa sexually services the male characters, and the male public via the vicarious form of the novel, she cannot be categorized as a prostitute, as she does not receive money in exchange for sex. As unremunerated work, it would be most accurate to describe her sexual "labor" as volunteer social work, or charity work. She declares, "I think of all Korean men as my lovers, except for those who live on other people's sacrifices." She once again clarifies her position to another puzzled man: "I do not belong to anyone. To no one. And I belong to everyone. This means I do not form any special relations with any individual in particular."[45] Her sexual relationship with each man is not an expression of any particular feelings or desires she has for him, but rather it is an impersonal act: serving an individual serves the general good of the (male) population. I-hwa's body is said to be the "source of water" for the (Korean) men, who were suffering from unrelenting thirst. Thus, her sexual acts take on a religious aura in the novel.[46]

I-hwa's sexual service performs psychological and physical healing, implicitly, of the trauma of modernization under the military regime. This sexual healing also takes place by infantilizing men, while transforming women into maternal figures. As I-hwa's spiritualized sexuality and sexualized spirituality comfort Korean men, the novel exhorts all Korean women to follow I-hwa's example. *Winter Woman* combines three positions of women in the symbolic order into one: mother, virgin, and prostitute.[47] The sexual role she plays for men in her life, and for the South Korean male public, provides maternal comfort and affect, while maintaining, paradoxically, her virginal purity and sacredness in her abstract and yet infinitely "promiscuous" sexual relations with men. I-hwa's symbolic and imaginary position as a "national lover" is essentially that of a Comfort Woman, further elevated to a supernatural, religious, moral height. The official name of the military and labor corps of the Japanese empire, in which Comfort Woman constituted a division, was Chŏngsindae; we might interpret the ideology implied in the name as a "corps of subjects who offer themselves freely to the empire." In the end, when she becomes Kwang-jun's helpmate in his noble project of rescuing the wretched of Korea, Kwang-jun declares her to be "my assistant, my comrade, and my Joan of Arc."[48]

What appears, at first, like a strange combination in *Winter Woman*— that of women's sexual freedom and subordination of that sexual freedom to the (masculine) nation—must be located in the contemporary changes that took place in regard to women's social position in 1970s South Korea. I-hwa's insistence on her total sexual liberty leads men to perceive her, at first, as one of the "women's lib" type of young women, as fashionable in South Korea as in the West at the time. Another forceful assertion of I-hwa's that seems to puzzle men is her rather trenchant critique of familism and her simultaneous refusal to get married. Again, this idea at first appears to resemble the 1970s feminist criticisms of patriarchy that were being imported into South Korea from the West. Both of these feminist ideas, however, are in fact appropriated as the novel's strategies for the containment of I-hwa. Her sexual liberty serves neither her desire nor her pleasure, as her sexual relations with men are sublated into a type of female masculinist nationalism. In her abstract and principled "promiscuity," she is in fact spiritually virginal and chaste. In her sexual "freedom," she "freely" subordinates her sexuality to Korean men. The novel implies that women can become sexually free only insofar as they serve men freely, without obligating them, for example, by wanting to marry them. Her refusal to marry is elaborated upon in her lengthy speeches about the evils of "family centrism." Again, at first, it appears as though her critique of family centrism is an effort at extricating women from the clutches of the patriarchal family structure. Her refusal to marry seems to advocate women's position as individuals outside the family, frustrating patriarchy's design to subordinate women through their interpellation in the domestic sphere as mothers, daughters, and wives. I-hwa's idea seems to coincide with the universal capitalist trend of liberating women from the strictures of familial and kinship systems, in order to directly incorporate them as individuals into the workforce, into the national collective. This change was, to some extent, in progress for working-class female rural migrants to urban areas in 1970s South Korea; they were becoming free social and economic agents in a limited fashion. As the middle-class heroine of *Winter Woman*, I-hwa's rejection of familism does circumvent the constraints of the bourgeois domestic sphere, but it perverts this process by mobilizing her voluntary sexual service (not paid sex work, as many working-class women did provide) into the national public sphere. I-hwa's national and nationalized sexual mobilization of middle-class feminine sexuality offers a counterpoint to the proletarianization of working-class female sexuality in numerous forms of waged labors, from factory work to prostitution.

One of I-hwa's "flaws," according to Sŏk-ki, one of her lovers, is her "political ignorance."[49] Sŏk-ki educates her about the political turmoil South Korea was experiencing under Park Chung Hee's dictatorship and its serious opposition from dissident students and intellectuals. Kwang-jun, her last lover in the novel, teaches her about the economic injustices that industrialization and modernization had brought upon the Korean underclass. While these male characters can be loosely associated with the dissident culture of the 1970s, the novel's general ideological stance can be summarized as an "enlightenment" perspective,[50] which essentially espouses the need for the elites' education of the masses. The "Enlightenment Novel" of the colonial era is a genre that was devised precisely to contest and contain the Marxist politicization of literature, and *Winter Woman* follows this ideological move; the political import of class problems and military dictatorship in the rapidly industrializing context is blunted down to social problems. The novel prescribes a "sexual-social solution" to the politico-economic problems of the nation, in the character of I-hwa, the saintly sexual healer who appears in the winter of South Korea to restore and redeem her compatriots.

If Cho Se-hŭi's opposition to the state and capital still maintains the family–(proletarian) class–(leftist) ethnonation nexus, via the filial daughter's sexual sacrifice, Cho Hae-il's *Winter Woman* dissolves the family as a mediating institution and inserts women directly into the ethnonational collective as further individualized and voluntarized agents whose sexuality is, however, completely subordinated to the (masculine) ethnonation; we have moved from a proletarian filial daughter to an ethnonational comfort woman. I would argue that the sacralization of (masculine) collectives has the effect of decommodifying the commodification of the female body and feminine sexuality; commercialized feminine sexuality can also be sacralized or sanctified on the one hand, while the reality of the defilement of its commodification must remain clandestine on the other hand. *Winter Woman* ascribes social and national value to I-hwa's "Madonna/Whore" sexuality by fusing the "Enlightenment Novel" genre, through which young South Korean women must be awakened to their role as comfort women for their men, with a popular literature subgenre that was fast becoming a pop culture phenomenon in the mid-1970s, namely, *hosŭtesŭ munhak* or "hostess literature," which I discuss in the next section.

Hostesses as Virtual Sex Commodities in Hometown of Stars

Hometown of Stars (1972) was another sensationally popular novel, again first serialized in the newspaper *Chosŏn Daily*. When it was made into a movie soon after, its enormous success at the box office came to signify a change in South Korean conceptions of sexuality, both female and male. *Hometown of Stars* is probably the most representative work of what came to be known as *hosŭtesŭ munhak* or "hostess literature" in the 1970s, if not the origin of such a popular literary genre. During the mid-'70s, South Korea began to see the effects of rapid industrialization. As the accumulating capital began to trickle down, college-educated white-collar professional men, especially those who worked for large and prestigious companies, constituted the core of the newly emergent middle class that was forming as a result. Their demand for sexualized service labors, such as bar hostessing and others, was met by the supply of young women who migrated from rural areas to the big cities, especially to Seoul. While one could find diverse variations of the very old East Asian idea of female companions at drinking establishments, differentiated according to class, in Seoul during the '70s the idea of "hostess" and "hostess bar" conjured up modern and urban young women and middle-class white-collar male workers—often referred to as *saelŏrimaen* or "salary men"—in Westernized settings.

Another peculiarity of the hostess culture must be located in the growing popular mass culture of the 1970s, such as distribution of televisions, accessibility of films, and even wider availability of newspapers and tabloids. It is no accident that a new category of sexualized service, that of bar hostess, was soon transformed into a popular literary and film genre. Indeed, bar hostessing as an occupation and the popular culture genres of "hostess literature" and "hostess film," in fact, almost simultaneously co-emerged rather than literary and film genres reflecting the already existing social phenomenon. Some of the hostesses practiced "part-time prostitution" (*kyŏmŏp maech'un*), to be distinguished from full-time prostitution. Their main job was to entertain male customers, although the nature of this entertainment could vary from mild sexual banter to strip shows. Sleeping with customers was not necessarily required, though it might be encouraged by the bar owners, and often desired by the hostesses themselves for higher income. Although this kind of sexualized female entertainment had always existed in both traditional and modern Korean culture, what was new at this historical juncture was the particularly modern ways in which female sexuality was being commodified and commoditized. The bar hostess in 1970s South Korea really became the cultural symbol of commodified and commoditized female sexuality, through the cinematic and popular culture representations that glamorized them, but which were largely divorced from the economic realities of their working-class lives. One of the major distinctions of the hostess's sexuality from other kinds of commercialized female sexuality is their double consumption, the fact that its sexualized entertainment service was not only consumed by male customers in the bars, but also that the novelistic, cinematic, and tabloid representations of their sexuality became the secondary objects of consumption for the male audiences of the 1970s.

Though mostly unengaged with the historical contexts of 1970s South Korea, *Hometown of Stars* frames itself through repeated references to the Park Chung Hee regime's militarized industrialization. Both in the beginning and at the end of the two-volume novel, the male protagonist catches sight of the same slogan: "Let's Build Our Nation as We Fight" *(Ssaumyŏnsŏ kŏnsŏlhaja)*. Here, the notion of "building" *(kŏnsŏl)* is closely related to the prevailing ideology of the Park regime, articulated in another ubiquitous motto, "Modernization of Our Nation" *(Choguk kŭndaehwa)*. The reference to "fighting" implies the militant posturings to be assumed by the South Korean population for anticommunist struggles against the North. The novel narrates the story of a young woman named Kyŏng-a, as a retrospective after the male first-person narrator, one of her lovers, learns from the local police station that Kyŏng-a has committed suicide. She was originally born into a middle-class home, but after her father's early death her family experiences financial difficulties and she gives up her college education after a semester to help her family. She works at a company as an entry-level worker in the accounting office, where she falls in love with one of her male coworkers. Although she strongly resists premarital sexual relations, she eventually gives in to his demands. As expected, he abandons her after a period of time. Although she later marries a much older, wealthy widower who pursues her, the marriage soon breaks up when he finds out that she had an abortion from a previous relationship. This becomes the starting point of her economic, moral, and sexual downward spiral. She then becomes a bar hostess in order to support herself, and this is when she meets the male narrator. After living together for a year, she leaves him when she feels that he has become tired of her. When they meet again after some time passes, we find out that she either has been living with a series of men or working as a bar woman of some kind, drifting from one place to another. As she becomes more and more dependent on alcohol, running out of men to turn to, she commits suicide. It is difficult to explain the explosive popularity of the novel in the '70s, with its rather common plot and trite characters, until we examine the relationship between the historic iconicty of the heroine and the urbanizing culture in which the novel places her.

Baudelaire wrote, "The prostitute appears as a commodity and a mass-produced article."[51] For the narrator of *Hometown of Stars*, chewing gum becomes a metaphor for her sexuality; he recalls that Kyŏng-a's nipples felt like a piece of "gum chewed and spat out."[52] The ephemeral usefulness and consummate disposability of both chewing gum and the prostitute make them exemplary modern commodities. The ubiquity of and yet haunting absence in commodities constitute a very strange contradictory relationship between the modern subject and his or her object—commodities— one that is seemingly plenitudinous and yet at the same time essentially impoverished. As if to resist her own destruction as a disposable commodity, Kyŏng-a's one very odd habit is to collect obsessively such trivial things as bus tickets, movie stubs, receipts, and so on. What interests us the most about *Hometown of Stars* are the ways in which the novel conceptualizes Kyŏng-a's sexuality in relation to the new experience of urbanization. I argue below that the novel relates "hostess sexuality" and its commercialized female body to the urban space through a figurative de-reterritorialization of the city and the body. I further explore how the deterritorialized feminine body associated with urbanization also signals the introduction of a virtual sexual commodity.

One of the ways in which modernization was made concrete was through the ongoing and fast-paced urbanization. The constantly changing landscape of the old city, Seoul, included the continual construction of buildings, the ever-expanding network of the mass transit system, and the growing ubiquity of squatters and their slums. With an exponential population increase from rural migration, the city was a familiar and yet profoundly foreign and alienating space for the majority of "Seoulites." Many of the professional men that hostesses served, also hailing from the countryside, also experienced living and working in Seoul as alienating, deterritorialized, and even emasculating. Thus, on the one hand, the male narrator's sympathy and affinity for Kyŏng-a establishes her as a symbolic surrogate for the ill effects—the social-psychological dimensions—of urbanization. On the other hand, the novel's repeated positing of Kyŏng-a's sexualized body as coinciding with the very territory of urban Seoul, transforms the shared sense of deterritorialized subjects—ones who lost their "hometowns" (*kohyang*), the same word used in the title of the novel, *Hometown of Stars*—between the professional class of men and hostesses, into the (re)territorialization of working-class women's bodies as sex or sexualized commodities. The male narrator would catch sight of Kyŏng-a's ghost "sit[ting] playfully on top of the neon sign of a city building."[53] Or he imagines her to be a pixie (*yojŏng*), flitting about the city at night and disappearing at dawn as the city wakes up. Yet these identifications between Kyŏng-a and the urban territory are ultimately reduced to Kyŏng-a's body, likened to the "back alleys of the city where we pee with no sense of responsibility."[54]

The novel's prevailing metaphor of Kyŏng-a as the "light that you see commonly on the streets of Seoul . . . like the florescent lights, neon signs, gas lamps of the peanut vendors that once bloom at night and then fade away,"[55] or as a small "pixie" that flickers and vanishes, figures her deterritorialized urban subjectivity as an ephemeral but glamorous specter. The wild popularity of this serialized novel, an old-fashioned medium, and its heroine Kyŏng-a, I argue, is related to the historical shift that the novel was part of and indeed helped to introduce—the production of female sexuality as a visual and virtual sexual commodity. The cinematic spectrality and ephemerality of such iconic images as Kyŏng-a sitting on top of a building like a billboard, or Kyŏng-a as a flickering pixie in the night city, performs this transition into the era of proliferating commodification of the female body and sexuality as virtual sex commodities.

For Peter Bailey, Victorian "para-sexuality," a commodified female sexuality that centers more on the visual relationship between male consumers and female sexual objects, removed from physical contact, replaced the preceding era's custom of barmaids moving about among male customers. Bailey argues that one of the effects of the removal and confinement of the Victorian barmaid behind the bar was the glamorization of her sexuality.[56] While South Korean hostesses served their male customers in close bodily proximity in the 1970s, contemporary mass cultural representations of hostesses in serialized novels, tabloids, and films generated the similar effect of glamorizing their commodified sexuality through the distance created by these cultural media.[57] In fact, "hostess sexuality" was a much more real and far-reaching presence as a virtual sexual commodity in the very material sphere of popular culture than in its nonvirtual counterpart.

When the narrator learns about Kyŏng-a's death from the police, the police detective complains about the increasing number of anonymous deaths in the city: "Every morning we wake up, we get dead bodies, at least several of them we don't have any way of identifying."[58] Kyŏng-a's body was one of them. They notify the narrator because they find his phone number in her handbag. This type of portrayal of social alienation in the urbanizing context already had its literary precedents in the mid-1960s,[59] but *Hometown of Stars* specifically relates this collective psychological condition to a commodification of feminine sexuality, most of all as an emblem. If Kyŏng-a's virtual "hostess sexuality" served to assuage the acute sense of alienation that male urban workers felt, Kyŏng-a in her death once again brings home the generalized anomie of urbanizing Korea: "The sexual act with Kyŏng-a was a confirmation of emptiness that was deeper than the ocean itself. Kyŏng-a was someone you could not know, the ultimate unknowable other. Kyŏng-a was the shadow of a city that was dissolved in the urban properties flowing in my body, such as neon signs, liquor glasses, buildings, traffic lights, newspapers, public telephones, the sense of alienation that one feels as one numerously bumps into the crowds all day long."[60]

PROSTITUTION AS WORK: SURVIVAL, MUTILATION, AND CLANDESTINITY

Whereas the main concern of both *Winter Woman* and *Hometown of Stars*, the social meaning of women's sexuality—nationalized or commercialized—displaces the significance of the working-class women's economic role in modernization, the very premise of the group of works I discuss below, *Children of Darkness* (1980) by Hwang Sŏk-yŏng, and "Yŏng-ja's Heyday" (1973) and *Miss Yang's Adventure* (1975) by Cho Sŏn-jak, is to politicize their subjectivity as the very articulation of their gendered, classed, and sexualized positions. *Children of Darkness* was written by Hwang Sŏk-yŏng, the foremost leftist writer of the 1970s and beyond. Veering away from his reputation as an orthodox socialist realist, this particular full-length novel details the street life led by petty criminals, street urchins, and prostitutes. "Yŏng-ja's Heyday," a short story, and *Miss Yang's Adventure*, a two-volume novel, are by Cho Sŏn-jak. Cho Sŏn-jak's short works are routinely anthologized as important literary achievements of the 1970s, although the enormous commercial success of the film version of "Yŏng-ja's Heyday" gained him notoriety associated with the popular genre of "hostess film." Although *Miss Yang's Adventure* never made its way into the canon, both of these works by Cho Sŏn-jak deal with the social phenomenon that affected a large sector of the population, that is, young female rural migrants who ended up in sex and sexualized service industries in Seoul, a topic for the most part excluded from the literary canon of the 1970s. Comparing these two writers on the topic of prostitution and the bottom life of working-class men and women, we note that while Hwang Sŏk-yŏng's portrait of the working class as a whole offers a sharper political resistance in his unrelenting realism, his representation of female prostitutes, though taking up a significant portion of the novel, is largely deterministic compared to his portrait of their male working-class counterparts. On the other hand, Cho Sŏn-jak's work, especially the longer work, *Miss Yang's Adventure*, is valuable in its focus on the complexity and multiplicity of the subjectivity of female migrants-turned-sex-workers.

Prostitution and Survival on the Street: Children of Darkness

Hwang Sŏk-yŏng's *Children of Darkness* is a complete deconstruction of preconceived notions about prostitution, placing it in its social, economic context where it comes into being and where it stays, that is, in the back-streets of the city. Of course, prostitution as an industry is stratified, with high-class and more organized types of prostitution at the top, but Hwang's interest mainly lies in the lowliest kind of prostitutes, those who exist alongside petty criminals and others who make a living on the street by day-laboring, begging, peddling, pilfering, and cheating, mostly among themselves and their slightly higher class customers or victims. The novel is a first-person narrative by a young man in his early twenties named Tong-ch'ŏl. Much less interested in the development of a character or plot, the novel is rather a series of vignettes that examines and explains the situation and logic of the economic activities performed in the backstreets of Seoul.

Tong-ch'ŏl, crippled as a child, once lived in a camp town, Tongduch'ŏn, with his mother and his older brother. His mother—it is implied—was a military prostitute, but after his brother is run over and killed by an American military truck, they leave the camp town. While his mother struggles to support herself and Tong-ch'ŏl by peddling on the street, Tong-ch'ŏl fast becomes a neighborhood delinquent and runs away from home. He eventually settles in a prostitution district and gets involved in the business as well as in other petty criminal activities. In the latter half of the novel, Tong-ch'ŏl and his friends pull off a big jewelry heist, but eventually he is caught and spends some time in jail. The very last part of the novel briefly describes Tong-ch'ŏl's conversion to Christianity and his efforts at both helping and organizing the street children while fighting the oppressive presence of the police and local authorities.

Children of Darkness catalogs a long list of "jobs" through which this sector of the population, consisting of mainly male children and teenagers as well as older men who make a living on the street, while their female counterparts appear to be almost exclusively occupied with sex work. These "jobs" for boys and men are known among them only by their slang expressions, incomprehensible to outsiders. Difficult to translate, these are only approximations: "back pusher, snitch, puncher, pimp."[61] They can be roughly divided into a few categories. For example, the job of the "back pushers" is a form of assistance to other laborers: they help push a rickshaw from behind and they receive a little money from the rickshaw man. Others would help bring customers to brothels or bars from the street and receive a small compensation from the owners. Another category of job, existing in a much more organized fashion for the street population, includes petty scams and thievery, such as pickpocketing and frauds involving gambling and betting on the streets. Of this category, the most lucrative and organized activity is that of trafficking in women, that is, abducting and selling women to bars and brothels. Another kind of work is peddling some small or cheap items, such as gum, pencils, or pens on the bus. Also readily available on the street was salvage—collecting recyclable bottles and newspapers—but such scavenging could easily turn into stealing from stores or houses. Peddling and scavenging also overlap with begging, although straight panhandling is, strictly, a separate category of work on the street.

Under such harsh and constrained circumstances, all of these categories of "work" easily slide into one another. There is hardly a clear-cut boundary between "honest" labor that is compensated "fairly" and a wide range of activities that are invented and reinvented for the sake of bare survival, necessarily involving multiple elements such as begging, cheating, and stealing, and necessarily exploiting the narrow margin of advantage over others, "others" often meaning those who are weaker and more vulnerable in the same class of people. We might call this complex mode of work "street labor," but the contingent, conditional, and metamorphic nature of this labor make it more a set of strategies of survival, or work of survival. On the one hand, survival as a mode of being becomes a kind of living labor precisely because of the fact that as an activity, it can be neither homogenized nor abstracted from the intimate circumstances out of which it arises.[62] Survival activities on the part of the street subjects are a pastiche of multiple, concrete responses to the demands of the ever-changing contexts of the streets. Their street labor exists as a convergence of the changeability and situatedness of their environment and their abilities to adapt to such an environment. An example of street labor would be a street character called Ppakkumi in Hwang's novel. As I mentioned earlier, Hwang Sŏk-yŏng gives a large number of these slang terms for different kinds of jobs, roles, or characters that are part of street life. Rather than a job or a role, Ppakkumi is a more general type: the word *ppakkumi* means "smart one," something like a smart aleck, slick boy, or trickster. Ppakkumi is the ultimate social economic type who must live and survive on the streets by the dint of his or her wits. Beyond their specific occupations or roles, all street subjects who survive are, in a way, ppakkumi, performing the labor of living by their wits.

In this context, Hwang Sŏk-yŏng's novel situates low-class prostitution as a specifically gendered and sexualized form of street labor. Sex is something women can sell, just as men can sell casual physical labor. Like other street labors, prostitution also intersects with begging, cheating, and stealing. For example, sex is offered in exchange for a bit of money that would buy minimal subsistence living, such as food, clothing, or temporary shelter; prostitution could also involve cheating and stealing from the customer. Prostitution has in common with other kinds of street labor the combination specific to those at the very bottom of the working-class life, the desperateness of their circumstances and their willingness to exchange anything they have—sex, physical work, or intelligence—for survival. Hwang Sŏk-yŏng's novel politicizes prostitution, often conceived as an identity, by extricating it from the space of morality and reinserting it, as a form of work, back into the complex socioeconomic matrix of street life.

Tong-ch'ŏl as a teenage runaway soon ends up in a "whore den" *(ch'angnyŏgul)* because it is a "comfortable place," where he performs various kinds of tasks for the prostitutes, including pimping, and in return he is taken care of by one of them, whom he calls "Older Sister" *(nuna)*.[63] The alliance between children and prostitutes is a logical one: they provide each other with different kinds of help, creating a family-like community in a rough environment. As a young man, Tong-ch'ŏl transitions into a *tunggi,* a slang term for *kidung sŏbang,* a male domestic partner who plays multiple roles as a husband, pimp, and business manager for a prostitute, providing needed services for women, such as protecting them from customers or dealing with territorial disputes with their competitors. He considers it one of the best jobs around, an "easy" job.[64]

Limiting its representation of prostitution to the street economy, the novel highlights workingmen's exploitation of their female counterparts. The most extreme case that Hwang exposes is *t'angch'igi,* a slang term for abducting and selling women to bars and brothels. What Hwang Sŏkyŏng describes in the novel as t'angch'igi and other related practices is similar to what Julia O'Connell Davidson calls in other global locations a "confined" brothel institution, which includes various coercive elements, such as abduction or entrapment, debt bondage, incarceration, and violent disciplinary measures.[65] Hwang describes this criminal activity as a meticulously planned and executed process that involves elaborate lies, teamwork, intimidation, and sexual violence exerted on young female rural migrants.

A team of t'angch'igi people would spot a potential victim, usually at the Seoul Station, often a recent migrant from the countryside who seems to be lost. One of the team members, usually a woman, approaches her by offering to help find the acquaintance or relative she may be looking for. Another person joins them to reinforce the Seoulite's good intention to help her, often pretending to be the first person's friend or relation. After physically securing her, they take her to their headquarters, a brothel or an inn. Once again, another elaborate ploy is staged in order to create a situation where one of the male members of the team would gain her confidence. This is the crucial part: this particular male member must become the savior of the potential t'angch'igi victim so that he will have an opportunity to rape her. The key event in t'angch'igi, apart from psychological intimidation and economic entrapment, is the sexual violence that is perpetrated on the victim in order to lock her into prostitution. Julia O'Connell Davidson reminds us also that the "initiation rape" is not simply a display of a brute disciplinary power, but it also establishes a more complex relationship of protection and dependency between prostitutes and their employers within the power structure of the brothel.[66]

To the victim's surprise, she now owes her "owner" a great deal of money, the money that the owner of the bar or brothel paid the t'angch'igi team, that is, the money with which the owner "bought" her from them: "I feel like something came over me. I can't believe I have to pay back the money I never spent."[67] Then she must proceed to beg the brothel owner to let her work there in order to pay back the money. As the realization of what has just happened sinks in, she must resign herself to her new situation through the false hope of escaping from her prison someday by working hard and saving up money. As she will soon realize, that will not happen any day soon, so she must once again adapt herself to the new environment that is her predicament. This process of t'angch'igi is similar to what a young female migrant over a longer period of time might experience in Seoul, but t'angch'igi compresses this structurally similar process of sexual, psychological, and economic victimization into a deliberately staged, scripted "reenactment" that takes place overnight. As we will see in *Miss Yang's Adventure*, the protagonist, Miss Yang, after over two years of valiant struggle in Seoul to survive without prostituting herself, eventually ends up in the same place, a brothel in a prostitution district, where Sun-im, one of the t'angch'igi victims in *Children of Darkness*, is kidnapped and begins working the next day.

To regard t'angch'igi as a compressed process of this kind of victimization is to grasp the overwhelming extent of determination of this group of women's path in 1970s South Korea. Sexual harassment and assault was, to an alarming degree, part and parcel of any feminized occupation in the '70s in South Korea, from manufacturing jobs to other service jobs such as bus conductor or domestic servant. From this larger pool of working women, it is those who suffer sexual harassment and violence in one form or another who are most likely to end up in prostitution. What Hwang shows us are the ways in which prostitution is situated in this contradictory space, where the trauma of sexual violence is preserved, while being simultaneously repressed in the prostitute's daily act of selling her sex and body. The prostitute must relive the sexual trauma again and again, and yet at the same time she must be forced to resign herself to feeling "comfortable" in her position. Tong-ch'ŏl's regret about a t'angch'igi he was part of acknowledges both the reality of intraclass gendered exploitation and his class camaraderie across gender differences in this way: "I always feel bad when I run into one of those girls I did a t'angch'igi on. It stays like a nail in my heart. It's like an octopus eating its own leg, like putting a knife into your own feet, isn't it? . . . One time I saw another t'angch'igi going on and I put a stop to it. But then again, of course, I ruined their livelihood."[68]

"Yŏng-ja's Heyday": Sex Work as Mutilation and Prosthetic Resistance

I have explored some of the parallels and connections made between South Korean military labor in Vietnam and prostitution in Cho Sŏn-jak's "Yŏng-ja's Heyday" in the previous chapter.[69] Here I would like to highlight and reemphasize a couple of dimensions of the story that pertain to prostitution, the depiction of sex work, first, as symbolic bodily mutilation, and second, as prosthetic resistance. The short story is narrated by a young veteran of the Vietnam War who now works as a *ttaemiri*, one who scrubs and washes people at a public bath in the outskirts of Seoul. On his visit to one of the cheapest prostitution districts, he happens to run into Yŏng-ja, whom he had known before going to war. At the time, Yŏng-ja was working as a housemaid for the owner of the small company where he was working as a welder. The narrator now learns that Yŏng-ja, who has lost an arm, makes a living as a prostitute. As they gradually get reacquainted, he learns that as a live-in domestic at his boss's house, she was already being sexually assaulted nightly by her employer and his son. She runs away to become a bus conductor, another common job for young female rural migrants. After she loses her arm in a fall from the crowded bus, she ends up in a prostitution district with nowhere else to go. The narrator makes a gift of a homemade prosthetic arm, a piece of wood tied together with some wires, which turns out to be a tremendous help in disguising her disability. The title of the story, "Yŏng-ja's Heyday," refers to this period when she thrives with the help of the prosthetic, which increases and improves her business. Shortly, however, the prostitution district faces a government crackdown. While Yŏng-ja and a couple of her coworkers are able to escape the police raids, about two weeks later the narrator finds her scorched body in the remains of a fire that had destroyed a block of brothels.

The young Vietnam veteran's deep resentment at his own position at the bottom of social ladder is articulated through his bitterness toward women of higher class, whom he designates as "regular" girls or nonprostitutes, as if prostitutes constituted a separate race of women. He expresses his anger in this way: "Actually, every time I saw those regular girls who are not whores, I just felt my spite rising."[70] In this passage, distinguishing "whores" from "regular girls" *(pŏndŭt pŏndŭthan)*, the narrator here characterizes prostitute women as a deformed or disfigured femininity. Yŏng-ja's one-armedness, the result of an occupational, industrial accident, also figuratively represents the mutilation of her sexuality and subjectivity as a sexually harassed and abused non–sex worker and later as a sex worker.[71] In a similar way that the mental trauma and bodily injury suffered in the war by Vietnam veterans emasculate them, Yŏng-ja's sexual damage places her permanently outside the category of normative femininity. However, Yŏng-ja's prosthesis enables her to achieve a supranormative subjectivity: by hiding her disability, the prosthesis brings her more business, while on the other hand when the men refuse to pay or try to run away, frightened by her disfigurement, she will use the prosthetic arm to defend the value of her labor. Yŏng-ja with a "righteous arm"—the literal meaning of the Sino-Korean word ŭisu, used for a prosthetic arm—emerges as a transcendent heroine, like the one-armed or one-legged swordsmen and women in martial arts films, to whom the story compares her.

The scorched bodies of Yŏng-ja and the other sex worker victims of the fire in the prostitution district remind the male narrator of the enemies he slaughtered in the war, the "blackened bodies of the Vietcongs burned to death from the flamethrower." The frequency and commonness of fires in prostitution quarters is not fictional, but real and historical. Bad electrical wiring, cramped quarters, and poorly constructed housing in the slums where brothels were located often led to fires, and the widespread practice of confining prostitutes to their rooms again was the cause of mass loss of lives in such fires. As the images of burned sex workers with those of the communist insurgents overlap in his mind, he hears her voice laughingly declare, "I am the one who set the fire."[72]

Sex and Sexualized Service Work as Clandestine Labor:
Miss Yang's Adventure

Cho Sŏn-jak's *Miss Yang's Adventure* is a full-length novel that has not been included in the national canon, although many of his other shorter works have been. One of the reasons for this omission may have to do with the somewhat ambiguous boundary in which the novel locates itself. While the material of the novel, prostitution, night life, and the underworld of related criminal activities, overlaps with that of the popular literary genre "hostess literature" *(hosŭtesŭ munhak),* discussed in the previous section of this chapter, the novel does not quite succumb to offering the kind of sexual pleasure sought by readers of the genre, and in fact sustains a politicized narration of the story of Yang Ŭn-ja, a female rural migrant to the city in her late teens, who is constantly threatened by and seduced into the world of prostitution.

The Secret Lives of South Korean Men

The narrative structure of the novel follows Ŭn-ja's movement through Seoul and through the series of jobs she takes in the city. There are basically two ways in which Ŭn-ja finds herself in a new job and in a new situation. It is through the network of female friends and coworkers and also through newspaper classified advertisements that she is introduced to bars and other sexualized service jobs. It is ultimately her close girlfriend who convinces her to take a job as a full-time prostitute at a brothel where she herself is working. This type of recruitment is easy for the owners of brothels and thus encouraged by them. The novel also structures a significant part of the narrative by having her answer various classified ads, and thus having her travel through the underworld of the sex and sexualized service industry. In certain cases these ads are meant to entrap women. Often a help-wanted ad for a typist or a female clerk is in fact designed to deceive and recruit women for bars and brothels. But others are just simply vaguer and vaguely alluring. This type of ad could be misleading for novices, but for more experienced female job seekers who can read the code, the intent of these ads is quite clear. At various moments in her urban life, Ŭn-ja, in desperation, decides to "tackle those help-wanted ads that were mystifying." Among many, one episode that follows her answering a particular ad stands out for its hyperbolic, parodic representation of the "mysteriousness" that seems to surround the prostitution industry. By the time Ŭn-ja answers the ad that reads "seeking those who want to achieve independence quietly," she has a pretty good idea what kind of job the ad might be for, just as the reader also does. Nonetheless, for this entire episode from her initial interview for the job to her leaving it, the narrative patently refuses to reveal to the reader exactly what is going on, while at the same time allowing the reader to conjecture exactly what transpires at Ŭn-ja's workplace. Ŭn-ja works at a relatively high class "tourist hotel" (kwang-wang hotel)—a type of hotel that caters to Korean upper-class and foreign tourists—in some capacity as a service worker. The narrative suggests that she is encouraged and even pressured to "go out" with the guests. Among her coworkers she gains the nickname "school girl Miss Yang" for sticking only to the "sacred part of the labor."[73]

This central episode of the novel illustrates two important aspects of nonmilitary or domestic prostitution. First, the narrative strategy of revealing and yet refusing to reveal Ŭn-ja's job performs this contradiction, that is, the ways in which prostitution exists in South Korean society: it is everywhere but it is nowhere. The narrative insistently uses such adjectives as "mystifying" or "mysterious" to describe these newspaper classified ads.[74] These adjectives in Korean, *arisonghan* and *pulgasaŭihan*, capture, with a somewhat humorous and satirical tone, the very modus operandi of the prostitution industry, its clandestinity. The moral unacceptability and illegality of ever-increasing prostitution in this era must be covered over with these euphemisms. Second, the particular ad in this key episode, "seeking those who want to achieve independence quietly," also instructs us as to what the clandestinity of prostitution means from the point of view of sex and sexualized service workers themselves. The classified ad already appears here as an interpretation of the job in Ŭn-ja's mind, rewritten and reimagined by the desperate situation of young female rural migrants into this fantasy of sex work as enabling one to achieve economic independence. It is what they want these jobs to be, a means to an end that would vacate the content of the means, the social stigma and the psychical and physical trauma and violence of sex and sexualized work. The essential part of the ad, "quietly," refers to the clandestinity of the job, desperately desired by the women themselves, while working to service South Korean men whose pleasure must also be clandestine. This episode further helps to illustrate the ways in which the social clandestinity of prostitution is structurally linked to its economic clandestinity, that is, the subterranean economic value of prostitution, its connection to other sectors of the economy by maintaining low wages for the manufacturing sector and sustaining the agricultural population.

Agency without Choice in Sex Work

One of the major strengths in the novel's treatment of the exodus of young women into Seoul is that it consistently endows the protagonist Ŭn-ja, and other female characters, with as much agency as possible while acknowledging rural poverty and gendered socioeconomic exploitation in the urbanization process as the ultimate determining conditions of their lives. Apart from the underdevelopment of rural areas under Park Chung Hee's industrialization policy, there were other cultural and social factors that propelled migration. Traditionally, these young women would have stayed home until marriage, helping out with domestic and agricultural work, but with the diminishing profitability of farming and the broadening range of employment for women, they were drawn to better economic opportunities and the idea of their own economic independence in the city. The availability of new cultural and leisure services and activities also play an important role in luring the young women into the urban areas. As the modernization process progressed, the gap in cultural consumption between the rural and urban areas came to be felt sharply. What rural women had heard about the cities, especially Seoul, stirred up "vague curiosity, vague hope, vague anticipation, and vague possibilities" in them. Rather than regarding female migrants as victims, the novel's slightly comical tone ends up highlighting the agency of the protagonist. The novel introduces Ŭn-ja, arriving in Seoul, as "an explorer who is stepping into the uncivilized territories [migaeji]."[75] She is an "adventurer" as the novel's title, Miss Yang's Adventure, indicates to us, one out to conquer the barbarous city folks, rather than be a meek sacrifice to them.

The centrality of Ŭn-ja's "mysterious" experience at the tourist hotel lies in the phrase "seeking those who want to achieve independence quietly" in the newspaper classified ad to which she responds. The appeal of this phrase to young women like Ŭn-ja was powerful. The very contradiction of their situation was resoundingly implied in this phrase; they so desperately desire to achieve a relative degree of economic independence, but again and again they must confront the reality that the only path open to them to achieve such a goal requires them to compromise their sexuality. If the clandestineness of their labor and identity is all they could hope for under such circumstances, they must also absent themselves as social and economic subjects of a nation-state. The notion of female migrants "who want to achieve independence quietly" encapsulates the irrepressible tension between the inexorable path on which they were placed and their frantic resistance to such overdetermined conditions. Ŭn-ja was "a mouse thrashing about in a trap, caught between her monthly salary and her daily humiliation."[76]

Ŭn-ja's tourist hotel experience becomes a kind of last stand to maintain her chastity from the mounting pressure. The battle has become too exhausting for her. A kind of liberation and awakening results from this state of mental fatigue; she realizes "how trivial her sexual purity was." She gives up her virginity "for free" to a male friend; her only consolation is that she received no money for it.[77] After this last stand, and after some more drifting in the world of sex and sexualized labor, Ŭn-ja eventually finds herself at a brothel where one of her friends works. Her friend and the brothel owner try to recruit her. She at first balks at the idea of full-time, full-fledged prostitution, but she finally succumbs to the persuasiveness of the situation.

What ultimately sways her to take the job is the stability of the work as a prostitute at the brothel. She had been drifting around from one boarding room to another, and from one job to another. Her experience in Seoul has been to try to escape, continually, each situation that has jeopardized her chastity. As she waits for her friend to be finished with her customer, she observes the life of a full-time sex worker as laid out in another girl's room. What impresses her more than anything is the fact that she has her own room, decorated with her favorite girly things, a diary with golden trim, a vanity with cosmetics, and an encouraging proverb up on the wall. She is also impressed with the transaction her friend has with her regular customer from the conversation she overhears; it resembles something of a relationship, in terms of their friendliness and stability. She feels the atmosphere in the house as warm, friendly, and communal, and her sense that these prostitutes are women like herself, that she is no different than they, is comforting rather than frightening to her. Rather than feeling superior to or separate from them, Ŭn-ja, for the first time, seems to feel a sense of camaraderie with the community of prostitutes gathered in this place. We can connect this incipient sense rising in Ŭn-ja to the more developed political sentiment expressed in "Yŏng-ja's Heyday." In one scene where a prostitute user tries to leave without paying Yŏng-ja, her coworkers come to her rescue with a lecture to the man about the "588 Republic" (588 is a nickname for one of the most famous prostitution quarters in Seoul), which they proclaim is "of the prostitutes, for the prostitutes, and by the prostitutes."[78] These literary moments from the 1970s trace themselves forward to the more contemporary politicization and collectivization of sex workers in real life, as we will see in this chapter's conclusion.

Her sense of her life up to this point in Seoul is described as "being once again thrown out" and "floating around." It has been like a "hot balloon, precariously and indefinitely floating around with no possibility of landing before it explodes." Now at the brothel, with her friend and everyone else urging her to stay, she feels a different kind of "seduction" to enter the final stop at the end of her long journey; the seduction of "the atmosphere of respite, lazy nostalgia, a cozy room . . . and the groundless sense of stability." Ironically and tragically, during Ŭn-ja's rough sojourn in Seoul only by entering full-time prostitution is she able to find a refuge from the world of infinite insecurity, danger, and violence. She is going to have to trade selling her body with the very least bit of security that the world would allow her. Only by selling her sex will she be able to afford a room of her own, where she can keep a diary and be able to reflect upon her own condition. The narrator describes Ŭn-ja's newfound home, a brothel: "Soon it became nighttime and Ŭn-ja was committed to one of the vacant rooms downstairs. That's right. There is no other word to describe it than to say, 'committed.' We usually call those who have been injured and lost their possessions and homes—due to war, fire, or flood—refugees. Refugees are supposed to be 'committed.' . . . As long as we are trying to understand Miss Yang Ŭn-ja as a refugee, we might as well make it clear what the disaster for her was. Wasn't it a blast of wind, the so-called modernization?"[79]

The novel concludes with a brief epilogue that narrates the present circumstance of Miss Yang, five years after she settled into the brothel. It suggests that Ŭn-ja has indeed achieved her financial independence by having become a sex worker serving Japanese businessmen. She seems to be very well-off, and yet still tormented by her guilt and morals. The very close of the novel finds her at the crossroads between accepting a marriage proposal from an admirer from her hometown and going to Japan to work on a more permanent basis—a fraudulent marriage to a Japanese man has been arranged for her. The story of a domestic sex worker ends as that of a transnational migrant sex worker.

Conclusion

Since the 1970s, the prostitution industry itself, as well as all of the related entities, such as state and local governments, NGOs, and consumers, has undergone a wide range of changes. I close this chapter with a preliminary discussion of some of these changes in contemporary South Korea. But first, I will analyze the lyrics of an iconic singer from the 1970s, Na Hun-a, as another way of capturing the lives and cultures of domestic migrants in general, beyond the particular population—young women—with which this chapter has been chiefly concerned.

The Cultures of Domestic Migrants

Many fictional characters I have discussed in the current and previous chapters, both male and female, represent the large sector of the rural population who became migrants to the urban areas, in particular to Seoul, during the 1960s and 1970s. Along with his rival Nam Chin, another young male singer, Na Hun-a, and his music were truly a social phenomenon of the 1970s. At the time, the profile of his huge fandom was believed to be the following: young women in their late teens and early twenties; originally from the countryside but now urban dwellers; mostly uneducated; often working in factories, as live-in domestics, and in other kinds of low-skill or menial service jobs. I would like to revise this relatively accurate portrait just a little by adding, first, that this fandom, imagined often as an army of young women infatuated with a charismatic young male singer, also included young women in occupations that were unmentionable, that is, prostitutes and sexualized service workers; and second, that despite the more conspicuous female fan base, I would argue that his songs, particularly their lyrics, indeed appealed powerfully to rural migrants of both sexes and all ages. As the broader issue of the formation of South Korean working-class culture as a whole remains outside the scope of this chapter, my discussion of Na's songs is limited to what I call the cultures of ("domestic") migrants.

Some of the recurring concepts in Na Hun-a's lyrics are *kohyang* ("hometown"), *t'ahyang* (literally, "other town," in the sense of not hometown or a strange place), *ibyŏl* ("parting"), and *hyangsu* ("homesickness"), as shown in the titles of what are still very famous and familiar songs, "Kohyangyŏk" (Hometown Station) or "Mŏnamŏn kohyang" (Distant Hometown). Indeed, the majority of his most beloved songs are about the ongoing historical phenomenon of migration in the 1970s. These songs, often with only several lines of lyrics, effectively capture the intense pain and sorrow of migrants' lives, brought on by the scattering of family members, a domestic diaspora. Na's more conventional love songs might be interpreted as a repository of these "diasporic" emotions, the general sense of loss, longing, nostalgia, and rootlessness, displaced onto romantic love. While these songs are filled with emotions about the lost hometown, they curiously never mention the subject's present location, the nonhometown, *t'ahyang*, that is, the urban setting and the urban life. The various factors that contributed to the sorrow of the protagonists of the songs in their urban life are, while implied, not specified: hard labor, meager wages, discrimination suffered due to their class status, lack of education, their regional dialects. All of the longing, rootlessness, and instability of migrants' lives stems from the hardship of their urban lives, the absent center of these songs. This curious and rich silence about the city in Na's songs points us to another meaning of Seoul, an idea, expressed in a short story by Kim

Sŭng-ok, "Seoul: 1964, Winter," that "Seoul is the place of concentration of every sort of desire."[80]

One of Na Hun-a's songs, titled "Kŏnbae" (Let's Raise Our Glass!), conceptualizes the migrant subject in this way, "You and I Both / Wanderers being hauled away."[81] This intricate phrase articulates the contradictory subjectivity of (domestic) migrant laborers as being forced to wander. The sense of agency, the free will of a "wanderer," intermingles with the simultaneous sense of overwhelming determination, being hauled around and dragged away. On the one hand, the migrants' sense of lostness and disorientation in their wandering steps has been systematically produced as the first stage toward reorienting them and rechanneling their bodies for industrial mobilization and proletarianization. On the other hand, their sense of themselves as wanderers, minimally free, is simultaneously experienced most profoundly. A song titled "Mŏnamŏn kohyanag" (Far Away from Hometown) describes a migrant's movement in this way:

> Under the faraway southern sky is my hometown I miss
> My beloved parents and siblings wait for my return
> *This strange town, a thousand miles away from home, unfamiliar streets, my*
> *steps wander and falter*
> Drinking my sorrow mixed with a glass of wine
> But my heart races toward my hometown sky. (emphasis added)[82]

A couple of Na Hun-a's songs, both extremely popular back then and still familiar to the generations who grew up in the 1970s and before, offer narratives that are more directly relevant to the topic of this chapter, young female rural migrants in Seoul. The first song, "18-se Sun-i" (An Eighteen-year-old Sun-i), is narrated by a young male voice:

> She said she would return when the apricot tree blooms
> But my love Sun-i does not know to return
> I must go, I must, to look for my Sun-i
> Has anyone seen such a person,
> Age, eighteen and name, Sun-i
> The fragrance of the flowers fallen makes me cry.[83]

Because Sun-i's trajectory, representing that of a multitude of young female migrants to the city, suggested by a common name Sun-i, is told from the perspective a young male lover left in the countryside, this narrative is able to feign ignorance as to what could have or might have or is most likely to have happened to Sun-i and others like her. It is this feigning about the Sun-i's of the era on the part of the mainstream society at large that *Miss Yang's Adventure* lays bare; Sun-i's fate, only faintly suggested by this song—Sun-i's "disappearance" and her subsequent "fall" like the fallen apricot blossoms—is fully figured in the tale of Ŭn-ja's urban adventures. Kim Sŭng-ok's "Seoul: 1964, Winter" sardonically tells the reader about five Mi-ja's, employed at five different bars in different parts of Seoul, implying the infinite duplicability of the experiences of these young girls. The story of five Mi-ja's suggests the contradiction of the migrant experience that is simultaneously a collective and yet a shockingly alienating one. Kim's story captures the somber mood of Seoul, a city that in the 1970s was beginning to overflow with the atomized mass, that is, rural migrants.[84]

In another song by Na, titled "Somun" (Rumors), the singer relates various rumors he has heard about his departed lover:

My beloved who left me suddenly
I never trust these rumors I hear here and there
A rumor has it that she is living in Pusan
Someone says they saw her in Kwangju
Another rumor would have it that she left for America for good
Or that she probably lives in Seoul
Or that she has changed beyond recognition
Or that she is still alone because of me.[85]

Here the song narrates another story of a (probably and relatively) young female migrant, possibly domestic or transnational; she is rumored to move through three Korean large cities or (again rumored) to have gone to America. With the phrase "that she has changed beyond recognition" in particular, this obscuring and obfuscating narrative again insinuates that the probable trajectory of her migration is related to the kind of work that is not mentionable, while holding out hope that she may be still chaste. These popular songs of the 1970s enable us to discern the patterns of suppression of the history of a group of people, stories that still have not been told.

Lastly, I would like to discuss the lyrics of two songs that point us in the direction of the broader construction of proletarian subjectivity in the industrializing era. The first song is titled "Chapch'o" (Weed):

The nameless weed on a windy hill where no one comes to visit
If it were a flower, then at least it would have fragrance
It is only a weed that has neither this nor that
If it only had feet, it would go look for its beloved
If it only had hands, it would beckon its beloved to come
It has neither this nor that
It has nothing.[86]

While the trope of "weed" or "grass" for people or proletariat is common enough, what stands out in these lyrics is a running reference to the idea of possession or possessiveness; "weed" is a thing to be pitied mainly because it possesses nothing. Unlike the more elite use of the trope of "grass" (p'ul) for "people" (minjung) in a famous poem by the leftist poet Kim Su-yŏng, titled "P'ul" (Grass), where grass is allegorically figured as heroic proletariat,[87] this song simply deplores the state of "weed" as possessing nothing. The anthropomorphic weed is spitefully lacking even feet and hands that would have performed proletarian labor.

Another song, titled "Ŏmae" (Mother), by Na Hun-a reveals an aspect of proletarian subjectivity, a deadly resistance to what I have called necropolitical labor:

Mother, mother, my dear mother
Why did she bear me?
To bear me, she should've borne me better
Not to bear me, she shouldn't have at all
Were I to live, life is hard and bitter
Were I to die, my life in its prime
This lot of mine is just awful.[88]

This particular song, both its melody and lyrics, is a modernized version of a type of traditional folksong, t'aryŏng, a lament. Both musically and lyrically, the song is a sustained outburst of intense emotions, bitterness, and resentment about the terrible hardship that he has experienced in life, without offering hope, promise, or any sense of positivity: the song refuses sublation. The only "solution" that the male proletarian subject can think of, or the only kind of resistance he may be able to put up, is to consider killing himself (the thought of which he stops by reminding himself of the preciousness of his youth), or at least to question his very birth by cursing his mother. We will see in chapter 4 that also for migrant workers from overseas, suicide, which means destruction of the self as a labor commodity, becomes the only resistance to necropolitical labor, labor that either harms or kills, that is, labor that is extracted on the condition of death.

Recent Government Crackdowns on Prostitution

Among the three models of intervention in the prostitution industry that governments around the globe tend to follow, "prohibition/abolition, regulation/registration, or deregulation,"[89] the South Korean state has adopted, historically, the official policy of prohibition, while permitting it to proliferate, and sometimes actively promoting it, by helping to create certain social conditions.[90] As we will see in the next chapter, the state has always cooperated with local U.S. military authorities, who have maintained the policies of registering military sex workers and regulating STDs and other health and commercial issues. The Roh Mu Hyun government's implementation of a new law, Special Law on Prostitution, in the fall of 2004, followed this historical tradition of cracking down on domestic prostitution, escalating it further up to a level more serious and severe than ever. It seems to have had multiple contradictory effects. Business in these districts was reduced by 50 percent, and the number of sex workers in the areas also decreased by 30 to 50 percent. However, it is safe to say that the government crackdowns have forced prostitution in these areas to go further underground, through the industry's resorting to new strategies, such as internet solicitation and infiltration into residential neighborhoods. It is also true that higher-class prostitution, which usually involves bars, salons, massage parlors, and other kinds of businesses that function as a cover for prostitution, is not affected by the government crackdown, which tends to focus on the known prostitution districts used by working-class men. The special law resulted in further diversifying the prostitution business, which had been already well on its way to becoming polymorphous and multifarious with the aid of new technologies.

Another consequence has been to force sex workers outside the country; some are opting to go abroad, to other Asian countries such as Japan as well as to the United States, in order to continue to make their living in the prostitution business. In other words, the law has turned more sex workers into global migrant workers. Although South Korean prostitution servicing Japanese, Americans, and overseas South Koreans persists, South Korean middle-class men have become consumers of overseas sex tourism in Southeast Asia.[91] Domestically they have also become consumers of the migrant sex work of Russian and Filipina women.

While some feminist and women's organizations approve of the radical reduction in the number of businesses in prostitution districts, other women activists, scholars, and sex workers themselves have also pointed out glaring problems with the special law, such as the absence of provisions to punish and/or educate male consumers and business owners; the main target for the authorities has been female sex workers. As these crackdowns have ended up robbing them of their livelihoods, one of the most important consequences of the special law has been sex workers' successful efforts at organizing themselves, and pushing for the opening of a public dialogue about the issue of prostitution. In the fall of 2004 and the summer of 2005, the National Association of Hant'ŏ and the Alliance of Women Workers of Hant'ŏ held a large-scale public rally, protesting the continuing enforcement of the Special Law on Prostitution. They have also designated a Sex Workers' Day as one of the ways to help bring awareness to the public that prostitution is a type of labor that constitutes their livelihood. Although some of the demonstrators wore sunglasses or paper bags over their faces, reminding us of the difficulty of organizing workers in the sex industry, a newspaper article commented that the image of their protest, fighting for their *saengjonkwon* (right to survival), was no different from what the South Korean public has been used to, that of other workers who have also fought for their right to work. One of the most trenchant critiques of the government by sex workers is their hypocrisy in placing sex workers in the so-called "protection facilities" *(poho sisŏl)* that resemble prisons and putting forward no practical or financially viable alternatives. The government does not lend any significant financial support to programs that are supposed to offer vocational training for sex workers who wish to leave the industry. Despite the Roh regime's reputation as "progressive," the government crackdowns or "rescue efforts" continue to function, as they have for several decades already, as a means of criminalizing sex workers without any concrete plans or programs.

Sex workers' associations are demanding that the government and mainstream society recognize their "right to sex work" *(sŏng nodongkwon)*, directly connected to their "right to survival" *(saengjonkwon)*. While many progressive feminist activists and scholars do support this position of sex workers, we must also take into account the rampant exploitation in the prostitution industry, consisting of practices that flagrantly violate the human rights of sex workers. Although some of the sex worker activists are rightly critical and resentful of certain women's organizations' tendency to regard sex workers simply as victims of human rights violations, the relations between their human rights and their "right to sex work and survival" are clearly very complex, requiring strategies of sorting out each situation carefully and protecting both rights that may be, at times, at odds with each other. I would argue that the claim by some sex worker activists that the negative image of the prostitution industry as relying upon human trafficking, incarceration, and physical, psychological, and sexual violence is the remnant of a bygone era, and that contemporary prostitution is a voluntary service work performed in exchange for monetary compensation, is at least an exaggeration, if not an outright misrepresentation of reality. At the same time, we do need to note the historical shift that the prostitution industry has undergone in the context of South Korea's economic development along the lines that Kathleen Barry argues as taking place globally, that is, a shift from a more militarized and physically and legally coercive mobilization for "prostitution," to sexual proletarianization that is economically motivated, or, put another way, whose only coercive forces and constraints are economic.[92]

While there is much on the issue of prostitution that requires investigation, research and debate on the part of all relevant groups, worker-activists, NGOs, and the state, I would argue, along with Julia O'Connell Davidson and others, for pursuing simultaneous and multiple strategies. On the one hand, abolition or prohibition as a state policy criminalizes prostitution unilaterally, without offering viable alternatives for sex workers or their employers, and without differentiating the economic and social stratification within the industry. On the other hand, deregulation without legal limits and boundaries can and does result in a range of human rights abuses and economic exploitation. While being able to imagine abolition of prostitution in one (ideal) future, by keeping in mind that prostitution is always already the product of a network of intersecting inequities, I would argue that regulation of the industry, which could serve the interests of diverse and hierarchized groups of people in prostitution, could be a simultaneously immediate and intermediate goal.[93]

Lastly, anticipating the last chapter on migrant labor, I would like to draw our attention to certain similarities between the proletarianization of sex and sexuality and the proletarianization of race and racialization. As prostitutes have been targets of the authorities' crackdowns, detention, and "reform" efforts, non-Korean migrant workers are similarly subjected to periodic bouts of crackdowns, detainment in facilities, and forcible deportations. While constituting major portions of the national economy, both of their respective sexualized and racialized labors are clandestine. The businesses, the state, and by extension mainstream South Korean society take advantage of the fatal weaknesses that both groups of clandestine laborers share—the illegality of their visa status in the case of migrant workers and the illegality of their occupation in the case of sex workers. Thus, for the state, businesses, and consumers of both labors, proletarianizing sex and race functions as a means of holding these clandestine laborers hostages. As we will see in chapter 4, one labor activist refers to migrant workers' attempt at integrating themselves into mainstream South Korean society by means of their labor activism as "coming out." We can argue that sex workers are now undergoing a similar kind of historical transformation, another "coming out," by taking their issues and rights to the public. Once criminals and then victims, both groups work toward their goal of becoming recognized as workers by the mainstream.

3 Military Prostitution

Gynocentrism, Racial Hybridity, and Diaspora

The numerous American military bases in South Korea constitute only a small segment of the United States' military presence in Asia, part of "a single security chain": "the 'Pacific Rim' must be strung with a necklace of American-controlled military bases: from Anchorage to San Diego, Hawaii, Vladivostok, Seoul, Yokohama, Cam Rahn Bay, Subic Bay, and Clark, Wellington, Belau, and Kwajalein."[1] Immediately after the withdrawal of the Japanese in August of 1945, the United States' military occupation of the southern half of the Korean peninsula began. Since the end of the U.S. military government's rule with the founding of the Republic of Korea in 1948, United States military forces have stayed on in over one hundred military facilities and fifty camps.[2] Over the course of half a century, the number of American troops stationed in South Korea has been, at any given time, no fewer than thirty-five thousand. As in those cities and towns near American military bases in multiple Asian nation-states, military prostitution in South Korea became an integral and vital part of both the local and the national economy, and everyday cultural and social life. In camp towns, known in Korean as *kijich'on,* located in impoverished rural parts of South Korea, where large American military bases tend to be located, the very bottom of the South Korean working class provide various kinds of day-to-day services to the occupying military, but the camp town economy is heavily dependent on bars and brothels, that is, sex and sexualized service industries. In the period of the last several decades, over a million women have worked as sex workers for American servicemen in camp towns around the country. Camp town sex workers have been the Comfort Women of postcolonial South Korea.[3] The most recent and significant change in South Korean camp towns, arising since the mid-1990s, has been the influx of Filipina and Russian migrant sex workers, who together make up 90 percent of the workforce in camp towns as of around 2005.[4]

Cynthia Enloe explains this process of the militarized industrialization of sex as the result of a conglomeration of multiple factors, such as politico-military strategic decisions on the part of national governments, organizational strategies and calculations of profitability on the part of local governments and the occupying military authorities, the presence of a large number of women regarded as a source of cheapened labor, and patriarchal-military assumptions about male sexual desires and needs and their relation to troop morale and combat readiness.[5] Below, I would like to offer a brief historical examination of some of the major agents and institutions in the camp towns of South Korea as they have been studied in existing literature on military prostitution. The main part of this chapter, then, attempts to provide critical readings of revisionist perspectives on these agents, institutions, and their positions, as represented by more recent cultural productions.

As Cynthia Enloe's pioneering work has forcefully demonstrated, international relations between nation-states—political, economic, and military— have appropriated, mobilized, and exploited femininity and feminine sexuality in the various roles women play as mothers and wives of soldiers, diplomats, and military sex workers during times of war and peace. Both the South Korean and the United States governments have been agents, strategically more and less active, who have shaped the broader contours, as well as the concrete practices of the militarization of camp town women. The South Korean state's willingness to become involved with camp towns and military prostitution varied from decade to decade, depending both on its relations with the United States and its own economic needs. Na Young Lee sums up these changes as moving from the "tacit permission" of the war-torn 1950s to "permissive promotion" and "active support" in the 1960s and '70s. The two major legal provisions made by the Park Chung Hee regime, almost immediately after his coup—the Prostitution Prevention Law, which excluded camp town prostitution from the general governmental crackdown on prostitution, and the Tourism Promotion Law, which designated camp towns as special tourism districts[6]—effectively demonstrate that the South Korean state saw camp town prostitution as a significant source of American currency, as it accelerated its industrialization efforts. Citing a Christian activist women's report, Katharine Moon writes that the state, through a government agency, the Korea International Tourism Association, "licensed and trained" prostitutes for foreign men, and the association publicly and routinely affirmed and praised the economic contribution of such prostitutes to the ongoing development.[7] Not unlike the case of other transnational labors of South Korea—such as military labor in Vietnam; the export of South Korean nurses, miners, construction workers, and emigrants; and the emergence of Asian migrant workers in South Korea—the Korean state played the role of brokering (sex) labor in camp towns. It also saw camp town prostitution as having social value in smoothing out relations between South Korea and the United States, both locally and internationally; camp town prostitutes were considered to be playing the role of "personal ambassadors" in their interactions with American servicemen.[8]

When American soldiers' salaries began to lose value in relation to the South Korean economy of the 1980s, which was climbing up the global hierarchy, the government lost interest in camp town prostitution and turned its attention to the so-called "kisaeng tourism," sex tourism catering mainly to Japanese businessmen, which was beginning to prove much more lucrative. The South Korean state's policies concerning the crimes and violence committed by American servicemen against South Korean civilians have been similarly fluctuating and opportunistic. Na Young Lee describes the state's shifting engagement and disengagement with the issues as "strategic vacillation," that is, the authorities either ignore or highlight violent crimes, rapes, and murders committed by GIs, often against South Korean military prostitutes, depending upon the perceived political usefulness of protest or silence at any given historical juncture.[9]

As Cynthia Enloe and others have pointed out, one of the constituent premises of military prostitution must be traced back to the ideologies of gender, interlocking and mutually reinforcing, such as masculinity's close association with militarism and militarization, the presumption of an inherent linkage between masculinity and sexual domination, and a conception of feminine sexuality as naturally disposed to traffic and commercialization. The necessary intersection of racist and neoimperialist ideologies with the gendered policies of the U.S. government and local military authorities further compounded the already existing imbalance of power between the two states, the United States and South Korea, and between South Korean camp town women workers and the U.S. servicemen.[10]

One of the more obvious and significant ways in which the disparity of power between South Korea and the United States manifests itself is the U.S.–ROK SOFA, the Status of Forces Agreement, created in 1966, stipulating the conditions of the U.S. military's presence and operations in South Korea. Various aspects of the treaty, such as the prosecution of criminal cases, civil suit procedures, and environmental issues, have been deemed unequal and unfair by South Koreans, including camp town residents who have been victims of violence and crimes committed by American servicemen, camp town activists, and antigovernment activists of the 1980s whose agenda came to embrace strong anti-Americanism. The American military in South Korea, which enjoyed virtual extraterritorial immunity before the ratification of SOFA in 1966, continued to operate under conditions that favored it against South Korea as a nation-state and against South Korean camp town residents in particular, even after two recent rounds of amendment to the SOFA in 1991 and 2001.[11] Local U.S. military authorities in South Korea exercise the greatest amount of control over camp town women via the medicalization of their bodies and sexuality—specifically through regular examination for STDs, the use of an identification system for sex workers to screen those who are "free" of STDs, and the legal–medical authority to quarantine those who are "infected" with STDs and confiscate their work permits. While the U.S. military's immediate concern is to protect their personnel from diseases, at the expense of controlling camp town women workers' lives and impinging upon their rights, the military medicalization of these women functions simultaneously as a broader mechanism of governing the camp towns at large.[12]

Historically, South Korean representations from journalism to literature have referred to *migun pŏmjoe*, crimes against Korean civilians perpetrated by American soldiers, understanding them as articulations of the American military's racism and sexism against Koreans, and camp town women in particular.[13] U.S. scholars and activists have also been very critical of GIs' role as consumers of sex work in Asia, and as material manifestations of hierarchized relations of race, nation, gender and sexuality, and class between GIs and Asian female sex workers. If the "mainstream" South Korean critique of GIs rises from the masculinist nationalist stance, this U.S. perspective mobilizes transnational feminism and race theories to analyze American soldiers in Asia.[14] Despite this very critical difference, both South Korean and American perspectives view American soldiers' relations with Asian and Korean sex workers as an instance of "sexual imperialism" that results from a complex of intersecting ideologies and power relations, such as militarism, imperialism, racism, and masculinism and sexism.[15] While agreeing with this point of view, this chapter also examines some of the new South Korean cultural productions that see American servicemen as historically, politically, and ideologically constructed— that is, as performing military work, an imperial counterpart to the South Korean neocolonized and subimperialist military work discussed in the first chapter.

During the 1960s and '70s, when the antigovernment South Korean labor movement arose, matured, and intensified against the Park Chung Hee military dictatorship's accelerated industrialization efforts, camp towns and their workers remained largely outside the domain of the activists' interests. Even the smaller number of Christian activists who fought against prostitution largely excluded camp town prostitution from their sphere of concern. During these years, we can argue that the most important activism in camp towns was carried out by the self-help groups organized by and for military sex workers. In the 1980s, we saw the entry of generally two types of external activists into camp towns: Christians and anti-American nationalists. While both groups of female activists contributed to improving the lives of camp town workers, their limits were set by their own priorities, shaped by their ideological or religious agendas.[16]

The most important focus in this chapter's narrative on camp town prostitution is, of course, female sex and sexualized service workers. Like young women who ended up in the domestic prostitution industry, those who were compelled into military prostitution came from similar backgrounds and circumstances; they were daughters of rural proletarian patriarchal families, whose subsistence living was being threatened further by the skewed developmentalist policies of the Park Chung Hee regime. Not only did their sexual labor in camp towns support their families and contribute to the national economy during the years of industrialization, but military sex work, along with transnational sex tourism, has also constituted the base of the global economy.[17] Sturdevant and Stoltzfus's book on military prostitution in Asia repeats at various moments one very apt caption for a series of photos that portray American soldiers at bars and clubs, enjoying themselves with Asian women who are also drinking, dancing, and smiling: "Men at play, women at work." Another quotation from a female worker explains this caption from a perspective invisible to the outsiders:

"I am laughing on the outside and crying on the inside."[18] This chapter will also shed some light on other groups in camp towns, whose lives are dependent and inextricably linked to women workers, such as biracial children and Korean men.

As the South Korean economy reached a certain level of development in the late 1980s, the value of the salaries of U.S. servicemen declined in relation to the increased wages of South Koreans. As the sector of working-class women who had been drawn into the relatively powerful camp town economy found more lucrative jobs within the diversified and thriving sex industry in the domestic arena, the import of military sex workers, mostly Filipina and Russian women, into South Korea began in the mid-1990s, in many ways following the precedent of Okinawa, where the demand for sex and sexualized labor had begun to be met by Filipinas since the mid-1970s. The South Korean state assisted in importing women by making legal provisions available, issuing visas, and managing the migrant sex worker population, brought in most often under the false pretext of Entertainment and Culture Visas (E-6). Korean men now participate in camp town economies, playing a revised role since the earlier era of industrialization, as part of organized crime networks that carry out human trafficking. One of the goals of this chapter is to bring to the fore the resistive aspects of camp town women's lives—indeed, to redefine what "resistance" might mean for those who have been severely constrained and disempowered by the circumstances of camp towns.

Although recent years have witnessed increased scholarly attention to the topic of military prostitution, these studies have been mostly from the social science fields, based on ethnographical fieldwork and empirical data and information. In contrast to these existing studies, this chapter, primarily an examination of literary and other cultural representations of military prostitution of the past and present, aims to offer a broader historical perspective on the changes that camp towns and their workers have undergone, and also to delve deeper into the ideological and symbolic values of the multiple and various historiographical perspectives of these cultural productions. South Korean cultural representations of domestic prostitution (serving South Korean male clientele) and military prostitution (serving U.S. troops) have tended to bifurcate. As we have seen in the previous chapter, domestic prostitution was rarely the subject of high literature, while it came to dominate the pages and screens of popular culture. On the other hand, military prostitution was a topic reserved for "serious" literature—leftist, masculinist, and nationalist—to be canonized as works of anti-American, anti-neocolonial, anti–military dictatorship resistance through the era of industrialization, from the mid-1960s through the 1980s.[19] If domestic prostitution consisted of twofold exploitation—consumption of sexualized labors of working-class women first, and then of their mass culture representations—I argue that military prostitution came to perform a symbolic labor for the (leftist and masculinist) nationalist camp. This particular signification turned working-class feminine sexuality in military prostitution into a sign of endangerment of ethnonational autonomy and integrity, that is, South Korea's hegemonized political, economic, and military relationship to the United States, giving military prostitution an exceptional status apart from all other female working-class sexualized labors, and overlooking the materiality of the lives and labors of camp town women workers.

After offering a critical survey of earlier representations of camp town and military prostitution from the 1960s and '70s, the second part of this chapter focuses on examining recent revisionist writings produced in the '90s. One such revisionist perspective brings the camp town patriarchy back from the margins of camp town literature, often represented as compromising compradors, or racialized or emasculated men in the earlier works, a perspective that desires to rehabilitate the camp town patriarchy as a legitimate sector of the larger working-class patriarchy. Another revision, which comes from a feminist perspective, attempts to de-allegorize camp town sex workers by detailing the day-to-day militarization, commercialization, racialization, and transnationalization of women's sexuality and work and, more importantly, by textualizing camp town women's everyday subversion and resistance.

The third revisionist perspective emerges in the voices of biracial children who are born and raised in the context of military prostitution. The majority of representations of camp town life in South Korean literature have excluded any extended portrayal of biracial children, who make up an important sector of the camp town population. My examination of Heinz Insu Fenkl's autobiographical novel, *Memories of My Ghost Brother*, explores the particular transnationality of camp town biracial children that arises through their dual dis-identification with both South Korea and the United States. This particular transnationality disrupts the boundary of South Korea as an ethnonation, while opening up the spaces of resistance in the interstices between ethnicities, nation-states, and empires.

The third and last part of this chapter shifts its attention to the relations between military prostitution and "diasporas." My reading of Kim Ki-dŏk's film *Address Unknown* will attempt to reconceptualize camp towns as a type of double diasporization from South Korea and the United States, and reenvisage their special "translocality." This section of the chapter also briefly examines the literal diaspora of camp town women—those who marry American servicemen and become immigrant brides and workers in the United States. Lastly, I discuss briefly the contemporary diasporization of Filipina and Russian military sex workers in South Korean camp towns, and their complex translocality.

ALLEGORIES OF MILITARY PROSTITUTION IN THE AGE OF AUTHORITARIANISM AND COMPRADOR CAPITAL

Discursive Production of the "Western Princess"

Throughout the 1950s, the appearance of female prostitutes catering to U.S. servicemen in literary works was chiefly related to the context of the aftermath of the Korean War, which had brought about economic devastation and a destruction of families, resulting in a large number of orphans and widows.[20] The South Korean literature of the postwar period registered such prostitutes as a marginal social category, reflecting the plight of these girls and women. In such canonical short works as "Shorty Kim" (1953), "A Stray Bullet" (1960), "Anna's Will" (1963), and "The Royal Tomb and the Occupying Troops" (1963), produced between the mid-1950s and the early '60s, the figure of the military prostitute remains fundamentally tied to her specific economic and social circumstances, without being transformed into the allegory for masculinist nationalism that she is to become later.[21] While military sex workers continued to be associated with working-class poverty, the next generation of women who entered military prostitution in the 1960s and '70s could no longer be linked to the same degree of desperation and the sacrifice of mothers and sisters typical in the previous generation in war-torn Korea. As South Korean industrialization, which mobilized a mass of young female labor, got underway, prostitution as a whole became generally separated out from the rest of the working-class female labor in mainstream society and in the public consciousness, despite the fact that not only were prostitutes drawn from the same gendered and classed population pool, but that there was also a constant flow of young women from factory, domestic, and other service work into sex work. Military prostitution for the U.S. troops in particular was further segregated from other sex and sexualized labors, and acutely stigmatized in the minds of South Korean people.

In conjunction with these changes, a new mode of conceptualizing military sex work that arose in the form of "camp town literature" or *kijich'on munhak*—a figuration of the camp town and the body of a female military prostitute as a metaphorical site of the U.S. hegemony over South Korea—can be linked to several other historical factors that came into play in the mid-1960s. The year 1965 was a watershed year for South Korea, for its complete integration into the U.S.-led global capitalist economy, and for the resubordination of its economy to Japan, by then already back on its way to becoming a superpower. South Korea began dispatching combat troops to the Vietnam War, in exchange for an influx of U.S. capital, in the form of investment, loans, contracts, and military salaries for its soldiers. South Korea's economic alliance with Japan was also crucial for capital flow, technology transfer, and the maximization of cheap Korean labor. The Park Chung Hee regime's normalization treaty with Japan was met with a vociferous opposition by dissident students and intellectuals, but the more important upshot of this opposition lay in their reassessment of South Korea's relations with the United States, rather than with Japan. The emerging dissident leftist nationalist faction reaffirmed to themselves the nature of American domination over South Korea as a new kind of colonialism, that is, neocoloniality, which was backed up by military occupation. The mounting anti-American sentiment was further reinforced by the dissidents' recognition of the military regime's comprador alliance with U.S. capital. I locate the postcolonial intensification and reinvention of South Korean ethnonationalism at this historical juncture as being defined in opposition to the neocolonial United States and the comprador military authoritarian regime. In this context, camp town literature—authored by male writers between the mid-1960s and late 1980s—becomes a major discursive site through which anti-Americanism would be articulated.

This figuration of the body of (working-class women) military sex workers as an infringement on the sovereignty of the (leftist masculinist) ethnonation is premised on a couple of intersecting assumptions. As Cynthia Enloe informs us, masculinist nationalism in the context of (neo)coloniality grasps women as its "most valuable possessions," who perform biological and social reproductive labor. Such valuation conceptualizes feminine sexuality and female labor as subordinate to the patriarchal family and the masculinist state. Furthermore, under colonial or neocolonial circumstances, the besieged national patriarchy's investment of women's sexual purity with the power to perpetuate national unity and cultural identity is even more intensified.[22] The idea of contamination and degeneracy, which is brought on by contact with the foreign other, what Ann Stoler calls "cultural-ethnonational hygiene" in the context of the Dutch colonization of Indonesia, operates also in the anti(neo)colonial ethnonationalist context of South Korea; it is a readily adoptable ideology for the (masculine) nation that is subjugated and dominated by another.[23] Camp town literature, as a literary subgenre, embodies this logic of masculinist nationalist resistance, "nationalism . . . that has sprung from masculinized memory, masculinized humiliation and masculinized hope."[24] It is a discursive site where the protest against the U.S. hegemony relies on an allegorization of the power hierarchy between South Korea and the United States in terms of gendered and sexualized relations; a raped, prostituted, and/or violated South Korean woman stands in for South Korea, as an American GI represents the U.S. imperial conquest. Through its allegorized construction of *yanggongju* ("Western princess," one of several derogatory terms referring to military sex workers for American troops), which elides the lived realities and material hardships of military sex workers, the literary subgenre attempts to restore and fortify the damaged masculine authority and diminished masculine national sovereignty of South Korea.

"Land of Excrement": Anti-Americanism as a Revenge Rape of a White Woman

"Land of Excrement" (1965) and "The Scream of a Yellow Dog" (1974) are arguably the most famous and representative examples of camp town fiction as masculinist national allegories of military prostitution. The elevated positions of these two stories in the South Korean literary canon are due to their open and bold anti-Americanism. Indeed, the author of "Land of Excrement," Nam Chŏng-hyŏn, was accused of violating national security and anticommunism laws for his forceful articulation of an anti-American stance, unprecedented in the post-Liberation era up to that point, 1965. In the trial of Nam Chŏng-hyŏn, the state charged that the fiction's anti-Americanism was tantamount to procommunism and thus constituted a threat to South Korean national security.[25] For its blunt opposition to U.S. imperialism and militarism in South Korea, and its equally unambiguous use of a gendered and sexualized allegory, it would not be an exaggeration to say that "Land of Excrement" definitively established the genre of camp town literature at this particular historical moment. In fact, we can locate the very dilemma of reading this story in the extreme conflict and contradiction between its brilliant success as a political allegory offering a vehement critique of U.S. imperialism and militarism on the Korean peninsula, on the one hand, and its equally brutal allegorization of women's sexuality—a symbolic violence perpetrated upon women, both Korean and white American—on the other hand.

The short story narrates an account of how a man named Hong Man-su, hiding in a mountain, has ended up surrounded by U.S. military forces who are ready to use an atomic bomb to destroy him. He has raped Mrs. Speed, the wife of Sergeant Speed of the U.S. Army stationed in South Korea, in order to "avenge" both his mother, who was raped by an American soldier when the U.S. troops came to occupy the southern half of the peninsula as the Japanese withdrew, and his sister, who later became a prostitute for American GIs and who is, for now, Sergeant Speed's mistress. The tale of Hong Man-su is a bare, stripped-down story, without any elaborate plot, psychological character portraits, or representation of historical details. Hong Man-su is introduced to the reader as the descendant of Tan'gun, the mythological founder of Korea, and as the tenth-generation heir to Hong Kil-dong, a fictional character from a Chosŏn dynasty novel, a righteous rebel with magical powers. Hong Man-su, whose name implies "Long Live Korea," is a rebel who stands up to the foreign power and its corrupt comprador partner. Although this political allegory acknowledges the socioeconomic position of Hong Man-su as a black market dealer of goods out of the U.S. military bases, and that of his sister as a military prostitute for American troops, these positions operate only as means of connecting the characters to the broader historical and ideological conditions that the nation as a collective confronts. Both masculine and feminine genders and sexualities function allegorically: Man-su as embodying ethnonational castration, and his mother's rape and his sister's prostitution as symbolizing the violation of ethnonational sovereignty.[26]

The description of an American GI's rape of Man-su's mother is also pared down, almost stylized. After the rape, his mother, whose "eyes lost the beauty of her soul,"[27] is said to spend several days naked as she loses her sanity. The purity of her soul, previously reflected in her beautiful eyes, can only form a harsh contrast with her current state of vileness and pollution. She soon passes away, and only her death performs a purificatory function. In her madness, she shoves Man-su's head into her genitalia, as if to transfer her trauma to him and to designate him as her avenger. The image of a five-year-old Man-su, whose head is pushed back into her "lewd parts,"[28] is that of a rebirth of Man-su as a neocolonized subject. Man-su's gaze into his mother's "magnified lewd parts," which were "dirty and terrifying but also intoxicating," seizes her sexuality and attempts to reterritorialize her body. Such a vision is said to have left a "deep wound in his heart."[29]

If Man-su's mother was a valiant resister to the imperialist/rapist, Man-su's sister is said not to mind her job as a prostitute for the GIs, and even to enjoy it. The corrupting influences of the empire have transformed the trauma of the initial neocolonial conquest, allegorized as a rape, into the ongoing domination, represented as the mundanity and normality of prostitution. The continuity posited between rape and prostitution further ignores the concrete socioeconomic contexts of military prostitution, while highlighting the allegorical politicality of the imbalance of power between the two nations; military prostitution is grasped as nothing more than institutionalization of the violence of imperial conquest as rape.

While as a filial son he had vowed to avenge his mother, as a brother to a military prostitute—Pun-i—Man-su is not able to rescue her; instead, he finds himself making a living off the situation by dealing in black market goods. When Sergeant Speed, who is Pun-i's boyfriend/customer, is visited by his wife from the United States, an opportunity for Man-su to avenge his women presents itself. Man-su's rape of Mrs. Speed seeks to restore South Korean masculinity by rectifying the unequal symbolic values associated with the respective feminine sexualities, yellow and white: "I just couldn't understand his way of thinking. . . . To my dismay, Sergeant Speed found fault with Pun-i's ample bottoms every which way. Comparing Pun-i's with his own wife's lower half, he would nightly abuse Pun-i with vile curses and violent words. . . . Every time I heard Pun-i's crying and screaming from Sergeant Speed's speedy kicks, I myself had to cry. . . . Then I became curious about Mrs. Speed's lower half, which Mr. Speed was always bragging about."[30] Man-su protests that while American men's sexual assault on Korean women does not even qualify as rape, his rape of Mrs. Speed brings on the White House's threat of nuclear attack.[31] Man-su's revenge rape of Mrs. Speed seeks to reverse the violence of U.S. imperialism by replicating the sexual violence upon the other's woman; the logic of anti-imperialist nationalism repeats and mirrors that of imperialism.

Man-su's curiosity about the "mysterious construction of [Mrs. Speed's] genitalia" appropriates feminine sexuality as symbolizing the mystery of the power of the empire, just as his mother's violated genitalia also allegorized the humiliation of the colonized ethnonation. Man-su's rape here is figured, on the one hand, as an intellectual quest into the secrets of the empire, while rape is a violent act of remasculinzation that seeks to overcome his castration. Through this discursive sexual violence, this racially castrated Korean male transforms himself into sexual predator, a sexualized version of the "yellow peril," unprecedented in South Korean literature and in South Korean discourses on its relationship with the United States. In this way, the story grasps the symbolic value invested in white feminine sexuality as central to the U.S. imperial project vis-à-vis its neo-colony, South Korea. Man-su's rape of the white woman threatens to blur the imperial and racial boundary that white American women play an essential role in solidifying.

The failure of Man-su's attempt to reverse and restore equivalent masculinity comes in the form of the United States' threat to explode an atomic bomb on the mountain where he is hiding. The entire narrative of the vehement critique of the United States, which takes place while he is besieged by the U.S. military, is a discursive explosion that aims at compensating for the equality that could not be accomplished in the material sphere. The language of his wish for his splendid death for the (masculine) nation is almost reminiscent of the kind of ultranationalism of the Japanese imperial military toward the end of the Pacific War, which sacralized and deified the deaths of male imperial soldiers. The destruction of his physical body, "turned to dust, scattered in the wind,"[32] by an American A-bomb would be as glorious as the death of Japanese imperial subjects, who were exhorted to fight unto death and to regard such deaths as beautiful and sacral as the shattering of a jewel. The explosion of the mountain where he is hiding, named Hyangmi-san (America Facing Mountain), is represented in parodic apocalyptic terms: "Amid the great explosive roar and splendid flash . . . Hyangmi-san will be blown to smithereens . . . So will their [Americans'] sacred mission."[33]

"The Scream of a Yellow Dog": Camp Town as a Dystopic Fairy Land

The narrative structure of "The Scream of a Yellow Dog," a short story by Ch'ŏn Sŭng-se, is set up as the travelogue of a man who journeys into an exotic land, a camp town. The male protagonist is pressured by his wife to get back the money that their former renter owes them. They learn that since her departure, she has become a prostitute in a camp town. He reluctantly sets out to find Ŭn-ju, who has changed her name to Tambi Kim. Representing the camp town as a magical dystopia, a place under an evil spell, this particular allegory of the camp town takes the shape of a fairy tale, also mediated by Hollywood films, in which a male hero sets out to rescue a damsel in distress. As soon as he steps into the town, he imagines what appears in front of him as a scene from a Western: "The streets were deserted, like the usual finale of a Western. A white soldier was standing stupidly with his yellow hair blowing in the wind, as if he were the righteous man who had just slain a villain." What he sees on the streets are mostly soldiers and prostitutes, and they appear and disappear as if on "magical streets." At night "the desolateness of the daytime, like magic, turned into rising heat." Each character he encounters—a wise old man, a crazy old woman, soldiers, and prostitutes—appears out of nowhere, as if disconnected from the social reality of which they are part. They appear like phantoms or ghosts, giving clues to or misleading the hero's search for Ŭn-ju (Silver Bead), who is lost under the evil magic spell. While Ŭn-ju, the pristine country girl in the male hero's imagination, is the object of his quest, he encounters many other prostitutes in the process. In contrast to the purity of Ŭn-ju in his mind, these prostitutes, who try to hook him, are portrayed as rough, foul-mouthed, and lewd. Their cavalierly seductive attitude, their apparent lack of shame in what they do, and their obliviousness to the nature of the town, convey to him the sense that they have lost touch with reality, imprisoned within the invisible walls of the enchanted town. As he combs the town to find Ŭn-ju, the protagonist encounters an old man who teaches the outsider "three key secrets" to survival in a camp town. The old man, with a Northern accent, is portrayed as someone who has transcended life's hardships and gained wisdom. The wise old man's advice to him, given in three Sino-Korean phrases, has the tone of a riddle: "Lose Face, Deny Decorum, Educate Hard." Encouraged by this encounter, the younger man presses on. He then comes across an old woman who is on a similar mission as his. She wears a long sash that says, "Yun Mi-sun, Age 19. Hometown, Chŏnbuk, Kŭmma. If you help me find my granddaughter, I will be forever indebted."[34] By the end of the story, he finds the grandmother dead in a ditch of water, with the writing on the sash all smudged. Grandmother has failed, offering the reader a chance to meditate on the difficulty of our hero's mission.

Unlike some of the hopelessly fallen women he encounters, the narrative suggests, Ŭn-ju lost her true identity only temporarily. Once he finds her, he is convinced that he can persuade her to lead a decent life by leaving the camp town and going back to her family in her rural hometown. He wants to restore her to what she was when he first knew her, a "typical country girl." When he finally finds her, despite his best efforts, he is unable to convince her and has to leave her as he found her. This last part of the short story, where he tries to persuade her, is what constitutes another essential ideological dimension of camp town literature, that is, a rescue and reform narrative. The rescue and reform narrative in a way rewrites the Hollywood Western mentioned earlier in the story; the Korean male hero takes the place of the white cowboy who comes into town to fight the villains—the occupying troops and consumers of military prostitution—rescue the woman, and restore peace. While this cannot happen in reality under the circumstances, and particularly not on a large scale, the ideological essence of the masculinist nationalist narrative vis-à-vis South Korean women is abundantly illustrated and advanced. The male hero disavows his knowledge of her fundamental predicament as a gendered and classed subject, and views Ŭn-ju's life as a military prostitute as a simple matter of a moral and lifestyle choice. In fact, her life as a military prostitute in a camp town is reduced, in his mind, to the camp town's association with the influences of Western civilization and modern culture that are sweeping South Korean society, causing Korean tradition and all that is good in what is simple, but "ours," to vanish:

> We don't need to be greedy. If we live within our means, then every turn of our lives could bring us peace. . . . We don't have to have to sit on a sofa and drink carrot juice made in a blender, or live in a carpeted house. Would driving a luxury car on a highway, or going to health resorts be the only affluence and peace? The unsophisticated and slow gait of our good-natured ancestors who have walked down the rice paddies, the sweaty palms of your hometown folks who just grab your hands, even their smelly breath. . . . Wouldn't all these give us a wonderful peacefulness? What if we don't speak English? Speaking just Korean well and correctly, wouldn't we have so much to say each other? Aren't Korean songs much better than rock and roll or soul music?[35]

In this amazing passage, for the protagonist and the text, military prostitution is completely taken out of its domestic and transnational social and economic contexts. Military sex workers' association with the United States, and by extension the West, is appropriated to allegorize not only political, economic, and military hegemony, but also the cultural imperialism of the United States, which was beginning to be felt in South Korea in the mid-1970s. At the very end of the story, when the protagonist is making his last pitch to Ŭn-ju to try to make an honest woman out of her, the narrative changes its form from a fairy tale to a kind of animal fable.

As the protagonist and Ŭn-ju say goodbye and part, they witness two dogs mating in the street. One is a large white male dog and the other is a smaller yellow female dog, marked as "the home-grown kind." What appeared to be a normal mating at first soon turns into a painful rape of the yellow dog by the white dog. The female yellow dog finally lets out a scream. As Ŭn-ju and the protagonist watch the process, the man says to her tearfully, "Ŭn-ju, yellow dogs must go with other yellow dogs, yellows with yellows."[36] These fictions portray camp towns, with their militarized-commodified sexuality, as the source of racialized sexual pollution and contamination and as a much more degenerate kind of commodified sexuality than domestically consumed sexuality: "The Scream of a Yellow Dog" compares camp town women to "lepers." Both "Land of Excrement" and "The Scream of a Yellow Dog" articulate not only the explosive male resentment against racial castration, but also a profound sexual xenophobia and fear of miscegenation. The ultimate goal that such masculinist nationalist camp town fictions serve is to police and discipline Korean women's desire and sexuality, seeking to instill what Ann Stoler calls "cultural-ethnonational hygiene."[37]

"America": Identificatory Adjustments to Allegories

"America" (1972), a novella by Cho Hae-il, maintains the form of a masculinist nationalist allegory overall, but it also departs from the above two works in significant ways. The gendered and sexual relations that allegorize the international power relations between the two countries are figured as much more complex articulations of the intersecting forces of gender, class, nationalism, and neocoloniality. The fact that its representation of the camp town is consistently informed by multiple historical contingencies begins, at least partially, to de-allegorize the subgenre.

The male narrator has just finished his military service and is on his way back home, but he finds himself suddenly "orphaned," due to the fact that the apartment building where his parents were living collapses and kills both of them. With no one to turn to, he arrives in a camp town, where an uncle of his is running a bar. His uncle is introduced to the reader as an adventurer who has taken interesting risks, and most of all as a survivor who possesses a type of worldly wisdom from having experienced much difficulty in life. The uncle flatly states to the protagonist that the camp town is not quite the unlivable place that many people deem it is.[38] It is, above all, a place where people make a living. The focus of the narrative is squarely on the camp town women sex workers, as it delves into a wide range of issues that concern their lives, such as multilayered economic exploitation, alcohol and drug problems, sexually transmitted diseases, violence committed by American servicemen, biracial children, and frequent suicides among the workers. The novella also offers a very positive representation of the local sex workers' association, established to provide mutual help to one another in the context of their utter exclusion from the normal patriarchal structure. Moving away from the earlier rescue-and-reform narrative, the text acknowledges military sex work as a job that, though not desirable, is not wholly illegitimate as a means of survival. The narrative's assertion of ethnonational masculinity takes a different form; as a young man just released from his military service duty, he not only enjoys being around many young women, but also the attention he receives from them. He becomes the most popular man around with all the sex workers. He does not feel competitive with Americans, who buy sex from the women, but rather he feels superior and sexually triumphant over them, since women offer themselves to him freely. The camp town is a place where prostitutes fight over a young and handsome Korean man like himself, "because he is Korean," according to a prostitute.[39] His sense of sexual reconquest of the Korean women in the camp town is also accompanied by his affinity and even identification with the women. When he first arrives in town, while he is taken aback by the unusual sight that a camp town is for a first-time visitor, he soon makes himself comfortable in the atmosphere by "making my own their deep intimacy with the life that their bodies exuded."[40] The novella's sympathy for camp town women derives from its positioning of the first-person male narrator as a quasi-insider, one who shares the daily life of poverty and stigma, while being simultaneously an outsider who observes the life in a camp town from a position of intellectual and social superiority. In the end, the novella proves to us, it is this identificatory positionality of the male narrator that functions more effectively to magnify and thus to recuperate the authority of masculinist nationalism.

"The End of the State Highway": De-allegorization and Moral Patriarchy

Ch'oe In-hun's very short story, "The End of the State Highway," published in 1966, can be considered a response to "Land of Excrement," which was published one year earlier.[41] If "Land of Excrement" can be said to have established the form of camp town literature as a masculinist nationalist allegory, Ch'oe's story from the mid-1960s precedes, in some ways, the feminist and other de-allegorizing narratives on camp town life from the late 1980s and 1990s that I will discuss in the second part of this chapter.

The story is set on the outskirts of a camp town, a transitional space between the camp town and its surrounding area. The narrative consists of an extremely matter-of-fact description of a state highway near an American military base, and in particular what happens on a rural bus traveling on the road. A young woman, who is easily recognized as a camp town prostitute, gets on the bus, traveling away from the camp town. Everyone on board, passengers and the driver, is male, except for the young woman. Soon a group of three drunken young men get on the bus and begin taunting and harassing her, making sexually explicit remarks in specific reference to her status as a military prostitute. The other passengers do not join the harassment, but they are complicit, passive participants, as they laugh at the lewd jokes made by the drunken young men. Unable to endure it any longer, she gets off the bus, only able to fire off one line of curse words, calling them all "sons of bitches."[42] In the middle of the road, she is seen to hesitate, and eventually to turn around and begin her walk back toward where she came from, in the direction of the camp town. The end of the story describes a little boy waiting for his older sister in another village, which, the reader gathers, must have been the young woman's destination.

The main objective of the story is to illustrate to us how a military prostitute is regarded by mainstream South Korean society, moving away from the ways in which a literary text, like "Land of Excrement" and others that followed it, allegorized the military prostitute and camp town as a space of resistance to U.S. hegemony. To most South Koreans, like the men on the bus, a *yangsaeksi* ("Western girl"), *yanggalbo* ("Western whore"), or *yanggongju* ("Western princess") is not a metaphor for the lost sovereignty of the nation, but simply a lower-class woman who has been degraded and polluted not only by her sex work but also by her association with foreign men. Ch'oe In-hun shows us how the majority of South Korean society regards them, that is, with contempt, scorn, and at best indifference. They exist as social pariahs, outside the purview of mainstream society and outside the boundary of the norms of patriarchy. This mainstream view presented in Ch'oe's story takes military prostitutes out of the allegorical abstraction and places them in the materiality of their racialized, sexualized occupation, shifting our attention from the allegorical transnational space to the material, domestic, national space. In place of allegorizing the military sex worker, the narrative chooses to allegorize the bus full of all male passengers as dogs. In this particular scene where she is about to get off the bus, after calling them "sons of bitches," the curse word, like magic, literally metamorphoses all of the men on the bus into dogs:

> "Sons of bitches—dogs! All of you!" she cries, barely able to leap off the bus as it starts to pull away. Loaded with dogs, the bus hesitates for a moment as if confused, then picks up speed. Driven by a dog, filled with dogs—some of the dogs with their paws up on the windows and barking— the bus barrels downs the state highway like a dog that's been kicked in the balls.[43]

In contrast to the men who became dogs, the young woman, who steps off the bus after her magic performance, takes on the most human aspect. The third-person narrator simply describes her external actions and expressions as she contemplates what to do next, all alone on the deserted state highway. The text does not ventriloquize her, but it makes palpable for the reader her sensibility and thoughtfulness: "She does not look anxious. Immersed in her own thoughts, she continues to gaze at the massive Salem box. She stands there, in the scorching sun, for about half an hour. Finally she walks in the direction she just came from—towards Salem. She walks for some time with tired steps, head down and wrapped in thought."[44] It is the text's refusal to speak for her that empowers her. As such a thinking subject, she is absolutely unallegorizable.

One of the things she was debating in her mind was which direction she will travel: should she go back to the camp town or go forward to visit her family? She contemplates this decision under a large billboard sign that advertises an American cigarette brand, Salem. The cigarettes coming out of the box are likened to artillery looming over her: "At the intersection, a massive replica of a Salem cigarette box towers over the landscape, large as a building. Out of the top of the green box, sitting somewhat askew on tall supports, a third of a cigarette the size of a chimney sticks out, aimed at the sky like a gun barrel. She gazes vacantly at that white gun barrel in the distance."[45] The young woman stands under the shadow of the United States militarism and capitalism, symbolized by a commodity, cigarettes.

The story also links South Korean development to American militarism by way of its central metaphor of "state highway" (*kukdo*). The narrative emphasizes the newly paved asphalt road that leads up to the American military base; it is repeatedly described as "rich," "oily," "burning under the hot sun." While the term *kukdo* means a "state highway," its Sino-Korean characters can also take on a metaphysical meaning, such as "the way of the nation." The path metaphor for the historical course that the Park regime set for itself, "choguk kŭndaehwa" (modernization of our fatherland), was already employed in the title of a Park Chung Hee book, one of several of his blueprints published for mass consumption, "Our Nation's Path."[46] Ch'oe In-hun's insistent reference to the "oily rich road" and the narrative's allusion to Park's idea of the nation's path illustrate the ways in which American domination of South Korea and the Park Chung Hee regime's own complicity with the empire are necessarily imbricated, how these two paths come together to become one. On this road, the young woman, a Western princess, stands alone and exposed under the burning sun of August.[47]

It is no accident that the American brand of cigarettes chosen by Ch'oe In-hun is "Salem." She is caught between two different kinds of Salem, the camp town and the larger community of South Korea. If she experiences racism and violence in the camp town, ruled by the American dollar and its neocolonial military authority, she suffers even worse discrimination and prejudice from her own people. She chooses her persecution in the American Salem over that in the South Korean Salem. The end of the short story shows us a little boy waiting for his big sister who has not yet arrived home. In recentering the boy waiting at the other end of the state highway, the short story situates the working-class male subject as the ultimate victim of American militarism and South Korean developmentalism. While the short story is quietly and yet vehemently critical of both the U.S. hegemony and the South Korean military dictatorship, I argue that the story reserves its harshest critique for South Korean patriarchy's moral degeneration. What I would call the critical masculinist nationalism of "The End of the State Highway" is, in a way, a much more sophisticated rescue narrative that calls for self-rectification, performing an even more effectively recuperative role in restoring the authority of masculinism and patriarchy than our previous example, "America."

Re-writing Military Prostitution in the 1990s: Camp Town Patriarchy, Gynocentric Sex Workers, and Biracial Dis-identifications

This section focuses on three major revisionist literary works on military prostitution and the camp town produced in the 1990s in South Korea and in the United States: *The Camp Town at Camp Seneca* by Pok Kŏ-il (1994), *Mudflats* by An Il-sun (1995),[48] and *Memories of My Ghost Brother* by Heinz Insu Fenkl (1996). The first two texts are the latest examples of the genre that radically reconceptualize the history of the camp town in the changed and changing context of South Korea in the 1990s. *Memories of My Ghost Brother* is a work written in English and published in the United States. While it is routinely classified—correctly—as a work of Asian American literature, here I would like to read it as a particular rewriting of a history of the South Korean working class and the U.S. empire in South Korea from the point of view of biracial children. All three texts deconstruct the dominant mode of representing camp town from the earlier decades, that is, the masculinist nationalist allegory. The de-allegorizing move is made from three varying perspectives: first, from that of camp town working-class patriarchy; second, from that of female military sex workers; and third, from that of biracial children.

The first two South Korean texts' deconstruction of camp town fiction occurred when South Korea could no longer be considered a neocolony of the United States. By the mid-1990s, South Koreans largely overcame the crippling and debilitating sense of colonization and victimization by American economic and military domination that they had suffered in earlier years. It is not at all a coincidence that what Pok Kŏ-il, the author of *The Camp Town at Camp Seneca*, calls a "non-allegorical"[49] story of camp town can be told at this particular historical juncture. The 1990s also saw the emergence of a feminist movement in all sectors of South Korean society, as the intense social movements of the '80s that centered on the masculinist conceptions of class and ethnonation began to dissolve with South Korea's gradual transition into liberal democracy. An Il-sun's two-volume novel on the lives of camp town women, *Mudflats*, came out of this broader feminist movement of the '90s. The third text, Fenkl's *Memories of My Ghost Brother*, can be situated in the U.S. multiculturalist context of the '90s, when Asian American literature and Asian American Studies became a more or less permanent, though marginalized, fixture in the cultural scene. Fenkl's autobiographical novel enables us to make critical connections, first, between U.S. militarism and the South Korean diaspora and second, between U.S. militarism in the greater Asian region and the transnational dimensions of camp towns.

Camp Town Patriarchy in The Camp Town at Camp Seneca

The novel *The Camp Town at Camp Seneca* is intended by the author to correct many misconceptions about camp towns held by members of South Korean mainstream society, and indeed thus to abolish the subgenre called "camp town literature."[50] The novel is written from the perspective of camp town insiders—a child, his family, and the villagers. This "insiders' perspective," offered to the reader as a critique of the existing camp town literature, recenters the town merchant community—importantly excluding the owners of bars and brothels—under a patriarchal leadership, wresting the attention away from what the novel implicitly suggests as disproportionately emphasized in the subgenre, namely, female military sex workers. In doing so, the novel intends to diminish the allegorical value placed on the prostitutes and to offer a comprehensive, "realistic" view of the life of a camp town. Although the novel frankly admits the serious dependence of the village economy on women's sex and sexualized work, and the villagers even express respect for their contribution, this particular de-allegorizing move radically marginalizes women sex workers, shifting its primary focus to the working-class patriarchy of the camp town, represented by the protagonist's father. The first-person narrator's father (whom I will just refer to as "Father" from here on) is portrayed as a model patriarch; though uneducated, he is wise, benevolent, and tolerant. Father first opens up the only drugstore in town and soon emerges as the leader of the village in its various dealings with the local government as well as with the U.S. military authorities, such as establishing an elementary school and an orphanage for biracial children. Father's role in the community is that of a moral leader, an educator, and a curer of ills. It is through such an idealized portrait of the patriarchal leadership of Father, "who always does the right thing,"[51] that Camp Town Seneca, in the course of the novel, is transformed into a near utopian community, where the usual problems of a military camp town community are resolved—a fantastically blessed place where villagers, prostitutes, and GIs live together in harmony. While candidly acknowledging the larger camp town community's vested interest in them, but simultaneously containing them within several, though central, episodes, the novel turns sex workers into passive recipients of the benevolent moral guidance and discipline of the camp town patriarchy. The novel challenges the (elite) masculinist nationalism of the previous allegories of camp town, which had in fact, ironically and yet logically, elided the men of camp town: it recenters, and thus remasculinizes, the working-class patriarchy of camp towns.

The novel's most significant departure from the earlier camp town literature lies in its revisionist representation of the relationships between the camp town patriarchy on the one hand and the South Korean state, its local governmental authorities and the local U.S. military authorities on the other. The target of criticism in the dominant perspective of camp town literature has been, of course, the American hegemony over South Korea and the presence of the U.S. military. What Pok Kŏ-il's novel does is to interrupt this equation between camp towns and South Korea; the novel's introduction of the specificities of the camp town working class dismantles the symbolic role that camp towns have played for the genre. To the residents of Camp Town Seneca, the United States does not exist as an abstract neocolonial power over South Korea. Rather, the United States that they experience takes the form of their day-to-day relationship with American GIs as their customers and neighbors, and with the local U.S. military as governing authorities and business and community partners. The subject of the South Korean state or its local manifestations remains outside the purview of traditional camp town literature. This particular revision of the subgenre reserves its most scathing criticism for the South Korean state and its local administrators. In a series of incidents, the novel illustrates the sense of betrayal and abandonment that camp town residents are made to feel by their own government.[52] Father states emphatically that the government, "looking at us as if the camp town gathered only some kind of freaks,"[53] had never supported them in any of their efforts to develop their community, such as bringing in electricity or building an elementary school, a police station, or an orphanage. Instead, Father contends, the government authorities only made their lives more difficult in numerous ways, such as by overcharging for health inspections of sex workers, confiscating black market commodities, or subjecting camp town residents to the arrogant, elite Korean military conscripts. Father's assessment points to the mainstream society's racializing alienation of camp town residents;

this community operates as an "internal" colony of South Korea and as an already diasporized, "external" colony of the United States.

Despite the fact that the narrator and Father both share this warm sense of loyalty to the local U.S. military authorities for their contribution to and cooperation with the town, it is much more accurate for us to view these community relations as those of governance, based on the virtual extra-territoriality that the U.S. military enjoys in South Korea; the U.S. military fills the power vacuum created by the South Korean state's prejudice and negligence. Under such circumstances, camp town residents were helpless to receive its assistance, but at the same time they were resigned to the abuses of power wielded by the local U.S. military, equally helpless to put up resistance. The injustices that they experience under the military-colonial authorities are painfully endured for the sake of having to continue to survive. Despite the implicit critique the novel levels at the leftist nationalists—critics of U.S. hegemony and authors of camp town fictions of the earlier era—the novel, in the end, aligns camp towns with the leftist nationalist conceptions of the ethnonation against the reactionary South Korean regimes. One of the stylistic strategies that the novel adopts for this realignment is to contain the intervention and interference of the U.S. military in the day-to-day lives of the camp town community by means of setting up four episodic chapters on the U.S. military, titled "The U.S. Military 1," "The U.S. Military 2," and so on. These chapters give us a general overview of the changing conditions of the U.S. military and their relations with South Korea as a whole and with camp town communities in particular. Outside these chapters, the lives of the camp town residents go on as if unrelated to, unaffected by, and autonomous from the U.S. military presence. Another narrative strategy of re-ethnonationalizing the camp town working class is to portray the origin of this particular camp town as a South Korean version of a pioneer village; the villagers were not "camp followers," but they were already waiting in the area before the U.S. military's arrival once they learned about the future installation of the base. The novel rewrites the American narrative of imperial conquest of Asians as "Indians" by comparing the first family to arrive in the area, the protagonist's family, to Robinson Crusoe. It is the villagers as pioneers who have built a civilization in the wilderness, not the U.S. military.

The fact that South Korea has moved from a periphery to a semi-periphery in global capitalism—Father says, "We are no longer a poor country"—makes it possible for Pok Kŏ-il to write an alternative history, in which the sovereignty of the camp town working-class patriarchy can be retrospectively and retroactively reimagined and recuperated. The economic relations between camp town residents and the GIs also change as a result; the end of the novel, set in the late 1980s, shows us the demise of this camp town, due to the fact that the relative poverty of American servicemen in relation to the increased wages of South Koreans makes the local U.S. military no longer the source of revenue and the foundation of the town economy. The U.S. military also has to modify its policy in order to accommodate these economic changes; now the GIs are allowed to be accompanied by their spouses, we are told in the novel, as they can no longer afford prostitution in the new economy.[54] The novel realigns the camp town working class with the ethnonation by conceiving of the camp town as a temporary place, a place that will disappear eventually and whose residents—in Father's words "handicapped" and requiring "protection" now—will be rehabilitated to become full-fledged members of the ethnonational community. The novel concludes, with satisfaction, that indeed the gradual economic rise of South Korea made it possible that camp towns, protectorates of the U.S. military, have been reconstituted as sovereign, modern, South Korean towns.

The novel's rewriting of camp town history succeeds in what it sets out to do, namely to contain U.S. neocolonial power, to assert the masculinity of the camp town working-class patriarchy, and to displace military sex workers to the margins of camp towns. The novel does treat a variety of problems that concern sex workers, such as murders of them by GIs, women's suicides, drug problems, biracial children, and their immigration to United States. But these issues, truly central to the power structure of camp town and beyond, are dealt with as if they were only one of many other day-to-day problems that the non-prostitution-related camp town residents experience. As the novel implicitly establishes the boundary between those members of the camp town population who are in businesses other than prostitution and the rest who are in prostitution—an untenable distinction since the entire economy of the camp town is in one way or another linked to the work of women—sex workers' problems are not the problem of the community of "non-prostitution" merchants and residents. Sex workers are only a burden to the hardworking and morally impeccable community. At one point, Father comes up with a "solution" to the problem of women as the source of the village's trouble: he will create a bar without women, a plan that, in the end, is quickly abandoned as an unrealistic venture. At another point in the story, the boy-narrator delights in the beauty and purity of the village covered under the white snow. As the village temporarily transforms into this land of magic and wonderment, the novel's desire is revealed: it would rewrite the tragic history of camp town as a fairy tale, told by a child, a fairy tale that excises, sanitizes, and covers up the real stories of camp town women: "*Camp Seneca was a fairy tale land—the pure snow that covered up everything*, the street lights that fell and froze on top of the snow, the buildings that became castles and trucks that became large animals for the snow that covered them. . . . Such a fantastic scene caressed my tired spirit"[55] (emphasis added).

Camp Town Matriarchy, Gynocentrism, and Lesbianism in Mudflats

If even the most sympathetic male writing on military prostitution does not go beyond understanding military sex workers as victims of the class system, U.S. neocolonialism, and even Korean patriarchy, An Il-sun's two-volume novel *Mudflats* offers us much more complex representations of camp town women's day-to-day negotiations and resistance to the multiply exploitative forces. Based upon An's two-year fieldwork in camp towns like Ŭijŏngbu, the novel might be classified as a fictionalized reportage, or we might call it an activist work of fiction. In contrast to the relatively large number of camp town fictions produced in the 1970s and '80s by male writers, women writers in general, from both the earlier and the more recent decades, have not really paid attention to this topic.[56] *Mudflats* is one of the few feminist literary works on military prostitution. Its author, An Il-sun, states in the preface that her immediate motivation for writing the novel was the 1992 murder of a camp town sex worker, Yun Kŭm-i, by an American serviceman, Kenneth Markle. The continuing anti-American sentiment from the 1980s student activism and its further heightening due to the imminent opening of the South Korean market to rice imports from the United States and President Bill Clinton's visit to Seoul made the Yun Kŭm-i case an incident that brought mainstream attention to camp town women in an unprecedented way. In the context surrounding the trial of Markle, Yun Kŭm-i, irrelevant and ignored as a military sex worker when alive, arose as an "ethnonation's symbol" when dead, not only for the activists involved but also for the South Korean public as a whole. Chŏng Hŭi-jin succinctly summarizes the meaning of the symbolic role that Yun, as a murdered military sex worker, took on as diverging in three ways: the Christian activists saw her murder as an issue of human rights and national sovereignty; leftist citizens' groups as that of anti-neocolonial nationalist protest against U.S. hegemony; and feminist activists as that of women's human rights and sexual violence.[57] An Il-sun's sharp condemnation of the sexual violence committed by the South Korean military in Vietnam and the ongoing consumption of overseas sex work by contemporary South Korean men, in her preface to the novel, points to the glaring hypocrisy—the absence of critique of the ethnonationalist (i.e., Korean) patriarchy and masculinism—that articulates itself as the first two responses to the Yun Kŭm-i case.[58] Furthermore, the novel's earnest efforts at representing the perspectives of camp town women, which have been hitherto left unheard and unknown, do, to some extent, chip away at the barrier between the elite feminist activist and scholarly representations and the lived experiences of military sex workers.

The novel begins with the trial of an American serviceman charged with two counts of murder. He is accused of having killed two sex workers, Ok-ju and Mi-ok. The story is told mainly from the perspective of Sŭng-ja, who was very close to both of the murdered women. While the two murders and the trial of the GI occupy the center of the novel throughout, and we are returned to the verdict at the end of the novel, the novel also offers us a historical and comprehensive view of the lives of camp town women, including the circumstances of, and motivations for, their entry into camp town life, the discipline and control the authorities exerted on their lives, the concrete realities of their occupation, and most importantly, a glimpse into the community of women among themselves.

Militarized Commercialization of Sex: Disciplinary Measures

The official power in the camp town is at its most systematic when it comes to the control of STDs; the control takes place through a militarized-medicalized discipline of the women's body. Although South Korean health authorities are part of the joint effort, *Mudflats* shows us that it is really the health department of the local U.S. military base that is in charge of constantly monitoring STDs. The systematicity and severity of the policing, in fact, places camp town women in the state of being always already criminalized, as each bar or club is required to display in a public space the pictures of all the women who have been determined to carry STDs at any given time. These women are designated as *kamyŏmwon*, or the "origin of contamination." Once a sex worker is "caught" carrying an STD, she will be incarcerated at an infirmary specially designed to quarantine and medicate her until she can be released again into the world of commercial sex. The obvious inequality in designating only sex workers, and not U.S. servicemen, as the cause of STDs is an ongoing source of anger for women toward the U.S. military. The system of quarantining workers leaves them with no income for the duration of their incarcerated treatment. Camp town women have aptly renamed this medical institution the "Monkey House" in English (Mŏngk'i hausŭ) for the purposes it serves— surveillance, discipline, and punishment of women. This nickname, however, reveals not only the psychological and moral degradation to which such disciplinary mechanisms subject women, but it also registers their resistive knowledge.[59]

Another apparatus through which the official power exercises itself is the "cultural education" of sex workers and military brides, organized jointly by the local South Korean government and the local U.S. military. This program is titled "culture lectures" (kyoyang kangjwa). While the term kyoyang (translated as "culture") in Korean refers to culture in the sense of refinement or education—with no connotation associated with ethnicity or race—the content of "culture lectures" in this context is to acculturate them into American and Western customs. These lectures regiment their minds and behaviors to transform them into Westernized commodities—made more palatable but without losing their exotic appeal—that will better suit the taste of their consumers.[60]

From the point of view of the South Korean capitalist state, the ultimate goal of enhancing the sexual service that camp town women provide the American military is economic. In Mudflats, a county chief gives a speech to camp town residents and sex workers in which he calls camp town sex workers "warriors of industrialization" (sanŏp yŏkkun), the ubiquitous catchphrase of the day, used to describe any and all workers. Toward these goals, he fawningly declares that camp town women have become "patriots without whom this country will be lost."[61] The most successful prostitutes in camp towns are indeed those who have mastered English, American cooking, and the overall American lifestyle. One of the murdered victims in Mudflats, Mi-ok, was such a case for these very reasons. When the American husbands whom they marry take it upon themselves to "educate" their brides in American ways, the cultural regimentation can sometimes take the form of mental and physical abuse. If and when such assimilationist endeavors on the part of their American husbands fail, divorce and abandonment in these women's lives may be often imminent.[62]

Reclaiming Economic and Sexual Agency

Mudflats portrays the complex and ambivalent ways in which prostitution in the camp town destabilizes sex workers' lives while at the same time provides new anchors and enables them to exercise a certain amount of economic and sexual agency. The destruction of the foundations for their previous familial and ethnonational identities before their militarized sexual proletarianization leads them to build new identities premised on a different set of factors, such as gynocentric communities, transnational and interracial relations, affirmative attitudes about sex and sexualized labor, and economic motivations. The capitalist South Korean state certainly viewed military sex work in economic terms, that is, as something between a labor "export" and sex tourism, and for the majority of camp town women themselves, the foremost reason why they ended up in camp towns as the very last resort was also economic. Some of them in fact were drawn to the reputation that camp towns have—the idea that they are places where "money goes around powerfully."[63] As the camp town is imagined as a special place where they can make the kind of money that they could only dream of on the "outside," the financial goals that they set for themselves become a significant part of their camp town identities. Their racially and sexually stigmatized identities are contested and refigured by their own determination about themselves—the ways in which they see the camp town as a temporary place and occupation that enables them to achieve another identity, one that is more socially acceptable.

When Sŭng-ja and Ok-ju first arrive in Tongduch'ŏn, one of the larger and more famous camp towns in South Korea, the woman owner of the business that they will work for, usually known as the "Big Mother," offers her assessment of camp town life. Trying to dispel outsiders' myths and prejudices, she emphasizes, "The camp town is not some alien land . . . and the Yankees are people, too. . . . By God, the camp town, like anywhere else, is where human beings live." And she goes on to tell the newcomers about the most important aspect of camp town life, money: "No matter what people say, it's undeniably a business . . . and you can leave this place as soon as you save up money." Although the extent to which this idea of "making a lot of money"[64] becomes a reality for camp town women is relative and unrealistic for most, what I would like to draw our attention to is the fact that their reconceptualization of their camp town identity as based on the financial remuneration of work and the translatability of money into futural social status is, though in limited ways, still empowering.

Another important facet of the camp town economy is the centrality of black marketeering in American goods out of the bases. The job of buying the commodities at the base, legally or illegally, was mainly that of female sex workers, who had close relations with GIs, whether as their short-term contract cohabitants, lovers, friends, or wives. For some women who became successful black marketers, sex work was only a secondary source of income, or even just a pretext or a situation that allowed them to have access to the more lucrative business of black marketing. Mi-ok, one of the murder victims in the novel, was one such case, an extremely competent businesswoman at the black marketing game who amassed a fortune; by the time she was killed, she was living comfortably in a Western-style two-story house with all the amenities. She manipulated a series of legal marriages to American servicemen—often men were also willing and active participants—for the purpose of black marketing.

Camp town women, in their economic role as black marketers, also participated in the informal, illegal (national) economy. In the devastation after the Korean War, and all the way through the decades of industrialization from the 1960s through the '70s, in the midst of shortages of necessities and demand for luxury items, the material value of "American-made" commodities, originating from the military bases and circulated throughout the country, was enormous. These goods, symbolic of America's wealth and power, were made available by camp town women's trafficking of their bodies, but their sexual labor was made to vanish, leaving only the magical fetishes of the "American Dream" for the South Korean bourgeoisie, the chief consumers of these goods. In O Chŏng-hŭi's famous work, "The Chinese Street," two young girls, playing with things "made-in-America" in a room rented out to a military sex worker, marvel at them, captivated by the goods that exude the aura and mystique of America. The novel *Mudflats* gives us a detailed inside look into the process, tracing these commodities back to their origin: the body of the sex worker. The close proximity between the female body and commodities and their material profitability suspends the abstract metaphorization of a woman's body as a site of (masculinist) national victimhood. The novel teaches us that camp town women's sex work and economic work as black marketers mediated between U.S. commodity imperialism, this "fantasy production" of America in the Third World, and the South Korean public.[65]

With unprecedented candor, *Mudflats* also delves into the bodily and affective dimensions of the process of commercializing feminine sexuality in the contexts of neocoloniality, militarization, and industrialization. The novel's portrayal of Sŭng-ja's first day at work at the club, the radically contradictory and ambivalent process of her mental and emotional adjustment to military sex work, is a shocking interruption of the mainstream society's preconceptions about military prostitution as well as sex work in general. At first, Sŭng-ja feels fearful and awkward about her job of sitting at the bar, drinking and having to speak English to customers, GIs, but the initial inhibition and humiliation Sŭng-ja feels on the job at the club is blunted with the aid of, first, alcohol, and later, drugs. The "good times" had by camp town women—Rose, one of the biracial children, says Mother always seemed "happy" in the club—come as a result of adjusting to the pressures and demands of the job, their emotional labor to anesthetize themselves. Learning the ropes and tricks of the job, Sŭng-ja finds out, really means the paradoxical and contradictory state of exerting all her efforts to let go of herself, that is, learning to lose her inhibitions and self-control. The narrator notes, "Sŭng-ja realized that she didn't need her mind or spirit but only her body. She felt that her behavior was becoming rougher without her intending it to become so. She was becoming someone other than herself." One of the requirements of the job is to empty oneself out, to erase the sense of self that one had before entering the camp town, producing oneself as a body that is a sexual commodity. Soon this means an erosion of any sort of stable identity for herself: "Her uprooted life was like a floating weed . . . she would be drifting by and meeting a GI was like catching a stone to rest. . . . Even a foreign soldier was something to hold on to. Otherwise, she felt that she would flow to a distant nowhere, swept up by the waves." The drugs given to the women by "Big Mother," the owner of the club/brothel, further carry out the process of routinizing the psychological violence the job requires them to suffer. The drug-induced "ecstasy of selflessness," "fearlessness," and anesthesia to sadness, replaces their identity. Alcohol, which Sŭng-ja feels gives her "power," becomes for her a "life-giving liquid."[66]

As scandalous as this may seem to the mainstream readers, the novel also describes how Sŭng-ja on her first day finds in the club scene a kind of "frankness," free of the "phony gestures or empty forms of other places." She finds this "exotic atmosphere to be somehow not unfamiliar" and she "felt herself to be at ease." In addition to the sense of liberation and refuge she feels in a camp town, away from the mainstream, Sŭng-ja's affirmative sentiments allow for a certain recognition of the camp town's own order, one that flouts the norms of the "outside" society. While the novel does portray the terror and shame Sŭng-ja and Ok-ju face when it is brought home to them for the first time what it means to be a sex worker—that they must have intercourse with their customers—it also points to the ways in which prostitution must be distinguished from other situations of sexual violence and exploitation. As Sŭng-ja watches the men (American GIs) and women (Korean bar girls/sex workers) dancing on the floor of the club, she senses a kind of pleasure that comes from social interaction, physical enjoyment, and sexual excitement. She feels the atmosphere of the club "grow warmer," and the club eventually turns into a "big vat of passion."[67] Sŭng-ja, a new arrival, becomes a witness to a kind of "enjoyment" that women seem to be drawing from such a context. Such experience of psychological and sexual "pleasure" on the part of sex workers, as profoundly ambivalent and complex as it is, can act as an effective way of restoring a certain amount of agency to their subjectivity, undermining the racial and gendered socioeconomic hierarchy of such commercial-sexual transactions.[68] The GIs themselves, in a way, become irrelevant, or they become relevant only as objects, as the women themselves are able to affirm their "pleasure." The 1950s and '60s representations of "excessive" sexuality associated with military prostitutes were meant to condemn the corrupting Americanizing influences on feminine sexuality, but Mudflats is able to offer a subversive reading of such a linkage.[69]

One of the ways in which women can further increase their economic and sexual agency in a camp town is by marrying an American, someone who will remove them from the camp town and from Korea. Husband-seeking in camp towns is a preoccupation for young women, an active and resourceful strategy of resistance to the prevailing instability of their lives. Mudflats describes both short-term contract cohabitations and formal marriages, which often form a continuum in terms of their premise as relationships of convenience and economic profitability. In both cases, women have relatively long and committed relationships with soldiers, providing companionship and domestic labor beyond sexual service. While contractual cohabitation, as compared to prostitution, offers women more financial security and some stability of monogamous relations, the still-commercial nature of this type of relationship does not remove them from the conditions of exploitation based on inequality of race, gender, and class. The close proximity between contractual cohabitation and marriage is further revealed by the relative volatility of these marriages—to which camp town women stake so much of their future—indicated by frequent cases of abandonment and a high rate of divorce.

Both contractual cohabitation and marriage in camp towns are really the latest versions of colonial concubinage, in which native women performed most of the domestic and social roles expected of a wife for European men in the colonies.[70] In their role as temporary *hyŏnjich'ŏ*, or "local concubine" to American servicemen, South Korean working-class women's advance into the space of transnational militarism and neocolonial capital takes places through their "domestic to domestic" transition,[71] providing domestic service for the American military and its soldiers—cooking, cleaning, laundering, and further serving as interpreters and cultural intermediaries.[72] The idea of domesticity is crucial to all forms of sexual service and relationships, whether it be a one-night commercial transaction, short-term cohabitation, or marriage. As Enloe argues, there is a certain modularity of domesticity in the ways in which both white and Korean middle-class women are set up as implicit models for camp town sex workers' performance as their temporary substitutes in the racial and class hierarchy of domesticity.[73] In a situation very similar to that of Dutch Indonesia, where colonial concubinage was allowed for the profit and benefit of the colonizing power, South Korean camp town women as cohabitants and wives are cheaper surrogates for American wives; the cost of allowing men to bring their American wives and families would have been a financial burden on the U.S. military budget. As the South Korean economy grew and wages increased, the U.S. military had to make concessions regarding their policies on the military personnel's dependents in South Korea.[74]

The profoundly contradictory kind of sexual and social agency that they are able to wrest, in an extremely constrained manner and to an extremely limited degree, from the context of military prostitution in a camp town may be described with a Korean notion, *ogi*, a combination of pride, stubbornness, and even spitefulness. One of the older women declares to young recruits with bravado, "I may not look like much, but the Japanese troops, the American military, there is no soldier that this bitch had not dealt with on her belly."[75] It is a kind of reversal where the difficulties that had been dealt her are turned around to become a source of strength and pride. Their recognition of the ostracism and degradation they suffered is transformed into the very source of affirmation and resistance.

Matriarchy, Gynocentrism, and Lesbianism in the Camp Town

In contrast to masculinist allegories of military prostitution, one of the aspects *Mudflats* brings out is not only camp town economic dependence on women's earnings from prostitution, but also the extent to which women are able to constitute themselves as agents of exchange and negotiation for their own profit.[76] The most powerful women in the camp town are those who own clubs, bars, and/or houses of prostitution, usually called Big Mother by other women who work for them. They participate, as major actors, in the highly exploitative economic structure of the camp town. While acknowledging this role, the novel generally portrays these women, with some exceptions, as more generous and less exploitative than their male counterparts, and especially emphasizes their social role as exercising a kind of matriarchal leadership and gynocentric protection over the women they employ. The fact that women are the breadwinners of the community has an unusual effect on the gender relations between Korean male residents and female military prostitutes. To the extent that financial responsibility and economic power are associated with masculinity, the camp town economy tends to masculinize the women while feminizing the Korean men who live off women's labor or rely on prostitution indirectly. The novella I discussed in the previous section, "America," describes a somewhat odd situation that takes place in the bars exclusively reserved for locals, that is, Koreans, where men do not pay, while only women, mostly sex workers, do, because they are always having a "gentleman's night." As the young male narrator, a newcomer to the camp town, soon figures out, in such bars it is men who become "comfort men" (*wianbu* 夫) to military sex workers, who perform the role of "comfort women" (*wianbu* 婦) to American servicemen. The novella illustrates the ways in which the intra-ethnic gender hierarchy is subverted by the particular economic relations of camp towns.

The racialized military sex workers' exclusion from the Korean patriarchal structure seems to transform the camp town into a feminine-identified space. One of the most distinguishing characterizations in women's writing on military prostitution is a portrayal of what we may call a "lesbian continuum," the continuity between intense female homosociality and female homosexuality in camp towns. This is not unique to the South Korean context, but rather a cross-cultural dimension of communities of women sex workers. Lesbian desires and relationships arise due to loss of erotic and romantic desire in the context of the commercialized nature of their relations with men. I would also argue that in the more or less exclusively female society of camp towns, women seem to take on dual gender and sexual roles; some are more masculine, while others are more feminine, but the same women can also play either more masculine or feminine roles, depending upon the circumstances. In both *Mudflats* and "Days and Dreams" (1983), a short story by Kang Sŏk-kyŏng, lesbianism emerges as a major issue. While "Days and Dreams" ultimately displaces lesbianism as another kind of relationship of convenience, essentially similar to its heterosexual counterpart,[77] *Mudflats* centers around both the intense emotional relationship between the protagonist Sŭng-ja and Ok-ju, one of the victims of the American GI's murder, and the sexual attraction and desires between Sŭng-ja and Mi-ok, the other murdered victim. In fact, the three characters form a kind of love triangle. The novel both reveals and conceals lesbianism in that Sŭng-ja's and Ok-ju's relationship, despite many textual evidences to the contrary, is represented, on the one hand, within the bounds of an acceptable and common, intense friendship between young women, while Sŭng-ja's and Mi-ok's relationship is explicitly portrayed as lesbian sexuality. From the first day, Sŭng-ja's and Ok-ju's closeness draws people's attention; they are said to be "like sisters," and people ask, "Are you dating each other?" Sŭng-ja's reaction to the news of Ok-ju's marriage to a young GI is portrayed as a lover's sickness, a sense of "betrayal," her illness that brings her "high fever" and hallucinations about Ok-ju.[78] It is Mi-ok, the most successful prostitute-cum-concubine-cum-black-marketer, who first expresses interest in Sŭng-ja and continues to make sexual advances toward her. Mi-ok, known as a "fearsome fox" who seduces and squeezes GIs for all they are worth, seems to reserve her most intense erotic feelings for Sŭng-ja. Sŭng-ja continues to resist Mi-ok's advances, but she theorizes Mi-ok's lesbianism and expresses her sympathy for it: "There was no sexual satisfaction when money was involved. . . . Because Sŭng-ja knew this, she had an inkling as to what Mi-ok was longing for. But no matter how lonely she was, she thought she must protect it."[79] As the rumor that Mi-ok and Sŭng-ja were *lesŭbiŏn* ("lesbians") begins to spread in town, the club owners quickly intervene to shut down the relationship that they perceived as threatening to their business. The novel's much more open exploration of Mi-ok's courting of Sŭng-ja illustrates her desire for economic partnership with Sŭng-ja as a significant constituent aspect of her lesbian desire. Mi-ok's future-oriented conception of herself perceives Sŭng-ja as not only a person she can depend upon emotionally, but also one with whom she can do business: "I don't give my heart just to anyone. You, Sŭng-ja, are different from others. I have an eye for these things. Once we save up some money, we are going to get out of here. . . . What really matters is money. When you have money, people suck up to you. If you have money, it doesn't matter if you have a past. Let's go to Seoul, and open a big fancy restaurant or a café." When Mi-ok realizes that Sŭng-ja's heart is only with Ok-ju, she declares that she would finally have to give up Sŭng-ja.[80] If *Mudflats*, on one level, tries to explain away Mi-ok's homosexuality, from the perspective of Sŭng-ja, by attributing the "cause" of her lesbianism to the sterility of the commercialized sexual relationship that women have with men, then it does not and cannot quite contain Sŭng-ja's intense emotional attachment to Ok-ju—provoking a great deal of jealousy from Mi-ok—within a South Korean normativizing understanding of lesbianism as a fleeting stage of pubescent sexuality. The contrast we see between Sŭng-ja's relationship with Ok-ju and her relationship with Mi-ok, we can argue, belongs in the categories of, respectively, what is acceptable and what is not.

In other words, an intense emotional relationship, without expressions of sexual desire, between women can be articulated, while sexual desire between women, as explicitly expressed by Mi-ok for Sŭng-ja, cannot be tolerated: Sŭng-ja must reject Mi-ok. Furthermore, we cannot attribute the particular emplotment of the novel, the fact that both Ok-ju and Mi-ok end up as the victims of the double murder committed by an American soldier, to sheer coincidence. Though surreptitiously, *Mudflats* offers an entirely different interpretation of the so-called "GI crimes," which had been one of the sources that fueled the production of masculinist nationalist allegories of the camp town. Given the centrality of lesbian relations in the novel, though embedded and disguised, what emerges as an implicit textual motivation for the character of the American GI who commits the murders against Korean female sex workers is not only his racism and sexism against Korean prostitutes but also his desire to interrupt lesbianism. The American perpetrator kills two women who were lesbians, or to be more precise, two women who were femmes. They were the two most beautiful women in the camp town and the objects of female masculine desire for Sŭng-ja, who is portrayed as male-identified.[81] Almost as if making a conscious decision, Sŭng-ja in her teenage years declared to herself, "Let's become a man! I am going to live like a man!"[82] Female same-sex desire operates as a kind of interruption of commodified heterosexuality, that is, as a critique of capitalist patriarchy and its commercialization of feminine sexuality. On the other hand, because of the contingent nature of lesbianism in such a context, there is a way in which the novel delimits and thus delegitimizes it. *Mudflats* rewrites the camp town history—what had been written, for the most part, as the narrative of emasculation and remasculinization—as a history of patriarchy's disavowal and destruction of female desires and female homosexuality.

Racialization, Racial Mobility, and Trans-racial Class Alliances in Camp Towns

Camp town women's association with American servicemen has conflicting and contradictory effects. On the one hand, it racializes them as foreign, excluding them from the proper boundary of the ethnonational community, while the very same association can be experienced by military sex workers themselves as a racial-social mobility. Whether they are racialized as white or black, which depends on with whom they mainly associate themselves, camp town women's sense of this painful exclusion often leads to their denationalization of themselves, their own active rejection of Korea. The military prostitute narrator of "Days and Dreams" says this about her coworker: "Her rude, ignorant life was the reason Sun-ja had this wild dream about going to America. She lost her love for her motherland, and the dream became an obsession."[83] The sense of their emotional detachment from Korea is often accompanied by camp town women's critique of, and resistance to, South Korean patriarchy in their comparison of it to American patriarchy, considered to be more liberal and egalitarian: "Why should we sacrifice our money and hearts to these Korean pricks? What good are they? GIs are cold as ice when they turn their backs on you but they'll propose if they like you.... Can you think of a Korean man who would propose to one of us?"[84] Nonetheless, rather than completely abandoning their Korean identity, whether in Korea or in the United States as immigrants, they deploy their relationship to Koreanness strategically against the racialization that they must face from Americans. In the novella "America," one of the ten pledges that members of the association of camp town women workers make is "Ssŭmbagwi is Korean."[85] Ssŭmbagwi is the name of their association, after the name of a local weed.

Military sex work starts out as a survival strategy and can later become a strategy of social and economic advancement. The other side of military sex workers' racialization resulting from their association with white

American servicemen is the effect of racial-social rise beyond the economic advantages. The consequence of their association with African American servicemen is more complex. While their association with African American men racializes them as black, if their relationship has the potential to lead to marriage and thus emigration to the United States, then their racialization is offset by the positive result of being able to escape their predicament in Korea. What became one of the most popular epithets for camp town women, *yanggongju*, "Western princess," points to this ambivalent, simultaneous racial-social upward and downward mobility. Their active efforts at Americanization afford them an opportunity to overcome the stigma and to transform themselves into respectable wives of American soldiers. In the case of military sex workers who come to orient themselves toward the United States, the transgressive and resistive dimensions of such an attitude are simultaneously mitigated by their incorporation into the long-standing racism and cultural imperialism once they moved to the United States.[86] As some of them, if not all, will experience the effects of the racial hierarchy and West-centrism that they appropriated to combat Korean patriarchy, their immigration to the United States can result in renationalization or a reattachment to a diasporic Korean ethnicity. The anticipated trajectory of their passage from the cruelty of rejection by their motherland to the United States as the land of, above all, their social rebirth and economic stability is rudely interrupted for many of the military brides as soon as they arrive.

Although relationships between camp town women workers and American servicemen never take place on an equal footing, we do witness, at moments in the revisionist camp town literature, the possibility of a camaraderie between them actualized—one that overcomes, partially and temporarily, the hierarchies of race, nation, and gender. This transracial, transcultural, and across-gender empathy occurs, sometimes, when Korean women recognize their class affinity with American men. When they realize that the enlisted men they married belong in the bottom stratum of American society, their disappointing knowledge can transform into something of a class alliance with their men. For those women who live with or marry African American men, the fact of their men's racialization becomes a basis of kinship, as the women themselves experience their own racialization imposed on them by Koreans and white Americans in camp towns. And lastly, but importantly, as discussed in chapter 1 on South Korean military labor in Vietnam, what can sometimes further bind these two groups of women and men is the recognition of their respective military and sexual proletarianization as soldiers and prostitutes, what brought them to the camp town in the first place.

The white American serviceman who murdered two women in *Mudflats*, Steven, had heard about the good times to be had with the cheapest women that could be bought in South Korea when he was stationed in Germany. As Cynthia Enloe points out, military labor is marketed in the United States to young men, just past their pubescent years, as an adventurous rite of passage to adult masculinity: see the world and become a man.[87] The novel, vaguely, attributes his motive for his murders of two military prostitutes to his disappointment in the reality of a camp town, which was not the exotic Orient of his fantasy. In this way, *Mudflats* does point to racist imperialist militarism as a cause of these murders committed by Steven, but Mi-ok and Ok-ju's deaths stubbornly remain as nonnational deaths in the novel. Their deaths are women's deaths, mourned by the women of the community and by one woman in particular, by Sŭng-ja, who loved both. Heinz Fenkl's *Memories of My Ghost Brother*, which I will discuss in the next section, similarly refuses to turn Gannan's suicide into a national death. In both of these texts, their deaths are positioned in the interstices between U.S. racist imperialist militarism and South Korean nationalism. If *Mudflats* deconstructs the masculine nationalism of camp town fiction of the earlier era, the novel, however, does not grasp military prostitution as a transnational phenomenon that links the territories and laboring bodies of South Korean camp towns to those of other nation-states in Asia under United States hegemony in the post-1945 era. The next section examines a Korean American text, *Memories of My Ghost Brother*, which explores South Korean camp towns as a transnational space, triangulating the militarized relations of power among the Korean peninsula, Asia, and the United States.

Racial Hybridity, Matrophobia, and Masculinities in Memories of My Ghost Brother

Heinz Insu Fenkl's *Memories of My Ghost Brother* is an autobiographical narrative of a biracial boyhood set in a South Korean camp town in the mid-1960s and early 1970s.[88] *Memories* is distinct from other camp town narratives discussed above in at least two important ways. First, it offers us the rare perspective of a biracial child, in this case a boy, when the majority of existing camp town fictions either simply disregard the presence or experience of this particular camp town population, or represent them as an emblem of the violation of South Korea's sovereignty and its racial purity. *Mudflats* is the only work that does pay a certain amount of attention to these children, though it primarily focuses on their mothers' point of view. *Memories* depicts the camp town as a transnational space through the experience of this community whose identity is necessarily divided, even more so than other camp town residents, between two cultures, two races, and two nationalities. Second, in contrast to South Korean fictions examined in this chapter, *Memories* is a work of Korean America that traces its history to a South Korean camp town. Its particular transnational perspective rises from the comparative and related contexts of the Asian diaspora, resulting from the U.S. military engagements in various parts of Asia, such as South Korea, Vietnam, Philippines, Thailand, and other locations and the Asian American biracial population that emerged from such militarized circumstances.

Biracial Children's Double Dis/Identifications: Korea and America

The transnationality of biracial children in camp towns is similar to the kind of racial hybridity Rey Chow speaks of, one of interstitial abjection.[89] In comparison to transnationalities of higher classes, characterized by flexibility, mobility, and multiple inclusion, camp town biracial children's transnationality is one of interstitial inflexibility and immobility, produced as a result of the combination of their nominally dual racial identity and their actual dual social and cultural exclusion. As white European fathers and colonial communities regarded the biracial children as the very embodiment of the threat that the darker-skinned colonized population posed for European civilization,[90] mainstream South Korean society, as neo-colonized counterpart, also looked on these biracial children as perilous to its racial purity and social integrity. More than other camp town residents, it is this very structure of division between two cultures that constitutes the subjectivity of the camp town biracial community. Their subjectivity is negatively constituted, through their very distance from both societies and cultures, while at the same time this very distance itself is what provides them with an intimate knowledge of two cultures, knowledge acquired from the margins of both.

Mudflats shows camp towns to be a matriarchal and matrilineal community where biracial children, often abandoned by their fathers, are placed into their mothers' family register, taking their mothers' last names. As their mothers are single working mothers, biracial children are also put in the communal care of other women coworkers. The case of Heinz Insu

Fenkl, the protagonist of *Memories,* is quite exceptional, as his parents were married and his father participated in his upbringing. Nonetheless, even Insu, whose father was away for extended periods—whether stationed in the DMZ or in Vietnam—grew up like many other biracial children, raised by a community of women. This means that their primary cultural identification is with the Korean language and culture of their everyday life. However, their native cultural identity as Korean does not entitle them to full membership in the national community. Painfully cognizant of this reality, unmarried mothers usually hope to have their biracial children adopted by American families as early as they can. In the case of Insu, his time in Korea was temporary until he would "return" to the United States. Unlike Insu, who is sent to an American school on the base, most of the fatherless biracial children of camp towns grow up in this space of contradiction, where their only cultural identification is with Korea, and yet they are politically and socially prevented from identifying with Korea as a national subject. Under such circumstances, they are encouraged by their mothers, in their hopes for a better life in United States, to identify with America, without any kind of cultural basis or knowledge, or indeed without any promise of realizing a possible adoption to the United States.

Mudflats follows the story of one particular female biracial child, Paek Rozŭ, or Rose Paek. Most biracial children, even when their fathers are not around, are often given English first names, as if to indicate their future destination, while they are compelled to take their mothers' last names. Rose is half–African American and half-Korean. Due to the other children's constant harassment of her at school, and the discrimination she experienced even in camp towns, any kind of identification with Korea was absolutely impossible for her. The rejection and alienation Rose experiences in relation to the Korean community orients her toward America. As a child, her longing for and fabulated identification with America was sustained by her mother's GI boyfriends, some of whom would take her to the base and treat her to all it could offer to stoke her imagination about America. However, GIs gradually and eventually lost interest in her as she got older. As she becomes so much more keenly aware of the utter impossibility of finding a place in Korean society, she, along with her mother, put all her hopes in the future of a possible adoption to America. Once again, they are disappointed; the older she got, the more difficult it became to find American families willing to adopt her. In her teenage years, she already found herself working as a prostitute away from her mother in another camp town where her marriage to an African American soldier, eventually and incredulously luckily, provides the only means of materializing her imagined connection with America.

Insu's experience with his German American father is more complex, since his disidentification with his father's race and nationality, in fact, coexists with the deep emotional connection Insu does make as a son to his father. Insu's father often takes him to the base to spend time together, showing him around, teaching him English, and telling him stories. Insu wishes to become a "dark-haired" GI when he grows up, as he bonds with his father. Unlike other fatherless biracial children in camp towns, whose connection to their fathers' country and its culture is merely imagined for the most part, Insu does live in two worlds—his mother's world and the camp town Korean community, and his father's world, the world inside and around the base where the GIs travel. Nonetheless, despite the father-son connection that develops, Insu cannot break away from his perception of his father's rejection of him; he hears about his father's shame at having a half-Korean child, and his embarrassment at having his Korean wife show up in front of his men. Insu sees himself from his father's perspective: "I would forever be tainted by a Koreanness that would make the words, 'gook' or 'dink' sound strange coming from my lips." While he feels excluded from, and envious of, the camaraderie between his father and his men, he also perceives this very camaraderie to be based on their racism against Asians. Apart from his filial emotions, Insu ultimately finds it impossible to identify either with his own father's ideological position, as a willing and proud imperial soldier of the United States, or with the United States itself as an empire that wages wars against Asians. Insu's father, Sergeant Fenkl, who was a German immigrant, carries a Nazi symbol with him during his tour in Vietnam: "Totems of the clan that kills people whose skin is the color of mine. Indelible." Although Insu, like other camp town biracial children and their mothers, longs to escape from life in the camp town to America, he cannot help but write the memoirs of a biracial childhood from a position that rejects an America that had already rejected him: "the dream country . . . that had vanished for me, . . . vast and mythic America we had believed in as children the day I set foot in the Westward Land."[91]

Ghostly Identities of Camp Town Biracial Children and Matrophobia

This double dis/identification with Korea and America leaves biracial children in a state of cultural limbo. Not being able to claim full membership in either culture, their identity and presence can only be described as ghostly in camp towns, which are internal and external colonies of both South Korea and United States. The prevailing trope of "ghost," signaled in the title *Memories of My Ghost Brother*, conveys the traces of their struggle to remain visible and alive, evidence of their having survived the colonizing forces, both Korean and American, that attempt to erase the cultural, social, and racial legitimacy of their being. Insu's book is written as a kind of literary rite of calling the ghosts of camp town biracial children, his "brothers," into our midst. Insu and Jamesŭ, one of Insu's best friends, a half–African American, half-Korean boy, make a pact to become "secret brothers," "a secret that is invisible to everyone else."[92] The two boys vow that if they betray each other, they will disappear like the names that they wrote on a windowpane with their fingers on a cold day. In this particular memoir, the ghostly fraternity of these boys is defined in relation to the text's matrophobic conceptualization of the power of camp town mothers, as we will see below.

I will focus on two moments in the book when the concept of their ghostly identity is brought out most expressly. Insu and his friends plan a heist, targeting a GI, as the children often either beg or steal from GIs in camp towns. On this particular day, they needed a relatively large sum of money for a sick friend who needed to buy medicine. They planned to steal a camera from a GI, an expensive but common item on the street, as GIs are also tourists. The elaborate scheme involves getting a GI to take a group photo with all of the participating boys. The extended description by Insu, the first-person narrator, of this snapshot recalls the ghostly subjectivity of a biracial boy in the arms of a young, anonymous GI. The narrator's description of the photo zooms in on one part: "He is holding a small, dark-skinned Korean boy as if he were a bundle of wild flowers . . . subtle angles of his face mark him as an Amerasian."[93] Apart from the dramatic irony that the young GI has no idea that his camera is about to be swiped by these friendly "Korean" boys, the passage conveys the irony of the relation that is a nonrelation between the youthful GI and the "Amerasian" boy he is holding. What the photo reveals to us is the fatefulness of the casual relationship, that of GI fathers and their sons (and daughters). The souvenir photo points to the haunting presence and absence of biracial children, called "souvenir babies" in the Philippines,[94] who are casually begotten and casually forgotten by their fathers. Insu, the narrator, is much less interested in assigning guilt to the would-be fathers, as the bright and innocent smile of the GI is emphasized, but the picture draws our attention to the larger historical forces that produced these offspring of the empire and their scattering, which can barely be made to appear only momentarily to us. This is the only time in the book that the term "Amerasian" is used. While the narrator may be forgiving toward the young GI in the photo, the ghostly subjectivity of camp town Amerasians, captured in the haunting photo, levels a powerful critique.

The ghostly subjectivity of biracial children is produced not only by the imperial forces and their male soldiers, but also by their Korean mothers. One of the meanings of "ghost brother" in the title of the book derives from a specific incident that Insu gradually finds out about toward the end of the book. Insu learns that he had an older biracial brother who had a different father. Sergeant Fenkl told Insu's mother that he would not marry her unless she gave up her son, and so she did. In the family photo album, Insu would eventually recognize that a boy who has a certain resemblance to himself was not him, but his older half-brother, who was sent to an orphanage and eventually adopted in the United States. Although Insu's father, in a way, is acknowledged as being responsible for this abandonment, the book curiously shifts the blame mostly to Insu's mother and by extension to other camp town women who have had to make similar choices. Insu's name for the "boy in the picture who looks like him but is not him," his "ghost brother," is "Kŭristo." When his father hears the name, he is of course surprised, and asks Insu what "Kŭristo" sounds like. When Insu cannot seem to figure it out, his father tells him "Kŭristo" is Christ, a Korean pronunciation of Christ. The novel renames his nameless "ghost brother" Christ, emblematic of a sacrificial act of being abandoned so that other biracial children (boys in particular), like Insu, can have a father and a family. The book gives us similar examples where women "traffic" in their sons—not daughters—for a chance to catch a husband and to emigrate to America. It is alleged by Insu's uncle that "Jamesŭ's Mother" probably drowned Jamesŭ so that she would be free to marry another man, a white GI this time. "Changmi's Mother" wants to secure her marriage to her lover by giving him a son, but when she learns that he is sterile, she plans to deceive him by offering someone else's son as his own. So, she is in search of an African American man who looks like her lover. It is the women's selfishness that exacts the Christlike sacrifices of biracial children, born and unborn. Insu's identification with the abandoned boy, his "ghost brother," is based on the contingency of his own birth and the utter exchangeability between his position and that of his ghost brother's; the moment he learns of the other boy's existence and his abandonment is when Insu himself becomes a ghost. From that moment on, Insu, too, lives on only as a ghost brother.

Just about when he is figuring out the secret of the ghost brother, Insu has repeated nightmares in which a female figure in a traditional Korean dress, with her long hair down her back, intrudes into his room. She always carries a bloody knife in her hand, and he wakes up just as she is about to stab him. This female ghost that appears in Insu's nightmares was an image made very popular in South Korean horror films in the 1960s, when Insu was growing up. The female ghost is, of course, his mother; Insu sees his own life as having survived the murderous intentions of his own mother. I suggest here that the matrophobic dimensions of Fenkl's book, combined with equally strong misogynist aspects, clearly articulated by the character of Insu's Korean uncle, is another interpretation of the powerful matriarchal, matrilineal, and gynocentric tendencies of the camp town that we observed in *Mudflats*. In fact, I would argue that Insu's matrophobia is the direct result of his uncle's own misogyny, passed on to Insu. He exhorts his nephew to distance himself from "those black marketeers, or whores": "None of them. They're just criminals and women selling their cunts to earn a living."[95] Both the uncle's misogyny and Insu's matrophobia work to counteract the powerful influences of women, to disempower them.[96]

Transnational, Transracial, and Transcendent Masculinity

In the case of Insu, the subjectifying category of masculine sexuality emerges as a transcendent category, one that still intimately intersects with ethnicity, which in turn comes to be detached from nationality, both Korean and American. At first glance, Insu's very close relationship with his uncle—his maternal aunt's husband, a Korean man—makes it appear as if he is identifying with Korean masculinity. However, the portrait of this uncle is very different from those of Korean males in the South Korean camp town fictions that we have examined in this chapter. These texts' presumption is working-class masculinity's necessary intersection with, or its subsumption by, nationality, and they attempt to restore working-class masculinity, alienated from its proper place, to Korean nationality. On the other hand, *Memories*' representation of the Korean uncle divorces him from nationality, despite appearances. Insu grows up listening to the uncle's retelling of Korean folktales. The ideological content of these stories may be summarized as stories of misogyny and remasculinization, such as his retelling of the stories of evil fox women, or an obedient ginseng hunter's wife who restores her husband's phallic power. While it is possible to read their overwhelming phallocentric content and appropriation of Korean tradition as calling for remasculinization of Korean ethnonational sexuality, I would argue that given the book's emphasis on the non-belonging of camp towns and their residents in the national space, this particular remasculinization can be said to restore a masculinity, which has been damaged by proletarianization, under-ethnonationalization due to Korean ostracism, and racialization by American neocolonization, to masculine sexuality, posited as an absolute category. With the help of traditional tales of mythological masculinity, Insu's uncle's masculinity is wishfully situated in a transcendent space. The uncle's fantasy of absolute phallic power is displaced onto Insu, who would conquer women of all races: "You can stick it in some white women, yellow women and black women."[97] The process of Insu's subjectification, foregrounding the primacy of the category of sexuality, I would argue, takes place through the uncle's fantastic tales of magical phallic power, which are transracial and transnational.

MILITARY CAMP TOWNS AND "DIASPORAS"

This last section of the chapter addresses three different ways in which military prostitution in South Korea has been related to diaspora: camp town subjectivity as internally diasporic, military brides' immigration to the United States, and migrant sex work in contemporary South Korea.

Labor, Death and Translocality in Camp Towns in Kim Ki-dŏk's Address Unknown

A relatively recent film by Kim Ki-dŏk, one of the most innovative filmmakers in contemporary South Korea, *Address Unknown* (*Such'wiin pulmyŏng*, 2001), offers another autobiographically inspired narrative of camp town life in the 1970s. *Address Unknown* tells the stories of three teenagers whose lives are interrelated in a camp town. Ch'ang-guk, a half–African American and half-Korean teenager, lives with his mother in an American school bus converted into a makeshift home in a field on the periphery of the town, and works for a dog butcher, Dog-Eye. Ch'ang-guk's mother, although lucid at times, appears to be nearly insane. Apart from stealing vegetables and grains from her farmer neighbors in the village, her main activity is to write letters to her "husband," Ch'ang-guk's father in the United States, whom she clearly has not heard from in years. These letters come back every time stamped "Address Unknown." Dog-Eye is Ch'ang-guk's sadistic and abusive employer, as well as his stepfather figure, since he claims Ch'ang-guk's mother as his lover. Dog-Eye served for three years at another U.S. military base as a Korean civilian worker, but now he works as a dog butcher. Dog butchers, formerly an untouchable caste, still occupy the very bottom rung of the socioeconomic order, and their pariah status is abundantly conveyed throughout the film. Eun-ok is another local teenager, whose eye has been blinded by a childhood accident, a shooting by her older brother. She is approached by a GI named James, who offers a deal: eye surgery at the U.S. military hospital in exchange for becoming his "sweetheart." With the recovery of her sight, she begins her sexual relationship with him. James is a discontented and rebellious American serviceman who eventually goes AWOL and is captured by the local U.S. military authorities by the end of film. Ch'ang-guk tries to break away from his job as Dog-Eye's assistant, a job he abhors, but is unable to do so because of Koreans' racist discrimination against him. Eventually, Ch'ang-guk murders Dog-Eye by hanging him—the same way Dog-Eye kills the dogs—and then kills himself by throwing himself into a muddy rice paddy. Upon discovering the dead body of her son, Ch'ang-guk's mother sets fire to her dead son and herself in the bus where they lived. A letter arrives from the States from a neighbor of Ch'ang-guk's father, relaying the news that Ch'ang-guk's father has died in an accident.

Like other revisionist works, *Address Unknown* attempts to de-allegorize camp town residents, prostitutes, GIs, and Korean men by showing the ongoing construction of their subjectivity. The film features no current sex workers, but only a teenager, Eun-ok, who forms a quasi-commercialized sexual relationship with a GI, after her disability draws her into a transaction with him. Another main female character in the film is Ch'ang-guk's mother; she is no longer a military prostitute, but her excruciating present is the historical result of her past as one. Eun-ok and Ch'ang-guk's mother respectively illustrate how one becomes a military prostitute and what becomes of military prostitutes afterwards. The most unprecedented de-allegorization in this South Korean text takes place with the American serviceman, James. The film's deliberate and careful portrayal of American soldiers as a collective of individuals who are responsible and respectful in their conduct toward local civilians is clearly meant to contradict the existing portrayals of American servicemen as allegorical articulations of hierarchized race, class, gender, and neocolonization.[98] Sexual imperialism, often expressed and performed by American soldiers—their pride in "being part of the greatest fighting force in the world," their sense of entitlement to sexual service, their abusive treatment of women as disposable commodities, and their misconceived notions about prostitution as voluntary— does coincide with and validate the notion of American servicemen as an imperial allegory that routinely appears in South Korean representations of them.[99] However, in *Address Unknown*, James is not a ready-made sexual predator or a violent rapist. Rather, the film shows the process through which the character, facing a variety of problems (difficulty in adjusting to the military, doubts about the American military's role overseas, cultural differences, homesickness, loneliness), gradually becomes violent toward Eun-ok, whom he had approached with a certain amount of genuine romantic interest and kind intentions to help with her medical issues. By the time we reach the scene in which an enraged James is choking Eun-ok, we have learned the various pressures of the low-ranking military work he volunteered to do. While the film makes it possible for us to imagine that another GI crime may have been an extension of this very scene, the film simultaneously unravels the logic of such GI crimes to show them as inextricably linked to the particular circumstances of the diasporized, imperialized military proletariat. His attack on Eun-ok is communicated to us as a suicidal desire taken out on one who is weaker and occupying even a lower rung in the imperial hierarchy, as he screams repeatedly to her, "Kill me, I have no hope." In *Address Unknown,* military prostitutes and GIs do not yet exist; rather, they are in the process of acquiring these identities.

Along with a de-allegorization of camp town characters, the other important setting of the film, the dog butchering business and the conditions and fate of the dogs, appears to take on an allegorical function. Very early in the film, the metaphorical equation between the dogs to be butchered and Ch'ang-guk is made, when Ch'ang-guk must get in the dog cage on the back of Dog-Eye's motorcycle as they go to work to pick up dogs. When Ch'ang-guk decides to kill Dog-Eye, he places him in the same dog cage on the motorcycle seat. Ch'ang-guk murders Dog-Eye by hanging, the way Dog-Eye kills dogs, as the dogs released from their cages pull the rope that hangs Dog-Eye.[100] What is it that makes the dogs and the human residents of camp town comparable? It is not so much the general sense that human lives are worthless, like those of the dogs; rather, it is the precise worth of dogs as lumps of meat—either living or dead—that functions as a metaphor for camp town human subjects. If dogs are weighed, bought, and sold by the pound, then human lives and their labors are similarly commodified, whether as military sex workers, like Ch'ang-guk's Mother or Eun-ok, or as civilian workers employed by the U.S. military, like Dog-Eye. Ch'ang-guk's even worse racialized marginalization in a South Korean camp town is further juxtaposed with the behavior of the condemned dogs; like them, he is utterly subjugated, helpless, submissive to his boss, Dog-Eye, and to the whole community. The most important parallel lies in their condemnation to death; the caged dogs live until they are butchered, while camp town residents—Ch'ang-guk, Ch'ang-guk's mother, Dog-Eye—live and labor until they die.

In a short story by Kang Sŏk-kyŏng, "Days and Dreams," a military prostitute depicts the camp town as an "island" between South Korea and the United States, a place that belongs to neither nation-state.[101] Camp towns within neocolonized South Korea remain closer to a traditional territorial colony, a place where a foreign military exerts various kinds of control and influence in all spheres of local life. The film *Address Unknown* makes this point via a succinct visual metaphor: the entire narrative is punctuated by a series of scenes of military jets flying over the rice paddies and of Apache helicopters hovering over the village. Ch'ang-guk's mother, who often speaks bits of English to other villagers, while exclaiming to them, "I will go to America!" is countered by a grocery store owner who yells back at her, "Speak Korean! This is Korea!" The grocer's declaration, which tries to reclaim the camp town as Korean, sounds hollow. If colonization is an experience of deterritorialization, whereby one's sense of locality and culture has been distorted and transformed by another occupying state's political, economic, and cultural domination, then the camp town is a slice of colonized territory in the American empire. Following Appadurai, if locality is "primarily relational and contextual rather than scalar or spatial" in a globalized world, then the complex process of delocalization and deterritorialization in the context of camp towns may be described as translocal.[102]

Although Appadurai's notion of translocality is closely connected to the more recent contemporary development of "technological interactivity," I believe the concept is still useful in thinking about South Korean camp towns of the industrializing era, from the mid-1960s to the 1980s. We might call this experience of (neo)colonial deterritorialization an imperial translocality that is generated by movements of people—the constant influx and outflow of American soldiers, immigration of Korean military brides to the United States, their return to South Korea in cases of failed marriages, children left behind in South Korea by American servicemen, their adoption to the United States—and the social relations and networks created by such movements. By imperial translocality I mean the ways in which the camp town's economy, culture, and society are transformed into a version of a deterritorialized American empire through these movements and connections. South Korean camp town residents are physically located in an external colony, and yet they maintain material connections to the United States through the work that they perform and the culture and language they are compelled to adopt. Camp towns may be said to be a deterritorialized locality of the U.S. empire, or a territorialized diaspora "within" South Korea. As camp towns are simultaneously segregated from the rest of South Korea as racialized ghettos, this further ends up intensifying the camp town residents' sense of connection (or desire for connection) to the United States. Their desire for the phantasm of America is in fact materially and experientially based on their (non)relation with both South Korea and the United States. This camp town translocality points to the double disjuncture between territory and subjectivity,[103] one articulated in camp towns in the form of those who are at once deterritorialized "American" subjects in the external colonies of the United States and deterritorialized "Korean" subjects in the internal colonies of South Korea.

Address Unknown articulates this deterritorialized translocal subjectivity most clearly in its exploration of the use of English in the camp town. Not only does Ch'ang-guk's mother's practice of addressing villagers in English remind them of their (neo)colonization, but more importantly, it is an eerily desperate and fantastic assertion of her deterritorialized imperial subjectivity, in some ways emancipatory vis-à-vis South Korea. When she asks the grocery store owner imperiously, "Where is [a] mackerel can?" and is met with the reply, "This is Korea! Speak Korean!" from the owner, she utters her subjectivity as one in transit or as translocally: "I will go to America!" Ch'ang-guk draws a bath for his mother in a makeshift tub made out of a metal suitcase. As he washes her body, he speaks to her in English, his tears flowing freely, "Mom, I am sorry. . . . I was wrong. . . . Please forgive me." Simultaneously, he tries to carve out the tattoo on her breast, which says, "U.S. Army, Michael." In this scene, as Ch'ang-guk tries to emancipate himself and his mother from the confining grips of the empire (in the form of a tattoo of Ch'ang-guk's father's name), his most heartfelt emotion—what constitutes his core self—must be spoken in the deterritorialized imperial language. As the imperial language subjugates him, it also liberates him from the other colonial power that Korea is.

A few central images from *Address Unknown* very accurately sum up camp town subjectivity. Ch'ang-guk's Mother's letter to her "husband" is continuously mailed to the U.S. address that she has for him, and it comes back every time with a red stamp, "Address Unknown." Like the letter she keeps on throwing at the United States, she hurls her body at the fence at the front gate of the local U.S. military base while screaming something about her husband and her wanting to go to America. The MPs, standing at attention, simply look on without the least reaction to her frenzy. Just as the letter she writes is thrown back at her, the MPs' nonresponse also hurls her back. The letter as an emblem articulates her subjectivity as one in a constant state of deterritorialization (from both and multiple places), in a state of movement or motion. In this film, extremely visual with very little dialogue, the most striking image is that of Ch'ang-guk's death. He throws himself headfirst into a wintry, muddy rice paddy. A few days later, when his mother and his friend, Chi-hŭm, discover his body, we see only the bottom half of his body, that is, his waist and two legs, frozen stiff, sticking out of the ground into the sky. The top half of his body is not visible, as it is buried underground.

The film's rather subtle treatment of Korean racism against African American soldiers and their biracial children, I would argue, brings out, even more effectively, the further intensified discrimination and alienation Ch'ang-guk suffers. The film's visual representation of Ch'ang-guk's racialization quietly captures his downcast gazes, his submissive, hesitant posturing, and his almost literal self-erasure and self-marginalization in various places of the camp town. Given the utter and extreme colonization that he experiences as the pain of deterritorialization from both Korea and the United States, his suicide seems the only logical conclusion, but the manner of his suicide seems to want to convey to us his impossible desire to belong to a place. His attempt at reterritorialization, an impossible autochthony, can only be performed in reverse; instead of being able to live rooted in a place, he can die with his head stuck in the ground.

Military Brides and Korean Diaspora in the United States

Another issue traditionally excluded in South Korean male and masculinist writings on military prostitution is the immigration of camp town women and their families to the United States as a consequence of their marriage to American servicemen. Similarly, in the U.S. historiography of Korean American immigration, the South Korean diaspora related to military prostitution has been largely marginalized, even though about 40 to 50 percent of South Korean immigration since 1965 can be traced to military brides.[104] I would like to turn briefly to *Mudflats'* representation of the immigrant experience of Ok-ju, one of the murdered victims in the story, as it accurately brings up a variety of issues that immigrant military brides face when they arrive in the United States. Ok-ju marries a white GI named Carl, with a baby from a previous relationship with another GI who abandoned her. Carl is described as an extremely gentle, sensitive husband, and a caring stepfather to Ok-ju's son, Johnson. After their marriage, they move to his hometown in Kansas. As Ok-ju adjusts to her new life in an American city in the Midwest, she must also adjust to the significant disparity between the fantasy she had about life in America and the reality she faces. She learns that the United States is a society stratified by class and race, and that her husband, a mere enlisted man from a working-class family, can afford, on his meager salary as a soldier, only a run-down apartment in the African American part of town. Despite the relative poverty she experiences on her arrival, she is nevertheless immensely happy to have escaped the life of prostitution in a camp town, grateful and eager to start her new life with her family. After putting Johnson in a daycare, Ok-ju gets a job at a dry cleaner run by a Korean immigrant. Everything seems to go well for Ok-ju and her family until Carl, who is deployed to Vietnam for six months, returns home, severely traumatized by the experience. He becomes an alcoholic and an extremely abusive husband and father to Johnson and their own daughter, Susan. His symptoms are described clearly as a case of post-traumatic stress disorder. As she faces difficulty at home, her Korean employer, who has always regarded Ok-ju, a military wife, with the usual prejudice and suspicion typical of the Korean community, fires her. She now has to clean houses and offices to support her children and her husband. As the meager pay for physically demanding work becomes more and more difficult for her to bear, she turns to a job in an "Oriental Massage Parlor," where she works as a masseuse and a part-time prostitute. She consoles herself by saying that she did the same kind of work in Korea and she can do it now in the United States, to support her family. One day when she comes back from work, she learns that Carl has strangled Johnson to death. This is the end of her immigrant life in United States and she returns to Korea, ending up in one of the camp towns again.

Both as military prostitutes and workers in South Korean camp towns, and as military brides in the United States, there is a deterritorialized continuity between women's transnational work on both sides of the Pacific. As military prostitutes, they are already diasporized in the "external" or "exteriorized" colony of the United States in South Korean camp towns, and their spatial and geographical movement to the United States as military brides situates them "back" into a literal diasporic location, often in racialized camp towns and ghettos, that is, "internal" or "interiorized" colonies of the United States. If their "sex work," which often includes other kinds of domestic labor, is a type of "offshore" work for the empire in the neocolonial outpost, then their work as spouses of military men within the United States becomes immigrant labor. These spaces, camp towns in South Korea and camp towns in the United States, are virtually and materially connected by physical movement across a national boundary. As unskilled labor, some of the immigrant brides in the United States end up in jobs similar to those they were doing or would have done back in South Korea, such as factory work (manufacturing in textile, clothing, electronic, or toys), agricultural work, or cleaning offices and homes, both during their marriages or after their divorces. More often than not, divorced military brides return to sex and sexualized service labor.[105] Their racialization in South Korean camp towns again forms a continuum with their experience in the United States, as they continue to be isolated and discriminated against by both the South Korean immigrant community and American mainstream society. Their move to the United States as immigrant military brides, however, also brings a series of changes in their material lives and consciousness. They realize that their husbands' socioeconomic position is not a constant, but something that changes, depending on their location within the broader empire; their husbands, as rank-and-file soldiers who occupy positions of wealth and power relative to Koreans, are no more than working-class military laborers in the United States. They experience significant disillusionment about their newfound relative poverty in the United States. Cultural differences and linguistic barriers—something that might have been overlooked with a bit more ease in South Korea—become a more serious obstacle, often making marriages unsustainable. Their position as military wives is extremely precarious, since divorce—at a rate as high as 80 percent—can threaten their more socially respectable positions as military wives, forcing them to go back to work in camp towns, often with children to support as single mothers.[106]

In both of their deterritorialized locations, in South Korean camp towns and in immigrant ghettos and camp towns in the United States, military sex workers' and immigrant brides' relationships to Korean identity is intensely complex and multifaceted. We have noted earlier camp town women's denationalization as well as their defensive nationalism. Dissociating itself from the Korean masculinism and patriarchy that the women have experienced, their Korean nationalism must be reconceptualized as antimasculinist and antipatriarchal. When they move to the United States, the nature of their relationship to Korea and Korean identity is not fundamentally altered, but rather intensified. Their diasporic nationalism continues to function as a means for them to protect themselves against the racism and sexism that they experience now within the boundary of the empire. The contradictory dimensions of their relationship with Korea, that is, their desire to cut off their ties with Korea and their need for them become further intensified. What emerges in Ji-yeon Yuh's ethnography of the lives of immigrant military brides is not only their strong desire to reclaim a Korean identity that has been suppressed by themselves and taken away by others, Koreans and Americans alike, but also what I would call their very specific and contextual nationalism and national identity built through their mutual association and aid in the United States as in South Korean camp towns. What they desire and assert is not so much a nostalgia or a longing for Korea, Korean nationalism, or identity in a totalizing sense, but rather very specific aspects of being Korean, such as speaking Korean, eating Korean food, sharing Korean culture and knowledge, and enjoying fellow Koreans' company. Here, their particular kind of diasporic nationalism might be conceptualized as multifaceted; it is, on the one hand, antistate nationalist, subnational nationalist, and antipatriarchal and antimasculinist nationalist, while it is, on the other hand, what we might call cultural and social nationalism. Korean identity is not necessarily something that must be adopted as a whole, but an identity whose related but discrete and separable dimensions can be selectively adopted. Their relationship to Korean culture, food, language, and people does not have to constitute an isomorphism with their relationship with various aspects of Korea as the nation-state that came to oppress them—the governing elites and bureaucracy, the class system, capitalism, and patriarchy.

Migrant Military Sex Work in Contemporary South Korean Camp Towns

If South Korean military sex workers were "labor exports" to Vietnam serving the U.S. military during the war, and to pockets of U.S. territory in

South Korea, the South Korean economic development of recent years has changed the racial makeup of the workforce in camp towns; since the late 1990s, South Korea has become an "importer" of camp town sex workers, mainly Filipina women and some Russian women, under the legal provision of the "entertainment visa." They make up a cheaper and more vulnerable workforce, paid one-third of what South Korean women are paid.[107] Once they are in South Korean camp towns, they are treated like migrant workers in other sectors, such as manufacturing and service; their passports are confiscated, and portions of their salaries are forcibly deducted and kept from them in order to prevent their escape. They are often physically and sexually abused by their Korean bar owners; over 90 percent of the complaints filed are against Koreans, rather than against American servicemen.[108] I also want to note the continuity between recent international marriages of South Korean farmers to Southeast Asian women—Vietnamese and Filipina—and the presence of Filipinas in South Korean camp towns. As I mentioned, South Korean men have also become users of Southeast Asian sex work, both in their own homeland and through overseas sex tourism. This continuity aligns South Korean men of different classes, no longer subaltern, with men of other advanced economies, American and others, as exploiters. If South Korean military prostitution now includes a migrant workforce from overseas, due to the relative wealth of the South Korean national economy, there is a way in which the enlisted ranks of the American military, largely made up of the racialized working class, have become transnational migrant militarized labor, serving the South Korean state and capital. One of the last scenes of the novel *The Camp Town at Camp Seneca* deals with a Korean merchant in the camp town who catches an African American soldier stealing a bag of instant ramen, which he does not have the money to pay for.[109] While the novel's own perspective on this scene is complex, it is an indisputable fact that American servicemen, who get paid the U.S. minimum wage, are no longer "wealthy," as they used to be in comparison to South Koreans in previous decades. In a contemporary South Korean camp town, an American soldier's reason for his preference for Filipina sex workers over South Korean women is the fact that they are both "foreigners."[110]

Katharine Moon points out that the kinds of reforms that had been made to address the conditions of Koreans working for the U.S. military, such as the SOFA amendment for the purpose of increasing the power balance between South Korea and United States and decreasing American abuses of power and diminishing violence and crime committed by its servicemen, can no longer address the exploitation suffered by the multi-national, multiracial workforce in South Korean camp towns.[111] Na Young Lee points out that as the women in camp towns changed from "ours" to "others," masculinist nationalist activism moved out of camp towns. Rather, Korean men are now involved in the trafficking of these migrant sex workers into South Korea. Ironically, this has resulted in South Korean men, once again, feeling victimized, as they are condemned by international agencies and laws (supported by the United States) for their human trafficking and violations of human rights.[112]

Furthermore, in the contemporary context where Russian migrant sex workers in camp towns service South Korean male clientele, in addition to the U.S. military, the intersecting and overlapping power relations among gender, class, race, and nationality became much more complex and difficult to delineate. As typical of the intermediate position of subempire that South Korea occupies, South Korean sex workers still migrate to wealthier locations, such as Japan and the United States. Migrant sex work in camp towns must be further examined in relation to international sex tourism, constituting the larger trend of globalizing sexual proletarianization, on the one hand, and in relation to the broader migration of labor in general on the other hand. This recent development once again reminds us of the serial substitutability and surrogacy of labor in general, and sex work in particular, in the global hierarchy of nations, races, and economies. If South Korean camp town workers once did—and still do—perform labors and provide service in place of U.S. women through the earlier era of industrialization, now women from even further peripheralized locations—Russia and the Philippines—have taken over Korean women's place in the contemporary capitalist global order. This very substitutability, we must remind ourselves, premises itself simultaneously upon the very unsubstitutability and inequality between those who are being substituted and those who are substituting.

CONCLUSION

I began this chapter with a look at works that deconstruct masculinist nationalist allegories of military prostitution, the dominant mode of representation throughout the era of South Korean industrialization under U.S. hegemony. In examining the revisionist works from the 1990s, my readings attended to the ways in which reinscriptions of military prostitution attempt to decouple the classed and gendered sexualities, both masculine and feminine, of camp town residents from their subordinated linkage to ethnonationality, their Koreanness. I have argued that the recentering of camp town patriarchy in Pok Kŏ-il's revision highlights the ways in which classed masculinity superseded their ethnonational identity in the specific circumstances of the camp town, that is, their denationalization in the face of the South Korean state's power vacuum and their neocolonization under the local U.S. military authorities. My reading of feminist representations also called attention to the gynocentrism, feminine homosociality, and lesbianism of camp town communities of women, especially the ways in which their particular militarized-commercialized feminine sexuality becomes detached from the ethnonation and are realigned with other women and men of other races. I also examined the ways in which camp town biracial children's dually dis-identificatory transnationalism, located between South Korea and the United States, transgresses the boundaries of culture, nation, and ethnicity and race, staking out subversive and resistive positions in the interstices of class and sexualities between nation and empire. In the third and last section of this chapter, I explored the relations between military prostitution and diasporas—the "internal diaspora" of camp towns, the the camp town diaspora in the United States, and the migration of military sex workers into contemporary South Korea. In reconceptualizing contemporary military prostitution in South Korea, all of the frameworks of the groups of literary works on the camp town that I treated in this chapter are inadequate to address these recent changes. With the exception of Fenkl's book, both groups—masculinist nationalist allegories and feminist revisionist works (exemplified by *Mudflats* and "Days and Dreams")—remain strictly within the ethnonational boundary, without considering the transnational connections that had already existed prior to the influx of migrant military sex workers into South Korean camp towns. In their ethnonationally and androcentrically based contestation against U.S. hegemony, the earlier camp town literature did not consider the always already transnational nature of U.S. imperialism and militarism that spans across various nation-states in Asia and beyond. The literal and physical movement of migrant sex workers into South Korean camp towns has, now and retroactively, made this transnational nature of U.S. empire and its militarism, its "empire of bases,"[113] obvious and undeniable to South Koreans.

Memories of My Ghost Brother succeeds in portraying the camp town as a place of survival by placing South Korean camp towns in the larger context of U.S. militarism across Asia. Insu remembers the snack bar on the base where he would meet his father and spend time with him: "I met my father at the Snack Bar in RC-4. It could have been any Snack Bar on any small U.S. army post, the same pastel-colored, vinyl-padded metal furniture, the same plastic trays, the same china, the same food." Fenkl is able to convey a sense of the universality of such conditions on bases and in camp towns across Asia between the mid-1960s and the mid-1970s: "I had walked down alleys. . . . [G]irls suck a GI's penis, boys would let a man fuck them and then pretend to be their family friend, stabbed with an Afro pick. . . . We were all doing our best to get money from the yellowhairs, longnoses, the Yankees . . . yangsaekshis, slicky boys, hustlers, pimps, . . . skulking through the narrow alleys . . . sewage, piss, stench. . . . [I]t gagged you."[114] The poignant contrast between the military bases that emanate wealth and power, and the poverty-stricken neighborhoods that surround them, populated by the natives of the lowest strata, is duplicated throughout the imperial outposts in various strategic locations in Asia. And in these neighborhoods, sexuality seems to be the universal commodity. Through his memory of his father's tour in Vietnam, Fenkl's book further elucidates the movement of imperial soldiers from one colony to another:

> While my father was on leave . . . [t]he U.S.S. Pueblo, an electronic spy ship, was captured off the coast of North Korea and all over the country, the military went on alert. My father went back up to his unit. . . . Later that month during the Vietnamese New Year's celebration of Tet, the NVA and the Vietcong simultaneously attacked over a hundred towns, cities and military installations all over Vietnam. It was the bloodiest offensive of the war. The outpost where my father had served near Nha Trang was overrun, and many of his friends were among the Killed-in-Action. The mood among the GIs in Korea became thick and black, full of hate for Asian people and tense with fear that the North Koreans might invade. The GIs were afraid to stay in Korea, but even more afraid that they might be shipped to Cam Rahn Bay to join some counteroffensive against the North Vietnamese. Houseboys and prostitutes were beaten more frequently: there were more fights in the clubs. The Korean army stayed on alert and continued to mobilize more men to send to Vietnam. There was constant news about the White Horse Division, the Tiger Division and the Blue Dragon Brigade.[115]

The passage above quietly illustrates not only the lateral dispersion of imperial military power throughout the region and its various neocolonial outposts, those already pacified and those to be pacified, but also the ways in which the decisions made at the highest echelons of power—commanders of nation-states, armed forces, and industries—are translated into the deaths and injuries suffered by their military proletariat and then further into the everyday brutality borne by those, again in multiple imperialized locations, who make a living by serving this imperial military proletariat.

4 Migrant and Immigrant Labor

Redefining Korean Identity

The history of modern Korea has been shaped by harsh colonization, participation in a series of wars—the Asia–Pacific Wars, the Korean War, and the Vietnam War—national division, and rapid industrialization, all of which entailed a violent social upheaval. Given this context, it is not surprising that one of the persistent themes in modern Korean literature is indeed that of exile, migration, and diaspora. Whether in "domestic" or "transnational" contexts, the sorrows of exile, nomadism, and homesickness pervade colonial and postcolonial literature, all the way up to the 1980s. And the experience of migration has always had, of course, material linkages to the conditions of labor. Post-liberation South Korea exported a variety of labor, including soldiers to Vietnam, construction workers to the Middle East, nurses and miners to West Germany, and emigrants to North and South America in the period from the mid-1960s to the early '80s. Most recently, however, South Koreans are experiencing the migration of others into their country—laborers, mostly from China, South Asia, and Southeast Asia. In an extremely short span of time, South Korea has moved from position of labor exporter to that of labor importer.

While the South Korean working class served as a transnationalized workforce for the U.S./Japan–dependent economy of the 1960s, '70s, and '80s, since the late '80s South Korea's emergence as a subempire has transformed other Asians into a transnationalized labor force for South Korean multinational capital. Politically, the year 1987 saw the end of over a quarter century of consecutive military dictatorships and the beginning of a gradual transition into liberal democracy. Economically, the Seoul Olympics of 1988 also marked a historical juncture in which South Korea became one of the more affluent parts of Asia, a destination for migrant workers.

Moreover, as South Korean companies also moved their production to off-shore locations in less developed parts of Asia, South Korean capital—both conglomerates and small-to-medium-sized businesses—came to employ a large non-Korean labor force. Since South Korean capital turned to migrant and offshore labor in order to continue to grow and maintain profitability, the bottom of the "South Korean" working class no longer consists of ethnic Koreans, but of other Asians, both within and outside of South Korea.[1] While the accumulation of wealth, made possible through the transnationalized, ethnicized labor of the South Korean working class (ethnicized vis-à-vis U.S. or Japanese capital) of the '60s, '70s, and '80s, laid the foundation for South Korea's "Democratization" in the late 1980s, South Korea's liberal democracy of more recent years has also been maintained by a new influx of ethnicized labor (ethnicized vis-à-vis South Korean capital and populace), that is, Chinese, Korean Chinese, South Asians, and Southeast Asians.

Migrant workers began arriving in South Korea in the late 1980s, and in the past twenty years, except for during the so-called IMF crisis from 1997 to 2000, the number has been steadily increasing. Though it is difficult to estimate the exact population figures, due to the fact that the overwhelming percentage of migrant workers are compelled to reside and work in South Korea illegally, the number of these workers is clearly on the rise and is projected only to increase at a more rapid rate in the future.[2] Migrant workers come from a great number of countries—over fifteen—from various parts of Asia, including South Asia and Southeast Asia, Central Asia, and some from as far as North Africa. South Korea is now home to migrant workers from China, Mongolia, Bangladesh, Thailand, Myanmar, Pakistan, Vietnam, the Philippines, Nepal, Uzbekistan, Kazakhstan, Morocco, Iran, and Russia. The majority of migrant workers are employed in the so-called 3D tasks, "dangerous, dirty, and difficult," in various manufacturing industries. There is also a critical shortage of construction workers needed for continuing urbanization. Through a special provision made in 2002, the shortage of service workers is being met by allowing Korean Chinese (ethnic Koreans from the PRC, often known in Korean as Chosŏnjok) to work in the industry.[3] While this particular ordinance excludes Korean Chinese employment in the "entertainment industry" (yuhŭng ŏpso), such as sex or sexualized service work in bars or the prostitution business, other ethnicized groups of women, such as Filipinas and Russians, are being imported for this particular sector through the government's issuance of "entertainment visas."

I argue in this chapter that South Korean migrant labor activism reacts to and engages with coexisting and overlapping historical conditions and systems. It is situated within the context of South Korea's transition from a mono-ethnic nation into a multiethnic immigrant nation, whose "labor import" is premised on its new status as one of the Asian subempires. Simultaneously, migrant labor activism emerges out of the recent rapid globalization process—which has encompassed all spheres, including international politics, transnational capitalism, and multinational culture industries—of which South Korea is part. This chapter pays attention to dual historical processes, in which South Korea as a nation-state still operates powerfully, governing and controlling various dimensions of "labor import" and migrants' work, while at the same time contemporary globalization has been eroding the nation-state system, disrupting the isomorphism among territory, people, and nation-state sovereignty.[4] I argue that the South Korean state functions simultaneously as a racial state that plays a major role in creating and maintaining a racially segmented labor market, and as a multicultural state that facilitates management of diverse ethnicized populations.[5]

The chapter then goes on to explore the ways in which migrant labor activism can appropriate both national and transnational structures and networks in order to push for progressive reforms and formulate resistive subjectivities. South Koreans and migrant worker–activists have recently begun to reconceptualize South Korea's labor importation around issues of immigration, social entitlements, and political representation, that is, matters of citizenship. In making the subject of transnational migrant work a domestic or intranational (rather than international) issue, a small minority of South Korean activists and migrant workers expedite the process of what they perceive as an inevitable outcome of continuing labor migration, that is, the reconfiguration of South Korea into a multiethnic nation. Following Appadurai and Sassen, this chapter illustrates the ways in which certain dimensions of globalization, such as the expansion of cultural and communication networks, the development of migrants' complex transnational and translocal subjectivities, and the emergence of a "new international human rights regime,"[6] operate subversively to counteract the powers of South Korea as a nation-state. Lastly, this chapter explores the ongoing process of the multiethnicization of South Korean society, in which Koreanness or Korean identity has incipiently begun to be decoupled from its exclusive association with the biologistic conception of ethnicity and ancestry on the one hand, and the performativity of Korean identity is being brought out through cultural assimilation and a Koreanization of the migrant population and their Korean-born and raised children on the other. I conclude the chapter by discussing the dual dimension of migrant subjects, who attempt to reterritorialize themselves in South Korea through cultural integration and "inflexible citizenship," while simultaneously maintaining themselves as deterritorialized subjects of multiple locations and nation-states, as they recreate and reinvent their translocal cultural identity.[7]

THE STATE, CAPITAL, AND LABOR TRAFFICKING

The South Korean State as a Racial State and a Multicultural State

While the South Korean state of the industrializing era played a central role in exporting labor, its transformation in recent years to a labor importer has created and maintained a racially segmented labor force through a range of laws and regulations that are designed to supply cheap labor for South Korean capital, bar social entitlements for migrant workers, and prevent their permanent settlement. The contemporary South Korean state, thus, heterogenizes the population by allowing labor migration in order to serve the needs of national economy, while continuing to insist on the conception of South Korea as an ethnically homogeneous nation by legislating political and social exclusion of migrant workers. Many state laws and government labor practices regarding migrant workers have either been inherited from the Japanese colonial period or borrowed from contemporary Japan. Either way, they constitute anachronisms that do not abide by the standards set by international human rights guidelines. Similarly, the pattern of collusion between the state and capital that we recognize in contemporary South Korea is also continuous with that of the previous era of South Korea's rapid industrialization. If the state collaborated with the conglomerates to extract cheap labor from the domestic population then, it now works with small to medium industries to import, manage, and govern the foreign migrant workforce. Through various legal provisions, and also by refusing to provide regulations or refusing to enforce them, the South Korean state sanctions and underwrites a racialized and racist labor exploitation of the migrant population; racism and state power are welded to each other.[8]

The South Korean state as a "racial state," to borrow Omi and Winant's term[9]—one that performs a key role in the ongoing racial formation of

South Korea—is further complicated by the ideologically complementary and compensatory role it plays in its purveying of official multiculturalism, which, Lisa Lowe reminds us, "takes up the role of resolving the history of inequalities left unresolved in the economic, political domains."[10] While the Justice Department of South Korea oversees the Immigration and Naturalization Service (INS), which for the most part bases its legal and illegal actions, such as arrests, detention, and deportation, on explicit racism and racial violence, at the same time, South Korean officials urge their "citizens to shift to a multicultural social consciousness."[11] The state demands that South Korean society embrace multiculturalism for the purpose of managing its diverse laboring population effectively, while disavowing the necessary political and social changes to support the multiethnic population. Just to name a couple of instances of its recent multicultural policies, the state makes special visa provisions for the children of migrant workers, offers Korean language classes for migrant workers and their children,[12] and sponsors multicultural events and festivals. One of such festivals in 2005 was even named "Migrant Workers' Arirang," after the traditional folksong *arirang*, which had been associated with Koreans' ethnonationally based oppression since the Japanese colonial period.[13] The highly precarious status of migrant workers in South Korea further raises the stakes for the compensatory function of official multiculturalism in South Korea. Furthermore, migrant workers' organization as laborers, as residents, and as (future and current) citizens, and their active resistance and contestation vis-à-vis the state and the South Korean mainstream society contribute, subversively, to the ongoing process of racial formation in contemporary South Korea, as we will see in the last section of this chapter.[14]

Laws and Regulations on Labor Migration and Migrant Labor

The most widely used, systematic method of exploiting foreign migrant workers is called the "Industrial Trainee System" *(sanŏp yŏnsusaeng chedo).* An "Industrial Trainee" is also called *kyoyuksaeng,* an apprentice or student. Under the pretext of technology transfer and the training of industrial workers,[15] this system imports a large number of workers from various Asian countries and offers salaries, stipulated by agreements between South Korea and the respective source countries, that are substantially lower than those of South Korean workers who perform similar types of work. Despite these fabricated rationales, the Industrial Trainee System is mainly used as a source of cheap and unskilled labor from other less developed

Asian countries. Under the pressure of labor activists, migrant workers, and even about half of the small to medium business employers, in July 2003 the South Korean National Assembly passed a law that began to allow a combination of two systems for foreign migrant labor, the existing Industrial Trainee System and the new Work Permit System (koyong hŏgaje). This new law also includes a provision for legalizing some of the undocumented migrant workers by offering amnesty for those who have stayed in South Korea under four years, while others with over four years of illegal residency were asked to leave the country voluntarily. This new law also made it possible, at least and only for migrant workers with legal status, to have rights equivalent to those of South Korean workers, including the right to strike.[16] However, the consensus since the implementation of the Work Permit System has been that the availability and acquisition of legal status for some of the migrant worker population has not accomplished much in terms of improving their overall working and living conditions.[17]

One of the ideological premises of the Industrial Trainee System in particular—but also, to a lesser extent, the Work Permit System and the general system of use of migrant labor—is this dis/connection between the workers' bodies and the location of their labor performed on the one hand, and their citizenship and the location of their nativity on the other. While their bodies are located in Korea, working, consuming, and living there, migrant workers are treated as if they were living in their own countries, where the cost of labor and living is cheaper than in Korea. In calculating their wages, the South Korean state and capital dissimulate that migrant workers' bodies, work, and life are somehow discontinuous with Korean society and the Korean territory where they are physically located. Their laboring and living bodies and their communities seem to constitute a deterritorialized colony within South Korea, or a colonized extraterritoriality, that is, a virtual island that is segregated from their surroundings. If the logic of this linkage between the laboring body and his or her native country, deemed indissoluble, operates to justify the low wages of migrant workers, the wage difference between receiving countries, like South Korea, and sending countries is experienced by migrant workers as a temporal issue. On the part of migrant workers themselves, an enormous motivation and temptation for them to come to South Korea, despite the hardship they expect, is this sense of temporal compression. That is, they can earn in one month in Korea and in other wealthier nations what they would have earned in ten years in their own countries. So if they could move from an industrial trainee job—that is, they are lucky enough to escape the "island" that the Industrial Trainee System constructs within Korea—to better paying jobs in Korean space and time, and then return to their own countries, their earnings from Korea can be calculated in terms of a temporal gain. But, more often than not, this gamble fails since, because of the harsh life and labor they endure, one year in Korea can be felt and experienced as ten years at home. Or one month in Korea can also mean the loss of all of their time, their future, if they lose a limb, their health, or their life. As a Nepali worker in Pak Pŏm-sin's novel *Namaste* puts it, "The three and a half years I lived through in South Korea is much longer than twenty years I lived in Nepal."[18]

For the undocumented migrant worker population in South Korea, labor laws are separate and unequal. While the South Korean constitution and labor laws prohibit discrimination based on nationality, unenforced laws are as good as nonexistent. The goal of migrant workers and labor activists is to have government authorities guarantee three major labor rights—the right to unionize, the right to strike, and the right to collectively bargain—by enforcing the laws guaranteeing them on behalf of the migrant worker population. Under these circumstances, one of the demands of workers and activists is for the state to legislate special laws that would protect at least the most minimal rights of migrant workers. For example, one of the most serious problems that migrant workers experience is delayed and unpaid wages. When this occurs, there are no official channels through which workers can address the issue, as a large percentage of migrant workers remain undocumented, which places them in a very vulnerable position. Currently, there are no fines or penalties for employers who fail to pay wages, nor are there any government agencies that administer or oversee the labor practices of the companies that employ migrant workers. Another example of an unenforced law is the state regulation established in 1995 that requires the employer to provide health insurance and compensation for industrial accidents. However, employers are either unaware of such laws or they simply do not comply with them, and the state turns a blind eye to such situations. Through its negligence and indifference, the South Korean state ends up being a silent and complicit partner to the criminal activities of the businesses that exploit migrant workers. The contemporary South Korean government repeats the notorious actions of its predecessors of earlier decades, who also actively and passively colluded with South Korean capitalists by refusing to enforce labor laws on behalf of South Korean workers.

While South Korea as a sovereign state still wields much power over the working conditions of migrant workers, through laws and regulations, globalization has precipitated the emergence of a "new international human rights regime" in which "human rights override the distinctions between citizens and aliens, undermining the authority of the state." Sassen argues, "Under human rights regimes states must increasingly take account of persons qua persons, rather than qua citizens. The individual is now an object of law and a site for rights regardless of whether a citizen or an alien."[19] While this is certainly a growing trend, and migrant workers in South Korea can and do appeal to these international rights and institutions, in reality the sovereign state's control, rather than the influence of the international human rights regime, still dominates migrant workers' lives and labor.

Government Crackdowns

State authorities carry out periodic crackdowns, rounding up undocumented migrant workers. Once they are captured and arrested by INS officials and the police, they are often detained in correctional facilities, despite the clear violation of international human rights that such a process constitutes. The brutalities committed against migrants by INS officials and the police seem to be common enough occurrences.[20] These general crackdown periods, also informally referred to as "big clean-up operations,"[21] are for the ostensible purpose of complying with the law—that is, identifying workers whose status is or has become illegal due to the expiration of their visas, and dealing with them accordingly—but they function, in fact, as a strategy of disposing of those who have stayed in Korea for an extended period time, that is, over a few years, in order to make room for a new crop of migrant workers—workers more vulnerable and more willing to work for cheaper wages. Needless to say, "big clean-up operations," the cleansing of the ethnicized workforce, serve as a powerful disciplinary mechanism.

During such periods of intense crackdowns, many migrant workers often opt to go underground rather than leave the country. Because they have spent already a large sum of money to come into the country, they simply cannot afford to return home without paying back the money that they owe their brokers, friends, and family. They also know that periodic crackdowns must stop in order for the supply of cheap labor to continue. The conditions of their hiding out during these "clean-up operations" are as miserable as their working conditions. They usually spend the majority of their time indoors, in cramped rooms where several workers live together. Since they have to use their savings, they often try to live on as little as possible, skipping meals and limiting their movements as if they were hibernating. Other survival strategies include living by such rules as having curtains drawn at all times, not using electric lamps at night, not gathering together with fellow migrant workers, and not using public transportation.[22] Hwang Sŏk-yŏng's novel *Children of Darkness*, which I discussed in chapter 2, describes a very similar type of situation, where petty street criminals, mostly teenage males, young men, and prostitutes, must also lie low during periodic "cleansing" operations by the local police. If Hwang's novel portrays the authoritarian state's criminalization of the underclass in late 1970s South Korea, the contemporary "liberal" state criminalizes the racialized migrant population who now make up the very bottom of the South Korean underclass. If migrant workers' labor takes place in carceral conditions, their waiting for the chance to work is also an imprisonment. Not only is their work made illegal, but their very existence in South Korea is also rendered illegitimate by a series of regulations of the state and the laws of the market economy. Just as "free labor" at the worker's disposal, in fact, means the opposite—that is, a condition of extreme constraint—"migrant labor" actually signifies the severe restriction of movement; workers migrate along predetermined paths, whether these paths are from periphery to semiperiphery or metropole, or from one job to another within a given country. Migrant workers who are deported are often forced to leave Korea without their wages, though they protest that with their fingers cut off and without their wages they cannot leave Korea. In the end, the crackdowns become a means of turning cheap labor into free labor. For example, in 1998 unpaid wages amounted to over 100 million dollars and the number of uncompensated victims of industrial accidents reached over five thousand.[23]

South Korean Employers

The fact that state authorities have not made a point of cracking down on the employers who use migrant labor, while simultaneously implementing harsh policies of detainment and deportation of migrant workers, eloquently reveals the state's intention to assist in the businesses' exploitation of foreign labor. Again, the situation is oddly similar to the state's position on prostitution: while it performs periodic and often severe crackdowns on female sex workers, it rarely if ever bothers with the other half of the business—the male users. Migrant workers themselves articulate this obvious contradiction: "If we are illegal, what of our Korean bosses who employ us? And what of the Korean economy, which uses our labor? Isn't South Korea itself illegal?" One of their slogans at rallies is, "Illegal Workers=Illegal Republic of Korea" (*Pulbŏp ch'eryuja=pulbŏp taehan minguk*).²⁴

The Democratic Labor Union (*minju noch'ong*) points to the Industrial Trainee System as the most prevailing, legalized, structural cause of the exploitation of migrant workers and of the violations against their human rights in South Korea.²⁵ The system revives a Japanese practice from the colonial period that was used to recruit Korean workers for factories in Japan proper. Its systematic nature of exploitation stems from the collusive network of multiple agents, the South Korean government (and, to some extent, the governments of the sending countries), South Korean employers, and, not the least of all, a South Korean organization called Chungso kiŏp hyŏpdong chohap chunganghoe or Chungkihyŏp (The Central Association of Small to Medium Businesses). While it is a nongovernmental organization in the private sector, in the tradition of crony capitalism that has flourished in South Korea, its connections with the government enables it to exert a significant amount of influence on labor policies. Chungkihyŏp functions as an intermediary between South Korean employers and the governments and labor brokers of the sending countries. In this process, the association ends up making a profit of roughly three hundred dollars per industrial trainee that it imports for South Korean employers, while also taking three hundred dollars from the overseas labor brokers. In 2001, the association's total profit from labor trafficking amounted to 3.6 million dollars.²⁶

The low wages of industrial trainees, who make about half of South Korean workers' pay, is justified under the pretext of "technology transfer," the idea that South Korean companies teach these workers skills to take back to their countries. Their status as apprentices or trainees, not full-fledged workers, thus rationalizes their low wage. It is further argued that industrial trainees are paid the wages they would have been paid in their own countries. In fact, the companies who do business with the countries of industrial trainees' origin are legally exempted from paying them the Korean minimum wage, according to a Labor Department provision.²⁷

When industrial trainees arrive and start working in Korea, a large percentage of them breach their contracts in order to take better-paying jobs. Their passports are taken away from them when they arrive, precisely to prevent such escapes. Sometimes they are locked inside their dormitories at the end of a workday. These companies also make use of a strategy called "forced savings deposit" (*kangje chŏknip*), devised for the express purpose of limiting the number of runaway trainees, whereby a fixed amount of money is automatically deducted from a worker's monthly salary and (supposedly) deposited in his or her savings account.[28] Again, this was a tactic used by Japanese companies in the colonial period against Korean factory workers. Workers have complained bitterly about the fact that they have never seen their savings account statement, nor do they have any kind of access to it. After deductions for their "forced savings deposit" and payment for room and board, industrial trainees are left with appallingly small amounts of money from their already low wages; the actual take-home pay for some can be as little as half of their official salary. One worker commented, "I have nothing left after I spend money to buy international calling cards to talk to my family back home."[29] Once workers run away from their trainee jobs, they have no way of recovering the monies put into these accounts. The forced savings deposit system provides the employers with one more way of making use of migrant labor for free.

RACIALIZATION, RACISM, AND RACIAL VIOLENCE

In a survey of eleven Asian nations that measured the quality of life for migrant worker populations in areas such as housing, education, health services, and entertainment, South Korea was ranked in the late 1990s as the number 1 nation in terms of the inconvenience and discomfort that migrant workers experienced in their work and living situations.[30] While the survey does not seem to have included questions directly related to racial discrimination, race is a central issue that affects all of the areas of living and working mentioned above, whether these aspects are regulated by laws or remain outside state governance.

Racialized Working Conditions

In February 2007, nine people died and eighteen were seriously injured in a fire at a detention center of the Yŏsu branch of the INS. The ironically named Yŏsu Protection Agency is a detention facility where migrant workers who have been arrested for their illegal status are incarcerated temporarily until their deportation. The rooms have windows with bars and doors with heavy double padlocks. Surveillance cameras are installed everywhere, including inside toilets, and those held here are let outside only for thirty minutes of exercise per day. Without a sprinkler system, when the building caught fire the detainees could not escape from their rooms, which were no different from prison cells.[31] While this tragic fatal fire happened to take place in a detention facility, migrant workers' day-to-day living and working conditions, in fact, constitute a continuum with the prisonlike conditions of the "protection agency." These conditions are most accurately described as carceral labor (kamgŭm nodong).[32] In order to prevent the workers from running away, their workplace is locked from the outside, just as their dormitories are bolted after work. This particular system of carceral labor reverses, in a way, Angela Davis's concept of a "prison-industrial complex," whereby a racialized population is first imprisoned for criminal offences, and then put to work while incarcerated.[33] In the case of migrant workers, the very premise of their labor in South Korea is incarceration based on their nationality and racialized status—the condition that predicates the import of their labor power into South Korea.

Another key factor that contributes to racialized working conditions for migrant workers is their South Korean coworkers' racism. In the construction businesses, where many Chinese and Korean Chinese workers are employed, South Korean workers have come to resent their presence as competitors. In some instances, South Korean workers have resorted to racial slurs, calling for "driving out the Chinks."[34] One migrant worker relates the story of how his boss started to beat him with a bat when he declined the cup of coffee offered to him.[35] This type of situation is comparable to both colonial Korea as well as to the immigrant labor market of the United States. Labor organizers and activist leaders try to remind workers of the need for their solidarity, but Korean workers are reluctant to be equated with workers of other races, whom they perceive to be racially inferior. In Puch'ŏn where a large number of migrant workers work and live, migrant residents of the city put together their own cultural event, to which they, as hosts, invited the Korean community. The event was named "We, too, Love Puch'ŏn." Yi Ran-ju, a Korean activist who works with migrant workers, calls this festivity a kind of kŏming autŭ ("coming out") of migrant workers.[36] Her use of this term, borrowed from English and used mainly in the context of the South Korean gay and lesbian movement, reveals racialized migrant labor in South Korea to be clandestine.

While the South Korean state is actively involved in bringing in migrant labor, the state's production of migrant workers' political invisibility, economic disposability, and social segregation simultaneously renders migrant workers and their labor clandestine. Its clandestinity intersects with that of other labors we discussed in the previous chapters: military labor and its paradoxical invisibility as a labor in contrast to its visibility as a national service; domestic prostitution and the irony of its ubiquity and clandestinity; and military prostitution and the contradiction of its simultaneous prominence as a national issue in "high" literature and its obscurity and erasure as a socially stigmatized labor.

Racialized Neighborhoods

In the past decade, migrant workers in South Korea have gradually begun to form their respective ethnic enclaves. Following Sassen, South Korean scholar Kim Hyŏn-mi calls Seoul a "global city" that now incorporates several districts occupied by various ethnic groups, including Vietnamese, Filipinos, Chinese, Korean Chinese, Mongolians, Russians, Central Asians, Nigerians, Ghanaians, and Egyptians.[37] Small cities, like Sŏngnam, Ansan, Yangju, Koyang, and Tongduchŏn, which have attracted migrant workers from various Asian countries and as far as from Africa, are now multiracial cities. For example, the Korean Chinese, who make up about 60 percent of the entire migrant worker population, have formed "Chosŏnjok streets," also known as *chaina taun* ("Chinatown"), in the Karibong District of Seoul. The Karibong District, a neighborhood near the major industrial complex called Kuro Industrial Complex, on the outskirts of Seoul, was a place where South Korean factory workers once lived and worked in the 1970s and '80s. During the period of rapid industrialization, it was a place where domestic migrant workers from the impoverished rural areas made a living—a home away from home, and a refuge that was not a refuge. It is a place that appears often in South Korean literary works of that period, as well as those that rewrite the history of the labor and dissident movement, works that deal with the hardships of the industrial proletariat.[38] The kind of housing that migrant workers can afford in these areas is known as *pŏljip*—"beehives"—or *tchokbang*, which may be translated as a "sliced room." They are literally a sliver of a room, where one person can lie down with little extra space. And such small rooms line each floor, indeed constituting a beehive-like formation. While South Korean factory workers were occupants of this type of housing in the 1970s and '80s, in recent years 80 to 90 percent of "beehive houses" have been occupied by migrant workers as the cheapest housing available.[39] Another type of housing the companies provide for migrant workers is called in Korean *konteinŏ:* these are metal shipping containers that have been converted into rooms. As these containers have no heating system built into them, in winter people can only use electric mats and blankets to keep warm.

There has been an increase in crime in these neighborhoods, including burglary, possession and sale of illegal drugs, assault, and murder. As the case often is in ethnic neighborhoods in other contexts, such as the United States, these crimes are committed against migrant workers by other migrant workers, usually within one ethnic community. This rise in the crime rate can be directly linked to the fact that migrant workers so often experience economic hardship due to unpaid wages.[40] As in other racialized contexts, the stress and pressure that migrant workers experience is taken out on the members of their own ethnic community, rather than being directed against those who are responsible for their racial degradation, exclusion, and misery.

Furthermore, migrant workers are also victims of racially motivated crimes committed by Koreans. Because of their illegal status, which makes them unwilling to report crimes to the police, migrant workers in these neighborhoods have become targets of local Korean gangs. As migrant workers resort to arming themselves as the only means of self-protection, the local authorities are concerned about the potential for racial violence between these two groups.[41] It is reported that victims of racial violence by South Koreans are most often migrant workers who are darker skinned, usually South Asians and Southeast Asians rather than Chinese, Korean Chinese, or other lighter skinned workers, such as Iranians.[42]

The city of Ansan is populated by a large number of migrant workers working in the so-called 3D industries, as well as by the very bottom of the Korean working class, who have also become domestic migrants.[43] It is known among Korean workers as the very end point, a place where one ends up when there is nowhere else to go. Ansan became the only and last place for these Koreans to be able to make a living, alongside foreign migrant workers, because of its abundance of "difficult, dirty, and dangerous" jobs and day laboring opportunities. However, in Ansan, such Koreans make up a minority. Ansan is not only a place where the majority population, migrant workers of various nationalities, live and work, but it is also a destination for migrant workers who work in other parts of South Korea, who pay monthly or biweekly visits in order to get together with their respective compatriots to exchange information, to eat their own ethnic food, and to share their homesickness. The streets of Ansan are lined with various ethnic restaurants, and there are more signs in Chinese and other languages than in Korean.

Invoking the title of a famous poem by Pak No-hae, "The Dawn of Labor," from the days of the South Korean labor movement of the 1980s, one newspaper article calls contemporary Ansan "The Dawn of Labor in Ansan." The lines cited from the poem that speak of the rural migrants to Seoul of the 1970s and '80s—"though we are neither migratory birds nor floating clouds . . . we came to Seoul"—are now applied to migrant workers from overseas. The newspaper article draws our attention to the transient nature of their lives. The instability, precariousness, and insecurity of rural migrants of Korean ethnicity of the earlier era are now made more profound by the racialized experiences of migrant workers. These ethnic ghettos are semicolonial or internal colonial territories. Migrant workers in contemporary South Korea remind us of Koreans as colonized migrants driven out to Manchuria, Japan, the South Pacific, or the United States. Their ghostly presence in South Korea, both indelible as well as fleeting, brings us back to the former era that has not yet gone by, back to a poem by the colonial poet Han Yong-un.[44]

The Karibong District was a place associated with "bitterness" (*han,* 恨) for South Korean workers, but now their *han* is being replaced by the even more intense and deeper *han* of migrant workers. The changing history of the Karibong District offers us a very clear example of this process of substituting workers of a formerly peripheral nation, South Korea, with (migrant) workers of currently peripheral nations. It illustrates the racialized surrogacy and serial replaceability of transnational proletarian labor. As in the U.S. immigrant context, such ethnic enclaves testify to the isolation and segregation of the ethnic population from the mainstream, while such areas become not only economic centers that provide various necessary services, but also communal havens that offer emotional respite and cultural interaction among the ethnicized residents. The racial ghettos of South Korea constitute these clandestine spaces of a subimperial nation-state, one that is multiethnic, and yet one that refuses to acknowledge its multiethnicity. However, they are not just disavowed multiethnic national spaces, but also transnational and globalized spaces that offer also unexpected resistances, as we will see in the next section.

Industrial Accidents, Injuries, and Deaths

About half of migrant workers fall victim to industrial accidents within the first year of their arrival.[45] Migrant workers say that their fingers that have been cut off and thrown out would fill up several hundred rice sacks. The haunting image of lost body parts once again alerts us to the continuity between South Korean workers of the previous era, and migrant workers who currently fill these dangerous jobs no longer wanted by Koreans. One of Hwang Sŏk-yŏng's famous portrayals of rural migrants-turned-urban poor, "A Dream of Good Fortune," describes a young male worker's loss of fingers at a furniture factory, and his meager compensation of thirty dollars for them.[46] As victims of industrial accidents, migrant workers often return home dead, arriving as a box of ashes or in a coffin. Some die from the violence committed by South Korean coworkers or bosses.[47] Furthermore, migrant workers' deaths are not limited to direct dangers to which they are exposed at their workplaces. Their deaths are often a result of a combination of related physical and psychological factors, such as overwork, malnutrition, depression, and alcoholism. Others return home as permanently disabled and mutilated bodies that carry the memories of their physical hardship and psychological pain that they suffered in South Korea. While South Korean law provides for financial compensation for the victims of industrial accidents and deaths, for both legal and undocumented migrant workers, a large percentage of victims and their families are unable to collect the money that they are due from damage to their bodies and the loss of their lives.

Much of the literary and popular cultural productions on rural migrants to urban areas from the 1970s highlights the sorrows of living and dying away from home in line with the traditional Asian worldview that considers death away from home as one of the worst misfortunes. South Koreans will also remember the return of their fellow citizens, soldiers, or construction workers, whether from the Vietnam War or from the Middle East as a handful of ashes. A book of photography of migrant workers, titled *Borderless Workers*, ends with a series of pictures that capture migrant workers' funerals. One sequence of pictures concerns "The Funeral of Nuzrŭl Islam, a Bangladeshi worker, 2001," as the caption below reads. It tells us that he became a victim of an industrial accident within the period of two and a half months of his arrival in South Korea. This sequence contains a picture of the preparation of his dead body, another of the grim looks of his fellow workers, and finally a picture of his coffin at the airport before it is loaded onto the airplane. His coworkers and compatriots stand around to say their final goodbyes to him as they wipe their tears. The caption tells us that the minister/activist Kim Hae-sŏng has become an expert in the required procedures for such funerals. A couple of other pictures show the basement of the Ansan Migrant Workers' Association building, in which boxes of the ashes of migrant workers lie stacked up on top of each other and next to each other. Next to the boxes, wrapped in Korean-style wrapping cloths, we also see photo portraits of migrant workers, which we assume were used for their funerals. One large picture shows the face of a middle-aged East Asian man, broadly smiling, in the darkness of the basement. The caption explains to us that the workers' illegal status during their lifetimes prevents their remains from leaving South Korea. They must continue to be exiles, even in death. Minister/activist Kim Hae-sŏng writes, "Every time I open the basement door, my ears ring with the murmurings of the dead, their stories of injustice, here in this place where we don't even have enough time to help the living."[48] Whether dead or mutilated, migrant workers and their suffering will forever connect them, materially, to South Korea as a community, a nation, and a place.

Organizing Migrant Labor

South Korean Labor Activists: Assimilationism and Semiperipheral Discipline

Suppressing its earlier internationalist tendency in the colonial period, leftist ideology in South Korea underwent a process of intense ethnonationalization in the context of the authoritarian states' mobilization of ethnonationalism for their developmentalist and anticommunist nation-building through the 1960s, '70s, and '80s. While the ideological premise for the dissident struggle was to situate South Korea and its authoritarian regimes in relation to U.S. neocoloniality, and thus to grasp the role of the South Korean working class as serving the interests of the neocolonial, comprador, capitalist structure, the student movement in its scholarly activities and politico-economic activism remained largely and staunchly ethnonationalist, unable, or unwilling, for the most part, to make transnational or

international connections. As South Korea transitioned into a liberal democracy in the 1990s, it also saw gradual dissolution of the student movement
and the subsequent reformulation of the South Korean left in general, and
labor activism in particular.

With the influx of migrant workers from overseas starting in the late
1980s, a sector of the South Korean labor movement began to turn its
attention to organizing the racialized workforce, changing its direction
from an ethnonationalist to a transnational or internationalist struggle.
The discourse of class and ethnonation from the '70s and '80s has recently
changed to that of human rights, the multiethnic nation, and internationalism. It was in May 2001 that the Democratic Labor Union (Minju noch'ong)
launched a new division for migrant workers, holding a ceremony in the
student union building at Yonsei University.[49] Those who are carrying on
the legacy of the democratization movement of the '70s and '80s are now
attempting to reinscribe the very meaning of the famous June Struggle of
1987, endeavoring to recast it from a nationalist struggle against military
dictatorships and class polarization to a struggle for the broader global
peace and antiwar causes and the "guarantee of human rights for migrant
workers."[50]

Below, I explore whether the racial hierarchy created and maintained by
the South Korean state and capital in the labor market might be duplicated,
however unwittingly, in the sphere of labor activism, even as South Korean
labor activism consciously and assiduously contests such dominant racial
ideologies and policies. Can the legacy of South Korean labor activism from
the 1970s and '80s become a "subuniversalist," and thus "subimperialist,"
internationalism, in the process of its "transmission" to migrant workers
and its "export" to parts of Asia to which migrant workers will return? I
examine the tension between South Korean activists' leadership as a form of
semiperipheral assimilation and discipline, and migrant worker–activists'
multiple strategies of resistance vis-à-vis both mainstream domination and
the problematic aspects of the progressive agenda.

In anticipation of a deadline approaching for forced deportation in 2004,
organized migrant workers began a demonstration at Myŏngdong Cathedral in the heart of downtown Seoul. In November of 2003, workers, along
with their South Korean supporters, camped outside the cathedral and
went on a hunger strike, which lasted for over a year.[51] Migrant workers'
labor activism is very much influenced by that of South Korean workers of
the earlier era. The similarity is immediately striking, for example, in all

aspects of the rallies and demonstrations. They seemed to have inherited many of the same militarized styles of protest, such as wearing headbands, shouting slogans, thrusting their arms forward, and so on.

In addition to instruction on Marxist theories, organizational methods, strategies of resistance, and Korean language and culture,[52] the curriculum for migrant worker–activists at Sŏngkonghoe University—one of the centers of South Korean activism in earlier decades, which is continuing the traditions of social movements with its efforts now focused on migrant workers—includes the history of South Korean labor activism of the 1980s. The South Korean activists' goal is to foster a group of migrant worker–activists who will take part in the domestic struggle and who, upon return to their native countries, will take on the role of leaders, internationalizing the lessons learned in South Korea. The linkages made by Korean activists between the struggles of South Korean workers of the earlier era and the challenges faced by the migrant workers of contemporary South Korea are meant to advance international and interethnic/ interracial solidarity and to promote education, acculturation, and assimilation of migrant worker–activists. But given the hierarchy of both the economies and the levels of democratization between South Korea and other Asian peripheral nation-states, the history of the South Korean labor movement, offered as part of the "curriculum," implicitly establishes the South Korean case as an archetype or a model to be followed by contemporary migrant worker–activists. The lessons of the South Korean labor movement seem to function here as ideologies of semiperipheral normalization and subimperialist universalism in their very progressivism, unintentionally replicating the hierarchy that exists in the sphere of global capitalism and international politics.

However, we also want to acknowledge the extent to which South Korean labor activism of earlier decades had been keenly aware of the problematic and contradiction-ridden nature of the relationship between the student leadership and workers.[53] This vigilance on the part of South Korean activists, which has been extended to their contemporary relations with migrant worker–activists, has helped to transfer the leadership role to migrant workers themselves, in organizations such as the Migrant Workers' Unions of the Seoul, Kyŏnggi, Inch'ŏn Area and various Migrant Workers' Broadcasting Stations. Nonetheless, the rhetoric of "autonomy of migrant workers" (chajujŏk ijunodongja), often and emphatically urged by Korean activists, still leaves us with a sense that the issues of cultural, national, and racial hierarchy, and the potential problem of progressivist subimperial universalism, are far from having been resolved.

Migrant Workers' Resistance: Assimilation, Anti-Koreanism, and Death

While nationality does serve as a basis for forming communities among migrant workers, it cannot function as the sole basis for solidarity and organization, due to the multinational, multiethnic nature of the migrant workforce. It is their anti-Koreanism—stemming from the contingent and situated basis of their shared experiences of exploitation by, and their rage against, the South Korean government, businesses, and society at large—that unites them and produces them as a pan-Asian, pan-ethnic, anti-subimperial collective. South Koreans, whose ethnonational identity has been shaped by the continual shoring up of a sense of victimhood in relation to Japanese colonialism and U.S. neocoloniality, now must grapple with their new position in the present global order that has created an anti-subimperial population, an anti-Korean political entity. For South Koreans, the familiarity and everydayness of such words as "anti-American" (*panmi*) or "anti-Japanese" (*panil*) are related to the history of Japanese colonialism and the U.S. hegemony. But now, it is time for South Koreans to add a new concept, one that places them at the receiving end of similar anti-(sub)imperial resistance—namely, "anti-Korean" (*panhan*) sentiments from migrant workers. Those who must leave South Korea with more debt than savings, with disabilities, with missing fingers and legs, and broken backs, and family members and relatives of others who leave South Korea as a handful of ashes, have only resentment and enmity for Korea and Koreans. In one of their protest rallies, Korean Chinese workers changed one of their placards to read "Taehan minguk" (大恨民國, Republic of Great Bitterness), rather than "Taehan minguk" (大韓民國, Republic of Korea). Their slogan plays on the homonymic characters "韓" (*han*, Korea) and "恨" (*han*, bitterness). Another slogan equates the characters, Republic of Great Bitterness/Korea, 大恨/韓民國 with the "Great Republic of Exploitation" (*ch'akch'wi taeguk*).[54]

Articulation of such powerful anti-Korean sentiments sometimes takes the form of various kinds of threats. Thai workers who once worked in South Korea and have now returned to Thailand have organized an anti-Korean association. Korean Chinese workers vow their revenge on South Korea. In fact, such intensity of hatred among former migrants to South Korea, both Chinese and Korean Chinese, has resulted in some danger for South Koreans who reside in China; there has been a series of kidnapping incidents targeting South Korean businessmen and their families.[55] Furthermore, such incidents receive a great deal of attention in the South Korean media, while criminal and exploitative actions of South Korean companies and employers are rarely reported. This, of course, further angers Korean Chinese and Chinese migrant workers. While the mainstream South Korean media reports incessantly on the so-called "Hallyu" phenomenon (the Korean Wave), marveling at how South Korean cultural products are loved in Asia, they do not ask why Korea is also hated both inside and outside of Korea among migrant and offshore workers.

Migrant workers' resistance takes multiple forms, as their very sentiments and emotions about Korea are necessarily ambivalent and conflict ridden. A recent novel by Pak Pŏm-sin, *Namaste,* highlights the aspects of migrant workers' resistance that articulate their desire for integration into Korea. One of the novel's central events is a fictionalized account of the long-term demonstration by migrant workers in 2003 at the Myŏngdong Cathedral. *Namaste* has migrant workers shouting four key slogans: "We, too, are workers" (in Korean in the original); "We make Korea" (in English in the original); "We love Korea" (in English in the original); and, "We have arrived in this land together" (in Korean in the original).[56] Their declaration of their status as *nodongja* ("worker") situates migrant workers in the broader historical development of the South Korean labor movement of the 1970s and '80s, which succeeded in creating a working-class consciousness, by specifically demanding that they be treated according to the workers' rights that South Korean workers had won for themselves earlier.[57] While this working-class consciousness was once very much bounded by ethnonationalism, migrant workers' claims today break open this boundary, placing *all* South Korean workers in the larger category of the international proletariat.

The next slogan, "We make Korea," brings attention to the fact that migrant workers' labor contributes to the South Korean economy and thus necessarily also to South Korea as a society and a national community. In repudiating South Koreans' treatment and misunderstanding of migrant workers as strangers, menial laborers, and sojourners, the third slogan, "We love Korea," in its expression of affection, articulates not only their desire for integration, but also their claim on South Korea. Their last slogan, "We have arrived in this land [*ittange*] together," can be interpreted as a call for uniting migrant workers. The ambiguity of the notion of arrival, implicitly countering the notion of autochthony often associated with ethnonational identity in South Korea, however, enables us to include South Koreans in the pronoun "we" in the sentence. Just as South Koreans have arrived from somewhere else, migrant workers have also arrived in this land. Migrant workers happened to be the most recent migrants to the Korean peninsula. In the words of Sin-u, a Korean character in the novel, "This is also Kamil's country." Kamil, a Nepali protagonist, replies, "I know. It has already become my country. That's why I protest. Because I love it."[58]

In the fall of 2003, in anticipation of an upcoming deadline for the voluntary departure of undocumented migrant workers that the government had set, there was a series of suicides committed by those who found no alternative to death. The meaning of such deaths cannot be reduced to cases of exceptional desperation. Rather, their suicides necessarily take on a collective political import in the context of exploitation and persecution. For example, the suicide of a Sri Lankan worker, Dakara, became a rallying point for an organized protest by migrant workers in the fall of 2003. A suicide note by a Korean Chinese worker, "Korea is sad!" (Hangugi sŭlp'ŭda!), offered a political indictment of South Korea.[59] In addition to the already desperate financial situations that most migrant workers are forced to put themselves in to be able to come and work in South Korea, once they are captured, they must pay a fine to the INS for each month that they have stayed illegally in order for them to be able to leave South Korea. This puts them in the bizarre situation where they have to go work illegally again in order to earn enough to pay the fine. Or sometimes the only way they can leave the country is to commit a minor offence and be forcibly deported. Given the fact that illegal work in South Korea has often been made possible by the heavy debt incurred not only by the workers as individuals but also by their family and friends, neither their bodies nor their labor power has been truly theirs to freely dispose of in the first place. And when the opportunity to work and thus to buy themselves and their labor power back is taken away, they can only release their bodies and discharge themselves of their indenturedness by disposing of their body itself. Their financial and social death is actualized or literalized through their physical death. As one worker stated, "I have no hope for the future. If I am going to die anyway, I am going to die in Korea."[60] A newspaper article interprets migrant workers' suicides as crying out, "In death, we will remain in Korea!"[61] This kind of negative investment in Korea works as a vindication for the part of their lives spent in the country. Another worker reasons that if he went back home now, his entire seven years in South Korea would be rendered "meaningless."

The meaning of such "meaninglessness" that forced deportation produces also lies in the fact that forced deportations destroy the sense of self-worth and identity created by the accumulation of time spent in Korea and the specific goals they set for themselves. When their lives in Korea as migrant workers have been reduced to the labor they perform, taking their jobs away through forced deportation is indeed to take away their lives, which exist only as hopes and dreams that years of hard labor in Korea might bring to realization in the future. Under such circumstances, those migrant workers who participated in the long-term protest at the Myŏngdong Cathedral stated that they went into the struggle "ready to confront death."[62] The progressive South Korean media places the dead migrant workers whose suicides articulate a vehement critique of South Korea in the category of "martyrs" (yŏlsa), along with many other South Korean workers who sacrificed themselves in the cause of their struggle in the 1970s and '80s.[63]

In their desire to remain in South Korea in death, we recognize vengeful ghosts who refuse to leave alone the living who have wronged them. A story from the colonial period, "The Homecoming of Bellybutton Pak," tells the experience of a peasant who leaves his village for Japan and dies in a flood upon his return home.[64] The short story is in the form of the peasant ghost's monologue, addressing one of the village elders as he is walking by the stream where his remains happen to lie. He implores the village elder to dig up and give to his family a bag of coins, which is buried under his ribs alongside the river rocks. The first-person narrative of the ghost, in his desperate and yet humorous appeal and complaint to his neighbor, leaves the reader, who is invited to identify with the village elder, with the voice of the peasant ringing in his or her ear. The picture I mentioned above of the remains of migrant workers in a basement in South Korea similarly speaks to the viewer of their han.

Once migrant workers participate in labor disputes, they immediately become targets of systematic efforts by INS officials and the police to deport them. This particular tactic of blacklisting workers-turned-unionizers was a powerful tool in deterring the spread of subversive ideas during the 70s and '80s. The authoritarian regimes deployed their bureaucratic, military, and police forces at all levels to carry out such functions as rounding up, interrogating, and torturing suspected labor activists, but now the

INS performs these tasks on migrant worker–activists. A South Korean activist notes that, both then and now, members of labor movements often mysteriously disappear. The difference now is that those migrant worker–activists who disappear will eventually find themselves on a plane returning back home, forced out of the country altogether. One article pointedly observes that to persecute and penalize those who are struggling against the violation of their human rights as workers is an added infringement on their human rights, their right to protest.[65]

In 2002 immigration authorities tried to forcibly deport a migrant worker from Bangladesh, Mr. Kobil, who had participated in a demonstration lasting over seventy days against labor abuses in South Korea. While migrant workers' right of assembly is not recognized by South Korea's racially discriminatory laws, which do not confer the status of laborer on migrant workers, his right to free assembly is, in fact, protected by international human rights regulations (in Korean, kukje inkwon kyuyak). Mr. Kobil refused to cooperate with the authorities, indeed charging the South Korean government with violation of international law.[66] Although the extent to which international regulations and laws can be enforced within the specific jurisdictions of a particular sovereign nation-state still remains in question, nevertheless, such international interdictions, at the very least, can be appropriated by workers and labor activists as a strategic weapon of empowerment and negotiation.

Multiethnicization and Multiculturalism

In 1993 Chandra Kumari Kurŭng, a Nepali "industrial trainee" working in South Korea, was picked up by the police; despite her repeated protest that she was a Nepali, the police decided that she was a mentally deficient Korean vagrant (hangnyŏja). She was first sent to a woman's shelter, and then eventually transferred to a psychiatric hospital, where she spent six years and four months. When one of the psychiatrists finally recognized the egregious mistake made by a series of institutions and their officials, including doctors and nurses, she was released and returned to Nepal. Subsequently, she was able to sue the Korean government and the psychiatric hospital that had detained her; the Seoul District Court ruled in her favor and ordered payment of a monetary compensation.[67]

This incredible story is indicative of the particular racial prejudices of South Koreans. On the one hand, many are very quick to discriminate against South and Southeast Asian workers, whose skin color and physical appearance are quite different from theirs, but they simply refuse to recognize differences—ethnic, cultural, and linguistic—when it comes to someone whose appearance resembles Koreans, like Chandra Kurŭng. Rather than seeing these differences in her, they can only see an inferior version of themselves—in this case, a mentally deficient Korean. Kurŭng's repeated pleas in her broken Korean that she was a Nepali worker apparently could not break through this barrier of prejudice.

Deracializing Oppression and Koreanizing Migrant Workers

In this context of South Korea's historical shift from a mono-ethnic to a multiethnic society, the terms that distinguish Korean nationals from foreigners are being readjusted and redefined. There seem to be essentially two separate categories of "foreigners": the term "foreigner" *(oegugin)* refers mainly to whites residing and/or working in white-collar jobs in Korea, while the term "foreign workers" *(oegugin nodongja)* seems to be reserved for nonwhite migrant workers. The difference between *oegugin* and *oegugin nodongja* is one of contrast between visibility and invisibility. Gradually gaining in use, we have also seen the term *naegugin,* which may be translated as "Korean national" or more literally "domestic or internal person."

In this new historical context, in which South Korea has become a multiethnic community, if not yet a multiethnic nation-state, the very determinations of what constitutes "Koreanness" are changing—at least within the small sector of progressives and labor activists. "Koreanness" can no longer be defined by blood, ancestry, or biologistic notions of ethnicity, but by residence occupied, material circumstances shared, and the language and culture acquired by a migrant worker population. In other words, "Koreanness," beyond its exclusive association with a single ethnicity, must be defined as a social, cultural, economic, and political identity that would include subjects of multiple ethnicities. We may call this process the "multiethnicization" of Koreanness. One of the ways in which this multiethnicization of "Koreanness" is illustrated is by a deracialization of language, by which I mean the decoupling of Koreanness from certain concepts and expressions that have been intensely and exclusively associated with Korean identity. Such common words as "hometown" *(kohyang),* "loss of hometown" *(manghyang),* "homesickness" *(hyangsu),* and "foreign (other) place" *(t'ahyang)* have been closely associated with the hardship and oppression that Koreans as an ethnic collective have experienced since the colonial period and through the periods of industrialization. The discourse of "*han*" that emerged in the 1970s is another prime example of such a racialized notion. The subtitle of a Korean book of photography on migrant workers, *Borderless Workers,* is "The Record of Tragic Bitterness of Foreign Workers and Korean Chinese." This use of "*t'onghan*" (tragic bitterness)— previously associated with ethnonational tragedies, such as the Japanese colonization of Korea, national division, or the Korean War—for non-ethnic Koreans disrupts the close linkage between the Korean language and the Korean race. The deracialization of the Korean language occurs when common phrases used in the 1970s and '80s at the height of labor and antidictatorship movement, such as "alienated people" *(sowoedoen saramdŭl)* and "workers of this soil" *(ittangŭi nodongja),* are applied to the migrant workers of contemporary South Korea. Another key word of that era, *minjung* ("people"), has expanded its referent now to include multiracial migrant workers residing and working in South Korea.[68] The comparability of the material histories and experiences of various ethnic and racial groups has necessitated this delinking of these concepts and sentiments from their exclusive association with Koreans as an ethnic collective.

The deracialization of these concepts points to a simultaneous process of Koreanizing migrant workers, demonstrated by migrant workers and their children who speak Korean, eat Korean food, and act Korean—that is, perform Koreanness. While the performativity of Korean ethnicity, embodied in the acculturation process of migrant workers, unravels the exclusivist notion of Koreanness, Koreanness is simultaneously in the process of being reconstituted as relatively inclusive and heterogeneous, ready to serve the interests of the South Korean state and capital. If Korean ethnic homogeneity was once essentialized for the purpose of postcolonial nation-building under the neocolonial circumstances in the earlier decades, the heterogenized, multiracialized Koreanness, differently and differentially essentialized, is starting to prove a more effective strategy in advancing the interests of the contemporary South Korean state and capital. On the other hand, the exclusionary form of Koreanness is not transcended but rather reformulated as a dominant ethnicity and culture, one that is subimperialist and subuniversalist, in relation to other Asian ethnicities and cultures that become minoritized, racialized, and suborientalized. South Korea has clearly made a transition from a mono-ethnic nation divided by class, to a multiethnic nation whose class stratifications are determined by, and intersect with, racial hierarchy. However, both the South Korean state and mainstream South Korean society's simultaneous disavowal of this historical shift renders the racialized migrant labor force and the issues of race and multiethnicity clandestine.

Multiculturalism and its Limits

The gradual multiethnicization of South Korea in recent years has brought about the emergence of multiculturalism as a broad principle, not only in the policies and practices of the government, but also in other kinds of public spheres, such as the mass media, education, and the activism of progressive NGOs; multiculturalism as a whole has now become an indispensable strategy for managing and expanding South Korea as a subempire. However, we certainly cannot equate all multiculturalisms. As I mentioned earlier, while certain dimensions of the activities of progressive NGOs and labor groups might have unintended subimperialist effects, their multiculturalist policies must be carefully distinguished from the much more conservative multiculturalism of the government and businesses. If in the 1970s, South Korea saw the appropriation of traditional Korean culture, especially folk culture, as an instrument of resistance against the state and capital, there is a way in which various national-cultural traditions of migrant workers are being deployed both by the state and capital on the one hand, and by the progressives on the other hand for opposing though sometimes overlapping purposes. Below I examine two examples in which we see the limits of South Korea's growing multiculturalism.

Educating Migrant Workers' Children: A Tree that Grows without Roots

A picture of young Sri Lankan parents at a ceremony marking the beginning of the school year for first graders at an elementary school on a cold spring day offers a revealing look at the psychological trauma involved in parenthood for migrant workers.[69] In the center of the photo, we have a close-up of a couple, a father and a mother, in formal attire for the occasion, both of whom wear a look of extreme anxiety and worry. To be exact, we read a look of anxiousness muted by fear. As if in a concentric circle, we also see rows of Korean parents, whose faces constitute an obvious contrast: as they are smiling and chatting with one another, they look relaxed, happy, and proud of becoming parents of first graders. Because the Sri Lankan couple have their backs to the other Korean parents, from the viewer's perspective it looks as if the couple's frightened look is caused by the gazes of the Korean parents who are facing the couple's back. The Sri Lankan couple's eyes are fixed on, we assume, their child, who is not part of this photo. The absence of the child further enhances the effect of the fearfulness that their faces exhibit.

Another small picture on the left side of the page shows, we assume again, their child. The Sri Lankan first grader is wearing a fairly large nametag, like the other Korean children. It shows his Korean name in Korean script, "Kim I-san." The caption explains to us that his Korean name was given to him by a local minister/activist, and that the name means "to move a mountain"—a symbolic articulation of the difficulty involved in finally winning the legal and bureaucratic battle of gaining permission for migrant workers' children to attend school. The child, standing alone and looking sad, appears even more frightened than his parents. His Korean name, though given through the good intentions of the activist minister, nonetheless alienates him further from his own identity in this assimilationist gesture. His look of fright sets him apart from his surroundings, and especially his Korean classmates, who are happily chattering away with each other.

The South Korean government has recently allowed the children of migrant workers to attend school, although they are not able to earn credits or graduate. In other words, they are being permitted to audit classes. To be able to offer full educational opportunities to the children of migrant workers is not quite feasible without much more serious financial support from the government. For now, NGOs are doing what they can by establishing nonaccredited schools taught by volunteers. One section on migrant workers' families in a book written by a South Korean labor activist is titled *A Tree That Grows without Roots (Ppuri ŏpsi charanŭn namu)*. This phrase alludes to the name of a cultural magazine (now defunct) that was started in the mid-1970s and that was associated with the dissident movement; its name, *A Tree Whose Roots Are Deep (Ppuri kip'ŭn namu)*, attempted to reappropriate Korean tradition and culture for opposing both the authoritarian state and the neocolonial power that supported it. The contemporary labor activist's rewriting of the magazine title as *A Tree That Grows without Roots* affirms the nature of the lives of the children of migrant workers, who are placed in adverse and hostile conditions. Challenging the organicist metaphor of the nation, it suggests that migrant workers' children and families can and will grow, despite the lack of cultural and social support from Koreans or Korean society. The image of a rootless tree is a powerful image, perhaps one uniquely appropriate for the age of deterritorialized and translocal identities. I will explore such dimensions of the migrant worker community later in this chapter.

World Cup Nationalism and the Multiethnic Korea

In June 2002 South Korea and Japan cohosted an important world soccer event, the World Cup. This sporting event became an occasion for the fiercest resurgence of South Korean nationalism in recent memory. While the South Korean national team's continuing victories were creating fervor among South Koreans, one South Korean reporter interviewed migrant workers. To his surprise, they said that, naturally, they always root for South Korea. Feeling a pang of guilt, in acknowledgement of all the ill treatment and inhospitality that they endure, he characterized their love of Korea as "unrequited love."[70] Migrant workers were shouting alongside Koreans what became the most common cheer sung by the audience, "Tae~han~minguk," which simply means "Republic of Korea." They cheered on the South Korean team with South Korean flags in one hand and their respective national flags in the other hand. This type of dual or bicultural national allegiance is something new and unfamiliar to South Koreans.

What is of more interest to us is the transformation that this singsong cheer, "Tae~han~minguk," underwent after the World Cup games were over. Soon after, in July of that year, the South Korean government declared that it would forcibly deport undocumented migrant workers who had stayed over four years, while offering amnesty to those whose stay in Korea amounted to less than four years. In gatherings protesting this declaration, migrant workers and their supporters used the same rhythm to which they had sung "Tae~han~minguk," this time to shout and sing "Ch'u~bang~ch'ŏlp'ye" (Abolish Deportation).[71] The fervor with which the cheer "Tae~han~minguk" was sung during the World Cup was a crystallized expression of a fascistic ethnonationalism that is very much alive and well in this age of multiethnic and multicultural South Korea. The combination of the rhythm, so familiar to the ears of Koreans, with a critical slogan, produced a disturbing jarring effect, bringing together the rhythm that stands for a supposed ethnic homogeneity and the motto that promotes racial diversity and equality. The discrepancy between the old rhythm and the new slogan dialogizes "Republic of Korea" with "Abolish Deportation."

SOUTH KOREA AS SUBIMPERIAL IMMIGRANT NATION

"The Korean Dream"

Vladimir Tikhonov's pointed critique of South Korean subimperialism notes that South Korea functions as a surrogate power for American, European, and Japanese capital.[72] In this section, I briefly survey a few aspects of South Korean society that point to its changed status from a mono-ethnic neocolony to a subimperial immigrant nation. The frequency of a term used in the Korean media, "the Korean Dream," referring to the desire of migrant workers from overseas to come to South Korea to work, seems at first puzzling.[73] Echoing the more globally famous term "the American Dream," the South Korean counterpart implies a certain desire for equation between Korea and America as a destination for immigrants and migrants, as the term "the Korean Dream" recognizes Korea's new place in the global hierarchy as a semiperipheral metropole. It reveals South Korean triumphalism, subtly reflecting a Korean desire to subordinate migrants of other races and nationalities. South Korea's interpellation into the "free world fantasy," its dream of development, has resulted in creating a Korean version of the "free world fantasy" for other countries that are less "developed" and less "free."[74] In the U.S. context, "the American Dream" has operated as an ideological apparatus that has promoted the assimilation of immigrants, while functioning as an instrument of racial rehabilitation and creation of an interiorized exclusion of immigrants of color in particular.[75] "The Korean Dream" operates in a similar fashion: the fantasy of "Korea," consisting of images, stories, and commodities, that fuels migration is the very mechanism of intepellation and discipline by dissimulating and camouflaging the reality of institutionalized racialized labor exploitation.

The emergence of Korean as a subimperial language, that is, a language that can help one to realize one's "Korean Dream," both within the domestic and overseas contexts, is becoming an undeniable historical phenomenon. In July 2003 the South Korean National Assembly passed a law that made it mandatory for migrant workers to take a Korean language examination as part of their qualification requirements.[76] In the communities of migrant workers and their Korean labor activists, public contests for Korean language speaking have become a common enough event. While the intentions of South Korean activists are positive and supportive, and

we can even acknowledge the kinds of benefits that migrant workers themselves draw from participation, such events necessarily confirm the status
of the Korean language as a subimperial language, as the need and desire
to learn Korean is directly linked to better jobs and wages, and to realizing
financial goals and personal dreams. Their passion for Korean might be
said to resemble Koreans' fervor for English as an imperial language in the
post-1945 era. Just as the Korean protagonist of "Kapitan Ri," first a Japanese colonial subject, then a neocolonial subject in North Korea under the
Soviet Union, and then again a neocolonial subject in South Korea under
U.S. hegemony, had to learn, in turn, Japanese, Russian, and English in
order to deracialize, empower, and assimilate himself,[77] for migrant workers the Korean language has become a language that can help them inte-
grate better into the power structure. Korean language books and Internet
sites specifically designed for migrant workers of various nationalities have
become very easily available. The *Hangyŏre* newspaper reports on a Korean
language instruction book created by a Vietnamese labor brokerage firm;
many Vietnamese workers in South Korea carry this book around with
them for its usefulness. It includes the following Korean phrases: "We are
also human beings"; "Please don't hit me"; "Can we have such and such
things in writing?"; "The company must deal with this problem"; "We cannot tolerate such actions"; and, "If you hit me again, I will move to another
company." Vietnamese workers stated that, although there are many other
Korean language books published by Koreans, all containing the usual
nice phrases, they are not suited for their specific needs.[78]

The Korean language that migrant workers in South Korea use shares
certain commonalities with the English language that residents of South
Korean camp towns had to pick up around the military bases, or the
English South Korean immigrants must learn for their survival, or the kind
of Korean language that Latino workers must acquire for their jobs at
South Korean immigrant businesses in the United States. If a (sub)impe-
rial language, as an instrument of oppression, makes it possible to partake
in the power structure by enabling assimilation, it can also be mobilized as
a strategy of resistance. Like the Korean language used by Vietnamese workers in South Korea and Latino workers employed by Koreans in the United
States, Koreans' Japanese of the colonial period, and Koreans' English
under the U.S. occupation and in South Korean camp towns possessed
such similarly resistive dimensions.

Economic Membership, Reterritorialization,
and Inflexible Citizenship

While ethnicity and citizenship are being decoupled, economic participation and citizenship are being linked. At the same time, we are mindful of the fact that the growing linkage between economic contributions and citizenship does not necessarily promote racial equality, but rather advances the racial segmentation of labor. In many immigrant contexts, notably the United States, the state and capital have traditionally utilized the labor of immigrant and migrant workers while simultaneously withholding their citizenship and civil rights.[79] As immigrants have done historically in the United States, migrants and immigrants to South Korea also invoke strategies of resistance, by which they situate themselves squarely within the framework of an immigrant nation-state and seek their rights as laborers, residents, and citizens.

One of the most immediate goals for the migrant worker community is to acquire the same basic three labor rights as South Korean workers—the rights to strike, organize, and collectively bargain. Migrant workers and their South Korean colleagues have recently won a small victory in the area of political participation by gaining the right to vote in local elections and run for local offices. This recent shift in demographics is beginning to interrupt the equation between ethnicity and citizenship that has been naturalized since 1945. The illegitimacy of their identity, which the South Korean state and capital have colluded to create, must in turn come to disrupt the legitimacy of the concept of an ethnically and culturally homogeneous Korea. In order for South Korea to move beyond the model of ethnonational community, the concept of citizenship must move toward the European model of postnational citizenship that recognizes economic contributions as a basis for social entitlements and political rights. Though deterritorialized and interstial, migrant workers nonetheless seek to reterritorialize themselves as members of their adopted national community. While in limited ways migrant workers exercise the flexibility of their membership in multiple national communities as we will see below, they simultaneously try to establish themselves as inflexible citizens of their new location in a nation-state, that is, to reclaim a level of isomorphism among their territorial residence, their political rights as legal national subjects, and their social and cultural integration into South Korea.

Pak Pŏm-sin's Namaste: *South Korea as an Immigrant Subempire*

This section first examines a novel by Pak Pŏm-sin, *Namaste*, which was serialized in the *Hangyŏre* newspaper in 2004. Since the publication of *Namaste*, other South Korean writers began to treat the subject of migrant workers, while at the same time encouraging and promoting migrant workers and activists to offer their own self-representations, as the earlier generation of student activists had done with South Korean workers in the 1970s and '80s.[80] Like *Namaste*, other literary works authored by South Korean writers also illustrate the serious political limits of mainstream representations of racial minorities. As has been the case with Asian American writing, we will have to wait for the second generation multiethnic Koreans to write the history and stories of migration and immigration in South Korea.

Namaste describes the contemporaneous labor struggle of migrant workers; the serialization of the novel overlapped with migrant worker–activists' 380-day-long demonstration at the Myŏngdong Cathedral. The novel is indicative of the overall adjustment of direction in South Korean leftist politics, from the intensely ethnonationalist labor movement of the 1970s and '80s to the contemporary subimperial context that calls for an international, interracial solidarity with migrant workers. In its unreserved critique of the appalling labor exploitation, racist policies, and practices of South Korean authorities and employers, and the xenophobic discrimination by the mainstream population, the novel as a whole is a major intervention that attempts to educate the South Korean public.

While acknowledging the progressive contributions of the novel, my reading critically explores the more unconscious and unintended dimensions of the emergent South Korean leftist multiculturalism. In the novel's narrativization of an interracial romance and its suborientalism, I argue, it foregrounds the gendered sexualities of the main characters in relation to ethnicity, class, nation, and subempire as constituent dimensions in realigning and reconstructing their subjectification in the subimperial context. In *Namaste*, Korean feminine sexuality is now redeployed and resubordinated in the transnational space of the Korean subempire, while the Korean masculine sexuality of elite leftist labor activism, now detached from its exclusive association with the ethnonation and its male-centered working class, forges linkages with a pan-Asian masculine proletarian or revolutionary subjectivity.

Suborientalist Subimperial Romance:
Korea as a Mother(land), Wife, and Pupil

Sin-u, a thirty-year-old divorcee and a returnee from the United States, discovers Kamil, a Nepali worker, unconscious in her yard. His "copper" skin and his supine posture remind her of a dead animal, but what returns him to humanity is the first Korean sentence that he speaks to her when he comes to: "The world is getting brighter."[81] His smile and his words become the center from which light, further enhanced by the brilliance of mountain cherry blossoms, radiates for Sin-u. Kamil has run away from a blue jeans factory, where he was being abused by his Korean coworkers. He and his girlfriend, Sabina, a fellow Nepali, move into one of the spare rooms in Sin-u's house. While Kamil is devoted to Sabina, because of her instability and possible infidelity he eventually comes to lean on Sin-u, and they gradually fall in love. The novel represents Sin-u's changing roles vis-à-vis Kamil: first, as a nurturing mother, next, as a supportive wife, and then, as an inspired pupil.

Sin-u's attraction to Kamil, five years younger than herself, is consistently described as maternal. The night before she meets him in her yard, she has a "birth dream," foretelling the birth of a sacred mountain man (sanin). Her love for Kamil, she acknowledges, is not quite what one feels for the "opposite sex," but rather "a tearful blood relation nursed in my own bosom."[82] In Namaste's representation of the current labor politics involving migrant workers, it might seem at first curious that the "progressive" dimensions of South Korea as an immigrant nation and subempire that oppose and criticize the racist and discriminatory practices of the mainstream is imagined as the feminine and feminized authority of a mother, given the fact that the South Korean dissident labor politics of earlier decades had always been intensely androcentric and patriarchalist. However, allegorization of an immigrant nation as a mother has been common enough in the U.S. context. Just to name a couple of texts, both a Filipino American novel, America Is in the Heart by Carlos Bulosan, and a Korean American novel, Native Speaker by Chang-Rae Lee, employ the figure of a white woman to symbolize the United States as a welcoming, embracing mother of immigrants of diverse races and ethnicities.[83] If the South Korean left's understanding of itself as a remasculinizing entity was premised on South Korea's besieged and emasculated position as a U.S. neo-colony, its transition to an emergent subempire that necessitates inclusion and assimilation of a multiethnic population regenders and resexualizes South Korea as a maternal polity.

The metaphor of immigrant subempire or nation as a mother lies in a continuum with the equally familiar metaphor of the colonizer as a parental figure, paternal or maternal. The figuring of an immigrant nation as an adoptive mother or as a (re)birth mother operates as an effective sign that performs the more complex task of assimilatory and integrative domination, that is, an "interiorized" colonization of immigrants and migrants.[84] It naturalizes the territorialization of the dominated immigrant and migrant subjects, through imagining filial, bodily ties, while obscuring the more violent strategies of hierarchized, racialized assimilation and exclusion. The immigrant (sub)empire, figured as a familial, generational hierarchy, infantilizes the immigrant or migrant. Along with its portrayal of Kamil as a godly man with a halo-like brilliance around him, and as a suffering man, "blood-stained," the novel also continually depicts him as a child in the beginning of their relationship. Sin-u is struck by her impulse to breastfeed him: "I wanted to be an old cow."[85] Behind the deployment of such a maternalism, I would argue, we actually find the South Korean left in the forms of a patriarchal and paternalist author. In installing maternalism as a surrogate, proxy subimperialist agent of multiculturalism, the leftist South Korean labor politics, as exemplified in *Namaste,* colludes with other subimperial interests by facilitating domination and assimilation, while at the same time establishing itself as the vanguard in charge of fostering the Asian masses' resistance and opposition vis-à-vis the state and multinational capital.

In *Namaste* the interracial romance narrative, then, grows into Kamil's proletarian bildungsroman. Kamil has been slated to become an ethnic proletarian martyr for transnational labor activism under the invisible authority and authorship of the South Korean left. Kamil says, "Korea's gift to me is that I became an adult here." Toward the end of the novel, when Kamil is about to martyr himself for the cause, he further elaborates: "the power to think, before I came to Korea, I did not have it. Either I put up meaningless resistance or I simply submitted. Korea taught me that."[86] The maternalism in the early part of the novel prepares Kamil for his transformation from an infant into a revolutionary in the latter half. Sin-u's character undergoes a conversion from a type of subimperialist memsahib to the domesticated, supportive wife of a transnational, pan-Asian male revolutionary subject.[87] The transnational alliance of Asian male workers returns the figure of a South Korean woman as a proxy subimperialist to her supporting role on the margin, similar to the one played by the older generation of South Korean women from the 1970s and '80s. With the suicide of a migrant worker, who throws himself under an oncoming subway train, Kamil undergoes "conscientization" (ŭisikhwa). He becomes a man for the first time, awakened to the significance of a "collective," while Sin-u critically reflects upon her womanly desire to hold Kamil to his familial obligations as a father and a husband. Admiring Kamil's leadership role in the protest, Sin-u says, "Unlike before, now I was in the bosom of a warrior."[88] The novel applies the epithet chŏnsa ("warrior"), along with another term, yŏlsa ("martyr"), to Kamil and his migrant worker–activist colleagues. If these terms, used to describe South Korean workers and their student activist allies of the 1970s and '80s, create solidarity across time and across racial and cultural differences, Kamil's very emergence as a transnational Asian revolutionary subject premises itself on the exclusion of Asian female workers' solidarity among themselves, as well as the possibility of their solidarity with Asian men as equal partners.

If Sin-u plays the roles of mother and wife in the novel's treatment of the issues of immigration and migrant labor, she plays Kamil's pupil in the novel's suborientalist engagement with Nepali thought, culture, and religion, a central aspect of the text. Although Sin-u also teaches Kamil Korean language, culture, and history, her lessons on Korea are meant to offer him more of a practical and material value. On the other hand, Sin-u's learning of Nepali and South Asian thought operates as a broader intellectual framework for the novel. The relationship between Korea and Nepal in Namaste parallels those between the West and its Orient and, later, between Japan and its Orient.[89] The degree of a nation-state's capitalist development and industrialization is inversely proportional to its access to the profundities and truths of the uncorrupt, sacred, and spiritual Orient. Sin-u's immersion into the mysteries of the Himalayas signifies South Korea's economic dominance over Nepal and other Asian nations precisely by conferring on them cultural and spiritual superiority. Kamil is Sin-u's "teacher" (sŭsŭng) in the highest sense of the word.[90]

Miscegenation and Dual Allegorizations of Asian Women:
Expansion of a Subempire or Creation of a Multiethnic Utopia?

Through Sin-u and Kamil's international and interracial relationship, which produces a biracial family, Namaste reconfigures feminine sexuality, now decoupled from its exclusive subordination to ethnonation, in relation to the changed status of South Korea as a subempire. The significance of the bi- or multiracial family in the novel as a performative history, I would argue, remains ambiguous. On the one hand, Korean feminine sexuality is surreptitiously (re)assigned the allegorical role of reproductive surrogacy for expanding the subempire, imagined as a racially mixed collective. Sin-u's suborientalist agency subordinates her reproductive sexuality to affirming South Korea's dominant status over Nepal, and further fortifying it through the reproduction of biracial subimperial subjects. On the other hand, we may also posit, given the novel's progressive stance in transnational labor politics, its creation of bi- and multiracial families gestures toward radically different conceptions of Korea and Asia as a multiethnic and multiracial utopian space, constituted not only through the labor movement but also connected through blood and kinship ties. From very early on in their relationship, Sin-u's description of her feelings toward Kamil is that of "blood relation."[91]

The novel's overall representation of Sin-u's pregnancy with Kamil's child is also intensely familistic. Shortly after her mother, who returned from the United States, passes away, Sin-u discovers that she is pregnant. The fetus is acknowledged as a reincarnation of her dying mother's approval of Kamil and of Sin-u's relationship with him. Sin-u's maternal affect toward the fetus is carried over to her protectiveness towards her biracial family as a whole. This is noted as a natural sentiment that rises from the deepest part of her soul: "The sense of obligation to protect my family was budding from the interior of myself." Her pregnancy with a biracial child, placed beyond national boundaries, becomes a process in which cosmic energy is shared and brought together.[92] The birth of the biracial child accomplishes this goal of unification of a (transnational and universal) Asian proletariat in a physical and material way. During her pregnancy, it is the fetus that connects Sin-u to Kamil, and ultimately to Nepal, which represents, for her, a path to enlightenment and universal truth.

Sin-u's own nationality and ethnicity as Korean is also transformed as a result of her relation with Kamil and their procreation: "I was born in *this land [i ttang]* through the mysterious opening of life creation. . . . [T]hrough the long and rough detour of America and following the path of fateful karma, I met Kamil, who came across the ocean, and that path was now open to the Himalayas and I believe that he came to show me the path."[93] Since the Park Chung Hee era and until recently, this particular phrase she uses, "to be born in this land" (*i ttange t'aeŏna*), has always suggested the autochthony of ethnonational subjects, an inalienable linkage between the body and the territory. Sin-u's musings about their karmic meeting, "namaste,"[94] deliberately and carefully detach her from this previous notion of "this land"; *ttang* could mean soil, land, nation, or earth. In the context of the novel, Sin-u's reference to *ttang* takes on a different import, and its translation could be revised as "I was born on this earth." *I ttang*, reinterpreted in this way, marks the transition of the South Korean proletariat from ethnonationalist autochthony to pan-Asian universal identity.

Then, the novel extends the familism that had been exclusively wedded to the ethnonation in order to imagine a multiethnic (Asian) collective, a transnational society that is similarly based upon blood and kinship. We also want to note here that this interracial, transnational family-community is limited to mixing within the Asian race. Given the extremely problematic portrayal of African Americans in the portion of the novel that describes Sin-u's immigrant experience in the United States, it is difficult to say this racially hybrid, blood-related polity would include mixing with other races, such as whites, blacks, or Latinos.[95] She gives birth to a daughter, and they name her Maya in Nepali, which means love, and Aerin in Korean, which means love of neighbor. We learn at the end of the novel that Kamil also had a child with Sabina, his Nepali girlfriend whose presence Sin-u had always felt as a threat to her relationship with Kamil. Ultimately, the two women in Kamil's life, Sin-u and Sabina, play a similarly allegorical role. Kamil, who represents the transnational Asian masculine revolutionary subject, must love both Sin-u and Sabina, who symbolize his split and yet compatible loyalties for both his native country and his adoptive country. Transnational Asian proletarian masculine subjectivity is, thus, produced through an appropriation and allegorization of double (or potentially multiple) Asian female sexualities, which are at once eroticized and maternalized.

The eighty-five-day-long protest ends with Kamil's self-immolation: he throws himself out of a high window in sacrifice. The epilogue of the novel brings the reader to the year 2021, roughly twenty years after Kamil's death. The novel has the two children of Kamil meet each other for the first time, Maya/Aerin, and a young Kamil. Two young people, a brother and a sister who share the same father, are on their way to visit his grave in

Nepal. This biracial family is rooted in two cultures, and yet at the same time inherently uprooted, diasporic, and transnational. While they are said to be *mujŏkja*, one who does not have a proper place to belong, both Maya/Aerin and young Kamil, who are cosmopolitan and elite, educated respectively in the United States and Britain, are comfortable in multiple locations.

Their futural deterritorialized citizenship in the cosmopolitan elite culture contrasts sharply with the very territorialized nature of the lives of contemporary migrant laborers in South Korea. As I have argued above, there is a way in which Sin-u and Kamil's biracial and multicultural family articulates a subimperialist desire, in which a woman's reproductive sexuality, now released from its total subsumption to ethnonationality, is reappropriated as a symbolic strategy of proxy conquest. A subempire, by definition, must be inclusive, not only of other ethnicities, but also of racially hybrid subjects. On the other hand, the novel also posits this multiethnic/racial/cultural family as a transnational utopian site of future solidarity for the pan-Asian masses. This duality in the novel, in my reading, is ultimately irresolvable, reflecting the contradictory desires of the South Korean left, where memories of intense domestic struggle, triumphalism of the new subempire, and lingering ambitions for international solidarity coexist. Such contradictions inhere in this particular historical juncture in South Korea, which registers the indeterminacy of a subempire that expands through incorporation, assimilation of "others," and diversification and heterogenization of "itself."

SOUTH KOREA AS A TRANSNATION AND MIGRANTS AS TRANSLOCAL SUBJECTS

Contemporary globalization, resulting in a significantly intensified rate and scale of mobility, has changed the very nature of the movement of people from more stable and simple kinds—immigration and temporary labor migration—to less stable and more complex kinds—what some have called "transmigration."[96] In this context, we may conceptualize South Korea not only as a stable immigrant nation-state-to-be, but also as what Arjun Appadurai calls a "diasporic switching point,"[97] stretching out and connected to the larger transnational network. Thus, for some migrant workers, South Korea may only be a temporary stop on their way to another country, as economic migration is propelled by their motivation to find better jobs, better pay, and better living conditions. Some sail to

Japan via secret channels, while others aspire to travel as far the United States. Yi Ran-ju, a South Korean activist who works with migrant workers, calls it a "migration chain" *(iju sasŭl)*, in which the hierarchy of national economies causes them to move up and down and around. This very movement, often carried out "illegally" or "secretly" *(milhang)*, and globally oriented, is itself a strategy of survival and resistance that challenges the conditions of living and laboring in particular national locations. As migrants move from one country to another, their cultural assimilation and adjustment becomes a double, triple, and multiple process. When she was visiting Korean migrant workers in Japan, Yi Ran-ju ran into a Southeast Asian man who used to work in Korea but had found a job working for a Korean business that deals with Korean tourists in Japan. His Korean language ability and cultural knowledge from his past gave him this unique niche that aided him in Japan, a higher place in the "migration chain."

While successful migrants are able to capitalize on their diverse cultural knowledge in their journey through various locations, we can be sure that others find such ceaseless movements exhausting and debilitating. The difficulty of such multiple migrations approximates a kind of transnational vagrancy, where migrant labor means the barest kind of survival—one that often risks nonsurvival. Nonetheless, we do want to acknowledge certain empowering dimensions of the transnational mobility of migrant workers, and this further helps us to revise our view of South Korea as not simply an immigrant nation-state, but rather as a "transnation."[98] Migrant workers' presence in South Korea is part of their multilocal and multi-directional mobility; the complex routes and trajectories of their diaspora, to some extent, relativize their attachment, hardship, and struggle in South Korea, as the potential and actual transnational mobility of migrant workers empowers them and helps destabilize the South Korean nation-state's immobilizing powers over migrant workers.

For Appadurai, translocality refers to the production of subjectivities that are deterritorialized from single national, social, or cultural contexts, through movements, and the use of, and exposure to, "technological interactivities."[99] Migrant workers' acquisition and maintenance of social ties, cultural knowledge, political memberships, and economic participation in more than one national location generate a peculiar type of locality that is deterritorialized in the transnationalizing and globalizing cultures and contexts, and yet thoroughly embedded in the local cultures and contexts. The newly formed ethnic enclaves of migrant workers in South Korea, which can be viewed as interiorized neocolonial spaces of a subimperial immigrant nation-state, can also be simultaneously reconceptualized as a site of translocal migrant worker activism, whose resistive agency emerges out of their personal and collective interstitial, transnational contexts. Another example of the production of such translocal subjectivity is the founding of various "migrant workers' broadcasting stations" (iju nodongja pangsongguk) since 2005, which include multilingual Internet sites, radio broadcasts, and paper newspapers. Migrant workers interact with one another, with their families and compatriots in their native countries and other locations, and with mainstream South Korean society, as activists, reporters, and community members, to voice and exchange information, concerns, and opinions.

Other kinds of cultural and artistic activities, such as organizing rock bands, writing songs and lyrics, mounting art exhibits, and writing essays and poetry, are also part of the process of production of migrant worker communities' translocal identities. A rock band consisting of seven migrant workers from Myanmar, in collaboration with workers from other countries such as Nigeria, Thailand, Nepal, and China, has put out an album titled in English *What Is Life?* with lyrics in Korean written by migrant workers. They speak of how exhausted they are, their having to fight with the machines, and their longing for their families and homelands, and they sadly acknowledge their illegal status in South Korea. Their songs are simultaneously a complaint, lament, protest, and appeal for solidarity among migrants from various parts of the world, as well as South Koreans. They articulate a migrant's sense of transnational and translocal identity, hybridizing their respective cultures, their knowledge of Korean culture, and their experience in Korea, with global popular culture. Another band formed by migrant workers is called Stop Crackdown. They sing, "Did you think that foreign migrant workers were just machines who only work? We, too, are human beings who like to sing." Their lyrics echo the dying cry of the most celebrated martyr of the South Korean labor movement, Chŏn T'ae-il: "We are not machines!" The name Stop Crackdown points to the ways in which their political and economic struggle to work and survive, and the artistic expression of such struggles, form an integral whole. They sing, "though trampled upon again and again, we get up again and we move on proudly. . . . We love Korea, we love Korea."[100]

Another song by Stop Crackdown, titled "Mix Language," collects some of the most frequently exchanged phrases and sentences among Koreans and migrant workers: How are you? / Company president, team leader, factory manager / Do this one and that / After these two, work on those / Do a good job / No defective goods please! / Are you done yet? / Finished your work? / Oh, dear! / Get the hell over here, you son of a bitch! / This is wrong / How many defective ones? / This one's expensive, buy that one / Are you really a foreigner? / Your eyes are pretty / You're good-looking / Mixing blood / Are you Nepalese? / Hey, it's too noisy / Do you have this in your country? / Is there a moon in Indonesia? [Yeah, there is a moon] / Does the sun rise in Nepal? [Sure, it does] / Don't you have spoons in your country? [That's why we eat with our hands] / How long have you been in Korea? [Twelve years!] / No more to say? / Take a break / Hurry, hurry / Mixing blood / No more to say? / Take a break / Hurry, Hurry / You're good-looking / Hurry, hurry /Hurry, hurry / Hurry, hurry / Take a break.[101]

As "transnationalism" itself is embedded in the global hierarchy, or rather, it is indeed an articulation of the global economic, racial, and cultural order, the concept and practice of translocality also partakes in this hierarchy. Migrant workers' particular investment in Korea, articulated in their expression of love for Korea, must be interpreted as resistive and subversive vis-à-vis their historically specific transnational and translocal identity situated in this global order. Transnational mobility and translocal identities, while liberatory with respect to one nation, culture, or location, are bound by another set of specific constraints and determinations.[102] The translocality of their cultural productions is anti-subimperial cultural nationalist, pan-Asian, pan–Third World, subversively Korean, and oppositionally global. As we have seen, migrants' subjectivity in South Korea is necessarily multiple, positional, and nonessentializable: as emigrants, they are their native nation-state's deterritorialized citizens; as immigrants, they are reterritorialized, assimilated Koreans; as transmigrants, they are translocal subjects situated beyond and between nations.

CONCLUSION

In this chapter, I have explored three dimensions of contemporary South Korea—the state, South Korean labor activism, and migrant worker–activists—in the overlapping and yet divergent contexts of South Korea both as an immigrant nation-state in the making, and as a globalized transnation. First, I have argued that the South Korean state performs the dual, complementary roles of legislating a racially segmented labor force and managing the same through its multicultural policies. I have raised the question of semiperipheral discipline in the sphere of labor organizing, that is, whether South Korean labor activists reproduce, unwittingly, a racial, national, and cultural hierarchy by establishing the history of the South Korean labor and democratization movement as a model to be followed by migrant worker–activists. Lastly, I have discussed the dual constructions of migrant workers, as both reterritorialized subjects of South Korea and translocal subjects in the globalized networks of culture, economy, and politics. I would like to conclude the chapter by touching on some of the related topics below that I do not explore fully above.

Female Migrant Workers and "Marriage Migrants"

An important category of female migrants that has become very visible in the mainstream media in recent years is "foreign brides" or "marriage migrants" from various Asian countries, those who marry Korean farmers and settle in the countryside. These brides began arriving about a decade ago; currently, there are roughly ten thousand of these women in South Korea. Many of them are Korean Chinese, while others are from Asian nations such as the Philippines, China, Thailand, Vietnam, and Mongolia. Most arrive in Korea through the arrangement of matchmaking services. Acknowledging their role as workers and immigrants, in addition to their role as a spouse, the South Korean media began to refer to them using the term kyŏlhon ijuja, or "marriage migrants." Both groups of women—female migrant workers and marriage migrants—often experience similar kinds of discrimination and violence from their South Korean male coworkers or spouses, who exercise their gendered, racial, class power over these women. For example, one Vietnamese female factory worker was beaten to death by her South Korean coworker and boyfriend. Perhaps not surprisingly, many marriages between South Korean farmers and Asian women do not work out, due to a variety of factors, including Korean husbands' abusive treatment of their wives. Although progressive NGOs, as well as even the mainstream media, make efforts to intervene on behalf of immigrant brides, and to educate the South Korean public, the racial and gender discrimination against these women and their biracial children is a growing social problem that South Korea, as a nation, must deal with now and in the future.

Female migrants constitute about one third of the entire migrant worker population residing and working in South Korea.[103] Apart from Russian and Filipina women who enter South Korea on "entertainment visas," recruited for sex and sexualized service industry jobs, female migrant workers also enter South Korea in search of factory or other service jobs in restaurants or sales. The fact that they often suffer varying degrees and kinds of sexual harassment on the job connects these different categories of female labor migration to one another; the fact of race, nationality, and class exploitation is always already compounded and complicated by simultaneous gendered and sexual proletarianization.[104]

Contemporary South Korean Diaspora: Cosmopolitanism, Education-Immigration, and Labor Migration

One of the peculiarities of a subempire consists of the multidirectional flows of migration. In conjunction with the recent influx of migrant workers into South Korea, there is also a continuing outflow of South Koreans to various locations around the globe, to the core countries as well as to the peripheral regions. The diversity of the contemporary South Korean diaspora is a stratified phenomenon. While the elite and upper class of South Korea continue to gravitate toward the metropolitan centers of Europe and North America with increased ease, frequency, and affluence, the South Korean middle class also continue to aspire to catch up with its elite counterpart in its desire for t'al-han'guk ("escaping Korea"); they may accomplish their ambition by travel and tourism, or by so-called "education-immigration," or by different kinds of study, training, and work overseas. Middle-class businessmen have also made advances into various Southeast Asian locations, such as Vietnam, Laos, Myanmar, Indonesia, and the Pacific Islands, finding lucrative the economic opportunities and ventures that developing countries offer.[105] The South Korean publishing industry provides guidebooks and manuals for the would-be adventurers, and the mainstream media regularly reports on the successful entrepreneurs in various locations. In something of a contradistinction to the triumphalism accorded the multinational corporations and their mythic success, the media often portray these overseas small- to medium-sized businesses in the tradition of pied-noir colonial settlers, all-sacrificing pioneers in the hinterland, educating the natives and selectively assimilating into local cultures, and ultimately patriotic expatriates. South Korean entrepreneurial migrants overseas function as deterritorialized and yet isomorphic sub-imperializing agents who expand the invisible yet tangible boundaries of South Korea as an economic nation-state. Their relative affluence and technological networks of culture and communication make it easier for these South Korean businessmen and their families, in contrast to migrant workers in South Korea, to maintain their national and cultural identity and to incorporate themselves into more metropolitan cultures (for example, by sending their children to private international schools), rather than being assimilated into the cultures of the dominated. On the other hand, the very bottom sector of the South Korean working class, including day laborers, construction workers, and sex workers, find themselves migrating to the neighboring wealthy nation, Japan, making up one fifth of its migrant labor force.[106] The deepening polarization of South Korea as a postindustrial semiperiphery has articulated itself in these radically contrasting out-migrations of its people.

Pan-Koreanism, Deterritorialized Subempire, and Renationalization

The recent emergence of South Korea as an economic power has also caused a reverse flow of diasporic Koreans from different locations back to South Korea. Chinese Koreans have entered South Korea, mostly as unskilled labor, while ethnic Koreans from North America have been attracted to the opportunities offered by big businesses in South Korea. The South Korean state has also made concerted efforts to organize and utilize various groups of ethnic Koreans from all parts of the world—Asia, North America, South America, and Central Asian states of the former Soviet Union—as potential sources of labor in the globalized economy. The incorporation of overseas ethnic Koreans into South Korean transnational capitalism is a stratified process that takes into account the economic and cultural standing of their respective nation-states. Whether racialized (as in the case of Korean Chinese) or Westernized or Americanized (as in the case of Koreans from North America), overseas ethnic Koreans are recruited to function as a transnational surrogate labor force in the interest of the expanding subempire. The idea of pan-Koreanism conceptualizes the overseas Korean population as part of the larger homogeneous ethnic body, despite, or rather because of, their cultural and linguistic heterogeneity, spanning the globe. The heterogeneity of homogeneous diasporic Koreans serves the new subimperial Korea. In the era of South and North Koreas' "economic cooperation"—including, among other ventures, the opening of the Kaesŏng Industrial Complex—in which we are facing the strange but real possibility of North Korean workers becoming "overseas" Koreans or "offshore" workers for South Korean capital, North Korea has now been reduced to one of South Korea's diasporic locations.[107] The global Korean diaspora that has resulted from the peninsula's domination by a series of foreign powers from the late nineteenth century through the early 1980s have now taken on the new role of contributing to the formation of Korea as a transterritorial or deterritorialized subempire.[108]

While this chapter has emphasized the incipient erosion of South Korea's mono-ethnicity and its national boundary, I also want to point to the simultaneous hardening of the ethnonational boundary. This re-nationalization, associated with the prevailing mood of triumphalism in South Korea, can also be concretely tied to the concerted efforts, on the part of the South Korean state and capital, to create a pan-Korean network abroad of diasporic Koreans in various locations on the globe whose Koreanness is similarly heterogenized and yet re-essentialized, as in the domestic context. As the South Korean state's management of migrants and diasporics inside and outside of South Korea, both exclusionary and inclusionary strategies, consists of models borrowed from imperial and postwar Japan and from the post–civil rights era United States, the South Korean governmentality over migrants and diasporics is culturally and temporally multilayered. In thinking about these two broad groups together, the migrant and immigrant population in South Korea on the one hand, and the ethnic Korean diasporic population overseas on the other, we see that Koreanness has become multiracial, multicultural, and multilocal. In both cases, Koreanness is multiply hyphenated for multiracial parentage, for multiple migrations and for multiple cultural identifications. Within South Korea we have, for example, immigrant Koreans, second-generation Koreans, Filipino Koreans, or Korean Chinese Koreans. And in North America we have Korean residents of Japan, Chinese Koreans, and Korean Chinese, who are now fast becoming part of Asian America. In the context of their overlapping similarities and the singular differences among these groups of various Koreans, some are already imagining and creating connections, interactions, and alliances that would be effective in carving out spaces of resistance to redefine and redeploy progressive, open-ended, and heterogeneous Koreanness vis-à-vis the hegemonic forces organized by the South Korean state, capital, and the mainstream media, despite the profound economic, cultural, and historical divides.

Through the process of rehierarchization and restratification of the global capitalist order in the post-1945 era, the South Korea that was a postcolonial and neocolonized space only twenty years ago has now been transformed into a subimperial space, to which postcolonial subjects from other parts of Asia are congregating, falling short of reaching other metropoles.[109] In the complex and contradictory terrain of South Korea, where multiple historicities and heterogenous spaces coexist, it has become increasingly difficult to separate the forces of oppression and resistance, as they have become entwined with each other; the legacies of coloniality and neocoloniality have become indeterminate in that they have rearticulated themselves in both directions, replicating colonial power as well as anticolonial resistance. If thirty-six years of colonialism brought about unprecedented changes to what was then known as Chosŏn, the history of labor migration over twenty years in South Korea, one which will continue into the forseeable future, has already laid the foundations for profound changes to come for what is still known as the Republic of Korea.

Postscript

The Exceptional and the Normative in South Korean Modernization

If Japan's reemergence as an economic superpower in the 1960s and '70s was touted as an instance of a model minority nation-state,[1] South Korea, along with other Asian "tiger" economies, followed in Japan's footsteps in the late '80s and '90s, another case of fulfilling the myth of the model Asian minority nation-state in the global capitalist context. In this last section of the book, in an effort to think through the in/validity of such discursive constructions, I would like to place South Korean development in the broader transnational context of the postwar era and consider briefly the ways in which the conditions of South Korean industrialization simultaneously overlapped with, and differed from, those of other Third World national contexts.

In the last half of the twentieth century, various Asian countries, such as Japan, the Philippines, Thailand, Taiwan, and South Korea among others, aligned with the United States, provided different kinds of labor for U.S. anticommunist military engagements in Asia (the Korean War and the "Vietnam Wars"),[2] gaining a range of economic benefits throughout the cold war era. They supplied products needed to carry out the wars and to maintain the local wartime economies; in this way, Asian industrial and manufacturing labor participated in U.S. militarism. Many Asian countries where the United States stationed its military—Japan, the Philippines, Thailand, and South Korea—provided military prostitution around the bases. The Philippines, in the course of its status as a colony and neocolony of the United States, also provided U.S. militarist ventures in Asia with a military proletariat in addition to military sex workers. In other words, U.S. anticommunist militarism in Asia was necessarily an integral part of the historical process of economic development and industrialization for the Asian allies of the United States.

The case of South Korea, however, departs in a few ways from its Asian neighbors, in its relation to U.S. militarism specifically, and to the global history of capitalism in general. South Korea's dispatching of its troops— its military proletarianization on behalf of the U.S. empire—became a crucial turning point in its economic development, through its forging of intimate relations with the United States and in its solidification of its position as a junior partner to the United States. South Korea's own experience of a "hot war," and its continuing confrontation with its own communist enemy, North Korea, further consolidated its position as a strategically central ally of the United States. South Korea, unlike some countries and regions of formerly colonized Asia, had already undergone industrialization under Japanese colonialism, and thus it possessed a certain infrastructure, and more importantly, it could draw on an interpellated elite class and a disciplined workforce.

As many have pointed out, since the beginning of modernity in Europe, the processes of military, industrial, and sexual proletarianization have been transnational phenomena. The European conquest of the rest of the globe in the late nineteenth century further complicated this multiple and intersecting proletarianization, which had already involved class, gender and sexuality, and nationality, by producing colonized and racialized military, industrial, and sexual proletariats. In the post-1945 era, the mode of mobilization of the global workforce has undergone a significant shift; global capital's need for racialized military, industrial, and sexual proletariats persists, but they are now either "offshore" workers in their "own" sovereign native nation-states, or they are migrant or immigrant workers in various imperial and subimperial locations.

South Korea has not been an exception in having supplied both kinds of transnational labor to other advanced nations during the decades of the 1960s, '70s, and '80s, and in more recent history, South Korea has also followed the norm of other newly industrialized Asian nations that have begun to utilize offshore and migrant and immigrant labors for their semi-peripheral economies. The "miracle" of South Korean development of the earlier and contemporary eras can be attributed to transnational labors at these two consecutive stages. First, South Korea deployed its own working class as transnational workers at home and abroad; when it had drained itself of its own cheap labor, it moved to appropriate other ethnicized labors, through offshore relocations and labor importation—that is, through subimperial external and internal colonizations.

Both South Korean industrialization under military dictatorships and the forces that opposed them—the democratization and labor movements—were intensely ethnonationalized through the three decades between the 1960s and '80s. And, until very recently, the South Korean historiography that recorded and interpreted these interlocking processes was equally bound within the ethnonationalist framework. As we have moved into the 1990s, when South Korea's demographics began to change noticeably due to the entry of migrant and immigrant workers, and South Korean capital was fast becoming a transnational enterprise, South Korean historiography also started gradually to readjust itself to the transnational framework, not only in terms of its contemporary history, but also in its exploration of its colonial and premodern pasts.

Another tendency in contemporary South Korean scholarship in various disciplines has been to "overcome" the category of ethnonation by a simple elision. Rather than think through the very complex historical process of the construction of modern ethnonationalism, for some the ethnonation has become a category that is no longer relevant in this new age; we see some South Korean historiography moving in a non-ethnonationalist, or even anti-ethnonationalist direction. In such an approach, the category of ethnonation, unthought and undisturbed, will remain reconstituted and even reinvigorated. A transnational historiography of modern Korea necessarily places the category of ethnonation, which has played an essential role in the very construction of modern Korea, in the interstices of other nation-states, and in the interstices between the category of ethnonation and other relevant categories such as race, sexuality, gender, and class.

Notes

INTRODUCTION

All translations of the passages cited from literary works from Korean into English are my own unless otherwise noted.

1. Virilio, *Speed and Politics*, 12.

2. Cho and Eckert, introduction to *Hanguk kŭndaehwa*, 11–56.

3. See, for example, Koo, *Korean Workers*; Hart-Landsberg, *The Rush to Development*; Lie, *Han Unbound*; Eun Mee Kim, *Big Business, Strong State: Collusion and Conflict in South Korean Development, 1960–1990* (Albany: State University of New York Press, 1997); Jung-En Woo, *Race to the Swift: State and Finance in Korean Industrialization* (New York: Columbia University Press, 1991); Dong-sook Shin Gills, *Rural Women and Triple Exploitation in Korean Development* (New York: St. Martin's, 1999); Seung-kyung Kim, *Class Struggle or Family Struggle?*; Yi Pyŏng-ch'ŏn, *Kaebal tokjaewa Pak Chŏng-hŭi sidae.*

4. Virilio, *Speed and Politics*, 30.

5. Ibid., 62, 43, 30.

6. Ibid., 83.

7. Barry, *The Prostitution of Sexuality*, 122–23.

8. I borrow the term "productive potential" from Escobar, *Encountering Development*, 21–101.

9. Mbembe, "Necropolitics," 11–40. Giorgio Agamben, *Homo Sacer: Sovereign Power and Bare Life*, trans. Daniel Heller-Roazen (Stanford: Stanford University Press, 1998), 119–88.

10. The etymological origin of the word "proletariat," dating back to the Roman Empire, means "serving the empire with one's offspring," according to the *Oxford English Dictionary.*

11. See An Yŏn-sŏn's discussion of the testimony of one of the surviving Comfort Women on how they were treated as a *somop'um*, "disposable commodity," in *Sŏng noyewa pyŏngsa mandŭlgi*, 103–4.

12. Mbembe, "Necropolitics," 11–40.

13. See Chuh, *Imagine Otherwise*.

14. Foucault, *History of Sexuality*, 140–43.

15. Ibid., 146.

16. Ibid., 103–14. Foucault goes only so far as to say that members of the bourgeoisie had first tried the new mode of governance through sexuality for themselves, only later to impose it upon the working class.

17. Ibid., 104.

18. Ibid., 114.

19. Weeks, *Sex, Politics, and Society*, 30; Walkowitz, *Prostitution and Victorian Society*.

20. In *The History of Sexuality*, Foucault is very wary of our reverting back to the notion of sexuality as a drive or instinct or energy that can then be conceptualized as something simply to be repressed and then appropriated for labor (114).

21. Foucault, *History of Sexuality*, 24.

22. Ibid., 146.

23. Ibid., 163.

24. Virilio, *Speed and Politics*, 31.

25. Ibid., 113. Virilio further describes this mass of proletarian workers as one deprived of will, mind, or emotion, as "creation of the presence in the world of bodies without will[;] . . . multitude of bodies with no soul, living dead, zombies" (76).

26. Military training has provided the model and principle for disciplinary procedures not only for various kinds of institutions, such as school, hospital, and prison, but also for "preventing civil disorder" in general (Foucault, *Discipline and Punish*, 169).

27. Ibid., 135.

28. Ibid., 137.

29. See Tadiar, *Fantasy-Production*, 55–56, 115.

30. Chasin, "Class and Its Close Relations," 77–78.

31. Chakrabarty, *Provincializing Europe*, 50.

32. Stoler, *Race and the Education of Desire*; Omi and Winant, *Racial Formation in the United States*, 77–91.

33. Stoler, *Race and the Education of Desire*, 60–61.

34. Nagel, *Race, Ethnicity, and Sexuality*, 14.

35. Miyoshi, "A Borderless World?" 78–106.

36. Omi and Winant, *Racial Formation in the United States*, 77–91.

37. Omi and Winant write in their influential book, "Race is an unstable, decentered complex of social meanings constantly being transformed by political struggles . . ." (cited in Lowe, *Immigrant Acts*, 10).

38. Lowe, *Immigrant Acts*, 60–83.

39. See Latham, "Introduction," 4–7.

40. Seungsook Moon, *Militarized Modernity and Gendered Citizenship in South Korea*, 1–43.

41. As economic development as such was the foundation of democracy, Park Chung Hee argued, true democracy was not possible when Korea had not reached a level of development. As Park's military dictatorship was further strengthened through a constitutional amendment that would ensure his reelection by a national assembly dominated by his own appointees in 1972, he put forth the idea of "Korean-style democracy."

42. See Eckert, *Offspring of Empire*.

43. The ideology of modernization became possible only after the end of World War II, as biology gradually gave way to notions of race and ethnicity as more culturally based (Latham, "Introduction," 4–5).

44. Seungsook Moon, *Militarized Modernity and Gendered Citizenship in South Korea*, 1–43.

45. Jin-kyung Lee, "Sovereign Aesthetics," 77–107.

46. Clifford Geertz, cited in Latham, *Modernization as Ideology*, 13.

47. Escobar, *Encountering Development*, 5.

48. I do not mean to elide other important factors that were at work in South Korean industrialization. In order to realize one of the most important pledges that Park Chung Hee made to the South Korean public following the coup, building an "autonomous economy" *(charip kyŏngje)*, one of the key things that Park did was to establish what became a central organization in his administration in the years to come, the Economic Planning Board (Kyŏngje kihoegwon) in 1961. The EPB, working closely with Park and his top advisors, became a powerful organ responsible for designing and executing the series of five-year plans, overseeing a chain of governmental departments. The fact that the office of the minister of the EPB was elevated to that of the vice prime minister in 1963 clearly illustrates the ways in which the military government prioritized economic development, forging an intimate and powerful relationship between military leadership in the political machine and the economic sphere that would come to include technocrats, academics, and industrial leaders. The EPB implemented four rounds of five-year plans in the course of Park's eighteen-year reign from 1961 to 1979. See Cho and Eckert, *Hanguk kŭndaehwa*, 116, 128.

49. The New Village Movement that followed attempted to stabilize the unevenness to some extent, proposing "uprooting poverty" in the rural areas as its foremost goal. While the movement traces its origin to the colonial period, the post-liberation version of the revitalization efforts of the rural area should also be linked to the U.S.-led modernization projects that were carried out globally, such as "villigization" programs in South Vietnam during the war (Latham, "Introduction," 6). The Strategic Hamlet program in South Vietnam may have uncanny connections with South Korean New Village Movement, considering the role that organization of villages played in promoting surveillance among villagers in the stringently anticommunist, militarized atmosphere of South Korea.

50. Lie, *Han Unbound*, 80, 99.

51. See, e.g., Eun Mee Kim, *Big Business, Strong State*; Jung-En Woo, *Race to the Swift*.

52. Yi Pyŏng-ch'ŏn, introduction to *Kaebal tokjaewa Pak Chŏng-hŭi sidae*, 49–50.

53. Hagen Koo, *Korean Workers: The Culture and Politics of Class Formation*, (Ithaca: Cornell University Press, 2001); Hart-Landsberg, *The Rush to Development*.

54. Lie, *Han Unbound*, 99.

55. Ibid., 100.

56. Ibid., 98–100.

57. Ibid., 245.

58. See Hwang Sŏk-yŏng's recent novel, *Sim Ch'ŏng: Yŏnkkoch'ŭi kil* (Seoul: Munhakdongne, 2007), which problematizes this very issue. Sim Ch'ŏng is a heroine of a folk tale who sells herself as a human sacrifice in order to pay off her blind father's debt.

59. Enloe, *Bananas, Beaches, and Bases*, 168.

60. Escobar, *Encountering Development*, 173.

61. Seungsook Moon, *Militarized Modernity and Gendered Citizenship in South Korea*; Eckert, "5.16 kunsa hyŏkmyŏng," 96.

62. Yi Pyŏng-ch'ŏn calls the role of the Vietnam War in the process of South Korea's development "the state strategy of utilizing war," and argues that the "triangle of South Korea-the U.S.-Vietnam" was an indispensable historical condition for South Korean development (see Yi Pyŏng-ch'ŏn, introduction to *Kaebal tokjaewa Pak Chŏng-hŭi sidae*, 53).

63. These twin slogans were, in Korean, "Charip kyŏngje" and "Chaju kukbang" (Yi Ki-jun, "Kukka kyŏngje chŏngch'aekŭi chedojŏk kiban," 146).

64. For the ways in which the South Korean military leadership was aided by the American government's military assistance, which not only provided weaponry and supplies, but also trained the South Korean military elites, see Eckert, "5.16 kunsa hyŏkmyŏng," 97.

65. Seungsook Moon, *Militarized Modernity and Gendered Citizenship in South Korea*.

66. Yi Pyŏng-ch'ŏn, introduction to *Kaebal tokjaewa Pak Chŏng-hŭi sidae*, 50.

67. Ibid., 59.

68. Ch'oe Ho-il, "Kukka anbo wigiwa yushin ch'eje," 173.

69. Escobar, *Encountering Development*, 34.

70. Sen, *Development as Freedom*.

71. Escobar writes about the powerful fear in the United States that not supplying poor countries with economic aid would result in their succumbing to the pressures of communism (*Encountering Development*, 34).

72. Escobar, *Encountering Development*, 5.

73. See T. Fujitani's discussion of Japan as a model minority nation in the cold war era ("Go for Broke, the Movie," 5).

74. An Yŏn-sŏn, *Sŏng noyewa pyŏngsa mandŭlgi*, 22.

75. Appadurai, *Modernity at Large*, 172–77.

76. Ibid., 172.

77. Cho Sŏn-jak, *Misŭ Yangŭi mohŏm*, 2:246.

1. SURROGATE MILITARY, SUBEMPIRE, AND MASCULINITY

1. See Han Hong-gu, "Betŭnam p'abyŏnggwa pyŏngyŏng kukkaŭi kil," 287–310. The number of South Korean soldiers in Vietnam averaged about 50,000 per year. About 5,000 South Korean soldiers died, and over 16,000 were injured in the war. Approximately 60,000 veterans and their children have suffered from the effects of Agent Orange. About 1.2 million Vietnamese died, and 3–4 million were injured during the war. See Tae Yang Kwak, "The Anvil of War: The Legacies of Korean Participation in the Vietnam War" (PhD diss., Harvard University, 2006).

2. Young, *Vietnam Wars*, 158.

3. See Heonik Kwon's *After the Massacre: Commemoration and Consolation in Ha My and My Lai* (Berkeley: University of California Press, 2006) on South Korean troops' massacres in the Vietnam War.

4. See Virilio, *Speed and Politics*, 3–36, 61–95. Domestic prostitution has attracted the attention of South Korean (often Christian) feminist activists; similarly, military prostitution for U.S. servicemen has generated much influential work in the United States in recent years. See Katharine Moon, *Sex among Allies;* Yuh, *Beyond the Shadow of Camptown.* See also Kim Hyŏn-mi's recent work on female migrant work in the South Korean "entertainment business" (*Gŭlobal sidaeŭi munhwa pŏnyŏk*, 147–80), and Cheng Sealing's "Sarangŭl paeugo sarange chukgo," 229–55. Also see Chŏng Hŭi-jin, "Chugŏya sanŭn yŏsŏngdŭrŭi inkwon," 300–358.

5. Mbembe, "Necropolitics," 11–40.

6. Ibid., 18.

7. See Meredith Woo-Cumings's notion of the developmental state in South Korea and East Asia, in her introduction to *The Developmental State,* 1–31.

8. See McClintock's notion of "commodity racism" (*Imperial Leather,* 207–31).

9. Yi Pyŏng-ch'ŏn, "Kaebal tokjaeŭi chŏngch'i kyŏngjehakgwa hangukŭi kyŏnghŏm," 17–65. Seungsook Moon, *Militarized Modernity and Gendered Citizenship in South Korea,* 1–43.

10. Hyung-A Kim, *Korea's Development under Park Chung Hee: Rapid Industrialization, 1961–79* (London: RoutledgeCurzon, 2004), 101, 111. Kwon In-suk, *Taehan mingugŭn kundaeda,* 46.

11. *Betŭnam chŏnjaeggwa hangukgun* [The Vietnam War and South Korean Military], produced by Kukbang hongbowon [Publicity Agency for National Defense], 2003, documentary available at *Wolnamjŏngwa hanguk* [The Vietnam War and the Republic of Korea], http://www.vietvet.co.kr (accessed May 17, 2010).

12. One of the many military marching songs of the era goes, "you, my beloved, will be in the land divided into North and South under the Vietnamese sky." See *Wolnamjŏngwa hanguk,* http://www.vietvet.co.kr, for the lyrics of the song "Maenghonŭn kanda" [The Brave Tigers' March].

13. See Kim Hyŏn-a, *Chŏnjaengŭi kiŏk/kiŏgŭi chŏnjaeng*, 100–105.

14. See *Wolnamjŏngwa hanguk*, http://www.vietvet.co.kr, for the lyrics, along with lyrics for "Chinjja sanai" [A Real Man], another popular military song.

15. See *Betŭnam chŏnjaeggwa hangukgun*, at *Wolnamjŏngwa hanguk*, http://www.vietvet.co.kr.

16. Kang Chun-man, *P'yŏnghwa sijangesŏ kungjŏng-dongkkaji*, 2:246–49.

17. Ibid., 2:248.

18. Armstrong, "America's Korea, Korea's Vietnam," 533.

19. For the notion of intersections between ethnicity and sexuality, called "ethno-sexuality," see Nagel, *Race, Ethnicity, and Sexuality*, 1–61.

20. See Han Hong-gu, "Betŭnam p'abyŏnggwa pyŏngyŏng gukkaŭi kil," 295.

21. Ibid., 300.

22. See the newsreel footage of the 1973 welcome ceremony at *Wolnamjŏngwa hanguk*, http://www.vietvet.co.kr.

23. "Sergeant Kim Who Returned from Vietnam" was sung by Kim Ch'u-ja in 1969. This singularly popular song was made into a movie with the same title in 1971. When we consider that most South Korean soldiers sent to Vietnam came from the countryside, it is not surprising that the film was regularly shown to middle and high school students in the provinces. The film is said to portray the returning Vietnam veterans' readjustment to life back in Korea "comically," performatively erasing the five thousand or so soldiers who did not return.

24. Available at *Wolnamjŏngwa hanguk*, http://www.vietvet.co.kr.

25. Debord, *Society of the Spectacle*, cited in Jeffords, *The Remasculinization of America*, 52.

26. Seungsook Moon, *Militarized Modernity and Gendered Citizenship*, 27–43.

27. I am borrowing T. Fujitani's term "visual domination" in his conceptualization of the Japanese emperor Meiji's role as modernizing in various state ceremonies, rituals, and pageants (*Splendid Monarchy*, 18–28).

28. See Seungsook Moon, "Begetting the Nation," 43–44.

29. Virilio, *Speed and Politics*, 12, 30.

30. "Industrial warrior" is a translation of the Korean term sanŏp chŏnsa (Koo, *Korean Workers*, 12–13). Virilio, *Speed and Politics*, 30.

31. Virilio, *Speed and Politics*, 77.

32. An Chŏng-hyo, *White Badge*, 75. An translated his own novel, first published in 1983 in Korea as *Hayan chŏnjaeng* (White War). The Korean original has three volumes, of which *White Badge* is the first volume. All citations from *White Badge* are from An's translation.

33. See Brian Thompson, "Surrogate Armies: Redefining the Ground Force," *Chairman of the Joint Chiefs of Staff Strategy Essay Competition*, January 1, 2002, 1–21. See also Joshua Kurlantzick, "Outsourcing the Dirty Work: The Military and Its Reliance on Hired Guns," *American Prospect*, May 1, 2003, 1–17.

34. Kang Chun-man, *P'yŏnghwa sijangesŏ kungjŏng-dongkkaji*, 2:248.

35. See Jeffords, *The Remasculinization of America*, 122–23.

36. Spivak, "Scattered Speculations on the Question of Value," 117.

37. An Chŏng-hyo, *White Badge*, 40.

38. Han Hong-gu, "Betŭnam p'abyŏnggwa pyŏngyŏng kukkaŭi kil," 300.

39. See *Betŭnam chŏnjaeggwa hangukgun*, at *Wolnamjŏngwa hanguk*, http://www .vietvet.co.kr.

40. Chalmers Johnson calls the post-1945 United States "an empire of bases, not of territories and these bases now encircle the earth" (*Sorrows of Empire*, 188).

41. Hwang Sŏk-yŏng, "Changsaŭi kkum" [The Dream of a Hero], in *Hwang Sŏk-yŏng chungdanp'yŏn chŏnjip*, 3:9–29.

42. Foucault, *History of Sexuality*, 1:53–73.

43. Hwang Sŏk-yŏng, "Changsaŭi kkum," 9.

44. Ibid., 28.

45. Ibid., 19.

46. Ibid., 22.

47. Ibid., 28.

48. See Kim Hyŏn-a's interview of South Korean veterans in *Chŏnjaengŭi kiŏk/kiŏgŭi chŏnjaeng*, 227–30.

49. An Chŏng-hyo, *White Badge*, 57.

50. Ibid., 71, 173.

51. Goldstein, *War and Gender*, 265.

52. Ibid., 349.

53. Robin Morgan, *The Sexuality of Terrorism* (New York: Norton, 1988), cited in Goldstein, *War and Gender*, 350.

54. Hwang Sŏk-yŏng, "Toraon saram" [One Who Returned], in *Hwang Sŏk-yŏng chungdanp'yŏn chŏnjip*, 1:119–20.

55. Jeffords, *Remasculinization of America*, 54–59.

56. Hwang Sŏk-yŏng, "Toraon saram," 118–19.

57. An Chŏng-hyo, *White Badge*, 201.

58. Ibid.

59. Major portions of Kim Hyŏn-a's book *Chŏnjaengŭi kiŏk/kiŏgŭi chŏnjaeng* consist of interviews with Vietnamese victims of the South Korean military's civilian massacres and rapes. It also tells us about various collective efforts on the part of Vietnamese to deal with these memories of trauma and the war crimes committed by members of the South Korean military (*Chŏnjaengŭi kiŏk/kiŏgŭi chŏnjaeng*, 51–98, 113–202).

60. Goldstein, *War and Gender*, 362.

61. See An Chŏng-hyo's *Hayan chŏnjaeng*, the original Korean version of *White Badge:* "I was a soldier who must act according to the commands given to me. I was trained to kill human beings and was compensated for such a job and I ultimately came to carry out the order that I kill. In such an act, the entity, 'I' cannot exist. 'I' does not know 'I' and 'I' am not 'I.' One who does not know what one does, one who can act

without motives, is what a soldier is. He is a small wheel that must turn according to the movement of the machine" (1:210).

62. An Chŏng-hyo, *White Badge*, 261.

63. "I could not erase self-hatred and shame. I tore another human being to pieces as if I were a primitive animal. . . . Unforgivable acts remained as a large stain on my soul. I was an executioner, with a black scarf around my face, wielding an axe wildly" (An Chŏng-hyo, *White Badge*, 261).

64. A recent U.S. documentary film, *Sir/No Sir* (dir. David Zeiger, 2006), records various kinds of rebellions and resistance by U.S. soldiers drafted for the Vietnam War, which amounted to an underground movement by soldiers and veterans with activities ranging from enlisted men's attacks on officers to 500,000 cases of desertion.

65. Hwang Sŏk-yŏng, "Molgaewŏlŭi sae" [Birds of Molgaewŏl], in *Hwang Sŏk-yŏng chungdanp'yŏn chŏnjip*, 3:181.

66. Ibid., 190.

67. Ibid., 182.

68. Ibid., 189.

69. Cho Sŏn-jak, "Yŏng-jaŭi chŏnsŏngsidae" [Yŏng-ja's Heyday], in *Hanguk sosol munhak taeg ye*, 108.

70. Ibid., 119.

71. Ibid., 120.

72. Hwang Sŏk-yŏng, "T'ap" [A Pagoda], in *Hwang Sŏk-yŏng chungdanp'yŏn chŏnjip*, 1:56.

73. See Tadiar, *Fantasy-Production*, 55–56, 115.

74. An Chŏng-hyo, *White Badge*, 71.

75. Pak Yŏng-han, *Mŏnamŏn ssongbagang*, 115–16. The two-volume novel is an expanded version of a novella published under the same title in a literary journal in 1977 (*Segye Munhak* [World Literature], Summer 1977, 260–365).

76. Considering the fact that disabilities as well as deaths have been excised from any official account of this military history, even such a clandestine remembrance from the 1970s offers resistance. There are very few South Korean literary representations of the Vietnam War where disabled veterans appear. An's *White Badge* "recalls" amputee veterans panhandling on city buses, as the Vietnam-bound soldiers nervously make fun of them by imitating their stylzed beggars' speech. The South Korean government has never acknowledged the South Korean POWs captured by the North Vietnamese, with the exception of five individual soldiers. The majority of these POWs seem to have been "returned" to North Korea. However, the South Korean government has officially categorized these POWs as either dead or missing in action (KBS, "Hyŏngnimŭn wolbukhaji anatda" [My Brother Did Not Go to North], *Ch'ujŏk 60bun* [60 Minute Investigation], TV news magazine).

77. Kim So-yŏng, "Kontakt'ŭ jonŭrosŏŭi janrŭ: Hong Kong akshongwa hanguk hwalgŭk" [Genre as a Contact Zone: Hong Kong Action Films and Korean Action Films], available at *T'to hanaŭi munhwa* [Alternative Culture], http://www.tomoon.org/index.asp (Seoul: Alternative Culture Corporation, 2002) (accessed May 18, 2010).

78. Cho Sŏn-jak, "Yŏng-jaŭi chŏnsŏngsidae," 132, 134, 136.

79. The veteran's recognition here offers us a glimpse into the suppressed stories of possible South Korean defection. I would imagine that this number would be much smaller than that of U.S. soldiers who deserted and defected during the war, but nonetheless the third volume of An Chŏng-hyo's novel *White War* explores the story of a South Korean soldier who defected and fought on the side of his former enemy, North Vietnam, and against his own country and the United States. The character, who settles in Vietnam after the war, asserts emphatically that he, a former fighter with the NLF, is not a citizen of the Republic of Korea, but a communist citizen of Vietnam (*Hayan chŏnjaeng*, vol. 3: *Ep'ilogŭrŭl wihan chŏnjaeng* [War for an Epilogue], 231–34).

80. Definitions from the *Oxford English Dictionary*.

81. The character of Rambo in the trilogy as a whole oscillates between Rambo as the emasculated victim of the state and Rambo as a national allegory for remasculinizing the United States in the wake of its defeat in the Vietnam War. For a thorough and extended discussion of the Rambo films, see Jeffords, *Remasculinization of America*, 116–43.

82. An Chŏng-hyo, *Hayan chŏnjaeng*, vol. 2, *Chŏnjaengŭi sup* [The Jungles of War], 20.

83. A recent South Korean movie, *Silmi Island* (*Silmido*; dir. Kang U-sŏk, 2003), is based on a true incident under Park Chung Hee's regime in which the recruitment, training, and dispatching of convicts to North Korea as espionage agents was aborted. The state is ready to "sacrifice" (kill) them, when it decides to abandon the plan.

84. Mbembe, "Necropolitics," 11–40.

85. For example, there is a ready continuity between the military prostitution available to the occupying forces and the soldiers' violent sexual subjugation of the local women. This is pointedly illustrated by a scene in Pak Yŏng-han's *Mŏnamŏn ssongbagang*, in which a South Korean soldier "buys" sex from a young girl with a box of rations and with a gun to her head, because he cannot quite trust her. We must also note the continuity between Vietnamese military sex workers and other Vietnamese women who were part of the armed resistance. There is a way in which military sex workers must be viewed as subjugated enemies who may still be resistant in their own ways. See Cynthia Enloe's *Maneuvers* for conceptualization of the continuity between rape and prostitution in militarized contexts.

86. An Chŏng-hyo, *White Badge*, 156–57.

87. Despite the obvious similarity, the term "camp town" is never used for these areas set up for South Korean soldiers in Vietnam, either in *White Badge* or *Distant Ssongba River.*

88. See Eng, *Racial Castration*.

89. An Chŏng-hyo, *White Badge*, 78.

90. Ibid., 162, 110, 105, 243.

91. Chakrabarty, *Provincializing Europe*, 50.

92. An Chŏng-hyo, *White Badge*, 45. Private Yun "Boar" Chilbok, enthusiastic for war and "born with all the qualities to make a good mercenary," ends up a casualty and is described by the narrator in this way: "He was born in a remote village. . . . He liked the army so much from the first day at the boot camp, because the military system gave him free meals and clothes and even boots and even soap and a toothbrush. . . . [H]e was really impressed by an army that was willing to pay him anything at all while he was doing absolutely nothing but enjoying himself playing a real soldier with a real rifle and all. . . . He had never dreamed in his childhood in his godforsaken mountain village that he would ever see a day when he might be paid as much as forty dollars a month and in American money at that" (207–8).

93. Hwang Sŏk-yŏng, "Nakt'a nukkal" [Eye of a Camel], in *Hwang Sŏk-yŏng chungdanp'yŏn chŏnjip*, 2:106–33.

94. Hwang Sŏk-yŏng, "Iut saram" [A Neighbor], in *Hwang Sŏk-yŏng chungdanp'yŏn chŏnjip*, 2:161–81.

95. An Chŏng-hyo, *White Badge*, 40.

96. Hwang Sŏk-yŏng, "Iut saram," 180–81.

97. Ibid., 163.

98. An Chŏng-hyo, *White Badge*, 47, 72, 40, 167.

99. Amy Kaplan, "Romancing the Empire," 222. See also Heinz Fenkl's novel, *Memories of My Ghost Brother*, set in a camp town in the South Korea of the late 1960s and the early '70s. It explores further in detail this issue of U.S. military engagement in Asia as continuation of its "domestic" territorial expansionism. The boy narrator, who is born of a Korean mother and a white American serviceman father, prepares a birthday gift for his father, who "liked to wear cowboy boots." At a craft shop at the base, he chooses his father's favorite design that he would engrave on the wallet for his father: "On one face of the billfold I stamped in his name in the kind of lettering you see on WANTED posters in Westerns"; "It was a North American buffalo like the one on the back of an Indian head nickel" (214–15). I discuss this novel more in detail in chapter 3, on South Korean military prostitution for U.S. troops.

100. Hwang Sŏk-yŏng, "Molgaewŏlŭi sae," 178, 182.

101. See Anne McClintock's notion of "commodity racism" in *Imperial Leather*, 207–31.

102. A Korean sergeant dresses up like an American in one of Hwang Sŏk-yŏng's stories ("T'ap," 65).

103. Hwang Sŏk-yŏng, "T'ap," 94.

104. A group of South Korean films produced between 1962 and 1968 deal with an anticolonial armed resistance movement located in Manchuria. Jinsoo An identifies these films as "Manchurian action films." They have also been humorously referred to as "Kimchi Westerns" as they seem to indeed borrow heavily from the Hollywood Western genre in terms of their depiction of the desert-like locale of Manchuria, Japanese imperialists as villains, and righteous horse-riding and shotgun-carrying Korean independence fighters. Although Jinsoo An's dissertation does not make the

link between this group of films and the Vietnam War, I believe it would be possible to think of these films as desiring to rewrite the earlier history—the defeat of anticolonial Korean armed resistance fighters by the Japanese military—through the ongoing South Korean military aggression in Vietnam. The images of anticolonial warriors in the "blank" territory of Manchuria—mirroring those of white cowboys in the "wild, wild West" of North America—evoke furtively the images of South Korean soldiers fighting communist Vietnamese. I would argue that this cycle of films, through their palimpsestic overlay of multiple, militarized, masculine images, helped to justify South Korea's contemporary military venture in Vietnam. For an extended analysis of these Manchurian action films, see Jinsoo An, "Popular Reasoning of South Korean Melodrama Films (1953–1972)" (PhD diss., UCLA, 2005), chap. 3: "Figuring Masculinity at Historical Juncture: Manchurian Action Films."

105. This is a portion of the lyrics of a popular song titled "Amerika ch'ainataun" [An American Chinatown], performed by a legendary South Korean singer, Yi Mi-ja.

106. Hwang Sŏk-yŏng, "Nakt'a nukkal," 132–33.

107. Ibid., 115.

108. Ibid., 119–22.

109. Ibid., 115, 118, 133.

110. Hwang Sŏk-yŏng began working on the novel in 1978 and completed it in 1989.

111. See Anne McClintock's notion of "commodity racism" in *Imperial Leather*, 207–31.

112. We have numerous representations of similar economic circumstances in the Korean War and the immediate post–Korean War era in South Korean literature. See, for example, Pak Wan-sŏ, *Namok* [The Naked Tree], trans. Yu Young-nan, Cornell East Asia Series (Ithaca: Cornell University Press, 1995).

113. Hwang Sŏk-yŏng, *Mugiŭi kŭnŭl*, 48. I am borrowing the English title from Chŏn Kyŏng-ja's translation (Hwang, *The Shadow of Arms*). However, translation of cited phrases and passages are my own.

114. Hwang Sŏk-yŏng writes: "There is not one Japanese soldier here, but the PX warehouse is jammed with their electronic products" (*Mugiŭi kŭnŭl*, 2:40).

115. Ibid., 1:66.

116. Ibid.

117. Ibid., 1:67.

118. O Chŏng-hŭi, "Chinatown," 215.

119. Hwang Sŏk-yŏng, *Mugiŭi kŭnŭl*, 1:67.

120. Georg Lukács, cited in McClintock, *Imperial Leather*, 212.

121. Hwang Sŏk-yŏng, *Mugiŭi kŭnŭl*, 1:67.

122. Susan Buck-Morss, cited in McClintock, *Imperial Leather*, 59. McClintock, *Imperial Leather*, 208.

123. Hwang Sŏk-yŏng, *Mugiŭi kŭnŭl*, 2:96. See also Hwang's not-so-novelistic exposition of the economic goals of U.S. militarist expansionism (1:162).

124. Ibid., 2:271.

125. Memoirs by Vietnam War veterans and veterans-turned-entrepreneurs have recently appeared. For example, see Pak Chŏng-hwan, *Nŭsi;* Yi Yong-jun, *Betŭnam;* Yi Ch'ae-in, *Kkongkkai Betŭnam yŏn'ga;* and Kim Ch'ŏl-su, *Saigon, Saigon. Saigon, Saigon* illustrates the global hierarchy of capitalist production and South Korea's and Vietnam's respective positions in it. As subcontractors, South Korean companies function as intermediaries between core economies and the Vietnamese workforce. Cho Hae-in's *Ssong Saigon* is a novel set in contemporary Vietnam. It is quite critical of South Korea's past involvement in the war and the abandonment of biracial children by South Korean men, and yet it does not make the connection between the past and South Korean men's contemporary participation as consumers in Vietnam's prostitution business. For a representation of Korean victims of Agent Orange, see Yi Tae-hwan's novel *Sŭlou Bulitŭ. R Point* (2006), directed by Kong Su-ch'ang, was a relatively commercially successful horror film set during the Vietnam War. The Broadway musical *Miss Saigon* was imported to South Korea in 2006 and seems to have been quite popular. Interestingly, a Korean American actor was cast for the role of an American GI as the romantic lead opposite the role of the Vietnamese female lead. *Hanoi Bride* was a television drama aired in 2005 by a major South Korean network, dealing with a love triangle between a South Korean male doctor; his brother, a farmer seeking a Vietnamese bride; and a young Vietnamese woman who is majoring in Korean in college. Her older sister, who had a relationship with a South Korean man during the war and was eventually abandoned by him, opposes her younger sister's interest in South Korean men. See chapter 4 for this issue of marriage migration.

126. Pang Hyŏn-sŏk, *Hanoie pyŏri ttŭda,* 111.

127. Pang Hyŏn-sŏk, *Labsŭt'ŏrŭl mŏngnŭn sigan* [The Time of Eating Lobster], in *Labsŭt'ŏrŭl mŏngnŭn sigan,* 74–179.

128. Ibid., 116.

129. Kŏn-sŏk's romantic relationship with Lien is predominantly portrayed as maternal, and their sexual and emotional linkage becomes his physical connection to Vietnamese society and Vietnam as a national territory. Lien is also a teacher; she teaches him Vietnamese and, most importantly, the history of the Vietnam War, through her gift of a Vietnamese classic, *The War Diary.*

130. The female ghost is meant to represent at least three characters in one: she is supposed to be a female guerrilla the South Korean squadron on the search mission fights and leaves to die; she is also a prostitute in a camp town for South Koreans; and finally, she is a female hostess at the hotel/resort built and used by the French military during their occupation of Vietnam. While the female ghost appears as the female hostess of the hotel, the ghost in white aodai is visually overlapping and deliberately confused with the others, the prostitute and the female guerrilla.

131. Kim Hyŏn-a, *Chŏnjaengŭi kiŏk/kiŏgŭi chŏnjaeng,* 203–54.

132. The third volume of An Chŏng-hyo's *White War,* published in 1993, deals quite extensively with this particular issue of biracial children left behind by South Korean soldiers and civilian workers in Vietnam.

133. Vietnamese women's sex labor and sexualized labors for South Korean troops during the Vietnam War, and their work for South Korean sex tourists and business-men in the contemporary market, form a continuity. If Pang's work either avoids alto-gether the issue of the South Korean male population as consumers of Vietnamese female sex work ("Chonjaeŭi hyŏngsik" [A Form of Existence] in *Labsŭt'ŏrŭl mŏngnŭn sigan*, 8–71), or romanticizes and legitimizes it as a love story (*The Time of Eating Lob-ster*), another contemporary work by South Korean writer Cho Hae-in, *Ssong Saigon* [Saigon River], is frank and explicit in its portrayal of rampant prostitution in Ho Chi Minh City and South Koreans' licentious participation in it. The novel portrays the economic domination of the city by multiple countries—European, North American, and Northeast Asian—represented by their transnational company men and male tourists. And this domination, through the market and commodities, is most clearly represented by the novel's description of the desperation and eagerness of the women who sell their bodies to foreigners. The novel, while sympathetic to Vietnamese women and their men, whose hostile defensiveness is painfully felt on the street, still treats the contemporary economic colonization with a cavalier attitude, an attitude that has forgotten the rage of South Korean men who were placed in a similar situation in earlier decades.

134. Tadiar writes, "the mode of production and signification of the free world fan-tasy appears as the regulatory ideal and strategy of development" (*Fantasy-Production*, 11, 146).

2. DOMESTIC PROSTITUTION

1. Barry, *Prostitution of Sexuality*, 51–58.

2. The popular literary texts I deal with on the topic of domestic prostitution in this chapter reached a certain iconic status at the time they were first published. The other popular texts on the topic include works by a detective novel writer, Kim Sŏng-jong, from the 1970s, such as his short story "A Prostitute's Death." However, though bestselling, his works did not quite attain the kind of prominence in the public con-sciousness as the texts I analyze in this chapter.

3. As the stringent male domination of the South Korean literary establishment continued all the way through the mid-1980s, we would have to wait until the late 1980s and 1990s to see significant participation by women writers in representing working-class women in general, and those in prostitution in particular. See, for exam-ple, works by such female writers from the 1990s as Kong Sŏn-ok, Kim Hyang-suk, and Kong Chi-yŏng. Kong Sŏn-ok's works represent a leftist nationalist feminist point of view on the intersection between working-class women and sex work (for the domestic clientele). See, for example, "Mokmarŭn kyejŏl" [A Parched Season], "Mok-sum" [Living Life], and "Hŭindal" [White Moon] in Kong's collection of short stories, *P'iŏra susŏnhwa*. See Sin Kyŏng-suk's *Oettan bang* for a representation of young factory women's lives in the 1970s. Although this particular novel excludes the prevalent con-nection and traffic between factory labor and prostitution that I examine in other

literary works in this chapter, it is valuable for an illuminating depiction of female factory workers and their politicization.

4. Davidson, *Prostitution, Power, and Freedom*, 3, 9, 121.

5. Written and directed by Patty Jenkins, 2003. Aileen Wuornos was executed in 2002 after being on Florida's death row for twelve years. A South Korean film by famed director Im Kwon-t'aek, *T'ik'et* [Ticket] (1986), also portrays a sex worker who responds to the abuse by killing a male user.

6. Davidson, *Prostitution, Power, and Freedom*, 134.

7. Jenkins, *Monster*.

8. Kim Won, *Yŏgong, 1970*; Yi Chong-gu et al., *1960–70nyŏndae nodongjaŭi chagŏpjang munhwawa chŏngch'esŏng*, and *1960–70 nyŏndae nodongjaŭi saenghwal-segyewa chŏngch'esŏng*; and Seung-kyung Kim, *Class Struggle or Family Struggle?*

9. One of the top writers from the 1970s and '80s, Yi Mun-yŏl, has a few stories that deal with the subject of prostitution and sexuality of working-class women. A story titled "Camels in the Kwidu Mountain" describes working-class housewives who, for various reasons, have found themselves in prostitution; like a roving caravan of camels, they follow around, with a blanket, older male mountain hikers to sell sex and sometimes coffee or snacks. The subjects of another short story, "Kuro Arirang," are young factory girls who have been sexually taken advantage of by a male college student labor activist. An interesting twist in the story is that the college student activist, who was disguised as a worker—a common strategy adopted by the student-activists of the 1970s and '80s, called *wijang ch'wiŏp*—turns out to be a young man from the working class who was pretending to be a student pretending to be a worker. Kuro Industrial Complex was one of the largest and most famous industrial complexes on the periphery of Seoul in the 1970s, employing a large number of young female workers in the so-called light industry that was the mainstay of South Korean development in the 1970s (Yi Mun-yŏl, "Kwidusanenŭn nakt'aga sanda" and "Kuro arirang," in *Kuro Arirang*, 11–26, 47–73).

10. Bell, *Reading, Writing, and Rewriting the Prostitute*, 44.

11. Cho Hye-jŏng, *Hangukŭi yŏsŏnggwa namsŏng*.

12. See Sŏk Chŏng-nam, *Kongjangŭi pulbit*.

13. Barry, *Prostitution of Sexuality*, 122–23.

14. See, for example, Kang Sŏk-kyŏng's "Days and Dreams," in which one of the characters says, "And I've heard that some of the girls are squeezed for money by their own families. If their families can't pity them, how can they take money the girls make by having their crotches ripped open and then use it for someone's tuition?" (17).

15. Nanette J. Davis, introduction to *Prostitution: An International Handbook on Trends, Problems, and Policies*, ed. Davis (Westport, Conn.: Greenwood Press, 1993), cited in Davidson, *Prostitution, Power, and Freedom*, 85.

16. Barry, *Prostitution of Sexuality*, 123.

17. The most popular of these weekly tabloid magazines among several competing ones was *Sŏndei Seoul* [Sunday Seoul]. While thinly veiled with a respectable-sounding

journalistic tone, the tabloids' articles, along with their visuals, offered, quite overtly and unabashedly, their readership sexual pleasure and gratification in the earlier and cruder form of virtual commodification of female sexuality. *Sŏndei Seoul* was established in 1968 and continued until 1991, but its heyday was the 1970s, the era of rapid industrialization under Park Chung Hee. For example, an article on the current state of the so-called *yullak yŏsong* (literally fallen women, one of the most common euphemistic terms referring to sex workers throughout the 1960s, '70s) is a rather detailed report from the point of view of a sympathetic male reporter on the recent crackdown on one of the famous prostitution quarters and its aftermath. However, the title of the article, "This Is How the Girls of the Night Are" ("Pamŭi agassidŭrŭn irŏt'a"), reveals the article to be another parasitic form of sexual exploitation (*Sŏndei Seoul*, January 19, 1969). The tabloid magazine reported on a multitude of sex and sexualized services. The variety itself seems truly amazing, while the magazine tends to focus on the more unusual types of services. It comments upon, in particular, the rise of what it calls the "*sallong*" (salon), as a new form of drinking establishment for the wealthy. "Sallongs" are modern bars with the kind of "hostesses" as sexualized or sex service workers that this chapter discusses (*Sŏndei Seoul*, March 23, 1969). *Sŏndei Seoul* also reported on the sex industries of other Asian countries, such as Hong Kong and Singapore, outlining their transnational dimensions and sensationalizing the particularly exotic, bizarre, or cruel sexual commodifications. South Korean male foreign correspondents found Korean sex workers in these overseas locations as well as Korean customers (*Sŏndei Seoul*, June 8, 1969; July 27, 1969).

18. Bell, *Reading, Writing, and Rewriting the Prostitute*, 40. While the vast majority of sex and sexualized service workers were young women, there was a small minority of young men who found themselves in this industry, catering to the female counterpart of the newly emergent bourgeoisie, housewives with much "leisure" time and money. *Sŏndei Seoul* reports on the more criminal dimensions of such commercialized sexual relations between these groups of men and women, where these young men extorted money from the older, wealthier housewives (*Sŏndei Seoul*, June 15, 1969; July 27, 1969). I discussed the case of the male prostitute Il-bong in the previous chapter, and it does seem that the category and phenomenon of male prostitution is not quite as exceptional as it might seem at first glance.

19. Kang Sŏk-kyŏng, "Days and Dreams," 1–27.

20. Yi Im-ha, *Kyejibŭn ŏttŏk'e yŏsŏngi toeŏtna?*, 96–106.

21. Hwang, "A Dream of Good Fortune," 116–49. Some aspects of this story seem to be based upon his reportage titled "Irŏbŏrin Suni" [Suni Who Is Lost], *Singdoa* (1974), 298–309.

22. Seung-kyung Kim, *Class Struggle or Family Struggle?*, 57–96.

23. Hwang Sŏk-yŏng, "Irŏbŏrin Suni," 307.

24. Hwang Sŏk-yŏng, "Kuro kongdanŭi nodong silt'ae," 117–27. In "Irŏbŏrin Suni," Hwang deals with several aspects of young factory women's lives that intersect with their sexuality as well as with sex or sexualized service jobs. For example, he

critiques the weekly tabloids whose articles on female factory workers simply become an excuse for journalistic exploitation of their sexuality (301). He also writes about the tragic reality of abandoned fetuses in the garbage dumps in the slum areas occupied mostly by factory girls. The neighborhood police officer reports that he had collected thirty-two dead fetuses in one year. Another aspect of factory girls' lives Hwang mentions, one that has already been discussed by many already, is the ways in which they coped with the stigma of being *kongsuni* (a belittling, if not derogatory, term for factory girls) and the inferiority complex imposed on them by the mainstream society. Their general tendency to spend a disproportionate amount of their salary on clothing, shoes, or cosmetics illustrates their desire to escape such social categorization (308). Many current studies, as well as literary and other cultural sources, tell us about the instances of "class passing," that is, the commonplace cases of factory girls attempting to pass as college girls. See, for example, Sŏk Chŏng-nam's autobiography, *Kongjangŭi pulbit*, for a more detailed discussion of the "shame" that they felt for being a factory worker, especially as a woman.

25. *Leji* is a Japanized pronunciation of "lady," applied to tea room attendants. It was still widely in use in the 1970s.

26. Julia O'Connell Davidson categorizes the type of prostitution where various legally permitted businesses, such as massage parlors, saunas, hotels or inns, night clubs, bars, restaurants, or barbershops, are used as "fronts" for prostitution, as "take-out" brothels. This is a very accurate description of one type of prostitution that also existed in late 1960s and '70s South Korea. See Davidson, *Prostitution, Power, and Freedom*, 18–29.

27. Kisaeng is a Korean counterpart to Japanese geisha. "Kisaeng tourism," and other kinds of sex tourism for foreign tourists in the industrializing era, are known for the extent to which the state was involved in not only sanctioning it but also actively promoting it. See Davidson, *Prostitution, Power, and Freedom*, 75.

28. Min Kyŏng-ja, "Hanguk maech'un yŏsŏng undongsa," 244–45.

29. Ibid., 245. The original Korean is "yullak haengwi pangjibŏp."

30. Ibid., 244–45. Julia O'Connell Davidson cites one South Korean minister's praise of sex workers servicing Japanese tourists for "contributing to their fatherland's economic development" (*Prostitution, Power, and Freedom*, 193).

31. Enloe, *Bananas, Beaches, and Bases*, 159.

32. Davidson, *Prostitution, Power, and Freedom*, 87, 193.

33. Min Kyŏng-ja, "Hanguk maech'un yŏsŏng undongsa," 239–99.

34. Enloe, *Maneuvers*, 68.

35. Enloe, *Bananas, Beaches, and Bases*, 36.

36. Enloe, *Maneuvers*, 65.

37. Enloe, *Bananas, Beaches, and Bases*, 28, 30.

38. Cho Se-hŭi, "Nanjangiga ssoa olin chagŭn kong" [A Dwarf Launches a Little Ball], in *Nanjangiga ssoa olin chagŭn kong*, 68–123.

39. The Korean term for "city redevelopment project" is *toshi chaegaebal kyehoek*.

40. Cho Se-hŭi, "Nanjangiga ssoa olin chagŭn kong," 111. Yŏng-hŭi's mother tells her in her dream how she tried to instill in her daughter the importance of sexual purity.

41. I must note that her name, which I have romanized here as I-hwa according to the McCune Reischauer system, is in fact the name of the most prestigious women's college in South Korea, differently romanized as Ewha. Established in the colonial period by American Protestant missionaries, Ewha Girls' High School and Women's College, one can safely argue, operates in South Korea as a certain symbol of femininity, femininity associated with intelligence, beauty, affluence, and elite family background. Despite a very strong feminist tradition that Ewha women have created and maintained since its inception, the particular kind of femininity associated with Ewha in the popular imagination has been largely recuperated into what we might call the sphere of elite domesticity. Therefore, the male fantasy that the novel suggests via the name of its heroine, I-hwa, must be read as a conjuring of the innumerable Ewha girls and young women.

42. Cho Hae-il, *Kyŏul yŏja*, 190.

43. Ibid., 143. After her first sexual experience, that is, rape, I-hwa says, "Everything feels vivid and important." Sŏk-ki replies, "Once you open yourself up, then that's what happens. That's called a human being's rebirth."

44. Ibid., 144.

45. Ibid., 559, 396.

46. Ibid., 399.

47. Bell, *Reading, Writing, and Rewriting the Prostitute*, 90.

48. Cho Hae-il, *Kyŏul yŏja*, 642.

49. Ibid., 143.

50. The term *kyemong*, from late-nineteenth century, precolonial Korea, was originally a translation of the Western term "enlightenment" and in the 1930s came to designate the conservative nationalist stance in opposition to the Marxist perspective. The masses simply become the beneficiaries of the enlightened and benevolent elites' condescension and charity. While *Winter Woman* gestures toward "political" resistance, in fact, the role that the central characters, Kwang-jun and I-hwa, play is closest to the famous characters of the colonial novels by conservative cultural nationalist writers, such as Yi Kwang-su and Sim Hun, who were part of the Pŭnarodŭ (To the People!) movement. In *Soil* by Yi Kwang-su and *Evergreen* by Sim Hun, the colonized country folk are the recipients of social work by the enlightened and educated students from Seoul, who try to help improve and modernize the peasants' way of life.

51. Charles Baudlaire, *Intimate Journals*, trans. Christopher Isherwood (San Francisco: City Lights Books, 1983), 3, quoted in Bell, *Reading, Writing, and Rewriting the Prostitute*, 44.

52. Ch'oe In-ho, *Pyŏldŭrŭi kohyang*, 60. See also An Nak-il, "1970nyŏndae taejung sosŏlŭi tugaji chŏnryak: Pyŏldŭrŭi kohyanggwa Yŏngjaŭi chŏnsŏngsidaerŭl chungsimŭro" [Two Narrative Strategies in Popular Novels of the 1970s: On *Hometown of Stars* and "Yŏngja's Heyday"], in Chŏng Tŏk-jun, *Hangugŭi taejung munhak*, 163–90.

53. Ch'oe In-ho, *Pyŏldŭrŭi kohyang*, 119.

54. Ibid., 60.

55. Ibid.

56. Bailey, *Popular Culture and Performance in the Victorian City*, 151–74.

57. See Allison, *Night Work*, and Silverberg, *Erotic Grotesque Nonsense*.

58. Ch'oe In-ho, *Pyŏldŭrŭi kohyang*, 57.

59. See for example Kim Sŭng-ok's famous short story "Seoul: 1964, Winter" ["Seoul: 1964, Kyŏul"].

60. Ch'oe In-ho, *Pyŏldŭrŭi kohyang*, 195, 263.

61. Hwang Sŏk-yŏng, *Ŏdumŭi chasikdŭl*, 20–22.

62. Chakrabarty, *Provincializing Europe*, 47–96.

63. Hwang Sŏk-yŏng, *Ŏdumŭi chasikdŭl*, 9.

64. Ibid., 73.

65. Davidson, *Prostitution, Freedom, and Power*, 29–35.

66. Ibid., 51.

67. Hwang Sŏk-yŏng, *Ŏdumŭi chasikdŭl*, 75.

68. Ibid., 78.

69. The film version of the short story was one of the biggest box office hits of the mid-1970s (*Yŏng-jaŭi chŏnsŏngsidae*, dir. Kim Ho-sŏn, 1975), known as one of the most representative films of the "hostess film" (*hosŭtesŭ yŏnghwa*) subgenre. While the film retained the same title as the original literary work, it loses almost all of the critical force of the story on the issues of the Vietnam War, as that part of the story is all but completely left out of the plot of the cinematic narrative. I would like to draw attention to one detail that was added in the film. When Yŏng-ja loses her arm from her fall while working as a bus conductor, she is compensated for her disability with a relatively small amount of money, which is nonetheless the largest sum of money she has ever seen in her life. The size of the settlement excites Yŏng-ja and her close friend about the possibility of turning it into capital for starting a small business, such as a beauty salon. But eventually Yŏng-ja decides to send all of it to her family in the countryside. One way or another, the incalculable value of Yŏng-ja's lost arm is translated into a calculable and calculated amount of cash.

70. Cho Sŏn-jak, "Yŏng-jaŭi chŏnsŏngsidae," 49.

71. Yŏng-ja's case, where her disability drove her into prostitution, is in fact not unusual at all but rather it is a common phenomenon. Physically disabled women, as well as mentally deficient women, have no other occupation to turn to except for prostitution.

72. Cho Sŏn-jak, "Yŏng-jaŭi chŏnsŏngsidae," 79.

73. Cho Sŏn-jak, *Misŭ Yangŭi mohŏm*, 176, 177, 189.

74. Ibid., 176.

75. Ibid., 95, 153.

76. Ibid., 70.

77. Ibid., 282.

78. Cho Sŏn-jak, "Yŏng-jaŭi chŏnsŏngsidae."

79. Cho Sŏn-jak, *Misŭ Yangŭi mohŏm,* 243, 244, 246.

80. Kim Sŭng-ok, "Seoul: 1964, Winter," 88.

81. In Korean, the sentence reads, "nŏna nana kkŭllyŏ kanŭn panangja" (Na Hun-a, *Na Hun-a chŏngok moŭmjip* [Collected Works of Na Hun-a's Songs], ALA Record Production, 2001).

82. Ibid.

83. Ibid.

84. Kim Sŭng-ok, "Seoul: 1964, Winter," 89.

85. Na Hun-a, *Na Hun-a chŏngok moŭmjip.*

86. Ibid.

87. Kim Su-yŏng, "P'ul" [Grass], in *Kim Su-yŏng chŏnjip* [Collected Works of Kim Su-yŏng] (Seoul: Minunsa, 2003), 1:375.

88. The male voice in the second stanza considers marrying for wealth another alternative to killing himself. Essentially, here the male proletarian character proposes prostitution as a solution to his plight (Na Hun-a, *Na Hun-a chŏngok moŭmjip*).

89. Davidson, *Prostitution, Power, and Freedom,* 196.

90. R. Miles defines the state in this way: "The state is not a political institution that manages the formal economy but rather . . . an institutional complex . . . which organizes social relations . . . to ensure the reproduction of a particular mode of . . . mode . . . it attempts to . . . secure by direct force and/or in law, the particular conditions considered necessary" (*Capitalism and Unfree Labor: Anomaly or Necessity?* [London: Tavistock, 1987], 81; cited in Davidson, *Prostitution, Power, and Freedom,* 192).

91. Enloe, *Bananas, Beaches, and Bases,* 19.

92. Spivak, "Scattered Speculations on the Question of Value," 117.

93. Davidson, *Prostitution, Power, and Freedom,* 208–9.

3. MILITARY PROSTITUTION

1. Enloe, *Bananas, Beaches, and Bases,* 85. On South Korean military prostitution under U.S. hegemony, see Katharine Moon, *Sex among Allies.*

2. Na Young Lee, "The Construction of U.S. Camptown Prostitution in South Korea," 10.

3. For a succinct history of the Japanese empire's mobilization of Comfort Women in the 1940s and its continuity and discontinuity with South Korean military prostitution for U.S. servicemen, see Yuh, *Beyond the Shadow of Camp Town,* 18–19. For an excellent discussion of the Japanese mobilization of Korean women for military and industrial prostitution during the World War II, see An Yŏn-sŏn, *Sŏng noyewa pyŏngsa mandŭlgi.* See also Kang Chŏng-suk, "Ilbongun 'wianbu' munje, ŏttŏk'e polgŏshinga?" 159–90. For a brief history of the scholarly and activist movements surrounding the Comfort Women issue, see Yi Hyo-jae, "Ilbongun wianbu munje haegyŏlŭl wihan undongŭi chŏngae kwajŏng," 181–238.

4. Na Young Lee, "The Construction of U.S. Camptown Prostitution in South Korea," 10.

5. Enloe, *Maneuvers*, 67, 70.

6. The Prostitution Prevention Law was called *yullak haengwi pangjipŏp* in Korean (Na Young Lee, "The Construction of U.S. Camptown Prostitution in South Korea," 119–22).

7. Moon, *Sex among Allies*, 43.

8. Ibid., 84–85, 102–3.

9. Na Young Lee, "The Construction of U.S. Camptown Prostitution in South Korea," 135.

10. Katharine Moon argues, very convincingly, that "the mere existence of power disparities between and among nations does not automatically translate into subordinated positions of women in a weaker state to men of a stronger state." In highlighting the transition from the 1960s to the 1970s, when South Korea lost its leverage vis-à-vis the United States and its local military authorities due to an American decision to reduce the number of troops stationed in South Korea, and had to make a variety of concessions in terms of cooperating with U.S. demands to address various issues in camp towns, from racial problems and control of STDs, Moon emphasizes the agency that South Korea had in the 1960s and lost in the 1970s as a "weaker state" in comparison to a "stronger state," the United States. In her study of the Clean-Up Campaigns of the 1970s, she also stresses the resistance of camp town women against the GIs, local U.S. military authorities, and the South Korean government (Moon, *Sex among Allies*, 48–56, 58–83).

11. In fact, the treaty was created to address the enormous imbalance existing at the time. Before 1966, the relations had been even more skewed, although clearly the 1966 SOFA did not create an equal condition.

12. Moon, *Sex among Allies*, 19, 127–48.

13. See Chuhan migun pŏmjoi kŭnjŏl undong ponbu, *Kkŭtnaji anŭn ap'umŭi yŏksa*.

14. For example, see Sturdevant and Stoltzfus, *Let the Good Times Roll*.

15. Ibid., 326.

16. Na Young Lee, "The Construction of U.S. Camptown Prostitution in South Korea," 152–62. See an excellent article, both comprehensive and detailed, on the history of camp town activisms by Chŏng Hŭi-jin, "Chugŏya sanŭn yŏsŏngdŭlŭi inkwŏn: hanguk kijich'on undongsa, 1986–1998," 300–358. The best-known Christian activist organization, Turebang (also known as "My Sister's Place" in English), was established in 1986 by Mun Hye-rim (a European American Christian activist, married to a Korean liberation theologian, Dr. Mun Tong-hwan) and Yu Pok-nim (a Korean female activist with the liberation theology background). Student activists' influx into camp towns began around 1990 as part of the official agenda of anti-American activist movement. Activism in camp towns was known as *kihwal*, short for *kijich'on hwaldong;* see also *nonghwal* (*nongch'on hwaldong*, farm activism), *konghwal* (*kongjang hwaldong,*

factory activism), *pinhwal* (*pinmin hwaldong*, slum activism), all of which college students participated in for various durations and with different degrees of commitment. Student activism in camp towns seems to have been a temporary phenomenon with a very specific historical relevance and political agenda, which in some ways distorted and exploited the predicament of camp town sex workers' work and their history. Those critical of *kihwal* argue that camp town activism must go beyond exceptionalizing camp town sex work in relation to the U.S.–South Korea relations and be included as part of the broader movement related to all prostitution. See Chŏng Hŭijin, "Chugŏya sanŭn yŏsŏngdŭlŭi inkwŏn: hanguk kijich'on undongsa, 1986–1998," 319–24.

17. Sturdevant and Stoltzfus, *Let the Good Times Roll,* 314.

18. Ibid., 79, 316.

19. Their anti-Americanism had been powerful since the mid-1960s, but it further intensified in the 1980s, after the Kwangju Massacre in which the United States was reported to have had a direct hand.

20. Yi Im-ha, *Kyejibŭn ŏttŏk'e yŏsŏngi toeŏtna?,* 96–106.

21. Song Pyŏng-su, "Ssyori Kim" [Shorty Kim], in *Ssyori Kim, Ch'ŏllo, oe,* 11–30; Ha Kŭn-ch'an, "Wangnŭnggwa chudungun" [The Royal Tomb and the Occupying Troops], in *Hanguk hyŏndae taep'yo sosŏlsŏn* [Representative Works in Modern Korean Literature] (Seoul: Ch'angbi, 1996), 9:265–89; O Yŏng-su, "Annaŭi yusŏ" [Anna's Will], *Hyŏndae Munhak,* April 1963, 55–91. There are less well-known, less canonical works that deal with the topic of camp town and military prostitution produced between 1950s and 1980s including O Sang-won, "Hwangsŏn jidae" [Yellow Area], *Sasanggye,* April 1960, 181–265; and three by Pak Sŏk-su—"Ch'ŏljomangsok hwip'aram" [Whistling Inside the Steel Fence], *Hyŏndae Munhak,* October 1982, 284–99; "Oeroun chŭngŏn" [A Lonely Testimony], *Sosŏl Munhak,* October 1985, 118–33; and "Tonggŏin" [A Live-in Lover], *Sosŏl Munhak,* February 1987, 273–98. Although a sizable number of texts can be classified as belonging to the subgenre of camp town literature, South Korean literary critics have not produced many scholarly articles or book-length studies on this topic at all. See Kim Chŏng-ja, "Hanguk kijich'on sosŏlŭi kibŏpjŏk yŏngu" [A Study on the Literary Strategies in Camp Town Literature], 117–44, and Pak Hun-ha, "Kijich'on sosŏlŭi chonjae pangsikgwa ideologi" [The Mode of Existence and Ideology of Camp Town Literature], 145–87, in Kim Chŏng-ja, ed., *Hanguk hyŏndae munhakŭi sŏnggwa maech'un yongu.*

22. The flip side, Enloe further suggests, is that such masculinist nationalists' investment in women's sexual purity and their labor simultaneously springs from their projection that women are the most "vulnerable" and "susceptible" to foreign forces' exploitation, assimilation, and cooptation (Enloe, *Bananas, Beaches, and Bases,* 54).

23. Stoler, "Carnal Knowledge and Imperial Power," 15.

24. Enloe, *Bananas, Beaches, and Bases,* 44.

25. Theodore Hughes, "Development as Devolution: Nam Chŏng-hyŏn and the 'Land of Excrement' Incident," *Journal of Korean Studies* 10, no. 1 (2005): 29–57.

26. Choi, "Nationalism and the Construction of Gender in Korea," 9–32.

27. Nam Chŏng-hyŏn, "Punji" [Land of Excrement], in *Punji*, 315.

28. Nam alters the Chinese character for "genitalia" (*ŭmbu*), exchanging the character *ŭm* with another homonymic character, *ŭm*, meaning "lewd."

29. Nam, "Punji," 323.

30. Ibid., 333.

31. While there are no hierarchized rape laws that are specifically related to different races, as in the cases of the earlier European colonies that Ann Stoler writes about, in cases of sexual violence, SOFA could be mobilized to give the best advantage to the imperial troops, while allowing the least for the neocolonized women. See Stoler's "Carnal Knowledge and Imperial Power," 20. The asymmetry of power between the two nations is codified in the SOFA laws, according to which cases, including those involving sexual assault, would be adjudicated when Koreans are victims of crime perpetrated by the U.S. military personnel. See Chuhan migun pŏmjoi kŭnjŏl undong ponbu, *Kkŭtnaji anŭn ap'umŭi yŏksa*. See also O Yŏn-ho, *Nogŭn-ri kŭ ihu*.

32. Nam, "Punji," 318.

33. Ibid.

34. Ch'ŏn Sŭng-se, "Hwangguŭi pimyŏng," 479, 488, 482, 483.

35. Ibid., 495.

36. Ibid., 497.

37. Stoler, "Carnal Knowledge and Imperial Power," 15.

38. Cho Hae-il, "Amerika," 358.

39. Ibid., 359.

40. Ibid., 356.

41. Ch'oe In-hun, "The End of the State Highway," translated from "Kukdoŭi kkŭt," in *Ch'oe In-hun chŏnjip* [The Collected Works of Ch'oe In-hun], vol. 8 (Seoul: Munhakkwa chisŏngsa, 1978). All of the citations from "The End of the State Highway" are from Theodore Hughes's translation of the story in *Manoa* (Honolulu: University of Hawaii Press, 1999), 15–20.

42. Ibid., 19.

43. Ibid.

44. Ibid.

45. Ibid.

46. Park Chung Hee, *Our Nation's Path* (Seoul: Dong-a, 1962).

47. In "The End of the State Highway" the funeral of one of the military sex workers becomes an occasion for public display of their sexuality and public critique of the multiple injustices that they suffer. If the *yanggongju* in the story is transformed into a visual spectacle of degradation and shame by the male bus passengers, then the portrayal of the funeral shows how they can voluntarily spectacularize themselves in protest of the mainstream society's ostracism and objectification. This funeral, with its traditional colorful decorations and improvisational wailers, becomes a carnival performance where the degraded prostitutes momentarily, through the sanctity and

universality of death, can be elevated to the position of protesting voices, reproaching, condemning South Korean and U.S. patriarchal societies.

48. *Ppaetpŏl*, the title of An Il-sun's novel, is the local nickname for Tongduch'ŏn, one of the largest U.S. military bases in South Korea. *Ppaetpŏl* means mudflats or the muddy part of the beach. Among local women, *ppaetbŏl* took on the meaning of being stuck in the muddy fields, not being able to move forward or backward.

49. The author writes that the novel is an autobiographical account of his experience growing up in a camp town. He dedicates his novel to his parents, who lived and worked in a camp town until their deaths (Pok Kŏ-il, "Afterword by the Author," in *K'aemp'ŭ senek'aŭi kijich'on*, 367).

50. Ibid.

51. Pok Kŏ-il, *K'aemp'ŭ senek'aŭi kijich'on*, 17.

52. The camp town residents' sense of abandonment by the South Korean state and mainstream society is accompanied by the sense of "protection" that they feel they receive from camp towns. Father uses the idea of a "protected district" *(poho kuyŏk)* in explaining the peculiarities of camp town to his son. He considers those who ended up in camp towns, including women, as having had special social and economic handicaps in life. One such handicap among camp town residents is being a refugee from North. The "easy" flow of money from the relatively wealthy GIs into the local economy of camp town, in a way, balances out the harsh stigma attached to camp towns.

53. Pok Kŏ-il, *K'aemp'ŭ senek'aŭi kijich'on*, 159.

54. The novel explains this U.S. policy change that allowed soldiers to bring their wives (ibid., 281).

55. Ibid., 269.

56. Kang Sŏk-kyŏng's "Days and Dreams" is one of the few such works by women writers from the early 1980s. Yun Chŏng-mo is another female writer from the 1980s who wrote about the issue of Comfort Women and camp town military prostitution. I would characterize Yun's ideological perspective as female masculinist nationalist, as these works tend not to be critical of South Korean patriarchy, while appropriating military sex work for the purpose of critiquing colonial and neocolonial domination by Japan and the United States. See *Emi irŭmŭn Chosenppiyŏtta, Kobbi*, and "Parambyŏgŭi ttaldŭl" [Daughters of Wind Walls], in *Pombi*, 199–294.

57. Chŏng Hŭi-jin, "Chugŏya sanŭn yŏsŏngdŭlŭi inkwŏn," 332–49.

58. An Il-sun, preface to *Ppaetpŏl*, 1:6. The novel's main character, Sŭng-ja, is loosely based on a camp town activist, Kim Yŏn-ja, who recently published her own autobiography: *Amerikataun wangŏnni: Kim Yŏn-ja chajŏn esei* [America Town's Big Sister: Kim Yŏn-ja's Autobiographical Essays] (Seoul: Samin, 2005).

59. Kang Sŏk-kyŏng, "Days and Dreams," 1–27.

60. Cynthia Enloe also mentions this in *Maneuvers*, 97–98.

61. An Il-sun, *Ppaetpŏl*, 1:267.

62. See Walkowitz, *Prostitution and Victorian Society*, 201–12. See also Enloe, *Bananas, Beaches, and Bases*, 82.

63. An Il-sun, *Ppaetpŏl,* 1:43.

64. Ibid., 1:43, 44, 45.

65. See Anne McClintock's notion of "commodity racism" in *Imperial Leather,* 207–31. See Tadiar, *Fantasy-Production,* 55–56, 115.

66. An Il-sun, *Ppaetpŏl,* 1:201, 92.

67. Ibid., 1:43, 45.

68. Kondo, *About Face.*

69. Maeng Su-jin discusses a military prostitute character, Sonya, in a 1960 South Korean film by Sin Sang-ok, *Chiokhwa* [The Flower of Hell], as a femme fatale whose excessive sexuality defies the traditional sexual mores. She attributes subversiveness to Sin's portrayal of Sonya ("Sŭk'ŭrinsogŭi aknyŏdŭl" [Villainesses of the Silver Screen], in Yu Chi-na and Cho Hŭb, *Hanguk yŏnghwa sekshuŏlit'irŭl mannada,* 114).

70. See Stoler, "Carnal Knowledge and Imperial Power," 16.

71. In her reading of "The Breast-Giver" Gayatri Spivak describes the working-class woman's commodification of her breast milk as a "domestic to 'domestic' transition," critiquing the Engelsian framework, theorizing family as the site of transition "from domestic to civil, private to public, home to work, sex to class." See Spivak, "A Literary Representation of the Subaltern," 248.

72. Stoler, "Carnal Knowledge and Imperial Power," 16–17.

73. See Enloe, *Manuervers,* 90, for a picture of a South Korean military sex worker in her room decorated both in Western and Oriental style.

74. Pok Kŏ-il, *K'aemp'ŭ senek'aŭi kijich'on,* 281.

75. An Il-sun, *Ppaetpŏl,* 2:84.

76. The masculine authorities, both South Korean and American, take different forms in camp towns. Some of the bars and brothels are owned by men, while others are run by women. Korean men in camp towns exert their patriarchal power as common-law husbands or lovers, as American men can also exercise their patriarchal authority as clients, lovers, temporary contract cohabitants, or husbands.

77. Kang Sŏk-kyŏng, "Days and Dreams," 1–27.

78. An Il-sun, *Ppaetpŏl,* 1:147, 149.

79. Ibid., 2:217. It is not clear from the context what "it" is.

80. Ibid., 2:258, 257, 255.

81. See Halberstam, *Female Masculinity.*

82. An Il-sun, *Ppaetpŏl,* 162.

83. Kang Sŏk-kyŏng, "Days and Dreams," 23.

84. Ibid., 21.

85. Cho Hae-il, "Amerika," 391.

86. Kelski, *Women on the Verge,* 4.

87. Enloe, *Bananas, Beaches, and Bases,* 23; Enloe, *Maneuvers,* 108–52. Apart from the context of military prostitution and overlapping with it, we should also note that there is a very high rate of cross-cultural homicide of prostitutes.

88. Korean American writers have produced a number of literary works on military prostitution of the Japanese colonial period and the U.S. neocolonial era. See Chang-rae Lee, *A Gesture Life*; and Keller, *Comfort Woman* and *Fox Girl*. For an insightful inquiry into the particularities of Korean American works on the issue of military prostitution, see Laura Kang's critique, "Conjuring 'Comfort Women': Mediated Affiliations and Disciplined Subjects in Korean/American Transnationality," *Journal of Asian American Studies* 6, no. 2 (2003): 25–55.

89. See Chow, "The Secrets of Ethnic Abjection," in *The Protestant Ethnic and the Spirit of Capitalism*, 128–52.

90. Stoler, "Carnal Knowledge and Imperial Power," 26.

91. Fenkl, *Memories of My Ghost Brother*, 17, 63, 253, 133, 172.

92. Ibid., 102.

93. Ibid., 160.

94. Moon, *Sex among Allies*, 34.

95. Fenkl, *Memories of My Ghost Brother*, 221.

96. On another level, as I also argued earlier, the camp town community is by default a matrilineal community, as the biracial children are abandoned by their fathers. By extension, their citizenship, through their exclusion from their fathers' country, also remains by default matrilineal. I would argue that this exclusion from patrilineage and patrilineal citizenship, which is a form of castration of male biracial children, results in shifting the responsibility to their camp town mothers and other women there. In other words, their patrilineal illegitimacy is rearticulated as matrophobia and misogyny.

97. Fenkl, *Memories of My Ghost Brother*, 17.

98. The film is careful in demonstrating American soldiers as conducting themselves responsibly outside the base, particularly through a series of scenes in which James is the only one who is veering from the normal boundaries of acceptable conduct, and he is either disciplined or restrained by American MPs or his fellow soldiers.

99. Sturdevant and Stoltzfus cite an anonymous ditty, from an American serviceman's point of view, that can be commonly found in Asian camp towns. This particular one, from a Filipino camp town, sums up, bluntly and succinctly, the racist and sexist view of male soldiers on prostitution and camp town women. The Asian woman in the ditty is described as "two slant eyes," who not only voluntarily has sex with the soldier, but whose sexual appetite for the man is insatiable. While the fact that he is paying for sex with a camp town woman is disavowed, the ditty's main emphasis is on the soldier-narrator's sexual performance, which leaves the woman wanting more. The last line of the song, which describes his own reaction to the preceding sexual transaction, reveals clearly the nature of his point of view: "You look back and say, 'Did I fuck that?!?!?!'" His earlier racist term for her, "two slant-eyes," has been transformed now into "that." It is almost as if the soldier himself is in disbelief, or is horrified to have learned that he had sex with "that," merely a thing that is not even recognizable as a human being

or a woman (Sturdevant and Stoltzfus, *Let the Good Times Roll*, 287). Sturdevant and Stoltzfus tell us that American soldiers often refer to the indigenous camp town women, using such racial slurs as "slope," "slant," and such racist and sexist terms as "moose" (or "house moose") or "Little Brown Fucking Machines Fueled by Rice" (or LBFM for short); see *Let the Good Times Roll*, 230, 326.

100. A couple of dog "characters" are treated as if they were human characters, by being given narratives and/or human traits. Chi-hŭm's dog and Eun-ok's puppy are such examples.

101. Kang Sŏk-kyŏng, "Days and Dreams," 22.

102. Appadurai, *Modernity at Large*, 178–99.

103. Ibid., 199.

104. There has been a general silence on this aspect of the history of South Korean immigration to the United States, due to the stigma associated with military prostitution, despite the fact that South Korean immigration to the United States has been centrally connected, first, to the Korean War and its effects, such as war orphans, adoption of camp town biracial children, and other military workers sponsored by American military personnel in the post–Korean War era, and second, to military prostitution in the following decades in the context of continuing U.S. military presence. See Yuh, *Beyond the Shadow of Camptown*, 164.

105. Yuh, *Beyond the Shadow of Camptown*, 111–12.

106. A documentary, *The Women Outside: Korean Women and the U.S. Military*, directed by Hye Jung Park and J. T. Takagi (1996), narrates a tragic incident involving a South Korean military immigrant wife in 1987. After her divorce from her American husband, Chong-sun France was left alone to support her two children in the military-base town of Jacksonville, North Carolina—an American camp town. She left her two young children alone without adult supervision to go work at a local bar at night. When she came home from work one day, she found one of her children dead, having broken his neck in the motel room where they were living. She was tried and sentenced to serve six years in jail.

107. Na Young Lee, "The Construction of U.S. Camptown Prostitution in South Korea," 207.

108. Ibid., 179–86.

109. Pok Kŏ-il, *K'aemp'ŭ senek'aŭi kijich'on*, 337–38.

110. Sealing Cheng, "Sarangŭl paeugo, sarange chukgo: k'jich'on k'ŭllŏbŭi GIwa p'ilip'in ent'ŏt'einŏŭi romaensŭ" [Learning Love and Dying for Love: Romance between a GI and a Filipina Entertainer], in Magdalenaŭi chip, *Yonggamhan yŏsŏngdŭl, nŭkdaerŭl t'ago dallinŭn*, 229–55.

111. See the conversation among Chŏng Yu-jin, Kim Ŭn-sil, and Katharine Moon, "Kukkaŭi anboga kaeinŭi anbonŭn anida," 79–105.

112. Na Young Lee, "The Construction of U.S. Camptown Prostitution in South Korea," 210.

113. Chalmers Johnson, *Sorrows of Empire*, 188.

114. Fenkl, *Memories of My Ghost Brother*, 249.

115. Ibid., 132.

4. MIGRANT AND IMMIGRANT LABOR

1. See Pak No-ja (Vladimir Tikhonov), *Hangyŏre Newspaper*, October 9, 2002. For a more comprehensive treatment of issues related to migrant labor, see the section titled "Ibangindŭrŭi nara, Taehanminguk" [Republic of Korea, Foreigner's Country], in Pak No-ja, *Tangsindŭrŭi Taehanminguk*, 2:171–216. Indonesian workers who work for Korean companies are organizing and confronting their Korean employers, but the association of Indonesian companies continues to lodge complaints against the governmental restrictions. The current relations between foreign/comprador capital and domestic labor in Indonesia are very similar to those that played out in South Korea during the 1970s and '80s. The mainstream South Korean media does not often report on labor problems that South Korean companies face abroad, as they tend to focus on the popularity of Korean products among foreign consumers, and the efficiency and great service that South Korean companies provide.

2. Seol and Skrentny, "South Korea," 481–513. See also Sŏl Tong-hun (Dong-Hoon Seol)'s in-depth sociological study of the migrant worker population in South Korea, *Oegugin nodongjawa hanguk sahoe*, and Sŏk, Chŏng, Yi, Yi, and Kang, *Oegugin nodongjadŭrŭi ilt'ŏwa sam*. For documentation of many cases of exploitation and abuse of migrant workers, see Oegugin nodongja taech'aek hyŏbŭihoe, *Oegugin iju nodongja ingwon paeksŏ*, 19–93 (this first part of the book consists of relatively brief descriptions of one hundred cases of human rights violations against migrant workers).

3. Korean Chinese or Chosŏnjok are descendants of Koreans who moved to China, starting in the late nineteenth century and throughout the colonial period. Some moved voluntarily in the earlier phase of colonial rule, while others in the late colonial period did so more forcibly and in an organized fashion under Japanese authority.

4. Appadurai, *Modernity at Large*, 191.

5. I am borrowing Lisa Lowe's understanding of these dual roles played by the state in the U.S. context, now relevant to the immigrant national context of South Korea. See Lowe, *Immigrant Acts*, 29.

6. Sassen, *Globalization and Its Discontents*, 21.

7. Ong, *Flexible Citizenship*, 1–26.

8. Stoler, *Race and the Education of Desire*, 77–91.

9. Omi and Winant, *Racial Formation in the United States*, 77–91.

10. Lowe, *Immigrant Acts*, 29.

11. The phrase in Korean is *tamunhwajŏk ŭisik*. See *Ijunodongja pangsongguk news* (Migrant Workers' Broadcasting Station), April 13, 2006, available at http://saladtv .kr/ (accessed, June 29, 2010).

12. Ibid.

13. Ibid., December 29, 2005, available at http://saladtv.kr/ (accessed, June 29, 2010).

14. For the notion of the compensatory function of culture, see "Heterogeneity, Hybridity and Multiplicity: Asian American Differences," in Lowe, *Immigrant Acts*, 60–83.

15. This special "benefit" is offered to South Korean companies that invest in foreign companies by offering technological know-how or export manufacturing equipment and industrial machinery to the countries where cheap labor is available (*Hangyŏre Newspaper*, September 27, 2002). See also Oegugin nodongja taech'aek hyŏbŭihoe, *Oegugin iju nodongja ingwon paeksŏ*, 124–48.

16. "Nodong chaengŭikwon," *Hangyŏre Newspaper*, July 31, 2003.

17. *Ijunodongja pangsongguk news*, September 2005, available at http://saladtv.kr/ (accessed, June 29, 2010).

18. Pak Pŏm-sin's *Namasŭte* [Namaste] was serialized in *Hangyŏre Newspaper* between January and December of 2004. I analyze the novel in detail in the latter part of this chapter. The serialized newspaper novel was later published in book form with some revision. This chapter refers to the serialized version, using the number of installments; the quote is from installment no. 67.

19. Sassen, *Globalization and Its Discontents*, 21–23.

20. *Hangyŏre Newspaper*, November 21, 1998. For many instances of such police and INS brutalities, see Oegugin nodongja taech'aek hyŏbŭihoe, *Oegugin iju nodongja ingwon paeksŏ*, 19–93, 122–23.

21. *Hangyŏre Newspaper*, November 21, 1998; the Korean term is *taech'ŏngso chakjŏn*.

22. *Hangyŏre Newspaper*, January 8, 2004.

23. *Hangyŏre Newspaper*, March 31, 1998.

24. Yi Ran-ju, *Malhaeyo, ch'andra*, 77–126.

25. *Hangyŏre Newspaper*, July 17, 2002.

26. Under the pressures of Chungkihyŏp, the South Korean government decided in 2002 to increase the quota set for industrial trainees from 80,000 to 130,000, disregarding the vociferous opposition to it by labor and human rights activists (*Hangyŏre Newspaper*, July 24, 2002).

27. *Hangyŏre Newspaper*, January 6, 2001.

28. *Hangyŏre Newspaper*, November 27, 2001. See also Oegugin nodongja taech'aek hyŏbŭihoe, *Oegugin iju nodongja ingwon paeksŏ*, 119.

29. *Hangyŏre Newspaper*, September 17, 2002.

30. *Hangyŏre Newspaper*, May 4, 1998.

31. *Ijunodongja pangsongguk news*, February 12, 2007, available at http://saladtv.kr/ (accessed, June 29, 2010). Oegugin nodongja taech'aek hyŏbŭihoe, *Oegugin iju nodongja ingwon paeksŏ*, 55–65.

32. *Hangyŏre Newspaper*, October 29, 2002. For other examples, see Oegugin nodongja taech'aek hyŏbŭihoe, *Oegugin iju nodongja ingwon paeksŏ*, 54–55, 65–66, 108.

33. Davis, *Angela Y. Davis Reader,* 61–110.

34. *Hangyŏre Newspaper,* November 28, 2001.

35. Kim Chi-yŏn and Kim Hae-sŏng, *Nodongjaege kukkyŏngŭn ŏpta,* 112–13. *Borderless Workers* is a book of text by Kim Hae-sŏng and photographs by Kim Chi-yŏn documenting the lives and struggles of migrant workers in South Korea.

36. Yi Ran-ju, *Malhaeyo, ch'andra,* 109.

37. See Kim Hyŏn-mi, "Kŭlobŏl toshi, Seoul" [A Global City, Seoul], in *Kŭlobŏlsidaeŭi munhwa pŏnyŏk,* 19–46.

38. See, for example, Yang Kwi-ja's *Distant and Beautiful Place* [Wonmi-dong saramdŭl], (Seoul: Sallim, 2004); Yi Mun-yŏl's short story "Kuro Arirang," from his collection titled *Kuro Arirang;* Yi Ch'ang-dong's retrospective film on the late 1970s and '80s, *Pakha sat'ang* [Peppermint Candy] (2000); among others.

39. *Hangyŏre Newspaper,* April 24, 2001.

40. *Hangyŏre Newspaper,* February 13, 2001.

41. *Hangyŏre Newspaper,* January 14, 1999.

42. *Hangyŏre Newspaper,* May 12, 2002.

43. *Hangyŏre Newspaper,* November 28, 2001. See Pak Ch'ae-ran's book on Ansan, *Kukkyŏng ŏpnŭn maŭl,* for an example of a nonacademic book that aims to inform and educate mainstream Koreans about migrant workers and multiculturalism.

44. *Hangyŏre Newspaper,* November 28, 2001. Han Yong-un, "I Saw You," in *Hanguk simunhak taegye* [Collected Works of Modern Korean Poetry], (Seoul: Chisik sanŏpsa, 1981), 2:54.

45. *Hangyŏre Newspaper,* October 29, 2002.

46. Hwang Sŏk-yŏng, "A Dream of Good Fortune," 115–49.

47. A Korean Chinese worker was beaten to death with a bat by his South Korean coworker. Kim Chi-yŏn and Kim Hae-sŏng, *Borderless Workers,* 46–47.

48. Kim Chi-yŏn and Kim Hae-sŏng, *Nodongjaege kukkyŏngŭn ŏpta,* 123.

49. *Hangyŏre Newspaper,* May 26, 2001.

50. *Hangyŏre Newspaper,* June 9, 2002.

51. *Hangyŏre Newspaper,* February 5, 2004, November 28, 2004. Like South Korean workers of the earlier period, migrant workers face the similar predicament of having to choose between joining the labor movement, thus giving up their jobs and pay, and not joining the movement, thus maintaining their livelihood and pursuing their personal goals. The former is clearly a personal sacrifice for the greater good, a decision reached with much difficulty.

52. *Hangyŏre Newspaper,* November 21, 2000.

53. See Namhee Lee, *The Making of Minjung,* 12.

54. Kim Chi-yŏn and Kim Hae-sŏng, *Nodongjaege kukkyŏngŭn ŏpta,* 11.

55. *Hangyŏre Newspaper,* December 4, 2002.

56. Pak Pŏm-sin, *Namasŭte,* no. 186.

57. See Hagen Koo's important book on the labor movements of the 1970s and '80s and working-class formation, *Korean Workers.*

58. Pak Pŏm-sin, *Namasŭte,* no. 197.

59. Kim Chi-yŏn and Kim Hae-sŏng, *Nodongjaege kukkyŏngŭn ŏpta,* 11.

60. *Hangyŏre Newspaper,* December 25, 2003.

61. *Hangyŏre Newspaper,* November 29, 2003.

62. *Hangyŏre Newspaper,* December 25, 2003.

63. *Hangyŏre Newspaper,* November 29, 2003.

64. Kim Sŭng-gu, "Paekkopjaengi paksŏbangŭi kwihyang," 1:327–36.

65. *Hangyŏre Newspaper,* September 3, 2002.

66. *Hangyŏre Newspaper,* November 13, 2002.

67. *Hangyŏre Newspaper,* November 15, 2002. A popular South Korean director, Pak Ch'an-uk, made a short film based on the story of Chandra Kurŭng, titled *Mitkŏna malgŏna: Chandra Kurŭngŭi iyagi* [Believe or Not: The Story of Chandra Kurŭng], 2003.

68. *Hangyŏre Newspaper,* May 18, 2005.

69. Kim Chi-yŏn and Kim Hae-sŏng, *Nodongjaege kukkyŏngŭn ŏpta,* 112–13.

70. *Hangyŏre Newspaper,* June 11, 2002.

71. *Hangyore Newspaper,* July 29, 2002, October 4, 2002.

72. *Hangyŏre Newspaper,* August 11, 2002.

73. For example, a book by Li Hye-sŏn, a Korean Chinese woman, on her and other migrant workers' experiences in South Korea is entitled *K'orian Dŭrim: Kŭ panghwanggwa hŭimangŭi pogosŏ* [The Korean Dream: A Report on the Wanderings and Hope] (Kyŏnggi-do, Korea: Aip'ildŭ, 2003).

74. Tadiar, *Fantasy-Production,* 1–24.

75. See Ruth Hsu's notion of "racial rehabilitation," cited in George, "But That Was in Another Country," 138. For the notion of exteriorized inclusion, see Balibar, "Racism and Nationalism," 37–67.

76. *Hangyŏre Newspaper,* July 31, 2003.

77. Chŏn Kwang-yong, "Kapitan Ri," 58–83.

78. *Hangyŏre Newspaper,* November 26, 2002.

79. Lowe, "Immigration, Citizenship, Racialization: Asian American Critique," in *Immigrant Acts,* 1–36.

80. For a critical analysis of new writings on the issues of migrant labor and multi-culturalism, see Hŏ Chŏng, "Ŏttŏk'e kukkyŏngŭl nŏmŭlgŏsinga?" [How Are We Going to Overcome the National Boundaries?], in *2000nyŏndae hanguk munhakŭi chinghudŭl* [Symptoms in Korean Literature of the 2000s], ed. Nam Song-u et al., 161–87 (Pusan: Sanjini, 2007). I cite some of these stories by South Korean writers, including Chŏng Yŏng-sŏn, "Kyŏul pi" [Winter Rain], in *P'yŏnghaengŭi arŭmdaum* [The Beauty of Parallels] (Kyŏnggido, Korea: Munhak such'ŏp, 2006), 281–303; Yi Hye-kyŏng, "Mul hanmogŭm" [A Sip of Water], in *T'ŭmsae* [In-Between] (Seoul: Ch'angbi, 2006), 8–30; Kim Chung-mi, *Kŏdaehan ppuri* [A Giant Root] (Seoul: Urikyoyuk, 2006); Yi Myŏng-rang, *Naŭi ibok hyŏngjedŭl* [My Half Siblings] (Seoul: Silch'ŏnmunhaksa, 2004); Kim Chae-yŏng, "K'okkiri" [An Elephant], in *K'okkiri* [An Elephant] (Seoul: Silch'ŏnmunhaksa, 2005), 9–38.

81. Pak Pŏm-sin, *Namasŭte*, no. 2.

82. Ibid., nos. 6, 40.

83. Carlos Bulosan, *America Is in the Heart* (Seattle: University of Washington Press, 1974). Chang-rae Lee, *Native Speaker* (New York: Riverhead Trade, 1996).

84. See Balibar, "Racism and Nationalism," 37–67.

85. Pak Pŏm-sin, *Namasŭte*, nos. 6, 40.

86. Ibid., nos. 67, 225.

87. See Jenny Sharpe's discussion of "memsahib" in *Allegories of Empire*, 85–110.

88. Pak Pŏm-sin, *Namasŭte*, no. 56.

89. See Edward Said, *Orientalism* (New York: Vintage, 1979). See also Stefan Tanaka, *Japan's Orient: Rendering Pasts into History* (Berkeley: University of California Press, 1995).

90. Pak Pŏm-sin, *Namasŭte*, no. 99.

91. Sin-u uses the word "p'ibuch'i," which has a very strong connotation for intimate and close blood relations (ibid., no. 25).

92. Pak Pŏm-sin, *Namasŭte*, nos. 128, 116.

93. I have translated *saengsŏngŭi barŭdo* as "opening of life creation" (ibid., no. 125). Kamil explains the Nepali word *barŭdo* as a transitional period (ibid., no. 46).

94. The novel explains the title, *Namaste*, as a Nepali word with a wide range of meanings, including "meeting, beginning of communication, a beautiful bridge between people, hello, goodbye, welcome" (ibid., no. 46). The word is originally Sanskrit and means "bowing to you."

95. The novel compares South Korean immigrants' experience in the United States to Asian migrant workers' experience in South Korea. Sin-u was an immigrant to the United States who returned to South Korea. She spent her teenage years in the United States, which she remembers overall as a painful time of loneliness, alienation, and racism. Her family, consisting of her parents and three brothers, were in Los Angeles at the time of the 1992 L.A. riots. The youngest of her brothers died in the violence, and the oldest brother moved to Washington, D.C., while the third brother and Sin-u returned to Korea. Both her parents remained with the oldest son, but her father, who was shot in the riot by an African American, soon passed away from the gunshot wound. Sin-u does not seem to have undergone any kind of assimilation during her immigrant life in the United States, while in contrast, Kamil's girlfriend Sabina's fifth year anniversary in South Korea is designated by Sin-u as her "fifth Korean birthday" (ibid., no. 19). Sabina's Korean age of five years, of course, transforms her into a child. Similarly, in contrast to his brothers, who experienced the United States as immigrants in painful and complex ways, Kamil is consistently portrayed as innocent and childlike. If the Korean immigrant experience in United States is one only of severe disillusionment, Kamil's experience in Korea, despite the many difficulties he must face, does end up leading him to the ultimate enlightenment, that is, the lessons to be gained from labor struggle. In comparing Kamil's and Sin-u's experiences, as a migrant worker and an immigrant, respectively, both of their romantic and sexual experiences

again play an important role in the novel's representation of their integration and/or lack of integration into the larger society. While Kamil finds himself nurtured and loved by Sin-u, and eventually having a child and starting a family in South Korea, Sin-u's alienation as a teenage immigrant, and the impossibility of her integration, is exemplified by her unwanted sexual encounter with an African American boy and the implicit rejection of her ethnicized sexuality by the white mainstream. The novel's choice for the character Sin-u and her family, to have been and still be immigrants to the United States, does serve in certain instances a progressive purpose. Sin-u's own experience makes her much more aware of, and sympathetic to, what Kamil and Sabina go through in South Korea. Migrant workers' sense of bitterness toward Korea is much more easily identified with through Sin-u, who experienced a similar sense of betrayal by the United States. Sin-u, who had her "American dream shattered" is much more sympathetic toward migrant workers who are having their "Korean dream shattered" (ibid., no. 83). It becomes a strategy of aligning the migrant labor from the periphery with the immigrant labor from the semiperiphery. She says, "There was nothing different between Kamil and me" (ibid.). But at the same time, in the absence of portraying alliances among minorities and ethnic immigrants in the U.S. context, the novel is more interested in building alliances among Asians, Asian migrants in South Korea, and Asian immigrants in the United States. This transnational Asian alliance seems to be formed in antagonistic relation to the United States, which is implicitly viewed as the white mainstream, to the exclusion of its racialized minorities—that is, the African American and Latino American population. We can pose the question of what kind of progressive political purposes such an Asian alliance, implicitly set against "white" America, , serves, if any. Does this exclusive Asian alliance in some ways replicate the concept of the Greater Asian Co-prosperity Sphere created by the Japanese empire in the 1930s? One of the novel's premises is a competitive comparison between South Korea and the United States as immigrant nations. Sin-u yells at her brother, "We are no better than the U.S., if not worse in fact" (ibid., no. 198). Sin-u's embracing of Kamil, along with his culture and religion, is implicitly contrasted with Americans' perceived lack of interest in, and appreciation of, minority cultures, including Korean, proving South Korea to be a superior immigrant nation than the United States.

96. Mahler, "Theoretical and Empirical Contributions," 73.

97. Appadurai, *Modernity at Large*, 172.

98. Ibid., 172–77.

99. Ibid., 178–99.

100. Their declaration of love for Korea is something that should give South Koreans a pause. One worker said that although he is being chased down by the INS, he still loves Korea, where he spent his entire twenties. It would be unimaginable for South Koreans to accept that a Korean migrant worker of the colonial period would declare that he or she loved Japan, to which he or she devoted his or her youth. And

yet, South Koreans do not tire of hearing how foreign migrant workers love Korea. While I do not doubt the sincerity of migrant workers' declaration of their affection for South Korea, I cannot help but think that this sentiment is necessarily a product of coercion, that is, part of their efforts to fit in and be accepted into a society where their presence and work are made invisible. Their articulation is, of course, no different from similar types of efforts made in ethnic immigrant communities of the United States. Conspicuous display of the Stars and Stripes on the windows of storefronts owned by immigrants would be one such example. Migrant workers inform South Koreans of their contribution to South Korea, "we are building Korea," as well as of the hardship that comes from being a "stranger" and being a laborer: their longing for their wives, children, and mothers, and their sorrow at seeing their coworkers be deported, and so on. Another project by migrant workers had a chance to be shown to the Korean public at a gallery in 2002. They named their exhibition "Mix Rice." "Rice" here, of course, functions as a symbol for the common grounds shared by various Asian ethnicities and nationalities, while the imperative "mix" reminds the audience of the necessity for integration of such diverse strands of Asian cultures and ethnicities. Just as the rice they eat comes in a variety of forms, so do the Asians. See *Hangyŏre Newspaper,* January 28, 2004.

101. The lyrics are composed by *Mix Rice* and the song was performed by Stop Crackdown. Both *Mix Rice* and *Stop Crackdown* are migrant worker–activist artist groups. I cite these lyrics from an article in a South Korean journal, Mixrice, "Mixterminal," *Bol* (Pol), Spring 2007, 104–18. "Mixterminal" is also the title of an Internet site that deals with a variety of issues related to migrant labor, including photos and art work. For more information, see http://www.mixterminal.net or http://www.mix rice.org (accessed June 16, 2010). When this song was performed, the lines in brackets in the English version were added as improvisations.

102. Guarnizo and Smith, "The Locations of Transnationalism," 11.

103. For a detailed statistical analysis and description of categories of female migrant workers, see Oegugin nodongja taech'aek hyŏbŭihoe, *Oegugin iju nodongja ingwon paeksŏ,* 111–16.

104. For specific instances, see ibid., 71–74.

105. Recent years have seen the publication of introductory or handbook types of books on overseas immigration or business ventures. See, for example, U Kil and Han Myŏng-hŭi, *Hangugŭl ttŏna sŏnggonghan saramdŭl* and *Segye 240 naraŭi hangugindŭl: tongasiaŭi kaech'ŏkjadŭl;* and Yi Sŏng-u, *Tandon 1000 tallŏro imingagi.* The cover of this last book lists the following countries in Korean in large letters: Laos, Cambodia, Myanmar, Thailand, Vietnam, Singapore, Malaysia, the Philippines, and Indonesia.

106. Yi Ran-ju, *Malhaeyo, ch'andra,* 90–95.

107. I would like to thank Naoki Sakai for encouraging me to make this connection between North Korea, the issues of reunification, and migrant labor in South Korea.

108. Guarnizo and Smith, "The Locations of Transnationalism," 8.
109. Sassen, *Globalization and Its Discontents*, xxx.

POSTSCRIPT

1. See T. Fujitani's discussion of Japan as a model minority nation in the cold war era in "Go for Broke, the Movie."
2. Young, *Vietnam Wars*.

Select Bibliography

Sources in English

Abelmann, Nancy, and John Lie. *Blue Dreams: Korean Americans and the Los Angeles Riots.* Cambridge, Mass.: Harvard University Press, 1995.

Adams, Vincanne, and Stacy Leigh Pigg, eds. *Sex in Development: Science, Sexuality, and Morality in Global Perspective.* Durham: Duke University Press, 2005.

Alexander, M. Jacqui, and Chandra Talpade Mohanty, eds. *Feminist Genealogies, Colonial Legacies, Democratic Futures.* New York: Routledge, 1997.

Allison, Anne. *Night Work: Sexuality, Pleasure, and Corporate Masculinity in Tokyo Hostess Clubs.* Chicago: University of Chicago Press, 1994.

Amott, Teresa, and Julie Matthaei. *Race, Gender, and Work: A Multi-Cultural Economic History of Women in the United States.* Boston: South End Press, 1996.

An, Chŏng-hyo. *White Badge.* New York: Soho, 1989.

Appadurai, Arjun. *Modernity at Large: Cultural Dimensions of Globalization.* Minneapolis: University of Minnesota Press, 1996.

Armstrong, Charles K. "America's Korea, Korea's Vietnam." *Critical Asian Studies* 33, no. 4 (2001): 527–39.

Bailey, Peter. *Popular Culture and Performance in the Victorian City.* Cambridge: Cambridge University Press, 1998.

Bales, Kevin. *Disposable People: New Slavery in the Global Economy.* Berkeley: University of California Press, 1999.

Balibar, Etienne. "Racism and Nationalism." In *Race, Nation, Class: Ambiguous Identities.* Edited by Etienne Balibar and Immanuel Wallerstein, 37–67. London: Verso, 1991.

Bao, Ninh. *The Sorrow of War: A Novel of North Vietnam.* Translated by Phan Thanh Hao. New York: Riverhead Books, 1993.

Barry, Kathleen. *The Prostitution of Sexuality: The Global Exploitation of Women.* New York: New York University Press, 1995.

Basch, Linda, Nina Glick Schiller, and Cristina Szanton Blanc. *Nations Unbound: Transnational Projects, Postcolonial Predicaments, and Deterritorialized Nation-States.* Amsterdam: Gordon and Breach Science Publishers, 1994.

Baudrillard, Jean. *The Mirror of Production*. Translated by Mark Poster. St. Louis: Telos Press, 1975.

Bell, Shannon. *Reading, Writing, and Rewriting the Prostitute Body*. Bloomington: Indiana University Press, 1994.

Beynon, John, and David Dunkerley, eds. *Globalization: The Reader*. New York: Routledge, 2000.

Bonacich, Edna, Lucie Cheng, Norma Chinchilla, Nora Hamilton, and Paul Ong, eds. *Global Production: The Apparel Industry in the Pacific Rim*. Philadelphia: Temple University Press, 1994.

Braziel, Jana Evans, and Anita Mannur, eds. *Theorizing Diaspora*. Oxford: Blackwell Publishing, 2003.

Breckenridge, Carol A., Sheldon Pollock, Homi K. Bhabha, and Dipesh Chakrabarty, eds. *Cosmopolitanism*. Durham: Duke University Press, 2002.

Casltes, Stephen, and Alastair Davidson. *Citizenship and Migration: Globalization and the Politics of Belonging*. New York: Routledge, 2000.

Chakrabarty, Dipesh. *Provincializing Europe: Postcolonial Thought and Historical Difference*. Princeton: Princeton University Press, 2000.

Chang, Grace. *Disposable Domestics: Immigrant Women Workers in the Global Economy*. Cambridge, Mass.: South End Press, 2000.

Chasin, Alexandra. "Class and Its Close Relations: Identities among Women, Servants, and Machines." In *Posthuman Bodies*. Edited by Judith Halberstam and Ira Livingston, 73–96. Bloomington: Indiana University Press, 1995.

Choi, Chungmoo. "Nationalism and the Construction of Gender in Korea." In Kim and Choi, *Dangerous Women*, 9–32.

Choi, In-Hoon [Ch'oe In-hun]. "The End of the State Highway." Translated by Theodore Hughes. *Manoa* 11, no. 2 (1999): 15–20.

Chŏn Kwang-yong. "Kapitan Ri." In Pihl, Fulton, and Fulton, *Land of Exile*, 58–83.

Chow, Rey. *The Protestant Ethnic and the Spirit of Capitalism*. New York: Columbia University Press, 2002.

Chuh, Kandice. *Imagine Otherwise: On Asian Americanist Critique*. Durham: Duke University Press, 2003.

Chuh, Kandice, and Karen Shimakawa, eds. *Orientations: Mapping Studies in the Asian Diaspora*. Durham: Duke University Press, 2001.

Collins, Jane L., and Martha Giminez, eds. *Work without Wages: Domestic Labor and Self-Employment within Capitalism*. Albany: State University of New York Press, 1990.

Connell, R. W. *Masculinities*. Berkeley: University of California Press, 1995.

Constable, Nicole. *Romance on a Global Stage: Pen Pals, Virtual Ethnography, and "Mail Order" Marriage*. Berkeley: University of California, 1995.

Cruiksank, Barbara. *The Will to Empower: Democratic Citizens and Other Subjects*. Ithaca: Cornell University Press, 1999.

Cumings, Bruce. "Occurrence at Nogŭn-ri Bridge: An Inquiry into the History and Memory of a Civil War." *Critical Asian Studies* (2001): 33:4.

Davidson, Julia O'Connell. *Prostitution, Power, and Freedom*. Ann Arbor: University of Michigan Press, 1998.

Davis, Angela Y. *The Angela Y. Davis Reader*. Malden, Mass.: Blackwell, 1998.

Debord, Guy. *The Society of the Spectacle*. Translated by Donald Nicholson-Smith. Brooklyn: Zone Books, 1994.

Desai, Vandana, and Robert B. Potter. *The Companion to Development Studies*. London: Arnold, 2002.

Douglass, Mike, and Glenda S. Roberts, eds. *Japan and Global Mirgration: Foreign Workers and the Advent of a Multicultural Society*. Honolulu: University of Hawaii Press, 2000.

Eckert, Carter J. *Offspring of Empire: The Koch'ang Kims and the Colonial Origins of Korean Capitalism, 1876–1945*. Seattle: University of Washington Press, 1991.

Ehrenreich, Barbara, and Arlie Russell Hochschild, eds. *Global Woman: Nannies, Maids, and Sex Workers in the New Economy*. New York: Henry Holt and Company, 2002.

Eng, David. *Racial Castration: Managing Masculinity in Asian America*. Durham: Duke University Press, 2001.

Enloe, Cynthia. *Bananas, Beaches, and Bases: Making Feminist Sense of International Politics*. Berkeley: University of California Press, 1989.

————. *Maneuvers: The International Politics of Militarizing Women's Lives*. Berkeley: University of California Press, 2000.

————. *The Morning After: Sexual Politics at the End of the Cold War*. Berkeley: University of California Press, 1993.

Escobar, Arturo. *Encountering Development: The Making and Unmaking of the Third World*. Princeton: Princeton University Press, 1995.

Espiritu, Ye Le. *Asian American Panethnicity: Bridging Institutions and Identities*. Philadelphia: Temple University Press, 1992.

Featherstone, Mike, Mike Hepworth, and Bryan S. Turner, eds. *The Body: Social Process and Cultural Theory*. London: Sage Publications, 1991.

Felski, Rita. *The Gender of Modernity*. Cambridge, Mass.: Harvard University Press, 1995.

Fenkl, Heinz Insu. *Memories of My Ghost Brother*. New York: Dutton, Penguin Books, 1996.

Ferguson, James. *The Anti-Politics Machine: "Development," Depoliticization, and Bureaucratic Power in Lesotho*. Minneapolis: University of Minnesota Press, 1994.

Foucault, Michel. *Discipline and Punish: The Birth of the Prison*. Translated by Alan Sheridan. New York: Vintage Books, 1979.

————. *The History of Sexuality*. Vol. 1, *Introduction*. Translated by Robert Hurley. New York: Vintage Books, 1978.

Fuentes, Annette, and Barbara Ehrenreich. *Women in the Global Factory*. Boston: South End Press, 1983.

Fujitani, T. "Go for Broke, the Movie: Japanese American Soldiers in U.S. National, Military, and Racial Discourses." In *Perilous Memories: The Asia–Pacific War(s)*.

Edited by T. Fujitani, Geoffrey M. White, and Lisa Yoneyama, 239–66. Durham: Duke University Press, 2001.

——. *Splendid Monarchy: Power and Pageantry in Modern Japan*. Berkeley: University of California Press, 1998.

George, Rosemary Marangoly. *Burning Down the House: Recycling Domesticity*. Boulder, Colo.: Westview Press, 1998.

——. "But That Was in Another Country: Girlhood and the Contemporary 'Coming-to-America' Narrative." In *The Girl: Construction of the Girl in Contemporary Fiction by Women*. Edited by Ruth O. Saxton, 135–52. New York: St. Martin's, 1998.

——. *The Politics of Home: Postcolonial Relocations and Twentieth-Century Fiction*. Berkeley: University of California Press, 1996.

Goldberg, David Theo, ed. *Multiculturalism: A Critical Reader*. Oxford: Blackwell Publishers, 1994.

Goldstein, Joshua S. *War and Gender*. Cambridge: Cambridge University Press, 2001.

Gonzalez, Gilbert G., Raul A. Fernandez, Vivian Price, David Smith, and Linda Trinh Vo, eds. *Labor Versus Empire: Race, Gender, and Migration*. New York: Routledge, 2004.

Grewal, Inderpal, and Caren Kaplan, eds. *Scattered Hegemonies: Postmodernity and Transnational Feminist Practices*. Minneapolis: University of Minnesota Press, 1994.

Grewal, Inderpal, Akhil Gupta, and Aihwa Ong, eds. "Asian Transnationalities." Special issue, *positions* 7, no. 3 (1999).

Guarnizo, Luis Eduardo, and Michael Peter Smith. "The Locations of Transnationalism." In Smith and Guarnizo, *Transnationalism from Below*, 3–34.

Halberstam, Judith. *Female Masculinity*. Durham: Duke University Press, 1998.

Hart-Landsberg, Martin. *The Rush to Development: Economic Change and Political Struggle in South Korea*. New York: Monthly Review Press, 1993.

Held, David, and Anthony McGrew, eds. *The Global Transformations Reader*. Oxford: Blackwell Publishers, 2000.

Hershatter, Gail. *Dangerous Pleasures: Prostitution and Modernity in Twentieth-Century Shanghai*. Berkeley: University of California Press, 1997.

Hicks, George. *The Comfort Women*. New York: Norton, 1994.

Hwang, Sŏk-yŏng. "A Dream of Good Fortune." In Pihl, Fulton, and Fulton, *Land of Exile*, 115–49.

—— [Hwang, Suk-Young]. *The Shadow of Arms*. Translated by Chun Kyung-ja. Cornell East Asia Series. Ithaca: Cornell University Press, 1994.

Jameson, Fredric, and Masao Miyoshi, eds. *The Cultures of Globalization*. Durham: Duke University Press, 1999.

Jeffords, Susan. *The Remasculinization of America: Gender and the Vietnam War*. Bloomington: Indiana University Press, 1989.

Jeffrey, Leslie Ann. *Sex and Borders: Gender, National Identity, and Prostitution Policy in Thailand*. Honolulu: University of Hawaii Press, 2002.

Johnson, Chalmers. *The Sorrows of Empire: Militarism, Secrecy, and the End of the Republic*. New York: Metropolitan Books, 2004.

Johnson, Marshall, and Fred Yen Liang Chiu, eds. "Subimperialism." Special issue, *positions* 8, no. 1 (2000).

Joseph, May. *Nomadic Identities: The Performance of Citizenship.* Minneapolis: University of Minnesota Press, 1999.

Kang, Sŏk-kyŏng. "Days and Dreams." In Kang Sŏk-kyŏng, Kim Chi-wŏn, and O Chŏng-hŭi, *Words of Farewell: Stories by Korean Women Writers.* Translated by Bruce and Ju-Chan Fulton, 1–27. Seattle: Seal Press, 1989.

Kaplan, Amy. "Romancing the Empire: The Embodiment of American Masculinity in the Popular Historical Novel of the 1890s." In *Postcolonial Theory and the United States: Race, Ethnicity, and Literature.* Edited by Amritjit Singh and Peter Schmidt, 220–43. Jackson: University of Mississippi Press, 2000.

Kaplan, Caren, Norma Alarcon, and Minoo Moallem, eds. *Between Woman and Nation: Nationalism, Transnational Feminism, and the State.* Durham: Duke University Press, 1999.

Keller, Nora Okja. *Comfort Woman.* New York: Penguin Books, 1997.

———. *Fox Girls.* New York: Penguin Book, 2002.

Kelsky, Karen. *Women on the Verge: Japanese Women, Western Dreams.* Durham: Duke University Press, 2001.

Kempadoo, Kamala, and Jo Doezema, eds. *Global Sex Workers: Rights, Resistance, and Redefinition.* New York: Routledge, 1998.

Kim, Elaine H., and Chungmoo Choi, eds. *Dangerous Women: Gender and Korean Nationalism.* New York: Routledge, 1998.

Kim, Jung Hwan. *Hanoi Seoul Poems.* Seoul: Munhakdongne Publishers, 2003.

Kim, Samuel S., ed. *Korea's Globalization.* Cambridge: Cambridge University Press, 2000.

———. *Korea's Democratization.* Cambridge: Cambridge University Press, 2003.

Kim, Seung-kyung. *Class Struggle or Family Struggle? The Lives of Women Factory Workers in South Korea.* Cambridge: Cambridge University Press, 1997.

Kim, Sŭng-ok. "Seoul: 1964, Winter." In Pihl, Fulton, and Fulton, *Land of Exile,* 84–101.

Kim-Gibson, Dai Sil. *Silence Broken: Korean Comfort Women.* Parkersburg, Iowa: Mid-Prairie Books, 1999.

Komai, Hiroshi. *Migrant Workers in Japan.* London: Kegan Paul International, 1995.

Kondo, Dorinne. *About Face: Performing Race in Fashion and Culture.* New York: Routledge, 1997.

Koo, Hagen. *Korean Workers: The Culture and Politics of Class Formation.* Ithaca: Cornell University Press, 2001.

Kristeva, Julia. *Strangers to Ourselves.* Translated by Leon S. Roudiez. New York: Columbia University Press, 1991.

Latham, Michael E. "Introduction: Modernization, International History, and the Cold War World." In *Staging Growth: Modernization, Development, and the Global Cold War.* Edited by David Engerman, Nils Gilman, Mark H. Haefele, and Michael E. Latham, 1–22. Amherst: University of Massachusetts Press, 2003.

―――. *Modernization as Ideology: American Social Science and "Nation Building" in the Kennedy Era*. Chapel Hill: University of North Carolina Press, 2000.

Lee, Chang-rae. *A Gesture Life*. New York: Riverhead Books, 1999.

Lee, Jin-kyung. "Sovereign Aesthetics, Disciplining Emotion, and Racial Rehabilitation in Colonial Korea, 1910–1922." *Acta Koreana* 8, no. 1 (2005): 77–107.

Lee, Namhee. *The Making of Minjung: Democracy and the Politics of Representation in South Korea*. Ithaca: Cornell University Press, 2007.

Lee, Na Young. "The Construction of U.S. Camptown Prostitution in South Korea: Trans/formation and Resistance." PhD diss., University of Maryland, College Park, 2006.

Lee, Steven Hugh. *Outposts 3onyof Empire: Korea, Vietnam, and the Origins of the Cold War in Asia, 1949–1954*. Montreal: McGill-Queen's University Press, 1995.

Lett, Denise Potrzeba. *In Pursuit of Status: The Making of South Korea's "New" Urban Middle Class*. Cambridge, Mass.: Harvard University Asia Center, 1998.

Lie, John. *Han Unbound: The Political Economy of South Korea*. Stanford: Stanford University Press, 1998.

―――. *Multiethnic Japan*. Cambridge, Mass.: Harvard University Press, 2001.

Light, Ivan, and Edna Bonacich. *Immigrant Entrepreneurs: Koreans in Los Angeles, 1965–1982*. Berkeley: University of California Press, 1988.

Limon, Martin. *Slicky Boys*. New York: Bantam Books, 1997.

Lowe, Lisa. *Immigrant Acts: On Asian American Cultural Politics*. Durham: Duke University Press, 1996.

Magubane, Zine. *Bringing the Empire Home: Race, Class, and Gender in Britain and Colonial South Africa*. Chicago: University of Chicago Press, 2004.

Mahler, Sarah J. "Theoretical and Empirical Contributions: Toward a Research Agenda for Transnationalism." In Smith and Guarnizo, *Transnationalism from Below*, 64–102.

Manderson, Lenore, and Margaret Jolly, eds. *Sites of Desire, Economies of Pleasure: Sexualities in Asia and the Pacific*. Chicago: University of Chicago Press, 1997.

Mbembe, Achille. "Necropolitics." *Public Culture* 15, no. 1 (2003): 11–40.

McClintock, Anne. *Imperial Leather: Race, Gender, and Sexuality in the Colonial Contest*. New York: Routledge, 1995.

Mies, Maria. *Patriarchy and Accumulation on a World Scale: Women in the International Division of Labor*. London: Zed Books, 1986.

Miyoshi, Masao. "A Borderless World? From Colonialism to Transnationalism and the Decline of the Nation–State." In *Global/Local: Cultural Production and the Transnational Imaginary*. Edited by Rob Wilson and Wimal Dissanayake, 78–106. Durham: Duke University Press, 1996.

Mohanty, Chandra Talpade. *Feminism without Borders: Decolonizing Theory, Practicing Solidarity*. Durham: Duke University Press, 2003.

Moon, Katharine H. S. *Sex among Allies: Military Prostitution in U.S.-Korea Relations*. New York: Columbia University Press, 1997.

Moon, Seungsook. *Militarized Modernity and Gendered Citizenship in South Korea.* Durham: Duke University Press, 2005.

Nagel, Joane. *Race, Ethnicity, and Sexuality: Intimate Intersections, Forbidden Frontiers.* Oxford: Oxford University Press, 2003.

Nagle, Jill, ed. *Whores and Other Feminists.* New York: Routledge, 1997.

Negri, Antonio. *Insurgencies: Constituent Power and the Modern State.* Translated by Maurizia Boscagli. Minneapolis: University of Minnesota Press, 1999.

Ngai, Mae M. *Impossible Subjects: Illegal Aliens and the Making of Modern America.* Princeton: Princeton University Press, 2004.

Nye, Robert A., ed. *Sexuality.* Oxford: Oxford University Press, 1999.

O, Chŏng-hŭi. "Chinatown." In Kang Sŏk-kyŏng, Kim Chi-wŏn, and O Chŏng-hŭi, *Words of Farewell: Stories by Korean Women Writers.* Translated by Bruce and Ju-Chan Fulton, 202–30. Seattle: Seal Press, 1989.

Omi, Michael, and Howard Winant. *Racial Formation in the United States: From the 1960s to the 1990s.* New York: Routledge, 1994.

Ong, Aihwa. *Flexible Citizenship: The Cultural Logics of Transnationality.* Durham: Duke University Press, 1999.

———. *Spirits of Resistance and Capitalist Discipline: Factory Women in Malaysia.* Albany: State University of New York Press, 1987.

Park, Jinim. *Narratives of the Vietnam War by Korean and American Writers.* New York: Peter Lang, 2007.

Parrenas, Rhacel Salazar. *Servants of Globalization: Women, Migration, and Domestic Work.* Stanford: Stanford University Press, 2001.

Pease, Donald, ed. *National Identities and Post-Americanist Narratives.* Durham: Duke University Press, 1994.

Pelley, Patricia M. *Postcolonial Vietnam: New Histories of the National Past.* Durham: Duke University Press, 2002.

Pihl, Marshall, and Bruce and Ju-chan Fulton, ed. and trans. *Land of Exile.* New York: M. E. Sharpe, 1993.

Rabinow, Paul, ed. *The Foucault Reader.* New York: Pantheon, 1984.

Sandoval, Chela. *Methodology of the Oppressed.* Minneapolis: University of Minnesota Press, 2000.

Sassen, Saskia. *Globalization and Its Discontents.* New York: The New Press, 1998.

Sen, Amartya. *Development as Freedom.* New York: Anchor Books, 1999.

Seol, Dong-Hoon, and John D. Skrentny. "South Korea: Importing Undocumented Workers." In *Controlling Immigration: A Global Perspective.* Edited by Wayne A. Cornelius, Takeyuki Tsuda, Philip L. Martin, and James F. Hollifield, 480–513. Stanford: Stanford University Press, 2004.

Serlin, David. *Replaceable You: Engineering the Body in Postwar America.* Chicago: University of Chicago Press, 2004.

Sharpe, Jenny. *Allegories of Empire: The Figure of Woman in the Colonial Text.* Minneapolis: University of Minnesota Press, 1993.

Shin, Gi-Wook. *Ethnic Nationalism in Korea: Genealogy, Politics and Legacy.* Stanford: Stanford University Press, 2006.

Silverberg, Miriam. *Erotic Grotesque Nonsense: The Mass Culture of Japanese Modern Times.* Berkeley: University of California Press, 2006.

Simon, Lawrence H. *Karl Marx: Selected Writings.* Indianapolis: Hackett Publishing, 1994.

Smith, Michael Peter, and Luis Eduardo Guarnizo, eds. *Transnationalism from Below.* New Brunswick, N.J.: Transaction Publishers, 2002.

Soysal, Yasemin Nuhoglu. *Limits of Citizenship: Migrants and Postnational Membership in Europe.* Chicago: University of Chicago Press, 1994.

Spivak, Gayatri. "A Literary Representation of the Subaltern: A Woman's Text from the Third World." In *Other Worlds: Essays in Cultural Politics,* 241–68. New York: Routledge, 1988.

———. "Scattered Speculations on the Question of Value." In *The Spivak Reader.* Edited by Donna Landry and Gerald Maclean, 107–40. New York: Routledge, 1996.

Stoler, Ann Laura. "Carnal Knowledge and Imperial Power: Gender, Race, and Morality in Colonial Asia." In *The Gender/Sexuality Reader.* Edited by Roger N. Lancaster and Micaela di Leonardo, 13–36. New York: Routledge, 1997.

———. *Race and the Education of Desire: Foucault's History of Sexuality and the Colonial Order of Things.* Durham: Duke University Press, 1995.

Sturdevant, Saundra Pollock, and Brenda Stoltzfus. *Let the Good Times Roll: Prostitution and the U.S. Military in Asia.* New York: The New Press, 1992.

Tadiar, Neferti Xina M. *Fantasy-Production: Sexual Economies and Other Philippine Consequences for the New World Order.* Hong Kong: Hong Kong University Press, 2004.

Theweleit, Klaus. *Male Fantasies.* Vol. 2. Minneapolis: University of Minnesota Press, 1989.

Tsuda, Takeyuki. *Strangers in the Ethnic Homeland: Japanese Brazilian Return Migration in Transnational Perspective.* New York: Columbia University Press, 2003.

Virilio, Paul. *Speed and Politics.* Translated by Mark Polizzotti. New York: Semiotext(e), 1986.

Walkowitz, Judith R. *Prostitution and Victorian Society: Women, Class, and the State.* Cambridge: Cambridge University Press, 1980.

Weeks, Jeffrey. *Sex, Politics, and Society: The Regulation of Sexuality since 1800.* London: Longman, 1989.

Williams-Leon, Teresa, and Cynthia L. Nakashima. *The Sum of Our Parts: Mixed Heritage Asian Americans.* Philadelphia: Temple University Press, 2001.

Woo-Cumings, Meredith, ed. *The Developmental State.* Ithaca: Cornell University Press, 1999.

Young, Marilyn B. *The Vietnam Wars, 1945–1990.* New York: HarperPerennial, 1991.

Yuh, Ji-yeon. *Beyond the Shadow of Camp Town: Korean Military Brides in America.* New York: New York University Press, 2002.

Yuval-Davis, Nira. *Gender and Nation.* London: Sage Publications, 1997.

Sources in Korean

An, Chŏng-hyo. *Hayan chŏnjaeng* [White War]. 3 vols. Seoul: Koryŏwon, 1989–93.

An, Il-sun. *Ppaetpŏl* [Mudflats]. 2 vols. Seoul: Kongganmidiŏ, 1995.

An, Yŏn-sŏn. *Sŏng noyewa pyŏngsa mandŭlgi* [Making Sex Slaves and Soldiers]. Seoul: Samin Publishers, 2003.

Ban, Re. *Kŭdae ajik sara ittamyŏn* [If You Are Still Alive]. Translated by Ha Chae-hong. Seoul: Silch'ŏnmunhaksa, 2002.

Cheng, Sealing. "Sarangŭl paeugo sarange chukgo" [Learning to Love, Dying for Love]. In *Magdalenaŭi chip, Yonggamhan yŏsŏngdŭl, nŭkdaerŭl t'ago dallinŭn*, 229–55.

Cho, Hae-il. "Amerika" [America]. In *Hanguk sosŏl munhak taegye* [The Collected Works of Korean Fiction], 65:352–430. Seoul: Tonga Publishers, 1995.

———. *Kyŏul yŏja* [Winter Woman]. 2 vols. Seoul: Chungangilbosa, 1985.

Cho, Hae-in. *Ssong Saigon* [Saigon River]. Seoul: Silch'ŏn munhaksa, 1997.

Cho, Hye-jŏng. *Hangugŭi yŏsŏnggwa namsŏng* [Women and Men of Korea]. Seoul: Munhakgwa chisŏngsa, 1988.

———. *Sŏngch'aljŏk kŭndaesŏnggwa peminism* [Reflective Modernity and Feminism]. Seoul: Ttohanaŭi munhwa Publishers, 1998.

Cho, I-je, and Carter Eckert. Introduction to Cho and Eckert, *Haguk kŭndaehwa, kijŏgŭi kwajŏng*, 11–53.

———, eds. *Haguk kŭndaehwa, kijŏgŭi kwajŏng* [Modernization of South Korea: A Miraculous Process]. Seoul: Wŏlgan chosŏnsa, 2005.

Cho, Se-hŭi. *Nanjangiga ssoa olin chagŭn kong* [A Dwarf Launches a Little Ball]. Seoul: Munhakgwa chisŏngsa, 1978.

Cho, Sŏn-jak. *Malgwalyangi toshi* [An Unruly City]. Seoul: Munje chakka sinsŏ, 1977.

———. *Misŭ Yangŭi mohŏm* [Miss Yang's Adventure]. 2 vols. Seoul: Yemungwan, 1976.

———. "Yŏng-jaŭi chŏnsŏngsidae" [Yŏng-ja's Heyday]. In *Hanguk sosŏl munhak taegye* [The Collected Works of Korean Fiction], 66:108–37. Seoul: Tonga Publishers, 1995.

Chu, Yu-shin, et. al. *Hanguk yŏnghwawa kŭndaesŏng: "Chayu puin" esŏ "angae" kkaji* [South Korean Cinema and Modernity: From *Madame Freedom* to *Fog*]. Seoul: Sodo, 2001.

Chuhan migun pŏmjoe kŭnjŏl undong ponbu [Activist Headquarters for Prevention of American Servicemen], eds. *Kkŭtnaji annŭn ap'umŭi yŏksa, migun pŏmjoe* [The History of Unending Injury: Crimes Committed by American Servicemen]. Seoul: Kaemasŏwŏn, 1999.

Chŏn, Sun-ok. *Kkŭtnaji annŭn sidaŭi norae* [A Seamstress's Song That Does Not End]. Seoul: Hangyŏre Newspaper Publishers, 2004.

Chŏng, Hŭi-jin. "Chugŏya sanŭn yŏsŏngdŭrŭi inkwon: Hanguk kijich'on yŏsŏng undongsa, 1986–1998" [Human Rights of Women Who Live by Dying: The History of Camp Town Movements in South Korea, 1986–1998]. In *Hanguk yŏsŏngŭi chŏnhwa yŏnhap, Hanguk yŏsŏng inkwon undongsa*, 300–358.

Chŏng, Tŏk-jun, ed. *Hangugŭi taejung munhak* [Popular Literature of South Korea]. Seoul: Sohwa Publishers, 2001.

Chŏng, Yu-jin, Kim Ŭn-sil, and Katharine Moon. "Kukkaŭi anboga kaeinŭi anbonŭn anida: Migukŭi kunsajuŭiwa kijich'on yŏsŏng" [National Security Is Not Individual's Security: U.S. Militarism and Camp Town Women]. *Tangdae pip'yŏng* [Contemporary Critique] 18 (2000): 79–105.

Ch'oe, Ho-il. "Kukka anbo wigiwa yushin ch'eje" [National Security Crises and the Yushin System]. In Cho and Eckert, *Hanguk kŭndaehwa, kijŏkŭi kwajŏng*, 149–82.

Ch'oe, In-ho. *Pyŏldŭrŭi kohyang* [Hometown of Stars]. 2 vols. Seoul: Saemt'ŏ, 1994.

Ch'oe, Wŏn-sik, and Im Hong-bae, eds. *Hwang Sŏk-yŏng munhak segye* [The Literary World of Hwang Sŏk-yŏng]. Seoul: Changbi Publishers, 2003.

Ch'ŏn, Sŭng-se. "Hwangguŭi pimyŏng" [The Scream of a Yellow Dog]. In *Hanguk sosŏl munhak taegye* [The Collected Works of Korean Fiction], 43:476–98. Seoul: Tonga Publishers, 1995.

Eckert, Carter. "5.16 kunsa hyŏkmyŏng, kŭ yŏksajŏk maekrak" [The May 16th Military Revolution and Its Historical Contexts]. In Yi, *Kaebal tokjaewa pak chŏng-hŭi sidae*, 93–114.

Han, Hong-gu. "Betŭnam p'abyŏnggwa pyŏngyŏng gukkaŭi kil" [Dispatching Troops to Vietnam and Militarization of South Korea]. In Yi, *Kaebal tokjaewa pak chŏnghŭi sidae*, 287–310.

Hanguk kukje nodong chaedan. *Bet'ŭnam chinch'ul kiŏp nomu kwalli annaesŏ* [A Guide to Managing Labor Relations in Vietnam]. Seoul: Hanguk kukje nodong chaedan, 2003.

Hanguk sahoe sahakhoe, ed. *Hanguk hyŏndaesawa sahoe pyŏndong* [Modern Korean History and Social Change]. Seoul: Munhakgwa chisŏngsa, 1997.

Hanguk yŏksa yŏnguhoe, ed. *Hanguk hyŏndaesa 3: 1960, 70nyŏndae hanguk sahoewa pyŏnhyŏk undong* [Modern Korean History: Korean Society and Social Movements of the 1960s and '70s]. Seoul: P'ulbit Publishers, 1991.

Hanguk yŏsŏngŭi chŏnhwa yŏnhap, ed. *Hanguk yŏsŏng inkwon undongsa* [A History of Korean Women's Human Rights Movement]. Seoul: Hanul Academy, 1999.

Hwang, Sŏk-yŏng. *Hwang Sŏk-yŏng chungdanp'yŏn chŏnjip* [Collected Novellas and Short Stories of Hwang Sŏk-yŏng]. 3 vols. Seoul: Ch'angjakgwa pip'yŏngsa, 2000.

———. "Kuro kongdanŭi nodong silt'ae" [The Labor Realities of the Kuro Industrial Complex]. *Wŏlgan chungang*, December 1973, 117–27.

———. *Mugiŭi kŭnŭl* [Shadow of Arms]. 2 vols. Seoul: Ch'angjakgwa pipyŏngsa, 1992.

———. *Ŏdumŭi chasikdŭl* [Children of Darkness]. Vol. 15 of *Chesamsedae hanguk munhak* [The Third Generation of Korean Literature]. Seoul: Samsŏng Publishers, 1983.

Im, Kye-sun. *Uriege dagaon chosŏnjogŭn nuguinga* [Who Are Korean Chinese?]. Seoul: Hyŏnamsa, 2003.

Kang, Chun-man. *P'yŏnghwa sijangesŏ kungjŏng-dongkkaji* [From P'yŏnghwa Market to Kungjŏng-dong]. 3 vols. Seoul: Inmulgwa sasangsa, 2002.

Kang, Chŏng-suk. "Ilbongun 'wianbu' munje, ŏttŏk'e polgŏshinga?" [The Problem of Japanese Military "Comfort Women": How Should We Examine It?]. In 20segi Hangukŭi yaman [Barbarisms in Korean History of the Twentieth Century]. Edited by Yi Pyŏng-ch'ŏn and Cho Yŏn-hyŏn, 159–90. Seoul: Ilbit, 2001.

Kang, In-sun. Hanguk yŏsŏng nodongja undongsa [A History of the Korean Women Workers' Movement]. Seoul: Hanul Academy, 2001.

Kim, Chŏng-ja, ed. Hanguk hyŏndae munhagŭi sŏnggwa maech'un yŏngu [Sexuality and Prostitution in Korean Modern Literature]. Seoul: T'aehaksa, 1996.

Kim, Ch'ŏl-su. Saigon, Saigon: Han hyŏnji kyŏngyŏnginŭi betŭnam chehŏmgi [Saigon, Saigon: A Memoir of a Manager in Vietnam]. Seoul: Ŏlgwa al, 2003.

Kim, Hae-sŏng, and Kim Chi-yŏn. Nodongjaege kukkyŏngŭn ŏpta: Oegugin nodongjawa chungguk tongp'oe kwanhan t'onghanŭi kirok [Borderless Workers: The Sorrowful Record of Foreign Migrant Workers and Korean Chinese in Korea]. Seoul: Nunbit, 2002.

Kim, Hyŏn-a. Chŏnjaengŭi kiŏk/kiŏgŭi chŏnjaeng [Remembering the War/The War Remembered]. Seoul: Ch'aek kalp'i Publishers, 2002.

Kim, Hyŏn-jin. Yŏphŭn [Leaf Scar]. 2 vols. Seoul: Taeingyoyuk Publishers, 2001.

Kim, Hyŏn-mi. Kŭlobŏlsidaeŭi munhwa pŏnyŏk [Cultural Translation in the Global Age]. Seoul: Ttohanaŭi munhwa, 2005.

Kim, Hyŏng-bae. Hwangsaek t'anhwan [Yellow Bullet]. 2 vols. Seoul: Padach'ulp'ansa, 2003.

Kim, Kyŏng-ae. Hanguk yŏsŏngŭi nodonggwa segsyuŏliti [Korean Women's Labor and Sexuality]. Seoul: P'ulbit Publishers, 1999.

Kim, Myŏng-sŏp, Yi Chae-hŭi, Kim Ho-gi, Kim Yong-ho, and Ma In-sŏp. 1970nyŏndae hubangiŭi chŏngch'i sahoe pyŏndong [Changes in Politics and Society in the Latter Half of the 1970s]. Seoul: Paeksansŏdang, 1999.

Kim, Sŭng-gu. "Paekkopjaengi paksŏbangŭi kwihyang" [The Homecoming of Belly-button Pak] (1939). In 1920–30nyŏndae minjung munhaksŏn [Selected Works of Proletarian Literature from 1920s and 1930s]. Edited by Chu Chong-yŏn and Yi Chŏng-ŭn, 1:327–36. Seoul: T'ap ch'ulp'ansa, 1990.

Kim, Tong-ch'un. Hanguk sahoe kwahagŭi saeroun nosaek [New Directions in South Korean Social Sciences]. Seoul: Ch'angjakgwa pip'yŏngsa, 1997.

————. Migugŭi enjin: Chŏnjaenggwa sijang [The American Engine: Wars and Markets]. Seoul: Changbi Publishers, 2004.

Kim, Won. Yŏgong, 1970: Kŭnyŏdŭrŭi panyŏksa [Factory Girls, 1970: Their Counter History]. Seoul: Imajin, 2005.

Kim, Yong-sŏng. Imin [Immigration]. 3 vols. Seoul: Miral Publishers, 1998.

Kong, Chi-yŏng. Pongsuni ŏnni [Pongsuni Sister]. Seoul: P'urŭnsup, 1998.

Kong, Sŏn-ok. P'iŏra susŏnhwa: Kong Sŏn-ok ch'angjakjip [Do Bloom, Narcissus: Collected Fictions by Kong Sŏn-ok]. Seoul: Ch'angjakgwa pip'yŏngsa, 1994.

————. Sangsuri namujip saramdŭl [People at the Sangsuri Tree House]. Seoul: Raedŏmhausjungang, 2005.

Kwon, In-suk. *Taehanmingugŭn kundaeda: Yŏsŏnghakjŏk sigagesŏ pon p'yŏnghwa, kunsajuŭi and namsŏngsŏng* [Republic of Korea Is a Military: Peace, Militarism, and Masculinity from a Feminist Perspective]. P'aju, South Korea: Ch'ŏngnyŏnsa, 2005.

Magdalenaŭi chip, ed. *Yonggamhan yŏsŏngdŭl, nŭkdaerŭl t'ago dallinŭn* [Brave Women Who Run with Wolves]. Seoul: Samin Publishers, 2002.

Min, Kyŏng-ja. "Hanguk maech'un yŏsŏng undongsa: 'Sŏng sago p'algi'ŭi chŏngch'isa" [The History of Korean Prostitution: The Politics of "Buying and Selling Sex"]. In *Hanguk yŏsŏngŭi chŏnhwayŏnhap, Hanguk Yŏsŏng Inkwonundongsa,* 239–99.

Munhaksawa pip'yŏng yŏnguhoe, ed. *1970nyŏndae munhak yŏngu* [On the 1970s Literature]. Seoul: Yeha, 1994.

Nam, Chŏng-hyŏn. *Punji: Nam Chŏng-hyŏn taep'yo chakp'umsŏn* [Land of Excrement: Representative Works by Nam Chŏng-hyŏn]. Seoul: Hangyŏre Publishers, 1987.

O, Yŏn-ho. *Nogŭn-ri kŭ ihu: Chuhan migun pŏmjoi 55nyŏnsa* [After Nogŭn-ri: The 55-year History of American Servicemen's Crimes]. Seoul: Mal, 1999.

Oegugin nodongja taech'aek hyŏbŭihoe [Committee on Foreign Migrant Workers in Korea], eds. *Oegugin iju nodongja inkwŏn paeksŏ* [A Report on Human Rights for Foreign Migrant Workers]. Seoul: Tasangŭlbang, 2001.

Pae, Kŭng-ch'an, Ch'oe Yong-ho, Chŏn Kwang-hŭi, Chŏng Yŏng-guk, and Sin Kwang-yŏng. *1970nyŏndae chŏnbangiŭi chŏngch'i sahoe pyŏndong* [Changes in Politics and Society in the First Half of the 1970s]. Seoul: Paeksansŏdang, 1999.

Paek, Mun-im. *Ch'unhyangŭi ttaldŭl: Hanguk yŏsŏngŭi panjokjari kyebohak* [Daughters of Ch'unhyang: The Incomplete Genealogy of Korean Women]. Seoul: Ch'aeksesang, 2001.

Paek, Wŏn-dam. *Hallyu: Tongasiaŭi munhwa sŏnt'aek* [The Korean Wave: Cultural Choice in East Asia]. Seoul: P'ent'agraem, 2005.

Pak, Chong-sŏng. *Kwŏlyŏkgwa maech'un* [Power and Prostitution]. Seoul: Ingansarang, 1996.

Pak, Chŏng-hwan. *Nŭsi* [A Siberian Crane]. 2 vols. Seoul: Munyedang, 2000.

Pak, Ch'ae-ran. *Kukyŏn ŏmnŭn maŭl* [A Village without National Borders]. Seoul: Sŏhaemunjip, 2004.

Pak, No-ja. *Tangsindŭrŭi taehanminguk* [Your Republic of Korea]. Vol. 2. Seoul: Hangyŏre Publishers, 2006.

Pak, Pŏm-sin. *Namasŭte* [Namaste]. Seoul: Hangyŏre sinmunsa, 2005.

Pak, Yŏng-han. *Mŏnamŏn ssongbagang* [Distant Ssongba River]. Seoul: Igasŏ, 2004.

Pang, Hyŏn-sŏk. *Hanoie pyŏri ttŭda: Sosŏlga pang hyŏn-sŏkgwa hamkke ttŏnanŭn betvŭnam yŏhang* [A Star Rises in Hanoi: Traveling with Novelist Pang Hyŏn-sŏk to Vietnam]. Seoul: Haenaem, 2002.

———. *Rabstŏrŭl mŏngnŭn sigan* [Time of Eating Lobster and Other Stories]. Seoul: Changbi Publishers, 2003.

———. *Sŭlou built* [Slow Bullet]. Seoul: Hwanam, 2004.

Park, Chung Hee. *Kukkawa hyŏngmyŏnggwa na* [The State, Revolution, and I]. Seoul: Chiguch'on Publishers, 1997.

Pok, Kŏ-il. *K'aempŭ senekaŭi kijich'on* [The Camp Town at Camp Seneca]. Seoul: Munhakgwa chisŏngsa, 1994.

Ri, Hye-sŏn. *Korian drim, kŭ panghwanggwa hŭimangŭi pogosŏ* [Korean Dream: A Report on Its Wanderings and Hopes]. Kyŏngido, South Korea: Aip'ildŭ Publishers, 2003.

Sin, Kyŏng-suk. *Oettan bang* [A Remote Room]. Seoul: Munhakdongne, 1995.

Song, Hyŏng-sŭng. *Naega ch'ehŏmhan k'aenada* [My Experiences in Canada]. Inch'ŏn, South Korea: Charyowŏn, 2002.

Song, Pyŏng-su. *Ssyori Kim, Ch'ŏllo, oe* [Shorty Kim, Railroads, and Other Stories]. Vol. 38 of *Hanguk sosŏl munhak taegye* [The Collected Works of Korean Fiction]. Seoul: Tonga Publishers, 1995.

Sŏk, Chŏng-nam. *Kongjangŭi pulbit* [Light of the Factory]. Seoul: Ilwŏlsŏgak, 1984.

Sŏk, Hyŏn-ho, Chŏng Ki-sŏn, Yi Chŏng-hwan, Yi Hye-kyŏng, and Kang Su-dol. *Oegugin nodongjaŭi iltŏwa sam* [The Life and Work of Foreign Migrant Workers]. Seoul: Chisikmadang, 2003.

Sŏl, Tong-hun. *Oegugin nodongjawa hanguk sahoe* [Foreign Migrant Workers and South Korean Society]. Seoul: Seoul National University Press, 1999.

Sŏng, Nam-hun, et. al. *Ŏdi p'indŭl kkoch'I anirya* [Flowers, No Matter Where They Bloom]. Seoul: Hyŏnsil munhwa yŏngu, 2006.

U, Kil, and Han Myŏng-hŭi. *Hangugŭl ttŏna sŏnggonghan saramdŭl* [Those Who Succeeded by Leaving Korea: South Pacific]. 2 vols. Seoul: Kŭmt'o, 2002.

———. *Segye 240 naraŭi hangukindŭl: Tongasiaŭi kaech'ŏkjadŭl* [South Koreans in 240 Countries: Pioneers of East Asia]. Seoul: Kŭmt'o, 2003.

Yang, Sŭng-yun, et. al. *Padaŭi silkŭ rodŭ* [Silk Road of the Seas]. Seoul: Ch'ŏnga Publishers, 2003.

Yi, Chae-in. *Kkonggi Betŭnam yŏnga* [A Love Ballad for a Vietnamese Girl]. Seoul: Cheobuks, 2005.

Yi, Chong-gu, et al. *1960–70nyŏndae hangugŭi sanŏphwawa nodongja chŏngch'esŏng* [South Korean Industrialization and Working-Class Identity in the 1960s and '70s]. Seoul: Hanul Academy, 2004.

———. *1960–70nyŏndae hanguk nodongjaŭi kyegŭp munhwawa chŏngch'esŏng* [South Korean Working-Class Culture and Identity in the 1960s and '70s]. Seoul: Hanul Academy, 2006.

———. *1960–70nyŏndae nodongjaŭi chagŏpjang munhwawa chŏngch'esŏng* [Working-Class Shop Floor Culture and Identity in the 1960s and '70s]. Seoul: Hanul Academy, 2006.

———. *1960–70nyŏndae nodongjaŭi saenghwal segyewa chŏngch'esŏng* [Working-Class Everyday Life and Identity in the 1960s and '70s]. Seoul: Hanul Academy, 2005.

Yi, Hyo-jae. "Ilbongun wianbu munje haegyŏlŭl wihan undongŭi chŏngae kwajŏng" [The Unfolding of the Movement to Resolve the Issue of Japanese Military "Comfort Women"]. In Hanguk yŏsŏngŭi chŏnhwayŏnhap, *Hanguk yŏsŏng inkwon undongsa*, 181–238.

Yi, Im-ha, ed. *Hanguk chŏnjaenggwa chendŏ: Yŏsŏng, chŏnjaengŭl nŏmŏ irŏsŏda* [The Korean War and Gender: Women Overcome the War and Stand Up]. Seoul: Sŏhaemunjip, 2004.

———. *Kyejibŭn ŏttŏk'e yŏsŏngi toeŏtna?* [How Did "Kyejib" Become "Yŏsŏng"?]. Seoul: Sŏhaemunjip, 2004.

Yi, Ki-jun. "Kukga kyŏngje chŏngch'aekŭi chedojŏk kiban" [Systematic Bases for the State Economic Policies]. In Cho and Eckert, *Hanguk kŭndaehwa, kijŏkŭi kwajŏng,* 115–48.

Yi, Mun-yŏl. *Kuro arirang: Yi Mun-yŏl sosŏljip* [Kuro Arirang: Collected Works of Yi Mun-yŏl]. Seoul: Munhakgwa chisŏngsa, 1987.

Yi, Pyŏng-ch'ŏn. Introduction to Yi, *Kaebal tokjaewa pak chŏng-hŭi sidae,* 17–65.

———. "Kaebal tokjaeŭi chŏngch'i kyŏngjehakgwa hangukŭi kyŏnghŏm" [The Political Economy of Authoritarian Developmentalism and the South Korean Experience]. In Yi, *Kaebal tokjaewa pak chŏng-hŭi sidae,* 17–65.

———, ed. *Kaebal tokjaewa pak chŏng-hŭi sidae* [Authoritarian Developmentalism and the Park Chung Hee Era]. Seoul: Changbi Publishers, 2003.

Yi, Ran-ju. *Malhaeyo, ch'andra* [Please Do Speak, Chandra]. Seoul: Salmipoinŭn ch'ang, 2003.

Yi, Sŏng-suk. *Maemaech'ungwa peminism: Saeroun tamnonŭl wihayŏ* [Prostitution and Feminism: For a New Discourse]. Seoul: Ch'aeksasang, 2002.

Yi, Sŏng-u. *Tandon 1000 tallŏro imingagi* [How to Emigrate with Only $1,000]. Seoul: Myŏngsang, 2003.

Yi, Tae-hwan. *Sŭlou bulit* [Slow Bullet]. Seoul: Silch'ŏnmunhaksa, 2001.

Yi, Yong-jun. *Betŭnam, ichyŏjin chŏnjaengŭi sanghŭnŭl ch'ajasŏ* [Vietnam: In Search of the Scars of a Forgotten War]. Seoul: Chosŏnilbosa, 2003.

Yi, Yŏng-hwan, ed. *Hanguk simin sahoeŭi pyŏndonggwa sahoe munje* [Changes in South Korean Civil Society and Social Problems]. Seoul: Nunumŭi chip Publishers, 2001.

Yonsei University Media Art Research Center. *Such'wiin pulmyŏng* [Address Unknown]. Seoul: Samin Publishers, 2002.

Yu, Chae-hyŏn. *Mek'ongŭi sŭlp'ŭn kŭrimja, indoch'aina* [Mekong's Sad Shadow, Indochina]. Seoul: Changbi Publishers, 2003.

Yu, Chi-na, and Cho Hŭb, eds. *Hanguk yŏnghwa seksyuŏlitirŭl mannada* [Korean Cinema and Sexuality]. Seoul: Saenggakŭi namu, 2004.

Yu, Kwang-ho, Min Kyŏng-guk, Yu Im-su, and Chŏng Chung-jae. *Hanguk che 3 konghwagugŭi kyŏngje chŏngch'aek* [Economic Policies of the Third Republic of South Korea]. Seoul: Hanguk chŏngsin munhwa yŏnguwŏn, 1999.

Yun, Chŏng-mo. *Emi irŭmŭn Chosenppiyŏtta* [My Mother's Name Was Chosenppi]. Seoul: Tangdae, 1997.

———. *Kobbi* [Shackles]. 2 vols. Seoul: P'ulbit, 1988.

———. *Nim: Yun Chŏng-mo ch'angjakjip* [Beloved: A Collection by Yun Chŏng-mo]. Seoul: Hangyŏre Publishers, 1987.

————. *Pombi: Yun Chŏng-mo ch'angjakjip* [Spring Rain: A Collection of Short Stories by Yun Chŏng-mo]. Seoul: P'ulbit, 1994.

Yun, Hŭng-gil. *Ahop k'yŏleŭi kuduro namŭn sanae* [A Man with Nine Pairs of Shoes]. Seoul: Munhakgwa chisŏngsa, 1977.

Yun, Su-jong, ed. *Tarŭge sanŭn saramdŭl: Uri sahoeŭi sosujadŭl iyagi* [People Who Live Differently: Stories of Minorities]. Seoul: Ihaksa, 2002.

NEWSPAPERS AND JOURNALS

Hangyŏre Newspaper
Hangyŏre 21

Index

Agamben, Giorgio, 5
Agent Orange, 76, 241n1, 248n125
"America" (Cho Hae-il), 94, 158;
  masculinist nationalist allegory in,
  140–41
"Amerika ch'ainataun" (song), 247n105
An Chŏng-hyo: Vietnam War themes of,
  51. See also White Badge; White War
An Il-sun: fieldwork of, 150; on sexual
  violence, 151. See also Mudflats
Ansan: Migrant Workers' Association,
  201; migrant workers of, 198–99,
  265n43
anti-Americanism, South Korean, 133;
  in literature, 131, 257n19
anticommunism: under Park, 29, 40–42,
  100; transnational, 37
Appadurai, Arjun, 32–33, 223; on
  mobility, 34; on translocality, 173,
  224
Asia: benefits of cold war for, 233;
  extension of American West, 65;
  military prostitution in, 129–30;
  "tiger" economies of, 233; transnational workforce of, 195, 267n95;
  U.S. capitalism in, 1; U.S. militarism
  in, 1, 48, 125; U.S. neocolonization
  of, 37
Asian American Studies, 146

Asia–Pacific Wars: Comfort Women in,
  4; effect on Korea, 185; Japan in, 15,
  30; proletariat of, 19
authoritarianism, comprador, 133

bar hostesses. See hostesses
Barry, Kathleen, 4, 80; on industrialization of sex, 79
Baudelaire, Charles: on prostitution,
  101
Bell, Shannon, 84
bio-power, 5; economy of, 8; in necropolitics, 8
biracial children, 74, 76; abandonment
  of, 168–69, 248nn125 132, 261n96;
  adoption to United States, 174,
  262n104; of camp towns, 36, 131,
  155, 163–64; cultural identity of, 165;
  dis-identification among, 131, 164–
  67, 181; exclusion of, 164; ghost
  identities of, 166–69; harassment of,
  165; matrophobia of, 169, 261n96;
  misogyny of, 169, 261n96; racial
  legitimacy of, 167; relations with U.S.
  soldiers, 167–68; subjectivity of, 164,
  168; transnationality of, 131, 164
"Birds of Molgaewŏl" (Hwang Sŏk-
  yŏng), 54, 56; ethnic identification in,
  65–66

287

Jin-kyung Lee is associate professor of modern Korean literature at the University of California, San Diego.